THE EIGHTY-FIRST ANNUAL MEETING OF THE AMERICAN ACADEMY OF POLITICAL AND SOCIAL SCIENCE

APRIL 15 AND 16, 1977
THE BENJAMIN FRANKLIN HOTEL
PHILADELPHIA, PENNSYLVANIA

The Annual Meeting will be addressed at each session by prominent scholars and officials and will be devoted to

AFRICA IN TRANSITION

Approximately 800 persons will be in attendance sometime during the two days of sessions, representing a wide variety of cultural, civic and scientific organizations.

Members are cordially invited to attend and will automatically receive full information.

- Proceedings of this 81st Annual Meeting will be published as the July issue of THE ANNALS

- FOR DETAILS WRITE TO: THE AMERICAN ACADEMY OF POLITICAL AND SOCIAL SCIENCE • BUSINESS OFFICE • 3937 CHESTNUT STREET, PHILADELPHIA, PENNSYLVANIA 19104

VOLUME 430 MARCH 1977

THE ANNALS

of The American Academy *of* Political *and* Social Science

RICHARD D. LAMBERT, *Editor*
ALAN W. HESTON, *Assistant Editor*

NUCLEAR PROLIFERATION: PROSPECTS, PROBLEMS, AND PROPOSALS

Special Editor of This Volume

JOSEPH I. COFFEY
Professor of Public & International Affairs
University Center for International Studies
University of Pittsburgh
Pittsburgh, Pennsylvania

PHILADELPHIA

Library of Congress Catalog Card Number 76-27888

The articles appearing in THE ANNALS are indexed in the *Reader's Guide to Periodical Literature*, the *Book Review Index*, the *Public Affairs Information Service Bulletin*, *Social Sciences Index*, and *Current Contents: Behavioral, Social, Management Sciences* and *Combined Retrospective Index Sets*. They are also abstracted and indexed in *ABC Pol Sci*, *Historical Abstracts*, *United States Political Science Documents*, *Abstracts for Social Workers*, *International Political Science Abstracts* and/or *America: History and Life*.

International Standard Book Numbers (ISBN)

ISBN 0-87761-213-7, vol. 430, 1977; paper—$4.00
ISBN 0-87761-212-9, vol. 430, 1977; cloth—$5.00

Issued bimonthly by The American Academy of Political and Social Science at 3937 Chestnut St., Philadelphia, Pennsylvania 19104. Cost per year: $15.00 paperbound; $20.00 clothbound. Add $1.50 to above rates for membership outside U.S.A. Second-class postage paid at Philadelphia and at additional mailing offices.

Claims for undelivered copies must be made within the month following the regular month of publication. The publisher will supply missing copies when losses have been sustained in transit and when the reserve stock will permit.

Editorial and Business Offices, 3937 Chestnut Street, Philadelphia, Pennsylvania 19104.

CONTENTS

CONTENTS

BOOK DEPARTMENT

PAGE

INTERNATIONAL RELATIONS AND POLITICAL SCIENCE

AFRICA, ASIA AND EUROPE

PAGE

LATIN AMERICA

UNITED STATES HISTORY AND POLITICS

SOCIOLOGY

ECONOMICS

PREFACE

The first nuclear explosion, in July 1945, prompted Dr. Robert Oppenheimer to recall the lines from the *Bhagavad Gita*, "I am become Death, the shatterer of worlds!"[1] Since that date, the face of Death has been seen on many more occasions, both in the attacks on Hiroshima and Nagasaki and in the hundreds of tests of nuclear weapons conducted by the United States and other countries. So far, however, the world has not been shattered; in fact, nuclear weapons have not been used in any of the conflicts of the past 30 years.

This fortunate outcome has been due in part to luck, in part to the fact that the five nuclear-armed powers (the United States, USSR, Britain, France, and China) have learned how to adapt their behavior to the requirements of the atomic age. But this age is one of rapid change, not least in the area of nuclear technology. Recent developments make it easier for states to produce nuclear weapons, and the incentives to do so remain high. Thus we may have, in the not-too-distant future, a world of 10, 20, or 30 nuclear powers, with a consequent increase in the complexity of interstate relations and in the likelihood that these may lead to nuclear war.

This issue of the ANNALS addresses itself to three aspects of nuclear proliferation: the prospect that new nuclear powers will come on the scene, the problems that their arrival may create, and ways of coping with those problems. To put the matter in these words implies that proliferation is undesirable—as I, for one, believe. This belief neither justifies the existence of five nuclear powers nor precludes acceptance of a sixth—or a seventh; rather, it reflects a concern about the potential consequences for peace and security of the proliferation of nuclear weapons. Whether this concern is well-founded, you may judge for yourself as you read further.

However, before you turn to substantive matters, I should like to thank the Center for Arms Control and International Security Studies of the University of Pittsburgh for its support of this endeavor, and most notably for its sponsorship of a workshop wherein authors (and critics) could discuss nuclear proliferation. In this way, good inputs were made even better.

JOSEPH I. COFFEY

1. Sri Krishna, *The Bhagavad Gita*.

ANNALS, AAPSS, 430, March 1977

"Quo Vadimus?"

By JOSEPH I. COFFEY

ABSTRACT: The arguments against nuclear proliferation are numerous and weighty. Further proliferation may increase the likelihood of nuclear war through accident, nuclear blackmail, or escalation of conflicts. Conversely, there are reasons for leaders to support their countries' right to acquire nuclear weapons for security, power status, or economic benefits. It is very likely that additional states will seek to produce nuclear weapons, and the technical information and expertise to design and manufacture a nuclear explosive devise are readily available. Problems of safeguarding nuclear facilities from nuclear diversion and sabotage and theft by terrorists are reasons for curbing nuclear proliferation and searching for ways to reduce incentives to proliferation both through responsible behavior by present nuclear powers and through the UN and international organizations. However, problems of organizational structure and decision-making processes will confront both nations and international organizations. Judgments as to the best way to slow, channel, and limit proliferation differ markedly; however, five suggestions are: (1) the promotion of détente; (2) amelioration of differences likely to induce proliferation, (3) establishment of policies to inhibit acquisition of nuclear energy systems by additional nations while offering alternatives; (4) application of economic sanctions against detonation of nuclear devices; and (5) a greater willingness to accord status to countries on the basis of factors other than nuclear capabilities.

Dr. Joseph I. Coffey is Professor of Public and International Affairs at the University of Pittsburgh and Director of the Center for Arms Control and International Security Studies there. He has previously worked as an analyst with the Bendix Corporation and at the Institute for Defense Analyses, and has served on the Army staff, in the Office of the Assistant Secretary of Defense (International Security Affairs), and on the White House staff. He is the author of Strategic Power and National Security, Deterrence in the 1970's, *and* Arms Control and European Security, *as well as numerous articles on arms control and defense policy.*

IN 1974, after a decade wherein the number of nuclear powers had remained at five, the Republic of India, by detonating a nuclear device, raised that number to six. Although India has not conducted further tests, nor taken any of the other steps required to create nuclear-capable forces, her action heightened concerns about the long-term feasibility of preventing nuclear proliferation, concerns which had already been aroused by a number of other factors.[1]

NUCLEAR PROLIFERATION: PRO AND CON

The arguments against "horizontal proliferation" are both numerous and weighty. As Dr. William Epstein points out in his article, further nuclear proliferation may increase the likelihood of nuclear war as a result of attempts at nuclear blackmail, or through the escalation of conventional conflicts involving nuclear-armed powers by accident, inadvertance, or miscalculation. Moreover, proliferation may intensify antagonisms between rival states and lead to shifts in local and regional power balances, creating a less stable and more quarrelsome world. In addition, proliferation may encourage build-ups in other armaments as smaller powers seek to keep or to restore military advantages and larger powers seek to bolster their air and missile defenses or to develop precision guided munitions for preemptive strikes. Since both courses divert resources from urgent social and economic needs, numerous leaders in many states oppose further proliferation.

Conversely, there are reasons why other leaders have supported the right of their countries to acquire nuclear weapons or, at least, to build up a capacity to produce them. As Dr. Epstein points out, one set of these reasons stems from the quest for security, with nuclear weapons offering the possibility of achieving military superiority, of preventing an adversary from gaining it, or of deterring him from attempting to exploit it, should he in fact acquire it. Another set of reasons derives from the desire to achieve or maintain great power status, to be assured of a seat at the "head of the table,"[2] to redress perceived inferiorities in the international hierarchy, or at least to enhance national prestige. Coupled with these are desires to demonstrate political independence and self-reliance and to end discriminatory treatment, such as applies to non-nuclear states under the Non-Proliferation Treaty (NPT). A third set of reasons for proliferation springs from the belief that nuclear weapons technology has potential economic benefits in the form of the development of peaceful nuclear explosives, spin-offs to civilian technology, and perhaps a better bargaining position, both with regard to the transfer of technology

1. As indicated in the introduction to part I, these included the dissatisfactions of many states with the seemingly discriminatory provisions of the NPT, with lack of real progress in SALT, and with the absence of firm guarantees of their security; the oil embargo of 1973, which spurred programs for the construction of nuclear reactors; increased sales of equipment which will enable more countries to build atomic weapons; innovations in nuclear technology, which promised to further enhance that capability; and an upsurge of terrorism, which induced fears lest extremists acquire—and use—nuclear weapons.

2. One could wish that these leaders would emulate the Irish chieftain seated "below the salt" at an Elizabethan banquet, who declaimed proudly, "Where O'Neill sits, there is the head of the table!"

and in negotiations on the terms of trade and the flow of capital from North to South. Thus, economic independence, as much as political independence, may be a major incentive to proliferation on the part of some states in the Third World.

Moreover, domestic factors may reinforce rational analyses of the advantages to be derived from nuclear weapons programs. Scientists and technologists involved in nuclear energy programs may see in such programs an opportunity to increase their power and influence, or an occasion to demonstrate what they can accomplish for the nation. Similarly, political, economic, and military elites may all see in nuclear weapons programs an opportunity to secure cherished group or national goals, ranging from that of controlled modernization to that of building up the armed forces. And governments faced with, or fearing, opposition from such elements may be driven—or tempted—to prolong their political life by endorsing nuclear weapons programs, or at least by keeping open their options to do so.

These are not the only factors affecting decisions to "go nuclear"; were they so, the world would by now be a nuclear-armed one. There are many countervailing considerations: issues of morality, concerns about cost, doubts about the utility of nuclear weapons, fear that their acquisition may again open a Pandora's box out of which newer and larger security problems may emerge. And there are ways of reducing the incentives to proliferation, both by holding out a carrot and by brandishing a stick.[3] Nevertheless, it is very likely that additional states will, over the next decade, seek to produce nuclear weapons or at least create a capacity to do so.

Should they wish to do this, the path is, as Dr. Frank Barnaby points out, both clear and easy to follow. Both the technical information and the expertise necessary to design and manufacture a nuclear explosive device are readily available. Moreover, all types of nuclear reactors generate plutonium (Pu-239), one of the fissile materials used in atomic weapons. (The other fissile material suitable for this purpose, U-235, can only be concentrated to the requisite degree in specialized enrichment facilities.) Thus, the spread of nuclear reactors occasioned by the growing demand for energy automatically spreads the capacity to produce atomic weapons.

This capacity does not depend solely on the availability of power reactors; research reactors also generate plutonium in sufficient quantities and small production reactors, whose output would be sufficient to build two low-yield atomic bombs a year, can be constructed at a cost of about $20 million. Moreover, if breeder reactors which produce plutonium in weapons-grade concentrations are introduced, countries will not even need the chemical processing plants which are now utilized to separate Pu-239 from other elements and isotopes in spent-fuel emissions. As new technologies for uranium enrichment, such as the centrifugal method or the jet nozzle procedure, become more widely disseminated, the ability to produce weapons-grade fissile materials may receive a further boost. And as one looks further ahead, laser techniques for enriching uranium and laser-induced fusion and fission offer the prospect of not only less expensive but more powerful weapons.

3. See William Epstein, "Why States Go—And Don't Go—Nuclear," and George H. Quester, "Reducing the Incentives to Proliferation."

In brief, many countries can now produce atomic weapons readily and fairly cheaply; the Indian nuclear explosion probably cost less than $500,000. As time goes on, more and more countries will acquire this ability, the cost of crude atomic bombs will go down, and more efficient (and effective) weapons can be built. Since many countries already possess rockets, missiles, and strike aircraft, they have at hand the means of delivering atomic weapons against their neighbors—and perhaps even against others on the same subcontinent. If not, such delivery vehicles can readily be bought or built; as Dr. Barnaby says, "A small but credible nuclear force . . . could be acquired for a few hundred million dollars . . . about the same cost as that of a modern cruiser."

NUCLEAR SAFEGUARDS

Furthermore, it is difficult to prevent diversion of fissile materials to the construction of nuclear weapons, even on the part of countries adhering to the Non-Proliferation Treaty and undergoing inspection by the International Atomic Energy Agency (IAEA). As Dr. Ryukichi Imai points out, "Measurement error alone [in a typical fuel reprocessing plant] will exceed [the amount of plutonium required for] one bomb. . . ." While the current inspection procedures of the IAEA provide for the timely detection of diversion from peaceful nuclear fuel cycles of significant quantities of nuclear materials, the word "significant" may have very different meanings to nuclear "haves" and "have nots." Moreover, the system of inspection covers only certain prescribed facilities in the countries which have signed the Nuclear Non-Proliferation Treaty and does not touch any in countries which have not signed it, safeguards there being worked out on a bilateral basis with countries supplying fissile materials and reactors. Accordingly, it is possible for some countries to build, or to utilize for the production of nuclear weapons, facilities which are not monitorable by anyone, as India did. Failing this, countries desirous of making atomic bombs could violate the inspection agreement in the hope that they would not be detected if they did so, nor suffer sanctions if they were detected, or they could abrogate the NPT, as they have a right to do. Thus, the system of safeguards against the diversion of nuclear materials is limited both in its application and in its consequences; as Dr. Imai points out, safeguards are not a substitute for political solutions to proliferation.

They are, equally, no substitutes for the physical safeguarding of nuclear facilities against sabotage and theft, which remains a national responsibility, or against the seizure of such facilities by armed gangs. As Dr. David Krieger notes, terrorists could readily acquire radioactive and even fissile materials and could, at some risk to themselves, fabricate crude atomic weapons. (This could be done even more easily by units of the military in revolt against their government or engaged in civil war; by paramilitary elements; or by organized revolutionary groups, such as the Irish Republican Army, the Palestine Liberation Organization, or the Argentinian Montañeros.) Both terrorists and revolutionaries could contaminate densely-populated areas with radioactive materials, could threaten the destruction of major targets, and could even wipe out leadership groups. One expert witness estimated that the detonation of a one-kiloton weapon outside the Capitol building during the delivery of a presidential State of the Union message would kill everyone in "the line of succession to the presidency—all the way to the bottom of the list."[4] Equally, terrorists or revolutionaries could direct atomic weapons, whether stolen, seized, or donated, against foreign targets, with the aim of breaking up a peace conference, disrupting a government, or simply inflicting enormous punishment. (Imagine what might happen at future Olympic Games if terrorists acquire a small-yield nuclear weapon!) Thus, to concern about the implications of proliferation for the behavior of states must be added those about the behavior of other actors in the international environment; as Dr. Krieger concludes, nuclear-armed terrorists or revolutionaries "could provide a significant threat to any society. . . ."

INCENTIVES AGAINST PROLIFERATION

This possibility reinforces other reasons for seeking to curb nuclear proliferation and lends urgency to the search for ways of reducing incentives to proliferation. This is not, however, a simple task, since these incentives are so varied in nature and so uneven in their impact upon potential proliferators.

As Professor George Quester suggests, one way of doing so may be to maintain—and perhaps even to increase—the U.S. commitment to states depending on this country for their security (as do the nations of Western Europe, Japan, Israel, Taiwan, and perhaps Iran) even while minimizing the American presence and American guarantees in areas where these might be both unwelcome and irrelevant to the problem of proliferation, as they would be to many countries in the Third World. Moreover, potential proliferators among such countries are more likely to be inspired by the prospect of political gains than by the necessity for military ones; since this is so, political disincentives should also be emphasized. Measures to be taken could include managing Strategic Arms Limitation Talks (SALT) in such a way as to downgrade the importance of nuclear weapons and remove the glamor attached to them; selectively supporting "no-first-use" policies and nuclear free zones in areas of the world where these are politically desirable, as may be the case in Latin America; ceasing all nuclear tests and deemphasizing peaceful nuclear explosives (PNE); and pressing potential Nth powers not to detonate a nuclear bomb, even if they construct one.

Economic measures may include placing greater emphasis on research and development of non-nuclear sources of energy, such as solar power; pushing alternative reactor designs and uranium enrichment processes which would be easier to monitor or whose end-products could be less readily fabricated into nuclear weapons; and promoting multinational rather than national reprocessing facilities. However, those states which are concerned about nuclear proliferation may also have to consider sanctions against states moving to produce nuclear weapons, sanctions

4. Theodore B. Taylor, Statement before the Subcommittee on Energy and the Environment of the House Committee on Interior and Insular Affairs, 26 February 1976, quoted in David Krieger, "What Happens If . . .? Terrorists, Revolutionaries, and Nuclear Weapons."

ranging from simple condemnation through denial of nuclear equipment or economic aid to military action—though the latter will certainly be more difficult to carry out than the former and may in consequence be less credible.

In all these efforts, the nuclear powers and other advanced industrial states should, according to Dr. Quester, be selective and varied in their approaches, and subtle in their application, thereby suiting the measures adopted to the problem and avoiding confrontations between the advanced and the developing countries. They should also recognize that even if these and other measures do not succeed in preventing further proliferation, they may curb it, slow it, or modify its nature—all of which are ends desirable in and of themselves. As the author says, "If India and Israel and one other country make it into the nuclear club by . . . [1985], this is not yet a world in which 'everyone has the bomb.' "

Whether proliferation can be slowed to such a crawl depends, according to Dr. Ashok Kapur, on a number of major developments, including responsible behavior by the present nuclear powers, a continuation of détente between East and West, some normalization of relations between the PRC and the USSR, as well as between the PRC and Western countries (including formal Chinese participation in SALT) and some amelioration of conflicts and confrontations in areas such as the Middle East and South Asia. Under such circumstances, Pakistan and Iran may not exercise their nuclear options (though Israel may) and Taiwan will probably hold off. South Africa may decide that atomic bombs will not deter black African support of revolutionary movements and hence may not produce them, while Brazil and Argentina may, despite their resentment of the double standard of the great powers, abstain from going nuclear. Even under these circumstances, however, we may see within a decade eight to ten nuclear powers rather than the present six.

Moreover, "normalization" of relations between China and the rest of the world may not promote interdependence among the states of South Asia, some of whom may then view proliferation as desirable. Or normalization may defuse South Asia, at the expense of arousing concerns elsewhere about security, with the result that other Asian states, such as Japan and South Korea, may go nuclear. Furthermore, if some diffusion of power does not take place, if tensions grow rather than shrink, or if improvements in Sino-Soviet relations are bought at the expense of détente, then, Dr. Kapur argues, "Global and continental relations . . . will have radicalized the shifts toward proliferation" and many more nations will acquire nuclear weapons.

Within this context, much depends on whether states which go nuclear simply demonstrate a capability or undertake serious (if technically deficient) programs for the development of nuclear forces. In the latter case, according to Dr. Lewis Dunn, the adverse consequences of even limited proliferation might be enhanced by accident-prone systems, by the possibility that these could be seized by dissident domestic elements, by their marginal survivability against a preemptive strike, and consequently by reliance on a hair-trigger launch-on-warning mode of protecting nuclear forces.

Futhermore, at least some countries acquiring nuclear weapons may look on these as potentially useful means of waging war, or as instruments for coercion rather than for deterrence, thereby further diminishing stability within several regions of the world. In those regions, one could accordingly expect to see nuclear arms races, small power nuclear wars, and perhaps catalytic wars. On a global basis, one could expect some erosion of existing alliances and possibly deliberate disengagement by the superpowers from associated states which acquired nuclear weapons—with mixed, but predominantly undesirable, consequences for peace.

Equally important is the fact that weapons systems lacking permissive action links (PAL) and other control mechanisms could be stolen and used by terrorists or seized and employed by dissident elements within a country. In some instances, it is conceivable that governments would find it desirable to sell—or to give—weapons to terrorists or to revolutionaries whose actions would further the interests of their countries or advance their own political and ideological objectives. One outcome could be increasing restrictions on individual liberties and group activities, perhaps growing political authoritarianism, and a consequent loss of support by regimes, all of which, according to Dunn, would contribute to the global anarchy which is likely to result anyway from interactions among 20 to 30 nuclear-armed states.

This does not mean that the world would necessarily go to Hades in a handbasket. Much would depend on the number of nuclear powers, their location, and the nature of their weapons program. Dunn suggests, therefore, continuing efforts to prevent proliferation or, failing that, to persuade countries to stay at the lower rung of the nuclear weapons ladder; attempting to influence both the design of systems for the control of weapons and doctrines for their employment by Nth powers; developing codes of nuclear behavior, to include a "no-first-use" policy; supporting regional arms control measures, to include hotlines and emergency verification procedures; seeking understandings among the global powers about their participation in regional conflicts; and continuing efforts to check the "growing risk of nuclear terrorism." Taken together, Dunn asserts, the preceding measures could comprise "the basic components of a strategy for managing in a proliferated world." Since, however, these measures require a changed global political environment and approaches other than business as usual, there may be "a gap between the gravity of the likely threats within a proliferated world and the potential effectiveness of politically acceptable responses to them."

BALANCED PROLIFERATION

Whether and how that gap is to be closed are questions to which no answers are possible, only speculations. One such speculation by Professor Thayer is based on the assumption that, in the short run, an acceleration of nuclear proliferation seems inevitable, that this will take place in a world wherein resources are finite and set limits to growth, and that these two factors, in juxtaposition, argue either for increasingly bitter conflicts over resources, leading to some form of nuclear holocaust, or to a complete social and political transformation into a world order very different from that described earlier by Dr. Dunn. In the near term, this transformation could be promoted by "balanced proliferation," that is, by the dissemination of weapons to another state or states once one country in a given region becomes an Nth power, accompanied by the concurrent dissociation of the superpowers from countries acquiring nuclear weapons. In short, Dr. Thayer asks us to recognize and accept the position that atomic bombs are essentially terror weapons; that stability depends, as Churchill once said, upon a balance of terror; that new countries possessing nuclear weapons are not likely to be any less sane, trustworthy, or rational than those now holding them; and that, under these circumstances, peace is to be maintained by adroit manipulations of nuclear capabilities.

In the longer run, however, one may find atomic weapons, whether built, bought, or donated, being used to ensure or to safeguard access to materials essential to growth. Governments will engage in economic competition to whose success nuclear weapons are essential, even as they are simultaneously reordering their societies and restructuring their economies into small, self-sufficient units which could better withstand a nuclear war, should deterrence fail or compellance lead to coercion. One may, alternatively, see acceptance of the thesis that in a world of finite resources, these belong to everyone, "to be *shared, distributed, allocated* on some agreed basis." In such a world, small essentially self-sustaining units may also be optimal, but more because such units will place fewer demands on resources than because they constitute more or less viable modules in the event of nuclear war. More importantly, the shared management of resources, both within states and among them, may reduce the need to exploit certain resources, among them nuclear energy, thereby facilitating "balanced deproliferation," in which not only nuclear weapons but also nuclear reactors are phased out. Whether, therefore, one arrives at the pessimistic outcome of nuclear armed autarchies competing for resources or the optimistic one of demilitarized entities cooperating in the management of resources, we are, says Professor Thayer, "fast approaching the demise of the nation-state as we know it."

Whether or not we arrive ultimately at a world in which international actors cooperate or compete, or indeed at any world other than one in which the survivors of a nuclear war scramble for subsistence, depends in part on how we manage affairs over the next decade or so. Dr. Colin Gray agrees with Professor Thayer that large-scale proliferation is inevitable (though not within that next decade), that proliferation may be accompanied by competition for shrinking resources, and that in the twenty-first century "a prime motivation pushing a state toward a nuclear-weapon capability may . . . be . . . a laudable desire to increase its international leverage for the end of ensuring an adequate supply of calories for a swollen population." However, Dr. Gray differs in believing that "the basic structure of world politics will not be radically changed"; that, despite a diffusion of power, the United States and the USSR will continue to outshadow all rivals; and that these two superpowers will, in support of their own interests, seek to impose a minimum of order in regions vital to them and to support valued allies—though not to the extent of accepting responsibility for nuclear actions taken by these allies. Moreover, he believes that both they and other powers, nuclear as well as non-nuclear, will still be concerned with reducing the risk of war and, to the extent possible, the damage from any war that might occur.

The first objective, Dr. Gray asserts, can be promoted by attempting to slow or to channel proliferation, by considering helping with Nth powers to develop more controllable and, within limits, more secure national nuclear forces, and by improving both warning systems and communication nets available to these powers. He also argues that it is unrealistic—and hence unreasonable—to try to deemphasize nuclear weapons by changing strategic concepts, as to a doctrine of "no-first-use"; by stressing certain conventional capabilities and denying others (such as fighter-bombers which could carry large, first generation atomic bombs); or by issuing nuclear guarantees—a move which would, moreover, run directly counter to the interests of the great powers in war avoidance. Under such circumstances, arms control policy aimed at reducing the risk of war may focus more on prudent actions to deal with particular cases than with sweeping measures of universal applicability. Moreover, policies aimed at reducing the damage from war may be unacceptable to new nuclear powers concerned with deterring (or winning) a local conflict. Thus, Dr. Gray concludes by saying: "Sad to predict, the first genuine opportunity for a non-marginal change for the better in the ways in which human beings provide for their security, will occur not as a consequence of the emergence of a nuclear-armed world, but rather as a consequence of nuclear war."

Professor Abraham Bargman turns his attention to a different way of maintaining peace and enhancing security in a nuclear armed world: through the United Nations. While recognizing the primary responsibility of the superpowers for the maintenance of peace, and the existence of relationships and institutions which compete with the United Nations, he sees the UN as playing a major role in three problem areas: disputes between states on nuclear rights and obligations; nuclear crises; and the reform of international institutions in a world of nuclear powers.

With respect to the first, Dr. Bargman notes both the lack of authority of the United Nations and the limitations on its responsibility, but he also sees it as likely to be involved in problems arising from (1) violations of treaty obligations with respect to proliferation; (2) withdrawals from such a treaty; (3) disputes and tensions stemming from specific nuclear activities; and (4) the development of measures to deal with new problems, such as nuclear terrorism. In his opinion, the Security Council of the United Nations has an important role to play in imposing sanctions on violators of the Non-Proliferation Treaty, in clarifying the justifications for withdrawal from that treaty, and in giving (or arranging) assurances against surprise attack to countries bordering on new nuclear powers, and the General Assembly has a similar role to play in developing measures against nuclear terrorism—and terrorists. He suggests that the United Nations can, and should, also play a role in nuclear crises. It can supplement actions taken by the superpowers to implement their "Agreement on the Prevention of Nuclear War" of 22 June 1973; it can provide a framework for decisions in crises involving other nuclear powers; and it can establish peacekeeping and other specialized forces for use in the aftermath of a nuclear crisis or a nuclear war.

Finally, Dr. Bargman points out

that the UN can press for measures which would denuclearize world politics such as nuclear disarmament or the internationalization of the production and stockpiling of fissionable materials. It can also prepare for such measures by concerted study of institutional changes which would make their adoption easier, establishing an international nuclear security planning group to examine the tensions associated with proliferation, to devise and propose measures to ameliorate them, and to carry out on an emergency basis crisis control measures, such as the supervision of nuclear facilities. Bargman says, "Is it not high time for governments to permit some of their best nuclear security experts to become part of an institution concerned only with the international implications of nuclear disputes, tensions, and crises? . . . [Certainly] all people and governments have a supreme interest in the avoidance of nuclear war."

STRUCTURAL AND DECISION-MAKING PROBLEMS

As Professor Michael Brenner points out, problems of organizational structure and decision-making processes will confront nations as well as international organizations. In the case of the United States, these problems will arise from the need to shift from consideration of bilateral stragetic relationships (in larger terms, the East-West conflict) to consideration of "the permutations and combinations of multi-player nuclear games." Among the objectives of these games will be to ensure stable deterrence by: (1) increased attention to defensive systems; (2) changes in strategic doctrine; (3) safer management of nuclear weapons; (4) improved strategic intelligence, and perhaps the pooling of intelligence with the Soviet Union as well as with other countries; (5) avoiding strains on U.S.-Soviet relations, such as might arise from undue emphasis on war-fighting capabilities against Nth powers; (6) projecting strategic images which slow and limit proliferation; (7) and devising both force plans and targeting options which will be suited to a nuclear-armed world.

Achieving these objectives will, Dr. Brenner argues, require a fundamental restructuring of the decision-making process in the United States, in order to achieve both closer synchronization of policy and more consistent implementation. While some version of the National Security Council format (wherein bureaucracies focus on, and develop options around, issues formulated by the president and his assistant for national security affairs) is the most suitable model, it should be modified to enhance the technical competence of central policy-making bodies, to divest these of their operational roles, and to assign to the departments and agencies of government more responsibility (and accountability) for the implementation of policies. It might even be altered to include the establishment of a cabinet-level "Committee on Nuclear Programs" which would: (1) outline national policies on strategic needs, military planning to meet those needs, and political initiatives; (2) exchange views on important strategic issues; and (3) critically evaluate the execution of policies and programs. This committee should also be the prime mechanism for decision making in crisis situations.

To the extent that the work of the committee involves, as it will, force planning and targeting doctrine, the president must exercise his authority to induce meaningful participation by the joint chiefs of staff; to the extent that its work affects alliance policy, as it also will, efforts should be made to persuade the allies to establish counterparts, such as a North Atlantic Treaty Organization (NATO) Political Planning Group. The aim, in this and other ways, would be to extend into the NATO and other alliances "the hoped-for-logic and coherence of U.S. decision making that will be a requisite for survival in the future."

Where Dr. Brenner dealt with the processes of decision making, Dr. Michael Nacht deals with their substance, commencing with the observation that U.S. policy toward states which have acquired nuclear weapons has tended to be based on previous bilateral relations with those states rather than on any consistent doctrine for coping with the consequences of nuclear proliferation. If the United States wishes to fashion a more coherent policy it has, according to Dr. Nacht, five options:

1. to exercise *malign neglect*, which means taking no effort to prevent proliferation, withdrawing from the international arena, and concentrating on the build-up of a military posture capable of defense as well as of deterrence;
2. to sponsor *nuclear realignment* by creating a ruling elite composed of the nuclear weapons states—augmented by those which subsequently acquire such weapons;
3. to practice *confrontation politics* in an effort to head off proliferation—or even to destroy the facilities and the delivery vehicles of states that have crossed the nuclear threshold;
4. to *promote equality* by closing the gaps between North and South in terms of levels of development, standards of living, and economic power—and hence, in terms of military capabilities and political influence;
5. to practice *adaptive continuity*, that is, to go on doing the same things as now, but to do them better.

As Dr. Nacht sees it, the fifth policy (which is both the most likely one and the preferred one) would be marked by attempts to control the spread of nuclear weapons through political-military strategies and through energy-related strategies. Measures under the former should include strengthening the NPT; pressing for Soviet-U.S. arms limitations; pledging the non-use of nuclear weapons against non-nuclear states, with the caveat that this would not apply to such states or their allies if they assist one or more nuclear-armed states in aggressive actions; adopting a comprehensive test ban treaty; extending and strengthening security guarantees; and imposing nonmilitary sanctions on a selective basis. Measures which might be adopted under energy-related strategies should encompass promoting suppliers' agreements which would further regulate the transfer of nuclear technology; exercising unilateral restraints on U.S. nuclear energy programs (as with respect to plutonium recycling and fast-breeder reactors); establishing multinational nuclear facilities instead of national ones; and increasing financial support to the IAEA.

Even if these measures fail to check proliferation, the United States should continue them, against an N + 1st power as well as against an Nth power. However, ongoing proliferation is likely to make the world a much more dangerous place, as well as to affect adversely United States security interests. If, therefore, there is a major shock to the system, such as might occur from the sale of a nuclear weapon or the use of one in anger, the United States may move more aggressively to halt further proliferation, employing coercive and military measures where necessary. Whether these, or any of the measures suggested earlier, can suffice to maintain U.S. security in a world of nuclear powers is, Dr. Nacht believes, an open question; nevertheless, he views the option of adaptive continuity as the optimal U.S. response.

SUMMARY

To sum up, nuclear proliferation may be almost inevitable; the question is not whether it will occur but among what countries, to what extent, and at what pace. The countries most likely to go nuclear are those whose security may be threatened in ways with which they cannot cope, either through the build-up of conventional armaments or through the establishment of secure relations with powerful protectors, countries such as Israel, Pakistan, South Africa, South Korea, and Taiwan. Another set of countries, such as Argentina, Brazil, and Iran, may be motivated less by military considerations than by political and economic ones, including the desire for increased status and prestige, the wish to enhance their influence in international negotiations, and the belief that nuclear weapons technology will promote economic development and accelerate the process of modernization. And still a third set, to include Japan and West Germany, may not seek nuclear weapons unless the political-military environment changes drastically and adversely—as might be the case if the Cold War were renewed and/or the United States tended to withdraw into itself.

As suggested by these lists, it is possible for the present nuclear powers—and especially for the United States—to influence the choices of some potential Nth powers through their own willingness to help settle disputes, to ameliorate tensions, and to offer both military assistance and security guarantees—though these latter measures may be counterproductive if they are done in competition with other nuclear powers and dangerous if they are extended while disputes persist among rivals who are backed by rival superpowers. In other instances, the potential influence of the nuclear powers upon Nth country choices may be less, either because they can acquire this influence only by deliberately giving up most of their own military and economic power (which is like asking them to commit suicide in order to diminish the risk of being murdered) or because the incentives to proliferation are beyond their control. They can, however, affect in larger degree the extent and the pace of proliferation—if they are willing to pay the price in terms of other objectives.

Judgments as to the best way to slow, channel, and limit proliferation differ markedly; to paraphrase former Secretary of Defense Lovett, whenever three people discuss nuclear proliferation, four different opinions emerge. At the risk of voicing that fourth opinion, I would suggest that the United States and other like-minded countries look to:

1. The promotion of détente, to include the normalization of relations with the People's Republic of China and, hopefully, between the PRC and other countries, including the Soviet Union. To the extent that the nuclear powers (and especially the two superpowers) behave responsibly, eschew confrontations, and demonstrate that they can,

despite their differences, live together in some degree of amity, they will both reduce fears that they will misuse their nuclear forces and demonstrate that these are not the ultimate determinants of national behavior.

2. The amelioration of differences likely to induce proliferation, as could those between Israel and her Arab neighbors and between India and other states in South Asia. These, even more than concerns about the armaments and the defense policies of the nuclear powers, are major incentives to proliferation, and their resolution would go far to slow the diffusion of nuclear weapons as well as to make the world a safer place—for other states as well as for those at loggerheads with each other.

3. The establishment of policies which not only would inhibit the acquisition by additional nations of self-contained nuclear energy systems but also would offer them viable alternatives to these systems, such as participation in nuclear research under international auspices, a share in multinational reprocessing plants, and, if necessary, free access to "peaceful nuclear explosives." (Whatever the costs of such measures, in dollars, in commercial advantages, or in other forms, they would be immeasurably less than the costs of adapting to a nuclear-armed world).

4. The concerted application of economic sanctions against states which detonate nuclear devices, which divert fissionable materials to the production of atomic weapons, or which refuse, after due notice, to allow whole-cycle inspection of their nuclear facilities, to include those they themselves have constructed. While the imposition of even limited sanctions may run counter to other national objectives (such as the maintenance of allied solidarity), and hence should not be undertaken lightly, their imposition against an Nth power may be essential if the N + 1st power is to be persuaded to forgo atomic bombs—or if either are to be induced to stop after the first nuclear explosion.

5. A greater willingness to accord status, and influence, to countries on the basis of factors other than nuclear capabilities or even military strength—factors such as economic capacity, level of development, or contributions to peace. In some sense this has already been done, as with Japan; but Brazil, India, Poland, and Sweden, to name just a few countries, have not been treated similarly or even comparably.

Whether these, or any other, policies will succeed even in slowing the pace of proliferation is questionable; as indicated earlier, many of the elements shaping decisions on whether to go nuclear are beyond the control of even the most powerful proponent of non-proliferation. What can be said, without question, is that unless such policies are adopted, proliferation will go on apace. And while one can scarcely argue that it is "right" for the United States (or the Soviet Union) to attempt to check the diffusion of power of which proliferation is both an instance and a symbol, one cannot argue either that it is right for those promoting that diffusion to do so by acquiring nuclear weapons. Surely there are other and less dangerous ways of advancing national interests. And conceivably, if both nuclear and potential nuclear powers look hard enough, they may find them—even if we, the authors of this work, have not.

ANNALS, AAPSS, 430, March 1977

Part I Introduction: Where We Are . . .

By JOSEPH I. COFFEY

Ever since the end of World War II, the nations of the world have pursued two basic (and inherently contradictory) goals: that of promoting and exploiting "atoms for peace" and that of controlling—and if possible eliminating—"atoms for war." In pursuit of the first goal, they have promoted research on nuclear technology, sponsored the development of nuclear reactors, and disseminated widely both the results of that research and the fruits of that development—thereby supplying knowledge and facilities which can be used to produce nuclear weapons. In pursuit of the second goal, that of controlling these weapons, some nations have sought to eliminate them completely, as the United States proposed in the Baruch Plan of 1946. Failing this, they have sought to prevent both "vertical proliferation,"[1] that is, the further development, accumulation, and deployment of weapons by the power(s) already possessing them, and "horizontal proliferation," the acquisition of nuclear weapons by additional powers.

In neither of these efforts have the nations sponsoring them been successful. The United States, which detonated the first atomic device at Alamogordo, New Mexico, on July 16, 1945, has since then both improved and vastly enlarged its stockpiles of nuclear weapons. In the 31 years since that first test, the Soviet Union (in 1949), the United Kingdom (in 1952), France (in 1960), and China (in 1964) have also "gone nuclear." On May 18, 1974, India set off a "peaceful nuclear explosive," which involves essentially the same technology as an atomic bomb, and became the world's sixth nuclear power, de facto if not de jure. And Israel, according to some reports,[2] has fabricated, though not tested, atomic bombs, thus raising the possibility that it may become the seventh.

These developments took place despite efforts to prevent proliferation, efforts which resulted in the conclusion of a number of international agreements. Among these are the 1963 Treaty Banning Nuclear Weapon Tests in the Atmosphere, in Outer Space and Under Water (known as the Partial Test Ban Treaty or PTBT), the 1967 Treaty for the Prohibition of Nuclear Weapons in Latin America (the Treaty of Tlatelolco), and, above all, the 1968 Treaty on the Non-Proliferation of Nuclear Weapons (known as the Non-Proliferation Treaty or NPT). While the International Atomic Energy Agency (IAEA) and the European Atomic Energy Community (Euratom), both established in 1957, were not created to prevent nuclear weapons

1. Definitions of these and other exotic terms will be found in the Glossary.
2. *The New York Times*, 15 March 1976, p. 1.

proliferation but rather to promote cooperation in the peaceful uses of atomic energy, they must be regarded as parts of the non-proliferation system insofar as they provide safeguards against the diversion of fissionable materials to the manufacture of weapons or nuclear explosive devices. And since the agreements that have been, or may be, reached at the Strategic Arms Limitation Talks (SALT) are in part an attempt to implement those provisions of the NPT calling for the cessation of the nuclear arms race and for nuclear disarmament, they also can be regarded as part of the network of arrangements intended to prevent the spread of nuclear weapons.

Several things have combined to bring into question the effectiveness of these arrangements. One was the action of India, which ended a 10-year period wherein no new power had detonated a nuclear device and which high-lighted the dissatisfactions of many states with the seemingly discriminatory provisions of the NPT, with the lack of real progress in SALT, and with the absence of firm guarantees of their security against attack. Another was the oil embargo of 1973, which spurred programs for the construction of power reactors as alternative sources of energy. A third was the fact that some of the developing countries sought (and some of the technically advanced countries were willing to provide) facilities for reprocessing fissionable materials from these reactors which would make these Third World countries independent of the nuclear powers—and which would facilitate their making atomic bombs, should they subsequently choose to do so. A fourth was the prospect that innovations in nuclear technology, such as the development of the fast breeder reactor, would further ease the difficulty of producing nuclear weapons. And a fifth was the upsurge of terrorism, which induced fears lest extremists acquire—and use—radioactive products, fissionable materials, or even nuclear weapons themselves.

In this part of the volume, we will look at the problems presented by these developments, beginning with a discussion of the reasons why states go—or don't go—nuclear, continuing with a description of the ways of fabricating atomic bombs and an examination of the safeguards against the diversion or seizure of fissionable materials, and ending with an inquiry into the prospects for reducing the incentives to proliferation. In this way we should both impart information about the problem of proliferation and suggest some ways of coping with it—thereby achieving the two principal objectives of any volume on public policy issues. Whether we succeed or fail you can judge as you read.

ANNALS, AAPSS, 430, March 1977

Why States Go—And Don't Go—Nuclear

By WILLIAM EPSTEIN

ABSTRACT: The incentives and disincentives for countries to go nuclear comprise a combination of military, political, and economic concerns and motivations. These vary over time for different countries. For countries allied to one of the two nuclear superpowers, concern about their military security is not a predominant factor, while it is the decisive one for the non-nuclear countries who are not under the nuclear umbrella of a superpower and who perceive serious threats to their security. For countries without acute security problems, the political and economic motivations are the predominant ones and these include such incentives as strengthening their independence and increasing their status and prestige in the world. The disincentives are largely potential, ranging from effective security guarantees through adequate supplies of conventional armaments to assurances concerning future supplies of fissile materials. Incentives to go nuclear appear to outweigh the disincentives. Only drastic measures by the nuclear powers in the way of security assurances, nuclear disarmament, and the creation of a more just political and economic world order can serve to prevent the emergence of a proliferated world.

William Epstein is a Special Fellow at the United Nations Institute for Training and Research and is engaged from time to time as a Special Consultant on Disarmament by the Secretary-General of the United Nations. He was for many years the Director of the Disarmament Division of the United Nations Secretariat. He is also a Visiting Professor at the University of Victoria in British Columbia, Canada. He has written extensively on arms control and disarmament, the non-proliferation of nuclear weapons, disarmament negotiations, and international organization. His most recent book is The Last Chance: Nuclear Proliferation and Arms Control.

The expression to "go nuclear" is used in this paper to mean the acquisition of a nuclear device, whether by manufacture or otherwise, whose availability has been publicly demonstrated by the carrying out of a nuclear explosion whether for military or peaceful purposes. For other definitions see the Glossary.

THE ESSENCE of the nuclear arms race is power—military, political, and economic. Almost all nations want to enhance their power and thus improve their positions in the world and increase their influence over the behavior of other nations. At the very least, many will wish to diminish their dependence on other states and to increase their freedom of action—outcomes which again may depend on their accretion of power.

The particular forms that this quest for power will take will, of course, vary; however, some states view nuclear proliferation as a means to this end. As spelled out below, they see nuclear weapons as promoting their security, enhancing their prestige, augmenting their influence, and improving their economic conditions. Whether, and to what extent, a given state will act on these views depends in part on its leaders' perceptions of the international environment and on their assessments of the best ways to achieve national objectives in that environment. It depends also, however, on the results of bureaucratic competition and on the pressures of domestic politics. Thus, the incentives and disincentives which are discussed below will apply differently to different countries at different times, according to both external and internal developments. In nuclear proliferation—as in life itself—nothing is simple!

MILITARY SECURITY

The dominant positive and negative incentives to go, or not to go, nuclear are those involving a country's military security. Problems of military security are paramount questions for all governments, and in the absence of any other satisfactory ways of ensuring it, defense based on military force is the customary preferred path. Whether the disincentives to go nuclear can be reinforced and made to outweigh the incentives will, to a large degree, depend on whether satisfactory alternatives can be found to the possession of military power as a means of ensuring security.

The desire to avoid the incalculable dangers and destruction of a nuclear holocaust—either another Hiroshima or a multitude of Hiroshimas—has been the most powerful disincentive to the spread of nuclear weapons. Nuclear weapons are still regarded with abhorrence as weapons of mass destruction. Fears of the open-ended proliferation of nuclear weapons were the main stimuli that led to the successful conclusion of the Non-Proliferation Treaty (NPT) in 1968. Strong support for the treaty came from two sources: the nuclear powers, who were its architects and chief protagonists, and the non-nuclear countries that had little potential and no likelihood of being able to go nuclear for decades to come (the "never-nuclears"). Because of their perceived common interest in preventing the major industrial states, such as West Germany and Japan, and such Third World countries as India, Israel, and Brazil, from going nuclear, the great and the small powers entered into a tacit alliance in an effort to prevent the near-nuclear and potential nuclear powers from going nuclear.

It was recognized that unless the process of proliferation was stopped all countries that could afford them would eventually acquire nuclear weapons, which would then become almost as common and universal as conventional weapons. Few doubted that this would mean almost inevitably a nuclear war of some kind. The danger lay not only in the possibilities of a nuclear war by deliberate intent and premeditation but, even more, the likelihood of such a war in a proliferated world occurring by accident, miscalculation, human or mechanical failure; ineffective command, control, and communication procedures; nuclear blackmail and terrorism; escalation of a regional conventional or nuclear war; or by sheer madness.

There is little support today for the "Gallois approach" which holds that the possession of nuclear weapons by additional nuclear powers, including adversaries among the smaller hostile ones, might have a mutually deterrent and stabilizing effect, as is claimed in the case of the great nuclear powers. It is because of the broad acceptance of the threat to international peace and security that would be posed by the further proliferation of nuclear weapons that the NPT, despite all its shortcomings, now has 100 signatories.

While the fears of the increased possibilities of a nuclear war with all its unthinkable consequences provided the main disincentive for the "horizontal" proliferation of nuclear weapons to new countries, it was the tremendous military advantages that flowed from the destructiveness of these weapons that provided the main incentive for both the "vertical" proliferation of their nuclear stockpiles by the nuclear powers and the acquisition of such weapons by additional powers. A list of such advantages which have motivated countries in the past, and may do so to other countries in the future, includes the following:

a. To achieve military superiority over an enemy or potential enemy (for example, the United States against Germany and Japan in World War II).

b. To prevent a perceived or potential enemy from achieving or maintaining superiority over you in either nuclear or conventional weapons (for example, each of the present nuclear powers).

c. To achieve an effective deterrent against a hostile nuclear power (for example, the NATO nuclear powers and possibly such potential nuclear powers as Israel, Iran, Pakistan, South Korea, and Taiwan).

d. To ensure that you will have a nuclear weapon capability or at least a nuclear option before an adversary does (for example, Argentina, Brazil, Egypt, Israel, Libya, and Saudi Arabia).

e. To achieve a greater degree of military independence without having to rely on the support of one or more nuclear powers (for example, Britain, France, China, India).

The USSR (in 1949), the UK (in 1952), France (in 1960), and China (in 1964) have each acquired nuclear weapons in part to deter a nuclear attack or threat by one of the nuclear superpowers. Each of these countries proceeded to acquire (more or less) invulnerable strategic nuclear weapons in order to be able to inflict an unacceptable amount of damage on the potential enemy. Once any country has gone nuclear, its rivals or competitors (whether adversary great powers or hostile neighboring small powers) are subjected to powerful pressures also to acquire nuclear weapons.

India, too, which had been one of the strongest and most active proponents of non-proliferation in the 1950s and early sixties, began to think in terms of nuclear deterrence after China exploded its first atomic bomb. Now that India has gone nuclear, domestic pressures on Pakistan to do so become practically irresistible. As Ali Bhutto remarked a few years ago, Pakistan will "eat grass" if necessary to keep up with India.

If Pakistan should go nuclear in order not to be defenseless against a possible Indian attack, it is hardly likely that Iran and Indonesia will refrain from going nuclear for similar security reasons. What new line or "firebreak" can be invented to keep Iran and Indonesia and eventually Bangladesh from going nuclear? It is easy to outline scenarios whereby Taiwan might feel it necessary to acquire a nuclear deterrent force against China or South Korea against either the USSR or China.

The logic of the "awful arithmetic" of nuclear weaponry is that the same reasons or arguments that led to the emergence of six nuclear powers can be used (whether rightly or wrongly is largely irrelevant) by the seventh, eighth, and ninth nuclear powers. The latter might be third-class nuclear powers who would have no really effective deterrent capacity against either the superpowers or the secondary nuclear powers for many years or decades. But a third-class nuclear power would certainly have an overwhelming military advantage in its own local area or region if it were the sole nuclear power there; it would have a deterrent capability against any local attack even if it lost its monopoly and one or more countries in the region acquired nuclear weapons. And it might believe it had some deterrent capability even against a nuclear power—at least enough to discourage ordinary nuclear threats or blackmail.

The domino theory would seem to have greater applicability to countries going nuclear than to countries falling to a political ideology. Whether it be regarded as the Nth-country problem or as a sort of chain reaction, the fact is that each time a country goes nuclear, it increases the incentives or pressures for its neighbors and other similarly situated countries to do so. So long as there was a sort of firebreak separating the great powers, who were permanent members of the Security Council, from all other powers, there was a chance of holding the line against the further horizontal proliferation of nuclear weapons. But once membership in the club is acquired by a middle or smaller power, the disincentive for other middle or smaller powers is greatly weakened.

If one other country should go nuclear, it would be difficult to keep the dam from bursting. Countries that had ratified the NPT might withdraw on three months' notice. As one country after another went nuclear, it would not take long for some parties to give notice of withdrawal. As the Shah of Iran said in September 1975 in an interview with the *New York Times*: "I am not really thinking of nuclear arms. But if 20 or 30 ridiculous little countries are going to develop nuclear weapons, then I may have to revise my policies. Even Libya is talking about trying to manufacture atomic weapons." There is no way of knowing how firmly he would stand on the figures 20 or 30. Depending on what countries went nuclear, the figures might be reduced to two or three.

The argument of a nuclear deterrent against a massive conventional attack may be perceived as having considerable validity for Israel against the Arab states, South Africa against black Africa, and Argentina against Brazil. In fact, apart from the example of these near-nuclear states, it can be used by any relatively advanced small state against any large neighbor whom it regards as a potential conventional adversary. It could apply to Cuba, Pakistan, Taiwan, and Turkey and a host of others, including Yugoslavia against the Soviet Union. Looking ahead to the more distant future, some scholars have even speculated about the possibility that some of the small Warsaw Pact powers in Eastern Europe might harbor such thoughts against the Soviet Union.

It was mainly for military reasons that a number of near-nuclear countries with vital security problems did not become parties to the NPT. They and some potential nuclear powers that had similar acute security problems wanted to keep their options open and are the most likely candidates to go nuclear over a period of time. The most important of these countries are: Argentina, Brazil, Chile, Cuba, Egypt, India, Indonesia, Israel, Pakistan, Turkey, South Africa, Spain, and Switzerland. Other countries that are parties to the NPT, but that have important internal or international security problems, include Iran, Libya, South Korea, Taiwan, and Yugoslavia; under the terms of the NPT they can, if they choose, withdraw on three months' notice.

A major disincentive for such countries going nuclear would be the provision of effective and credible security guarantees. Such guarantees can be provided in a number of ways:

a. By positive guarantees to come to a country's aid if it is threatened or attacked with nuclear weapons. The most effective guarantee is by a treaty of military alliance. Thus, the members of the NATO and Warsaw Pact alliances who come under the nuclear umbrella and defense commitments of one of the superpowers have no particular need or incentive to go nuclear. The same is true of countries having bilateral treaties of alliance such as Mongolia, Japan, South Korea, and Taiwan. Short of such formal, public, legal, military commitments, however, it is doubtful whether any country would regard a security guarantee as being sufficient to ensure its security. Even U.S. allies, such as France, South Korea, and Taiwan, have doubts at times about the adequacy and permanence of alliance guarantees. The stationing of American troops on their territories has tended to reinforce the commitment. Except for France, in whose case other incentives were important, none of the U.S. allies has demonstrated any present intention of going nuclear, although several, including Taiwan, have acquired an option to do so.

The resolution of the UN Security Council of June 17, 1968, and the declarations of intention made by the US, USSR, and UK in the council that they would "seek immediate Security Council action to provide assistance, in accordance with the Charter," to any non-nuclear party to the NPT against which nuclear weapons are used or threatened, are subject to the veto and are not regarded by non-nuclear powers as providing any effective or credible guarantee.

b. By negative security assurances, whereby the nuclear powers would pledge never to use or threaten to use nuclear weapons against non-nuclear powers who did not have nuclear weapons on their territories. At one time, during the negotiation of the NPT, the non-nuclear powers regarded such assurances as important, and they still would prefer to have them. The United States, however, has refused to give such assurances for fear that they would be regarded by its NATO allies as undermining its commitment to them. In any case, the faith of the non-nuclear powers in the usefulness of such assurances has eroded over the years, and they would regard such negative assurances as providing little or no incentive to forbear going nuclear.

c. By the nuclear powers fulfilling their NPT obligations to pursue efforts to halt the nuclear arms race and achieve measures of nuclear disarmament. Here, too, the success of such efforts was at one time regarded as an indirect way of increasing the security of all countries, but faith in such efforts has also been eroded by the failure of the nuclear parties to the NPT to stop testing nuclear weapons or achieve any actual measures of nuclear disarmament. Only drastic nuclear disarmament that would reverse the nuclear arms race might serve to provide any real incentive against nuclear proliferation.[1]

d. By being assured of a supply of conventional arms that would ensure a threatened country's ability to deal with any potential conventional attack. A guarantee of such a supply of arms would clearly help to remove or lessen the need or desire of such beleaguered countries as Israel, South Korea, or Taiwan to go nuclear.

e. If a strong police force was available to the UN Security Council either to defend any country from a nuclear or conventional attack or to take military sanctions against any country that went nuclear in violation of its NPT obligations, and if the nations of the world believed that the UN force would be used for those purposes, this would provide good reasons for a country to forgo nuclear weapons. The possibilities of this occurring in the near future, however, are remote.[2]

POLITICAL PRESTIGE

It has become obvious to all countries that the acquisition of nuclear weapons and the technology for making them enhance a nation's prestige and status in the world, not just in military terms, but also in other ways. States possessing these arms are given greater weight in the entire range of foreign policy matters. They are brought into more top level international discussions of all kinds, and their views are treated with greater respect. Because of their nuclear weapon capability, the United Kingdom and France, who have fallen behind Japan and West Germany in economic strength, are still regarded as great powers, and China and India, who are much further down the list, are also treated as having achieved great power status. Brazil and Iran, which regard themselves as potential great powers, may very well be attracted to going nuclear by the larger voice they would receive not only in regional but also in world affairs.

Thus, states may seek, through the acquisition of nuclear weapons:

a. To maintain or achieve great power status. The best examples of the former are the secondary nuclear powers: The UK, France, and China. India at the present time and per-

1. For a contrary view, see George Quester, "Reducing the Incentives to Proliferation."

2. See Abraham Bargman, "The United Nations, the Superpowers, and Proliferation."

haps Brazil and Iran in the future are examples of the latter.

b. To be assured of a seat at the "head table" in international forums. This would apply mainly to the larger and more developed countries.

c. To enhance their prestige within a region or grouping of states.

d. To redress a perceived inferiority in the international hierarchy. This would apply mainly to former colonies that wish to achieve a status of equality with the former colonial powers.

e. To remove discriminatory aspects affecting their status, such as the distinction between nuclear and non-nuclear powers, the ban on conducting peaceful nuclear explosions, or having to accept international safeguards on all their nuclear activities.

f. To demonstrate political independence and self-reliance and to be able to resist political pressures from the nuclear superpowers.

On the other hand, the political pressures exercised in manifold direct and indirect ways by the nuclear powers and by some of the more important developed non-nuclear countries can provide disincentives to a country going nuclear. In addition, a beleaguered country might risk losing the direct and open political and moral support of one or more nuclear powers in world councils and in interstate relations. As indicated above, a country that has the capability to go nuclear can gain some enhanced political stature and prestige by a deliberate decision based on moral grounds to refrain from doing so.

ECONOMIC BENEFITS

Economic considerations are, in large part, a close parallel to or reflection of the political considerations. They affect both the developed and developing countries.

a. It is widely believed that the peaceful applications of nuclear energy, particularly as a source of cheap power, could be a major factor in promoting a country's economic position and improving its standard of living. It is also still believed that there are important "spinoff" benefits in the form of peaceful uses from the technology acquired as a result of know how in the field of nuclear explosions, despite the contrary evidence from the experience of Canada, West Germany, Japan, and Sweden.

b. Although there are growing doubts about the potential benefits of peaceful nuclear explosions, the Soviet Union and most of the developing countries continue to have great hopes for them, hopes which are fed by the May 13, 1976, US-USSR Treaty on Underground Nuclear Explosions for Peaceful Purposes.

c. Some countries are interested in building up a peaceful nuclear industry because of the potential military spinoff benefits. Even if they have no present intention of going nuclear, as has been repeatedly stressed by leaders in Brazil, Iran, South Africa, Taiwan, and other countries, they have the good feeling that by developing their nuclear industries they are acquiring a nuclear option in case the time comes when they might want to exercise that option.

Thus, the symbiotic nature of the peaceful and military uses of nuclear energy is perceived as providing spinoff benefits in both directions. The military spinoff from peaceful uses appears to have more validity than the reverse.

d. In any case, countries interested in nuclear energy—India, Brazil, and Iran are the best examples—would like to be in the very front rank of technology. They believe that the acquisition of advanced nuclear technological capability will help close the economic gap between themselves and the rich countries and will elevate their economic power and prestige. In this field, as in the political, national nuclear power industries are coming to be regarded somewhat like national airlines.

e. It is generally accepted that, once a country has established a domestic nuclear power industry, it can readily go nuclear at very low cost, since the major costs would have been taken care of in the creation of the nuclear industry. For example, it has been reported that the cost of India's underground explosion was less than $250,000. Nuclear weapons also provide a "bigger bang for a buck," that is to say they yield greater military benefits at much less cost than modern conventional arms and forces. The actual cost of manufacturing the warhead is relatively cheap—in the range of tens of thousands of dollars. This cost benefit is of particular interest to countries that are content to use aircraft and other existing means of delivery. It would not, of course, apply to countries that might want a range of sophisticated nuclear weapons and delivery vehicles.

f. Perhaps most important of all the economic incentives is that countries, particularly those that were former colonies, perceive the acquisition of nuclear capability in the economic as well as the military and political field as freeing them from dependence on the superpowers and former colonial powers, giving them a larger degree of economic independence, and avoiding the dangers of some form of nuclear neocolonialism.

g. Finally, some Third World countries that are committed to the creation of a new world economic order may perceive the acquisition of a nuclear option as giving them greater bargaining leverage with the rich industrial countries and greater power to resist nuclear blackmail in the economic as well as in other fields or even to try to exploit their own nuclear blackmail. With problems posed by poverty, population, hunger, energy resources, pollution, and multinational corporations likely to intensify rather than abate in the future, it is not unlikely that this incentive will also increase as time passes.

While it is not popular to discuss disincentives in terms of "carrots" or "sticks," these are the main instruments available to governments for influencing the actions of other governments, and there are a number of these which might induce a country to forgo nuclear weapons:

a. A guaranteed source and supply of nuclear fuel to operate their power reactors can constitute a strong incentive to countries not to go nuclear. If nuclear power provides a significant portion of a country's energy requirements, it is a matter of major economic importance that its supply of nuclear fuel be maintained and not interrupted.

b. Conversely, if a country knew that it would lose its source of supply if it went nuclear, the threat of such an embargo might have the desired effect. It is important, however, that the risk of an embargo be clear and certain. Only Canada terminated its nuclear assistance program to India after the Indian explosion and, at the time of writing, it is not clear whether the United States and other countries will do so. Failure to impose such economic sanctions, even limited to the nuclear field, can create a presumption against imposing them in the future in other cases.

c. Similarly if a country knew that it could not acquire any nuclear facilities or technology unless it agreed to become a party to the NPT or to accept equivalent restrictions and safeguards, this, too, would provide an important reason for not going nuclear. Apparently, Libya and South Korea were induced to become parties to the NPT in order to obtain nuclear reactors, and South Korea reportedly was persuaded to abandon its plan to acquire a plutonium reprocessing plant from France in order to ensure the continued availability of nuclear and other assistance from the United States. Some observers have argued, however, that these countries joined the NPT in order to be able to obtain nuclear reactors and technology so that they could acquire a nuclear weapons option and go nuclear at some later time if they chose.

d. If the London Suppliers' Club could agree on strict rules and standards for the supply of nuclear equipment, materials, and technology under conditions that would, to the extent that this is possible, prevent nuclear weapon proliferation (which they have not as yet done), this would probably constitute the most powerful feasible incentive for countries not to go nuclear.

e. Since the build-up of stocks of spent fuel can create an environmental hazard, particularly for heavily populated states or small countries, the willingness of supplier states to accept the return of spent nuclear fuel or to arrange for its storage elsewhere could constitute some incentive to such countries to agree not to reprocess their fuel and thus make it more difficult for them to go nuclear.

f. Assurances of economic and financial support extending beyond the nuclear field can provide a strong inducement to countries not to go nuclear. If it were to extend to matters of far-reaching import such as specific elements of a new world economic order, it could become a most important incentive that might help to create a new political and moral climate that would strongly favor the maintenance and strengthening of the non-proliferation regime. Here, again, the threat or possibility of discontinuing such support could prevent or inhibit a country from going nuclear.

GENERAL OBSERVATIONS

There is no way in which to measure or quantify the respective inducements and motivations outlined above with any degree of precision. Nevertheless, certain observations can be made with some degree of confidence. It would appear to be almost axiomatic that considerations of military security are the predominant ones. For countries facing real threats to their survival, independence, or integrity, the paramount and decisive incentive is security, and all others pale into relative insignificance. Such acute problems fortunately afflict only a few countries, and special measures may be necessary with regard to them if, indeed, any measures can be effective for long.

For such countries, it may be necessary to work out or allow for some special status or category in which they would not be strictly nuclear or non-nuclear. This category would consist of states such as Israel, which is reported to have some assembled or almost completed nuclear weapons that it can explode at any time. It might include such other countries as Argentina, Egypt, Pakistan, South Korea, Taiwan, and South Africa. It might restrain or slow down the trend of proliferation if such countries developed their capabilities and kept their options open without actually exploding any nuclear device. This category might also include such states as Australia, Canada, West Germany, Italy, Japan, the Netherlands, Spain, Sweden, and Switzerland, with very advanced nuclear technologies and capabilities, that could easily and quickly go nuclear but have no desire or need to do so at present. They may, however, wish to acquire a nuclear option if a number of other states do so.[3]

Whether a country decides to go nuclear or not depends on reasons that are of particular importance to that country: how it views its needs and interests in the context of the military, political, economic, and moral climate of the world. Governments will be responsive to the reactions and pressures of public opinion in their countries, which will be shaped by developments in neighboring countries rather than by developments in the policies and actions of the nuclear powers that do not directly affect them.

Within each country, there is a whole spectrum of competing and often conflicting opinions, with different groups struggling to make their point of view prevail. It can usually be expected that the military-industrial complex, scientists and bureaucrats associated with it, and the more conservative elements in a country will favor the acquisition of nuclear weapons, while the more liberal elements, peace groups, and scientists in universities and other academic institutions will oppose that course of action. One particular impetus to the acquisition of nuclear weapons has been provided by the scientists and technicians involved in nuclear energy programs. In the cases of France and India, it was these who became the active—and indeed the primary—proponents of nuclear weapons development.

In some circumstances, because of intractable economic and social problems which create internal political dissatisfaction and unrest, domestic politics rather than international considerations may provide the impetus for going nuclear. By exercising that option, a government can win the support of opposing or wavering military, political, and scientific elites and other influential groups, as well as the general public. There is some evidence that the Indian explosion was motivated, at least in part, by the need of that government to gain popular support.

Some success on the part of the nuclear powers in moving toward real nuclear disarmament could at least help to postpone the decisions of non-nuclear countries to acquire a nuclear option and capability. Any time gained in this respect will make possible further debate and reflection; it will allow more time for wiser counsels to prevail and for taking action to manage and shape events so as to reduce the pressures for going nuclear. In short, the achievement of substantial progress toward nuclear disarmament by the

3. See Ashok Kapur, "Nth Powers of the Future."

nuclear powers would provide incentives and pressures for the non-nuclear countries to refrain from going nuclear.

THE LINKAGE BETWEEN VERTICAL AND HORIZONTAL PROLIFERATION[4]

The theory has been advanced by a number of persons that there is, in fact, little or no linkage between vertical and horizontal proliferation. Those who propagate this theory hold that what the great powers, and in particular the superpowers, do or do not do to limit and control the nuclear arms race has little to do with whether any non-nuclear power will or will not go nuclear.

While there might be some force to this argument in terms of logic or of rational behavior, the actions of nations in fact are determined more by political, emotional, and psychological factors than by logic or pure reason. If nuclear powers, and not just the superpowers, proclaim and justify their acquisition and continued possession of nuclear weapons as a deterrent against any attack, conventional as well as nuclear, how can they deny the validity of this theory or concept for the other powers? If the possession of nuclear weapons will deter the Soviet Union and the United States, or the Soviet Union and China, from attacking each other, why would they not also deter any attack in an acute crisis between any other pair of adversary states? Since the posture of the nuclear powers seems to be aimed at the highest level of deterrence, particularly in a qualitative or technological sense, it seems clear that they consider that the possession and continued improvement of these weapons are indispensable. As long as the nuclear powers continue to believe and behave in a way that demonstrates they feel more secure with nuclear weapons than without them, it seems hardly likely that they can persuade the non-nuclear powers of the opposite. Certainly they are not in any strong political position, and even less of a moral position, to urge the benefits and value of non-proliferation on the latter. Their example and precept would, on the contrary, undermine the position of the moderates and provide powerful arguments for military and political groups within any wavering country of the need to go nuclear.

The failure of the two superpowers, despite their commitments in the NPT to agree on a comprehensive test ban (that is, a ban on underground tests) and their agreement on the Threshold Test Ban Treaty in July 1974 and the Peaceful Nuclear Explosion Treaty in May 1976 (which permit individual nuclear explosions for both military and peaceful purposes up to a yield of 150 kilotons), serves to highlight the matter. The non-nuclear countries are becoming increasingly disillusioned by what they regard as the blatant cynicism of the superpowers.

Among the nuclear powers, only China has clearly and unequivocally declared that it would never be the first to use nuclear weapons and that it would never use nuclear weapons against non-nuclear states, and it has called on all other nuclear states to make similar declarations. No other nuclear power has made a similar declaration, though the Soviet Union and France have at different times and in less categorical terms indicated that they would favor such

4. For a more detailed discussion of the subject, see William Epstein, *The Last Chance: Nuclear Proliferation and Arms Control* (New York: The Free Press, 1976).

a policy if it were agreed by all the nuclear powers. The United States, however, has not only refused to make any such declarations but, in fact, after its withdrawal from Vietnam, expressly reaffirmed the policy of first use of nuclear weapons, if necessary, to repel a conventional attack in Europe or against South Korea. This policy could result in heightened incentives in non-nuclear countries to acquire nuclear weapons, not only to deter a local or regional conventional attack, but also as a response to nuclear threats or blackmail against them by nuclear powers. Although they could never hope to match the major nuclear powers, they might well conclude (as did General de Gaulle) that they could achieve some degree of nuclear deterrence against the nuclear powers by counter-threats of "tearing off an arm."

What the nuclear powers and other great powers do determines not only the military but also the political and moral climate in the world. If the superpowers demonstrate that they intend to halt and reverse the nuclear arms race and are, in fact, engaged in doing so and in living up to their legal and moral obligations, they will create a climate that favors nuclear arms restraint and that discourages or weakens the elements within other countries that want to go nuclear. Their cessation of the nuclear arms race would have a positive effect on world security and would begin to diminish the aura of prestige that is attached to the possession of vast stockpiles of nuclear weapons. It might also release human and material resources for scientific and technological development of the peaceful uses of nuclear energy and for making them more safe. It would begin to lessen the central role that these weapons play in the defense systems and power positions of the nuclear states and reduce their psychological involvement and preoccupation with nuclear weaponry. Above all, it would enhance the moral position of the nuclear powers and put them in a better position to urge other states not to go nuclear.

On the other hand, the continuing failure of the nuclear powers to stop nuclear tests, to halt the arms race, and to achieve measures of nuclear disarmament will provide, if not genuine reasons, then at least excuses for other countries to go nuclear. It will certainly strengthen the arguments and positions of the nuclear hawks and weaken those of the doves in the non-nuclear countries. As the nuclear powers militarize the world with both nuclear and conventional weapons, the development of regional arms races and of an arms race climate in the world become inevitable. And such an arms race climate will not stop with the acquisition of conventional armaments.

Even if the link between vertical and horizontal proliferation has been exaggerated or exploited by the non-nuclear powers, there can be little doubt that maintaining the legitimacy of nuclear weapons and of the nuclear arms race will facilitate the further spread of these weapons.

It may be difficult or even impossible to prove that, if the nuclear powers completely fulfilled all of their obligations concerning nuclear disarmament, it would necessarily or even to any important extent prevent other countries from going nuclear. The non-nuclear powers might fall back on other arguments or excuses relative to their security, their prestige, their economic and technological development, or the discriminatory nature of the NPT. On the other hand, it is easier to provide evidence that the failure of the nuclear powers to implement their nuclear disarmament pledges has been a factor in damaging or weakening the NPT. The constant repetition of statements and warnings by near-nuclear and other non-nuclear powers that they cannot or will not give up the option to go nuclear so long as the nuclear powers do not give up the vertical proliferation of these weapons, irrespective of how sincerely it is meant, makes it easier for non-parties to stand apart from the NPT. It might also provide a ready excuse some day for any of the non-nuclear parties to the NPT to withdraw from the treaty under the procedure provided for, and thus lead to the final collapse of the non-proliferation regime.

CONCLUSIONS

It is almost universally accepted, with very few dissenters, that the further proliferation of nuclear weapons reduces everybody's security and poses appalling dangers for humanity. The fact that there are 100 parties to the NPT, despite widespread criticism of the treaty and doubts about its effectiveness, testifies to the belief that it represents an accepted means for at least restraining the horizontal proliferation of nuclear weapons.

In assessing the continued viability and credibility of the non-proliferation regime, it becomes apparent that the incentives for states to go nuclear seem to far outweigh the disincentives. Countries facing serious threats to their survival or security pose the greatest challenge. Those non-nuclear countries that are not under the nuclear umbrella of any of the nuclear powers and have no alternative means of ensuring their security feel that they may ultimately have to rely on nuclear weapons and in the meantime are developing nuclear weapon options. Other countries, not faced by such security threats, but desiring to reinforce their independence or to increase their political and economic status and prestige also appear to have strong motivations to go nuclear. Past experience and future prospects are that when any state goes nuclear a chain reaction or domino effect compels its potential adversaries to do likewise.

Only strong inducements involving some combinations of tangible military, political, and economic rewards and punishments could provide the necessary disincentives sufficient to override the more immediate perceived benefits of going nuclear.

The implementation of far-reaching measures that would produce such inducements would require the political and moral leadership of the existing nuclear powers in creating a more secure, more disarmed, and more just political and economic world order that could remove or reduce the needs and desires of other states to go nuclear. Up to the present, the weight of the evidence is against that happening and the prospects are for a proliferating world.

ANNALS, AAPSS, 430, March 1977

How States Can "Go Nuclear"

By FRANK C. BARNABY

ABSTRACT: As indicated by this article, the processes of nuclear fission are well known, the technology for building nuclear reactors is highly developed, and the demands for energy are inducing the construction of more (and more widely distributed) power reactors. Since each reactor is a source of plutonium, this means that the material needed for atomic weapons will be available in large quantities to many countries. Moreover, the technical information needed to fabricate nuclear weapons can be found in unclassified literature, the experts needed to do this are available, the equipment required can be bought in the open market, and the costs are comparatively small. Hence, any state wishing to "go nuclear" can readily do so, and the means of preventing (or even hampering) this are few indeed.

Dr. Frank C. Barnaby has been the Director of SIPRI (Stockholm International Peace Research Institute) since October 1971. Before that he was the Executive Secretary of the Pugwash Conferences on Science and World Affairs and a research physicist at University College, London. He is the author of The Nuclear Future *and* Man and the Atom *and has written or edited books and articles on disarmament issues.*

NUCLEAR weapons,[1] or their components, may be bought, stolen, acquired as gifts, or produced indigenously. Indigenous production requires a nuclear reactor—research, power, or production—and access to a reprocessing facility, or it requires a uranium-enrichment plant. And it is based on the acquisition, through these means, of one of the two sorts of fissile material used for atomic bombs: plutonium-239 (Pu-239) and uranium-235 (U-235).

FISSILE MATERIALS

A new nuclear-weapon country is most likely to base its atomic-bomb program on plutonium; uranium-enrichment is a complex and expensive process. Thus, an understanding of the process whereby plutonium is produced is essential to an understanding of the ways in which nuclear weapons can be fabricated.

Ordinary uranium consists of a mixture of three kinds of atoms, each with different numbers of neutrons in its nucleus: U-234, U-235, and U-238. But only U-235 and U-238 are of any practical consequence; the percentage of U-234 in natural uranium is exceedingly small.

A neutron can cause fission in U-238 only if its velocity exceeds a certain value. But too few of the neutrons available for sustaining the fission process have this critical velocity and a chain reaction is not possible using only U-238. A nucleus of U-235 will undergo fission when any neutron, even one moving very slowly, collides with it, and a chain reaction is possible using U-235. Consequently, the fission process of greatest practical importance consists of the capture of a neutron by a U-235 nucleus, resulting in the formation of a nucleus of the isotope U-236, which rapidly splits into two fragments, nuclei of elements of medium atomic numbers called fission products.

It invariably happens that the total sum of the masses of the fission products and the fission neutrons is less than the mass of the U-236 nucleus. The energy accompanying fission is equal to this mass difference multiplied by the square of the velocity of light. Although the mass difference involved is very small, the velocity of light squared is an enormous number and, therefore, the amount of energy liberated is very large. In fact, the complete fissioning of one gram of U-235 would release about 23,000 kilowatt-hours of heat.

Pu-239 is produced when U-238 nuclei absorb slow neutrons. The U-239 nuclei so formed do not undergo fission but are ultimately transformed into Pu-239 by radioactive decay. A U-239 nucleus decays by emitting an electron which is, so to speak, shot out of the nucleus like a bullet—a process called beta decay. Beta decay occurs when one of the neutrons in a radioactive nucleus spontaneously changes into a proton. A new element is formed by this event, since the new nucleus contains an additional proton. Thus, when U-239 decays, an isotope with an atomic number of 93 is produced, namely neptunium-239 (Np-239). And Np-239 is also radioac-

1. By "nuclear weapon" we normally mean a weapon based on a nuclear explosive, derived either from the fission or the fusion of atomic nuclei. For further definitions, see the Glossary.

tive, undergoing beta decay to produce Pu-239 (atomic number 94) (figure 1).

In a nuclear reactor, plutonium is produced in steadily increasing quantities as the uranium fuel is consumed by fission; nuclear reactors are, therefore, of fundamental importance for proliferation.

NUCLEAR REACTORS

Nuclear reactors, like atomic bombs, depend for their operation on nuclear fission. The fission process alone is, however, insufficient for the practical utilization of nuclear energy, either in reactors or bombs. This can only be achieved because fission, which is initiated by neutrons, is also accompanied by the emission of neutrons and these are, in turn, able to initiate further fission in neighboring nuclei. Provided that at least one neutron can be made to split another nucleus, a self-sustaining process or chain reaction can be produced and energy generated continuously. In a nuclear reactor, a fission chain reaction is initiated and maintained under control, normally using uranium—either natural uranium or that enriched with uranium-235—as fuel.

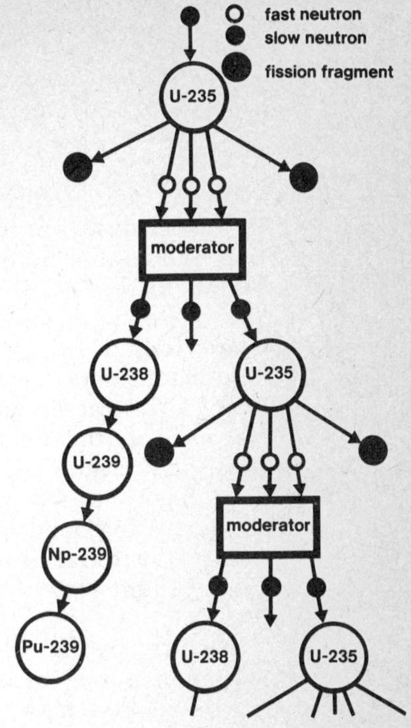

FIGURE 1

The chain reaction—showing the fission of uranium-235 and the subsequent capture of neutrons by uranium-238 leading to the production of plutonium.

A reactor is essentially a furnace where a self-sustaining chain reaction can be controlled and the heat produced put to useful work—usually the production of electricity. Natural uranium by itself cannot be used to produce the chain reaction because of the large proportion of U-238 contained in it. But there is a solution to this problem. This is to mix natural uranium with a substance—called a moderator—whose nuclei are small in size so that if a fast neutron collides with one of them it will lose a large fraction of its velocity, just as a billiard ball will lose velocity when it collides with another one. The neutron's velocity is, thus, rapidly "moderated" down to the low velocity at which it can be efficiently captured by a U-235 nucleus, producing fission, and at which it will have a relatively high probability of avoiding capture by a U-238 nucleus (figure 1).

In a typical power reactor, the fuel, moderator, and coolant are enclosed in a pressure vessel. Heat is removed from the fuel elements in the reactor core by the coolant, which flows over them. The coolant then flows through a heat exchanger where it turns water in a secondary circuit into steam, used to drive a turbine generator which produces electricity.

Several hundred types of reactors have been built or suggested—based on possible permutations of alternative fuels, moderator materials, and coolant materials. But only three types of power reactors (all of which are fueled by uranium) have significant commercial importance. Each is characterized by: the material used as the moderator—graphite, light water (ordinary water), or heavy water (in which the hydrogen is replaced by deuterium)—and the material used as the coolant—gas, light water, or heavy water.

Light-water reactors, by far the world's most common power reactors, have been developed mainly in the United States; in them, ordinary water is used both as the moderator and the coolant. Graphite-moderated, gas-cooled reactors have received most attention in the UK and France, mainly because they were first adopted for plutonium production for the nuclear-weapon programs of these countries. Heavy-water moderated power reactors are much less common than the other two types, mainly because their development was inhibited by the scarcity and relatively high cost of heavy water. Canada, in particular, has based its nuclear program on these reactors.

Currently under development is a fast-breeder reactor, which differs from other types in that it produces more fuel than it consumes. It is possible, by a suitable design, to convert U-238 in the core of the reactor and U-238 placed in a "blanket" around the core into plutonium. "Breeding" occurs because the chain reaction proceeds with a greater neutron surplus than is possible in an ordinary reactor. The stockpile of fissile material is, therefore, steadily increased, and about every 10 years an amount of fuel equal to twice that put in initially is accumulated. Thus, enough fuel becomes available not only to keep the reactor operating but also to fuel a new one of the same size.

Some exploratory work has been carried out on the possibility of using thorium in fast-breeder reactors. If the naturally-occurring isotope Th-232 is introduced into the reactor, some of the nuclei will capture neutrons, producing atoms of the isotope Th-233 which decays to protactinium-233. Protactinium-233 decays, in turn, to U-233. The nuclei of U-233 are fissionable by slow neutrons and, therefore, it is a potentially valuable fissile material like U-235 and Pu-239. U-233 could be, but has so far not been, used to produce atomic bombs.

PLUTONIUM PRODUCTION FROM NUCLEAR POWER REACTORS

The uranium fuel is normally put into a reactor in the form of cylindrical metal-clad elements. When nuclear power reactors are operated for the most economical production of electricity, the plutonium they produce is not suitable for use as the fissile material for very efficient atomic bombs because the fissile isotope of plutonium—Pu-239—is contaminated by the presence of other isotopes of the element, particularly Pu-240. "Weapons-grade" plutonium should contain no more than 10 percent of these other isotopes, and preferably less.

Under normal operating conditions, the fuel elements are left in the reactor for periods of between three and four years, and the plutonium recovered from the spent fuel elements then typically has a Pu-239 content of about 70 percent.[2] This plutonium would be usable in atomic bombs, though relatively large amounts would be needed for a given explosive yield and the physical size of the weapon would be comparatively large. Moreover, Pu-240 is an extremely unstable isotope and undergoes fission spontaneously. Therefore, steps would have to be taken to prevent the device from overheating due to this spontaneous fission. More seriously, because of the likelihood of pre-detonation, the yield of the device would be unpredictable. For these and other reasons, the construction of such a weapon would be a relatively complex task, but the result would be an effective weapon nonetheless.

The operational parameters of nuclear power reactors vary according to type, but it is possible to calculate crudely the world's plutonium production. The net conversion ratio—Pu-239 extracted/U-235 destroyed—for the total mix of reactors expected in the world over the next decade, is likely to be about 0.35. And an average thermal-to-electric conversion efficiency of about 30 percent can be reasonably assumed. This means that about 2.97 grams of U-235 will be destroyed and about 1.04 grams of Pu-239 produced for each megawatt-day of electricity generated. Nuclear power plants will be generally operated for 255 days per year. Therefore, on the average, one megawatt of nuclear capacity will produce annually about 265 grams (255 × 1.04) of Pu-239 for extraction.

The total nuclear electrical capacity in 1980 (taking this year as an example) will be about 300 GWe (gigawatts of electricity), and this will produce about 80,000 kilograms (265 × 300) or 80 tons of Pu-239. This plutonium could become available in 1983—the three-year delay being the time during which the fuel is kept in the reactor and the time needed for the extraction of plutonium from the spent reactor fuel elements. About 40 percent of this plutonium will be produced in the countries which do not now have nuclear weapons. This amount of plutonium corresponds in theory to the production of about 50 atomic bombs, each with a yield equivalent to that of 20,000 tons of TNT, per week in these countries. By 1980, the world will have accumulated about 300,000 kilograms of plutonium—enough for some 9,000 to 10,000 low-yield atomic bombs.[3]

ATOMIC WEAPONS

Any country with a nuclear power reactor has in its territory, in continuously increasing amounts, the basic fissile material for effective

2. If a nuclear power reactor were to be used to produce "weapons-grade" plutonium, the fuel elements would have to be removed after only a few weeks so that the amount of Pu-240 produced would be suitably limited.

3. Few people have a clear idea of how extensive the spread of nuclear technology around the world has already become or how rapidly it will most probably continue. At the end of 1975, 168 nuclear power reactors with a generating capacity greater than 20 million watts of electricity (MWe) were producing a total of about 75,000 MWe in 19 countries (table 1).

By 1980, 29 countries are expected to have installed nuclear power reactors with a total electrical generating capacity of about 220 MWe, about 11 times the 1970 figure. Looking further ahead, it is probable, according to the latest predictions, that the 1980 figure will be multiplied more than 16-fold by the year 2000. By this time, if the present trend continues, nuclear-power reactors will be commonplace on all continents.

TABLE 1

WORLD NUCLEAR POWER CAPACITY IN OPERATION, AS OF 31 DECEMBER 1975 AND PROJECTED FOR 1980

COUNTRY	TOTAL NUCLEAR POWER CAPACITY 1975 MWE (NET)	NUMBER OF POWER REACTORS 1975 (>20 MWE)	TOTAL NUCLEAR POWER CAPACITY 1980 MWE (NET)	NUMBER OF POWER REACTORS 1980* (>20 MWE)	THEORETICAL CAPACITY FOR 20 KT ATOMIC BOMB PRODUCTION 1980 (BOMBS/YEAR)
Argentina	319	1	919	2	25
Austria	—	—	692	1	15
Belgium	1,650	3	3,446	5 (1)	85
Brazil	—	—	626	1	15
Bulgaria	864	2	1,728	4	45
Canada	2,539	7	7,802	15	200
Czechoslovakia	110	1	1,838	5 (3)	45
Finland	—	—	1,500	3	35
France	2,706	10	14,462	22	—
German DR	926	3	1,786	5	45
Germany, FR	4,060	8	13,320	18	330
Hungary	—	—	864	2	20
India	587	3	1,229	6	30
Iran	—	—	1,200	1	30
Italy	542	3	1,422	5	35
Japan	6,287	12	19,066	28 (4)	450
Korea, South	—	—	1,769	3 (2)	45
Mexico	—	—	1,308	2	30
Netherlands	499	2	499	2	12
Pakistan	125	1	125	1	3
Romania	—	—	432	1 (1)	10
Spain	1,073	3	8,365	11 (1)	210
Sweden	3,184	5	8,264	11 (1)	210
Switzerland	1,006	3	5,933	8 (4)	150
Taiwan	—	—	2,158	3	50
UK	4,539	29	10,697	39	—
USA	36,593	54	86,690	103 (5)	—
USSR	5,464	18	19,624	36	—
Yugoslavia	—	—	1,400	2 (1)	35
Totals		1975	1980	Total theoretical bomb production capacity in non-nuclear-weapon countries 1980	2–200 bombs/ year
Countries†		19	29		
Reactors		168	345		
Capacity (*MWe*)		73,073	219,164		

SOURCE: *World Armaments and Disarmament, SIPRI Yearbook 1976* (Stockholm: Almqvist & Wiksell, Stockholm International Peace Research Institute, 1976), p. 42.

* The numbers in brackets indicate the number of reactors included in the total figure for reactors planned for operation in 1980 but not under construction as of 31 December 1975.

† The People's Republic of China has constructed one or two power reactors but only to supply electricity for its military uranium-enrichment plant.

atomic bomb production and the capacity to produce the fissile material for very efficient atomic bombs. But plutonium can also be produced in some research reactors. A research reactor is designed primarily to supply neutrons for experimental purposes or for the production of radioactive isotopes for medical, agricultural, or industrial use. It may also be used for training, materials testing, and so on.

Israel is an example of a country which does not have a power reactor but which has accumulated a stockpile of plutonium produced in a research reactor. Other countries which have large enough research reactors to produce significant quantities of plutonium include Australia, Denmark, Norway, and South Africa.

If breeder reactors are widely used, plutonium will become correspondingly more widespread. The elements from the breeder blanket, in which U-238 is converted into plutonium, will normally contain weapons-grade plutonium (95 to 98 percent Pu-239). The plutonium in the spent fuel elements from the core of the reactor will, moreover, usually contain almost 70 percent of Pu-239, which is about the same constituency as the plutonium in the spent fuel elements from a typical thermal reactor. Second and subsequent generations of breeder reactors may actually be fueled with weapons-grade plutonium.

The plutonium produced in reactor fuel elements is removed in a chemical reprocessing plant. The current worldwide capacity for reprocessing reactor fuel is relatively small (table 2). But the nuclear industries in many countries with significant nuclear-power programs are now demanding new reprocessing plants. The main argument given for this demand is that plutonium is needed to fuel future breeder reactors. The main reason against reprocessing is that it increases the chance of the proliferation of nuclear weapons.

Irrespective of its peaceful nuclear program, a country may decide to acquire and operate clandestinely a reactor specifically for military purposes. The components for a nuclear reactor capable of producing enough plutonium annually for, say, two atomic bombs with yields of 20 kilotons can be obtained easily (and secretly) on the open market. A graphite (or heavy water)-moderated reactor of about 120 megawatts thermal (equivalent to 40 MWe), producing about 20 kilograms of plutonium-239 per year, would be sufficient for this purpose.

The reactor could use natural uranium as fuel, so that no uranium-enrichment facility would be required. So many countries have domestic supplies of uranium which is easily mined and milled, that access to uranium should be no difficulty. The cost of constructing a reactor of this type would not exceed $20 million. The plutonium produced in the reactor fuel elements could be removed in a small, laboratory-scale plant so that access to a commercial reprocessing plant would not be necessary.

In summary, weapon-grade plutonium for an atomic-bomb program may be obtained from (*a*) a power reactor by removing fuel elements in time, (*b*) a research reactor of suitable size, (*c*) the blanket elements of a breeder reactor and, (*d*) the core elements of a later-generation breeder (figure 2). Plutonium for effective atomic bombs may be obtained from a power reactor operated under normal conditions for electricity production or from the core elements of a first-generation breeder reactor. Other than for (*d*) above, access to a reprocessing plant would be necessary to remove the plutonium from the reactor fuel elements. But for low production rates, equivalent to that necessary for a few bombs per year, a small reprocessing unit would certainly suffice. Not only are the construction plans for such a reprocessing unit in the open literature, but the materials

TABLE 2

Summary of the Nuclear Status of Countries Having at Least One Nuclear Reactor or One Element of the Nuclear Fuel Cycle on Their Territory

Country	Power Reactors 1975	Power Reactors 1980	Uranium Enrichment Capability*	Fuel Reprocessing Capability*	Uranium Resources <$30/lb	Uranium Producer 1975–76	Research Reactor in Operation‡	Breeder Reactor Program	NPT Status§	NPT Safeguards Agreement**	Non-NPT Safeguards Agreement with IAEA‡	Member of IAEA‡	Member of Euratom††	Member of NEA‡‡
Algeria					+							+		
Angola					+									
Argentina	+	+			+	+	+				+	+		
Australia			P		+	+	+		R	*		+		+
Austria		+					+		R	*		+		+
Belgium	+	+		*p*§§			+		R	S		+	+	+
Brazil		+	P	P	+		+				+	+		
Bulgaria	+	+					+		R	*		+		
Canada	+	+	P		+	+	+		R	*		+		+
Central African Republic					+				R					
Chile							+				+	+		
Columbia					+		+		S		+	+		
Czechoslovakia	+	+			+		+		R	*		+		
Denmark					+		+		R	*		+	+	+
Egypt							+		S			+		
Finland		+			+		+		R	*		+		
France	+	+	O/C/P*p*	O/C/P*p*	+	+	+	+		nw		+	+	+
Gabon					+	+			R			+		
German DR	+	+					+		R	*		+		
Germany, FR	+	+	O/C	O/C/P	+	+	+	+	R	S		+	+	+
Greece							+		R	*		+		+
Hungary		+					+		R	*		+		
India	+	+		O/C	+	+	+	+			+	+		
Indonesia							+		S		+	+		
Iran		+					+		R	*		+		
Iraq							+		R	*		+		
Israel							+				+	+		
Italy	+	+		P*p*	+		+	+	R	S		+	+	+
Japan	+	+	P	O/C/P	+	+	+	+	S		+	+		+
Korea, South		+					+		R	*		+		

Mauritania					+									
Mexico		+			+	+	+		R			+		
Netherlands	+	+	O/*p*				+		R	S		+	+	+
Niger					+	+						+		
Norway							+		R	*		+		+
Pakistan	+	+		P			+				+	+		
Philippines							+		R	*		+		
Poland							+		R	*				
Portugal					+	+	+				+	+		+
Romania		+					+		R	*		+		
South Africa			O/P		+	+	+				+	+		
Spain	+	+		O	+	+	+				+	+		+
Sweden	+	+	P	P	+		+		R	*		+		+
Switzerland	+	+					+		S		+	+		+
Taiwan		+					+		R		+			
Thailand							+		R	*		+		
Turkey					+		+		S		+	+		+
UK	+	+	O/*p*	O/C/*p*	+		+	+	R	nw		+	+	+
Uruguay							+		R	S	+	+		
USA	+	+	O/P*p*	C/P*p*	+	+	+	+	R	nw		+		
USSR	+	+	O	O	+	+	+	+	R	nw		+		
Venezuela			P				+		R		+	+		
Yugoslavia		+			+		+		R	*		+		
Zaire			P		+		+		R	*		+		

SOURCE: *World Armaments and Disarmament, SIPRI Yearbook 1976* (Stockholm: Almqvist & Wiksell, Stockholm International Peace Research Institute, 1976), pp. 46–7.

* Commercial- or pilot-scale facility on country's territory: O = in operation; C = under construction; P = facility planned or under consideration; *p* = additional capacity planned for existing facility.

† The Nuclear Energy Agency (NEA) has defined world uranium resources in two ways: first according to the type of resource in geological terms, second according to a hypothetical market price. Geologically, ore deposits are classified as *reasonably assured resources* (RAR) or *estimated additional resources* (EAR), the difference being the reliability of the geological estimate. There are three price categories (per pound U_3O_8): (a) less than $15; (b) $15 to $30; and (c) $30 to $100 (these categories correspond to $10, $10–15 and $15–30 in the NEA's 1973 report). The recent escalation of the market price of uranium emphasizes that the NEA price levels should not be interpreted too literally in making economic assessments of nuclear power costs but they nevertheless serve as a useful indication of the competitive value of a country's uranium resources.

‡ As of 31 December 1975.

§ As of 31 December 1975. R = ratified; S = signed.

** As of 31 December 1975. * = in force; S = signed; nw = nuclear-weapon state.

†† Euratom = European Atomic Energy Community.

‡‡ NEA = Nuclear Energy Agency of the Organization for Economic Cooperation and Development (OECD).

§§ The Eurochemic reprocessing plant in Mol has been shut down and future reopening is doubtful, but under consideration.

SOURCES: See sources to table 1B.1. page 33: *Facts on Nuclear Proliferation*, a handbook prepared for the committee on Government Operations, US Senate, by the Congressional Research Service, Library of Congress (Washington, US Printing Office, 1975) pp. 105–107 and 127–129. *Oversight Hearings on Nuclear Energy—International Proliferation of Nuclear Technology*. Hearings before the Subcommittee on Energy and the Environment of the Committee on Interior and Insular Affairs, US House of Representatives, 21, 22 and 24 July 1975 (Washington, US Government Printing Office, 1975) pp. 42–43; Poole, L. G., "World Uranium Resources", *Nuclear Engineering International*, Vol. 20, No. 224, February 1975, pp. 95–100; "The Nuclear Fuel Cycle", *Nuclear Engineering International*, Vol. 20, No. 237, December 1975, pp. 1015–1020; Rippon, S., "Reprocessing—What Went Wrong", *Nuclear Engineering International*, Vol. 21, No. 239, February 1976, pp. 21–27.

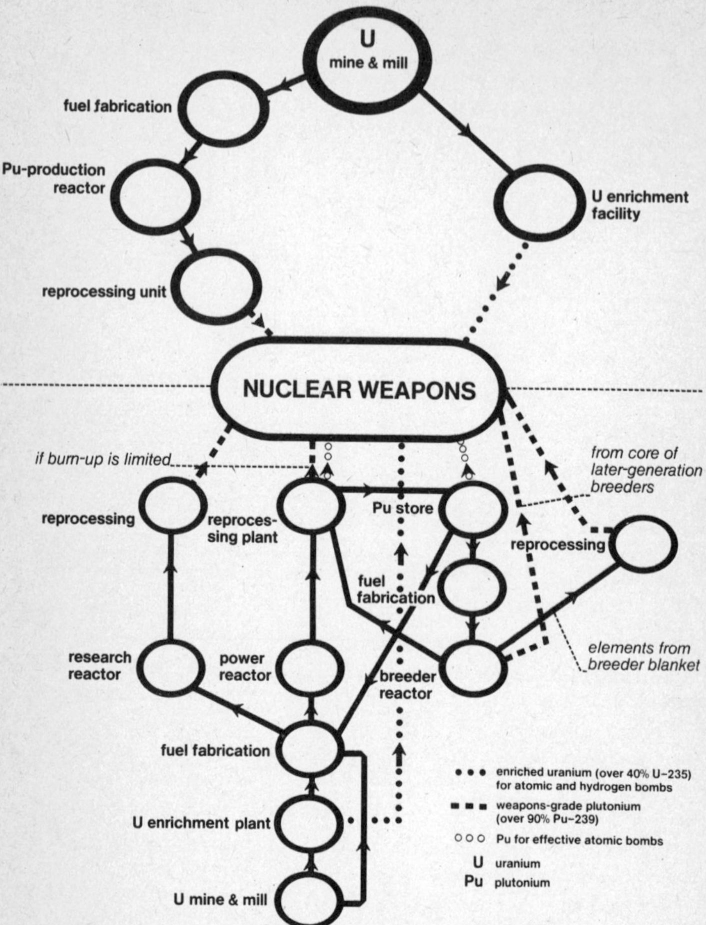

FIGURE 2

Direct Routes to Atomic Weapons. All these operations may be done under military control on a small scale and secretly at a cost of about a million dollars per weapon for a couple of dozen weapons.

Indirect Routes to Atomic Weapons. Nuclear explosives may be produced as by-products of a peaceful nuclear-power program. The cost of so producing a nuclear explosive device may be no more than a few hundred thousand dollars.

required to build one are also readily available.

Although a country with a large peaceful nuclear program may be able to divert clandestinely, over time, enough plutonium for a modest number of atomic bombs if it were intent on doing so, the risk of detection would be considerably less if a small reactor and reprocessing unit were bought secretly for military purposes. It would, however, be difficult to hide the rapid production of enough plutonium for a large number of atomic bombs. Such an operation would require the use of large reactors and of a large reprocessing plant, and would probably be embarked upon without any attempt at secrecy.

THERMONUCLEAR WEAPONS

A thermonuclear weapon has, as its core, a mass of fissile material—in effect, an atomic bomb. This core is surrounded by a quantity of lithium deuteride and all of this is usually enclosed in an outer shell of uranium. For reasons that have not so far been made public, U-235 is the preferred (if not the essential) fissile material for efficient thermonuclear weapons—it seems that Pu-239 is much inferior for this purpose. When the fissile material in the core explodes, much heat and many neutrons are released (as in an atomic bomb). The neutrons convert some of the lithium-6 surrounding the core to tritium, and the heat causes some of the deuterium nuclei to fuse both with tritium nuclei and with other deuterium nuclei. These deuterium-tritium and deuterium-deuterium fusion (or thermonuclear) reactions are accompanied by the release of a large amount of energy and the production of high-speed neutrons. These neutrons are fast enough to cause some of the U-238 in the outer shell of the weapon to fission, thus releasing still more energy and more neutrons. A typical thermonuclear weapon is, thus, a fission-fusion-fission device.

The central fission trigger is required to provide the enormous temperature required to ensure that thermonuclear reactions take place. And access to a uranium-enrichment facility is necessary to obtain the material for this trigger. For use in nuclear weapons, the concentration of U-235 has to be increased from its natural value of 0.72 percent in uranium ore to a value of over 40 percent. For use as reactor fuel, uranium is normally enriched to values of less than 4 percent.

Because U-235 and U-238 are chemically identical, it is necessary to use a physical method to separate and enrich them. Three methods are feasible for large-scale uranium enrichment: the gaseous diffusion, the gas centrifuge, and the jet nozzle techniques.

The gaseous diffusion method is based upon the fact that in a gaseous mixture of two isotopic molecules, the molecules of the lighter isotope will diffuse more rapidly through a porous barrier than those of the heavier one. Seven diffusion plants now exist: three in the United States and one in each of the USSR, the UK, France, and China. These plants were all originally built for military purposes but, apart from the Chinese one, they are now mainly used to produce enriched uranium for power reactors. No plant has been built outside the present nuclear weapon countries.

The centrifugal method of separating isotopes in gaseous form is based on the principle that the gravitational force on a particle is proportional to its mass. Significant separation can be achieved by the use of a centrifuge, which provides a field of force analogous to gravity but much more powerful. Gas centrifuge technology has been developed mainly in the UK, the Netherlands, and the Federal Republic of Germany.

A third technology being adopted for large-scale uranium enrichment is the jet nozzle procedure, based on pressure diffusion in a gaseous mixture of uranium hexafluoride and an additional light gas (helium or hydrogen) flowing at high speed through nozzles along curved walls. The heavier molecules are less deflected and enriched in the stream with the largest curvature. A small 10-stage pilot plant was built at Karlsruhe (Federal Republic of Germany) and has been operating at full-scale capacity since 1967. It is probable that the jet nozzle technique is the basis of the South African enrichment plant.

Because of the association of highly-enriched uranium with thermonuclear weapons and its use, with plutonium, in the most efficient atomic bombs, the spread of uranium-enrichment plants has acquired much significance. Attention has so far been mainly focused on plants large enough for commercial use. But a small enrichment facility—a dozen or so centrifuges, for example—would be adequate to produce the kilogram quantities of suitably enriched uranium per year needed for the development of a modest nuclear-weapon program. The high degree of enrichment necessary would be obtained by recycling the uranium again and again through the system.

NUCLEAR-CAPABLE DELIVERY SYSTEMS

The atomic bomb dropped on Hiroshima had an explosive yield equivalent to about 12,000 tons of TNT (12kt) and it weighed about 4 tons. The yield-to-weight ratio—a measure of the efficiency of a bomb—was, therefore, about 3,000. A modern U.S. nuclear warhead—the Minuteman-III independently targetable re-entry vehicle, for example—has a yield of about 200 kt and weighs about 0.1 tons. The yield-to-weight ratio is, therefore, about 2 million—almost the maximum theoretically attainable with a thermonuclear weapon.

A new nuclear-weapon power should today have little difficulty in producing an atomic bomb with a yield-to-weight ratio of about 20,000, even at an early stage in its nuclear weapon program. Such a weapon with a yield of about 20 kt would weigh about 1,000 kilograms. A warhead with these characteristics could be transported by any of the delivery systems listed in table 3. To take a few examples: the A-4 Skyhawk has a maximum weapon load of about 4,500 kilograms, the F-104 Starfighter about 2,000 kilograms, the F-4 Phantom about 7,000 kilograms, the Mirage V about 4,000 kilograms, the Canberra and Buccaneer about 3,600 kilograms, and the Ilyushin-28 about 2,200 kilograms. Surface-to-surface missiles like the U.S. Lance and Pershing, the USSR Scud, and the Israeli Jericho are all nuclear capable. Moreover, the technology of a peaceful space program could produce, as by-products, guided missiles suitable for short, medium, and long-range delivery of nuclear warheads. And even atmosphere-sounding rockets could be modified to short-range ballistic missiles.

Few, if any, countries would have difficulty in acquiring one of the delivery systems in the table. It should also be remembered that most civilian airlines have aircraft—like the Boeing 707, for example—more sophisticated than the B-29

TABLE 3

SOME OF THE NUCLEAR-CAPABLE AIRCRAFT AND MISSILES IN THE ARSENALS OF COUNTRIES WITH ADVANCED NUCLEAR TECHNOLOGY

COUNTRY	NUCLEAR-CAPABLE DELIVERY SYSTEMS
Argentina	Aircarft: A-4 Skyhawk, Canberra, Mirage III E
Belgium	Aircraft: F-104G Starfighter, Mirage V SSM: Honest John
Brazil	Aircraft: Mirage III E
Bulgaria	Aircraft: Ilyushin-28, MiG-21 MF Fishbed SSM: Scud, Frog
Canada	Aircraft: F-104D Starfighter
Czechoslovakia	Aircraft: Ilyushin-28, SU-7 Fitter SSM: Scud, Frog
FR Germany	Aircraft: F-104G Starfighter, F-4F Phantom II SSM: Honest John, Pershing, Sergeant
German DR	Aircraft: MiG-21 MF Fishbed, SU-7 Fitter SSM: Scud, Frog
Hungary	Aircraft: SU-7 Fitter, Ilyushin-28 SSM: Scud, Frog
India	Aircraft: Canberra, SU-7 Fitter, MiG-21 MF Fishbed
Israel	Aircraft: F-4E Phantom II, A-4 E/H Skyhawk, Mirage III/Kfir SSM: Jericho
Italy	Aircraft: F-104G/S Starfighter SSM: Honest John, Lance
Japan	Aircraft: F-4E Phantom II, F-104J Starfighter
South Korea	Aircraft: F-4D Phantom II SSM: Honest John
Netherlands	Aircraft: F-104G Starfighter SSM: Honest John
Pakistan	Aircraft: Canberra, Mirage V, Mirage III E
South Africa	Aircraft: Canberra, Buccaneer, Mirage F-1, Mirage III E
Spain	Aircraft: F-4C Phantom II, Mirage III E, Mirage F-1
Taiwan	Aircraft: F-100 A/D Super Sabre, F-104G Starfighter

NOTE: Aircraft combat radii (kilometers): 3,000–6,000: Canberra, Buccaneer, A-4 Skyhawk; 1,000–3,000: F-4 Phantom, Su-7 Fitter, F-104G Starfighter, Mirage III E, Ilyushin-28; remainder under 1,000.

Surface-to-surface missile ranges (kilometers): Jericho 1,000, Pershing 720, Scud B 280, Lance 139, Sergeant 135, Frog 75, Honest John 40.

bomber which dropped the atomic bombs on Hiroshima and Nagasaki. These could be provided with the avionics needed to convert them into effective long-range bombers capable of delivering even very crude (that is, heavy) atomic bombs. Thus, even without turning to exotic weapons like the cruise missile, almost every country capable of making atomic bombs is capable of delivering them, at least against neighboring states.

COST OF NUCLEAR FORCES

The development and production of even modest nuclear forces used to be a costly enterprise. The British and French nuclear forces, for example, cost well over $10 billion. The development of the nuclear warheads was a major part of this cost.

The 1974 Indian nuclear explosion, however, is said to have cost only about $500,000, including the cost of the plutonium and preparation of the test site. The Indian event showed that a country with a significant peaceful nuclear program can, by the diversion of relatively small financial and manpower resources, produce nuclear explosive devices as, so to speak, a by-product of its peaceful nuclear activity. The nuclear-weapon powers—the U.S., the USSR, the UK, France, and China—began their nuclear programs specifically for military purposes and only later initiated peaceful nuclear programs. Today, as the Indian example shows, this procedure is likely to be reversed.

Cost is clearly no longer a significant barrier to the acquisition of atomic bombs based on plutonium, even if a reactor is bought specifically and solely for the purpose. The production of highly-enriched uranium for use as the trigger material for hydrogen bombs would be much more costly because of the expense of developing even a small uranium-enrichment facility. For many countries, however, particularly the smaller ones, an atomic warhead with a yield of about 20 kt is adequate against most strategic military targets provided that the delivery system is relatively accurate—and against cities, even if it is not. (For tactical purposes, accurately delivered warheads of much lower yield are normally sufficient.) Since such delivery systems are comparatively cheap and easy to acquire, a small but credible nuclear force based on indigenously-produced atomic bombs could be acquired for a few hundred million dollars—about the price of a modern cruiser.

CONCLUSIONS

The technical information required to design and manufacture a nuclear explosive device is now readily available and so is the necessary expertise. Many people, numbering in the thousands, have direct knowledge of nuclear-weapon design and this number inevitably grows continuously. All the operations leading to the manufacture of nuclear weapons by governments could, as we have seen, be performed on a small scale and in secret, separately from a peaceful nuclear power program. For these reasons, effective and credible control of fissile material is very difficult.

International safeguards, of the type operated by the International Atomic Energy Agency (IAEA), cannot prevent the diversion of nuclear material even from safeguarded facilities; they can only detect it, after the event. Using the best technology available, no safeguards system can be perfect. There will soon be so much plutonium produced in each of many countries that if a very small percentage is unaccounted for, this would still amount to enough plutonium to make theoretically a large number of atomic bombs. We will soon reach the point at which enough plutonium could be diverted clandestinely to produce a "bomb-a-week"—though not, fortunately, by a single country.

To prevent further proliferation of nuclear weapons is obviously going to be an extremely difficult task. It will even be difficult to slow it down appreciably. There are, however, some technical measures which could hinder proliferation, including a moratorium on the construction of reprocessing plants and breeder reactors (at least until the necessity for these reactors has been definitely demonstrated) and the multinational ownership of uranium-enrichment plants under IAEA control.

Looking further ahead, the application of such developments as laser techniques and rotating plasmas for uranium enrichment, and laser-induced fusion and fission, should be avoided unless shown to be absolutely necessary. Laser enrichment, now in the research state, may turn out to be the cheapest method of separating uranium isotopes, at least on a relatively small scale. And laser-induced fusion, if developed to the point at which it could be used in weapons, may prove to be the most dangerous development of all, so far as nuclear-weapon proliferation is concerned. Hence, controls over nuclear technology may be essential if one is seeking to control proliferation.

ANNALS, AAPSS, 430, March 1977

What Happens If . . .? Terrorists, Revolutionaries, and Nuclear Weapons

By DAVID KRIEGER

ABSTRACT: This paper explores what may happen if terrorists or revolutionaries are able to develop nuclear explosives or the ability to dispense radioactive materials. Continued proliferation of so-called peaceful nuclear technology will increase the likelihood of this happening. The consequences are substantial, since nuclear technology would provide terrorists or revolutionaries with a lever for threatening or carrying out acts of mass destruction against a society. Deterrence would be ineffective against terrorists who are unidentified and/or unlocatable, or at least believe themselves to be so. Complications would arise, which could potentially trigger an international war, if nuclear-armed terrorists or revolutionaries deliberately misidentify themselves. The solution to the problem would require perfect safeguarding of nuclear weapons and special nuclear materials on a global scale. The record in the United States, a technologically advanced nation with an established nuclear program, suggests that perfect safeguards are unlikely to be achieved. Thus, future policy-makers may face a significantly enhanced threat from terrorists or revolutionaries in possession of a nuclear weapon.

David Krieger is a research political scientist living in Santa Barbara. He was formerly Director of the International Relations Center at San Francisco State University and a staff member at the Center for the Study of Democratic Institutions.

TERRORIST and revolutionary activities spring from deep wells of social and personal discontent, and it seems unlikely that these wells will dry up of their own accord, or that social changes will soon cap them. Thus, we can predict with a high degree of certainty that terrorist and revolutionary activity will continue.

THE FUTURE OF TERRORIST AND REVOLUTIONARY ACTIVITIES

Terrorism is nongovernmental public violence or its threat performed by an individual or small group and aimed at achieving social or political goals which may be subnational, national, or international. Revolutionaries have the specific goal of bringing down a government, and to this end their actions may range from nonviolent to terrorist to organized military activities.

The victims of terrorist activity may be:

—victims of convenience (that is, easy targets) such as passengers aboard a hijacked airliner
—newsworthy victims such as Olympic athletes
—representatives of groups perceived to be exploitative, such as, diplomats, industrialists, politicians, or even tourists from a given nation
—individuals or groups believed to provide an effective "bargaining chip." For example, any of the above could be held hostage in order to extort money, have prisoners released, change government or corporate policies, and so forth.

Terrorists may also threaten inanimate objects. They may target social or political symbols; for example, attempting to bomb the Washington Monument or Independence Hall. They may also seek to control or destroy vulnerable functioning technologies, such as computer centers, communication systems, or power generating stations. Any of these events could result in the death of innocent people who happened to be "in the wrong place at the wrong time."

Terrorist activities seem to have increasingly taken on an international character in the past decade. The U.S. State Department has published a memorandum stating:

> . . . since 1968 there has been a marked increase in international terrorism as a means for the attainment of political goals. Simultaneously, there has been a major development of intelligence, training, financial and operational collaboration among terrorist groups in different parts of the world. . . . Technological advances afford the terrorist opportunities he never had before: an instant world-wide audience . . . new types of weapons, a plethora of vulnerable targets.[1]

Thus, at least in the eyes of the State Department, international terrorism is becoming better organized, with better financing and weapons, and plenty of targets.

Based on past incidents, certain general motivations for terrorism can be suggested:

—to attain national or global publicity for a cause
—to achieve certain limited political and/or financial goals
—to demonstrate the weakness of an established government

1. Fahey Black, "Terrorism," *GIST* (Washington, D.C.: U.S. Department of State, March 1976).

—to manipulate a government into an unnecessary and discreditable use of force
—to create a situation where one can be hunted, killed, or put on trial with notoriety and excitement

Motives range from clear political objectives to hazy quasi-suicidal propensities. Globally, it would appear that there is a large body of persons whose lack of sufficient satisfaction and excitement in their lives makes them potential criminals or terrorists. We cannot say with certainty what catalysts will convert individual dissatisfaction and thirst for adventure into political terrorism. We can only suggest that we have no valid reason to believe that the discontent from which terrorism arises will soon diminish or that terrorism will decline in the foreseeable future.

Revolutionaries may be defined as individuals and groups acting with the primary intention of bringing down a government and replacing the fallen government with one more in accord with their own value system. Revolutionaries may, of course, act from either a left or right perspective and may be comprised of poor and maltreated elements of society or of well-to-do and well-established elements discontented with government policies. In the latter case, national military forces or a branch thereof will often play a major role in overthrowing an existing government. Most Latin American nations, for example, are now governed by military regimes which forcibly supplanted preexisting governments. Naturally, a large, well-organized revolutionary movement, which included a trained military force could pose a greater threat to take possession of nuclear weapons or nuclear weapon materials than could a smaller, less powerful terrorist organization. Also, nuclear weapons may come into the possession of former revolutionaries who become legitimized by the assumption of power within a state and who persist in their revolutionary aims and aspirations, thereby transforming the threat from a national to an international one.

THE NUCLEAR DIMENSION

It is the specific purpose of this paper to explore what may happen if terrorists and revolutionaries are able to develop nuclear explosive or dispersal capabilities. Thus far, only a few national governments possess nuclear weapons, and each has taken strong (although possibly insufficient) precautionary measures to prevent their nuclear bombs or special nuclear materials which are convertible to explosives from falling into unauthorized hands.

Whether terrorists and revolutionaries of the future will be able to achieve a nuclear weapon capability depends upon several factors. These include:

—the sympathies and political stability of regimes possessing a nuclear weapon capability
—safeguards applied by regimes possessing uranium enrichment and/or nuclear fuel reprocessing plants and their political stability
—the durability of safeguarding procedures for special nuclear material nationally and internationally over time

At the present time, only five nations are acknowledged members of the nuclear weapon club: the United States, USSR, UK, France, and China. India tested what it described as a "peaceful" nuclear explosive in 1974, having created it with materials originally supplied by the United States and Canada for its nuclear power program. India's example illustrates how, under poor safeguards, nuclear electricity generation can lead to nuclear weapons.[2]

The stability of regimes possessing nuclear weapons is important, since opportunities for terrorists or revolutionaries to take possession of stockpiled nuclear weapons could arise as a result of a coup or revolution. The nations currently possessing nuclear weapons appear stable enough at present, but will this always be so? Imagine, for example, the government of China being unable to continue to assert control over the entire country after repeated, devastating earthquakes and factional struggles. A splinter group of army officers seizes control of a few nuclear missiles and (*a*) threatens to employ them against Japan unless a large sum is paid; (*b*) uses the weapons without warning against the USSR which is suspected of having caused the earthquakes in China by geological warfare; or (*c*) is convinced by a revolutionary student group to turn over the weapons to it to prevent capitalists from regaining a foothold in China.

Should there be a rapid proliferation of nuclear-weapon states, which at this time seems rather likely, future nuclear-weapon states may be less stable than current nuclear powers and thus more likely to lose their nuclear weapons to terrorists or revolutionaries. Nevertheless, of the various ways for terrorists or revolutionaries to gain nuclear weapons, taking them forcibly from a government would be relatively difficult unless the power of the revolutionary force approached that of the government. Far simpler would be to convince a sympathetic government to give one or more weapons away. We can imagine, for example, another Middle Eastern nation clandestinely creating nuclear weapons in the same way Israel is purported to have done and then turning some of them over to a terrorist group with whom its leader sympathizes. Or the nuclear weapon may be given to the terrorist group as payment for other activities the national leader wants accomplished. In either case, the agreement would most likely be secret, so that the national donor would not be held culpable for the terrorist use of the weapon. The situation could become even more confused and dangerous if the terrorist group claimed publicly to have received the nuclear weapon from an innocent party, thereby generating a retaliatory response against the innocent party. In certain cases, this could conceivably result in international war.

The above example, as with others, points out the difficulty of drawing a hard line between national goals and terrorist goals. In the future, as in the past, national leaders may work clandestinely to achieve certain goals through the activities of terrorist groups. Some of these goals may involve the use of nuclear weapons, and others may involve the trade of nuclear weapons for terrorist services rendered. Based on past performance, can we doubt that certain national leaders would be capable of such behavior? Moreover, we cannot safely dismiss

2. In addition to the five nuclear-weapon nations and India, Israel is widely thought also to possess nuclear weapons developed from its nuclear reactors.

the possibility that these leaders will eventually acquire nuclear weapons or that other leaders of this disposition will come to power in nuclear-weapon states of the future.

Nations possessing nuclear spent fuel reprocessing plants will have at hand the plutonium necessary for constructing nuclear weapons. Reprocessing plants will make it possible for nations possessing them to develop nuclear weapons or, depending upon the degree of safeguarding applied, for terrorists to obtain bomb-grade materials from the reprocessing facility. Since a certain amount of material is unaccounted for in processing, it is impossible to know with certainty whether it was in fact, diverted. Uranium enrichment plants would offer less opportunity for diversion by terrorists or revolutionaries unless highly enriched uranium was being produced, and most enriched uranium for power plants is not weapons-grade.

It is widely acknowledged by the experts in this area that a sophisticated terrorist group would be capable of constructing nuclear weapons with information and equipment publicly available, once sufficient plutonium or highly enriched uranium had been obtained. Former nuclear weapons designer Theodore Taylor, for example, and his co-author, Mason Willrich, stated in their Ford Foundation Energy Policy Project study:

> It is difficult to imagine that a determined terrorist group could not acquire a nuclear weapon manufacturing capability once it had the required nuclear weapon materials. In this regard, a terrorist's willingness to take chances with his own health and safety, and to use coercion to obtain information or services from others, should be contrasted with the probably more conservative approach of persons engaged in crime for money.[3]

Agreements are currently being pursued by France and West Germany to sell nuclear reprocessing facilities to less developed countries, including Brazil and Pakistan. The United States has opposed such technology transfers as promotive of nuclear weapons proliferation, but other nuclear exporting countries have not been ready to forgo the potential profits.

Regardless of the apparent present stability of national regimes acquiring reprocessing facilities, it remains impossible to assure that in the future such countries will not have leaders with terrorist sympathies or that, in the chaos of a civil war, nuclear materials would not fall into the hands of avowed terrorist groups. Similar considerations may be applied to nations with nuclear power facilities.

Nuclear power plants, while not prime potential sources of special nuclear materials, are major potential targets for terrorist attack; in effect, they are huge radiological weapons which terrorists could sabotage, spreading deadly radioactivity far downwind. We will discuss this possibility further in a separate section of this paper.

SAFEGUARDING SPECIAL NUCLEAR MATERIALS

A major factor in determining the ease with which terrorist groups may attain nuclear weapons will be the extent to which effective national and international safeguards over special nuclear materials are

3. Mason Willrich and Theodore B. Taylor, *Nuclear Theft: Risks and Safeguards* (Cambridge, Mass.: Ballinger Publishing Company, 1974), p. 115.

devised and enforced. The issue of nuclear safeguards became a subject of public and congressional concern in the United States largely through the persistent efforts of a former nuclear weapons designer Theodore B. Taylor. In his Ford Foundation study with Mason Willrich, it was argued forcibly that "without effective safeguards to prevent nuclear theft, the development of nuclear power will create substantial risks to the security and safety of the American people and people generally."[4]

Elsewhere in their study, the authors considered the possibility of terrorists gaining nuclear materials. They wrote:

> One wonders how in the long run nuclear power industries can develop and prosper in a world where terrorist activities are widespread and persistent. For if present trends continue, it seems only a question of time before some terrorist organization exploits the possibilities for coercion which are inherent in nuclear fuel.[5]

The study by Willrich and Taylor was published in early 1974. Congressional interest was stirred, but little action was taken. In early 1976, the Director of the Nuclear Regulatory Commission's Division of Safeguards, Carl H. Builder, wrote a memorandum, which subsequently became public, in which he expressed concern that ". . . some or even many of our currently licensed facilities may not have safeguards adequate against the lowest levels of design threat [of theft] we are considering. . . ."[6] This level was defined as one insider and three outsiders. And the House Subcommittee on Energy and the Environment, in February 1976, summarizing testimony presented to it, noted that "although the witnesses differed on the severity of the threat, it is obvious there is insufficient security against threats the NRC considers plausible."[7]

Thus, more than two years after Taylor and Willrich called national attention to nuclear safeguarding inadequacies, the problems remain far from being solved. Taylor himself provided rather extraordinary testimony at the subcommittee hearings mentioned above. Rather than offering confident answers to safeguarding problems, Taylor indicated that he found himself faced with certain questions he was unable to answer after years of effort to do so. Specifically, regarding safeguards, he asked:

> What levels of risks of nuclear violence, whether caused by nations or criminal groups, are acceptable to society worldwide, and who should decide what these levels should be? By what process is the worldwide public to be assured that international and domestic safeguards against purposeful nuclear violence will, in fact, be effective, in the sense that residual risks will be both known and considered acceptable by the public?[8]

Taylor's questions speak eloquently to the intractability of the problems of potential nuclear violence and nuclear safeguards. The

4. Ibid.

5. Ibid., p. 169.

6. Carl H. Builder, "Adequacy of Current Safeguards," Memorandum to R. A. Brightsen, U.S. Nuclear Regulatory Commission, 19 January 1976.

7. "House Subcommittee Chairman Calls for Improved Nuclear Security," Subcommittee on Energy and the Environment, House Committee on Interior and Insular Affairs, news release of 3 March 1976.

8. Theodore B. Taylor, Statement before the Subcommittee on Energy and the Environment of the House Committee on Interior and Insular Affairs, 26 February 1976.

safeguarding problems which Taylor was instrumental in raising seem further from solution now than when he initially raised them.

I have concentrated on U.S. safeguarding difficulties because it seems a valid assumption that if the world's richest and most technologically advanced nation cannot adequately deal with these problems, then other nations will be even more likely to fail. The supposed safeguards provided by the International Atomic Energy Agency (IAEA) are basically an inventory accounting system administered by the agency's small technical staff. The IAEA is able to recognize diversions after they occur, but is helpless to prevent diversions. It provides no physical security against diversion, nor does it have any capability to track down and recover diverted materials.

It appears that neither national nor international safeguards will prove adequate to prevent terrorists from going nuclear. In the following sections, we will consider what sort of world we may expect with nuclear armed terrorists.

WHAT TERRORISTS AND REVOLUTIONARIES CAN DO WITH NUCLEAR WEAPONS

With a nuclear weapon at their disposal, the coercive leverage of a terrorist or revolutionary group is multiplied enormously. Terrorists could threaten the destruction of any number of key targets, including a nation's capital city, a major dam, or a nuclear power generating station. Nuclear threats against any of these targets could cause widespread panic and intense pressure on the government to accede to terrorist demands.

The government involved would be in the difficult position of not knowing with certainty whether the terrorists were bluffing. One wonders how much risk a government would take if the terrorists publicly presented a credible description and photographs of their nuclear weapon and a small sample of special nuclear material. As a matter of policy, the U.S. government refuses to negotiate for the release of Americans who have been kidnapped. Would it adopt a similar no-negotiation policy for the "release" of Americans who were in effect being held hostage by a nuclear bomb threat to New York or Chicago?

Nuclear terrorists would have the advantage of choosing whether or not to identify themselves for publicity purposes. But even while identifying themselves, they could remain unlocatable and thus untargetable for retaliation. This, of course, nullifies the basic premise of deterrence theory, namely that a nuclear attack can be prevented by fear of retaliation. Clearly, if terrorists cannot be located, they have no need to fear retaliation, and thus deterrence in this context becomes meaningless. Further, some terrorists may be assumed to be so alienated that they would not be deterred even if located and certain to die if they carried out their threat. Of course, a nuclear bomb could be detonated remotely, even in another city, by telephone signal.

An interesting variant of the above would be for the atomic terrorists to claim to be a group on which they desired to bring public enmity, or upon which they desired to inflict the retaliatory might of the threatened nation. When terrorists have deliberately misidentified themselves, one wonders whether or not national leaders would be capable of responding intelligently, under possibly panic conditions.

Were the terrorists to have more than one nuclear weapon, their position would be even more powerful. After they exploded one, it would be virtually impossible to reject their subsequent demands. Even if they had only one weapon which they used and bluffed a second weapon, it would be extremely difficult to attempt calling the bluff in the face of their already demonstrated capability and the likely overriding public sentiment to avoid further destruction at virtually any price. One successful nuclear extortion threat, or one actual nuclear bombing, would also undoubtedly instigate many similar threats. Distinguishing credible extortionists from hoaxers would increase in difficulty.

The sorts of situations we are now considering would very likely result in state-of-emergency declarations and the assumption of unlimited police powers by the threatened government. Responding to nuclear threats could undermine civil liberties and put democratic governments to their severest test.

Revolutionaries within a given nation would be unlikely to use nuclear tactics against a population center of their own people. They might, however, be willing to act against a military target or a government symbol. Revolutionaries could also act without identifying themselves if they perceived the action to be in their interest. Revolutionaries would probably be less inhibited in terrorizing a foreign government they desired overthrown. Theodore Taylor has pointed out that a nuclear weapon with a one-fiftieth kiloton yield (1,000 times less powerful than the yield at Hiroshima) detonated in a car on Pennsylvania Avenue would produce sufficient radiation to kill anyone above basement level in the White House, and that a one kiloton weapon (still 20 times less powerful than the Hiroshima bomb), if exploded just outside the exclusion area during a State of the Union message, would kill everyone inside the Capitol building.[9] Taylor states of the latter possibility:

> It's hard for me to think of a higher-leverage target, at least in the United States. The bomb would destroy the heads of all branches of the United States government—all Supreme Court justices, the entire cabinet, all legislators, and, for what it's worth, the Joint Chiefs of Staff. With the exception of anyone who happened to be sick in bed, it would kill the line of succession to the Presidency—all the way to the bottom of the list. A fizzle-yield, low-efficiency, basically lousy fission bomb could do this.[10]

The situation referred to by Dr. Taylor would involve no threat, no warning—simply the explosion, the death and destruction, and the ensuing chaos and panic. Terrorists or revolutionaries in possession of a nuclear weapon would have the option of exploding it without warning. Some groups might find this preferable both to avoid identification with the act and to avoid capture. By deliberately misidentifying themselves, terrorists might be able to catalyze domestic repression and/or international war.

RADIATION DISPERSAL DEVICES

To construct a nuclear bomb requires either about 11 pounds of plutonium or about 45 pounds of

9. John McPhee, *The Curve of Binding Energy* (New York: Farrar, Strauss and Giroux, 1973), pp. 221–22.

10. Ibid., p. 222.

highly enriched uranium. It also requires some expertise and at least several weeks of work by a small well-trained team. With lesser amounts of time, expertise, and plutonium, terrorists could prepare radiological weapons which could be used for extortion or contamination of chosen targets.

Plutonium is an extremely toxic carcinogen. In a study done by the U.S. Atomic Energy Commission, it was calculated that the release of 4.4 pounds of plutonium oxide as a fine powder would entail 100 percent probability of developing bone or lung cancer up to 1,800 feet downwind from the point of release, and a 1 percent risk as far as 40 miles downwind.[11]

The immediate impact in terms of deaths and recognizable injury would be far less with a radiological weapon than a nuclear bomb, but the psychological and economic impact of forcing the evacuation of a large area and the costly and lengthy decontamination procedures involved could make radiological weapons attractive to terrorist and revolutionary groups. Additionally, radiation dispersal devices would be far easier to prepare than a nuclear bomb, requiring only a basic knowledge of nuclear chemistry. Terrorists who threatened the release of plutonium oxide in a population center would have to be negotiated with seriously, particularly if they included a sample of plutonium with their threat letter. It would be virtually impossible for authorities to prevent the release of plutonium oxide when it could be done by simply attaching a leaking container of the material to a city taxicab or dropping it from the window of a tall building.

Dr. Edward Martell, a nuclear chemist with the National Center for Atmospheric Research, has stated: "in the not too unlikely event of a major plutonium release, the resulting contamination could require large-scale evacuation of the affected area, the leveling of buildings and homes, the deep plowing and removal of topsoil and an unpredictable number of radiation casualties."[12] The evident potential for creating the economic and social chaos—of forcing evacuation of a major city, say New York or Washington, D.C.—might prove a substantial lure for political terrorists in possession of plutonium. They might feel safer putting the diverted plutonium to immediate use rather than running the risk of organizing the talent and taking the necessary time to construct a nuclear bomb.

Radiation dispersal devices could also be used against more specific targets, particularly ventilated buildings. Feasible targets might include legislative chambers, stock exchanges, embassies, corporate headquarters, political conventions, power plants, and communication centers. Willrich and Taylor have calculated that the indoor release of one gram of powdered plutonium oxide could provide lethal dosages for inhabitants within a 500 square meter area and significant contamination requiring some evacuation and clean-up over a 50,000 square meter area. The indoor release of 100 grams of plutonium, about one-quarter pound, would give lethal inhalation dosages for 50,000 square meters and sig-

11. "Generic Environmental Statement on Mixed Oxide Fuel" (U.S. Atomic Energy Commission WASH-1327, August 1974), vol. 4, p. v-48.

12. Edward H. Martell, cited in Roger Rapoport, *The Great American Bomb Machine* (New York: Ballantine, 1972), p. 47.

nificant contamination over 5 million square meters.[13]

The above calculations are for an oxide of plutonium-239, the most common isotope of plutonium produced as a by-product of the nuclear fission process. A 1,000-megawatt light-water nuclear power reactor produces approximately 440 pounds of plutonium annually. A less common isotope of plutonium produced by the fission process is plutonium-238. This isotope decays at a rate approximately 280 times faster than plutonium-239, having an 87 year half-life rather than 24,400 years, and thus is approximately 280 times as toxic. Plutonium-238 is worthy of our attention, since it is being used to power cardiac pacemakers. Each pacemaker contains approximately one-quarter gram of plutonium-238. Extrapolating from the figures given by Willrich and Taylor, the one-quarter gram of plutonium-238 in a single pacemaker could provide lethal dosages over an indoor area of 37,500 square meters and provide significant contamination requiring some evacuation and clean-up to an area of 3,750,000 square meters. It would seem imprudent at best to dismiss the possibility of terrorists gaining a significant radiological weapon by the removal of an implanted nuclear heart pacemaker from a hapless victim, particularly when the recipients of nuclear pacemakers are periodically mentioned in the press.[14] At the present time, 20 such pacemakers are being manufactured and implanted monthly in the United States. A decision is pending on whether or not to proceed with nuclear heart pacemakers on a larger scale.

Since the major radiotoxic danger of plutonium derives from inhalation, sophisticated terrorists could theoretically contain the plutonium without hazard to themselves until they are ready to release it. If they chose to release it by time-bomb, they could be out of the area when the release occurred.

Douglas DeNike, a long-time scholar of nuclear terrorism, has painted this frightening scenario for the use of radiological weapons by terrorists:

> Perhaps the end will come with a whimper rather than a bang. Covert radiological warfare could cripple any nation without its immediate awareness. The downtown cores of the hundred largest American cities, for example, could be made uninhabitable by two foreign students on their summer vacation. The whole job would require roughly 100 pounds of power-reactor-grade plutonium or strontium-90 particles. A pound of either one, tied to the underside of a taxicab in a leaking container, would create an insidious cancer-induction hazard over several square miles.[15]

While the health effects of the radiological contamination might not be felt for many years, the psychological and economic effects of announcing the contamination, as the terrorists would surely do, would be substantial, particularly if evacuation and decontamination were necessitated.

As with a nuclear bomb, the leverage of terrorists generally would

13. Willrich and Taylor, *Nuclear Theft*, p. 25.

14. See, for example, "Government Owns Part of His Heart," *Santa Barbara News Press*, 26 February 1976. For a fictional account of nuclear terrorism with a cardiac pacemaker, see my story, "The Ordeal of Harry Dalton: A Parable for Our Times," *Science Forum*, vol. 8, no. 6 (December 1975), pp. 3–7.

15. L. Douglas DeNike, "Nuclear Terror," *Sierra Club Bulletin*, November-December 1975.

increase after the initial terrorist release of radionuclides. It would be extremely difficult for officials of a threatened city to resist terrorist demands when another city had already been required to evacuate.

NUCLEAR FACILITIES AS TARGETS FOR TERRORISTS AND REVOLUTIONARIES

As we enter the fourth quarter of the twentieth century, nuclear power plants are being increasingly relied upon to supply electric power. While a majority of people probably continue to view nuclear power as a great technological achievement, a growing minority see nuclear power as a symbol of technological arrogance. It is becoming increasingly widely understood that a meltdown of a nuclear reactor core could result in the release of volatile radioactive materials which could take thousands of lives and cause billions of dollars in property damage. The amount of potential damage remains a hotly debated issue, but the most recent Nuclear Regulatory Commission (NRC) document on this issue, the "Reactor Safety Study" (Rasmussen Report), estimates a worst-case accident would cause 3,300 early fatalities, 45,000 cases of early illnesses, and $14 billion in property damage.[16] This study argues that the chances of a nuclear accident killing more than 1,000 people are extremely low, the likelihood of occurrence being once in a million reactor-years for 100 nuclear plants, about the same risk as this number of people being killed by a meteorite. The study, however, excludes consideration of intentional destruction of a nuclear reactor which could set the probability of a core meltdown at unity.

In 1972 airline hijackers threatened to crash a Boeing 727 into the Oak Ridge, Tennessee, nuclear installation. The site was evacuated, and the terrorists did not carry out their threat. James R. Schlesinger, who was at that time U.S. Atomic Energy Commission (AEC) chairman, commented on the incident that

> . . . if one intends to crash a plane into a facility and one is able to persuade the pilot that that is the best way to go, there is, I suspect, little that can be done about that problem. The nuclear plants that we are building today are designed carefully to take the impact of, I believe, a 200,000 pound aircraft arriving at something on the order of 150 miles per hour. They will not take the impact of a larger aircraft.[17]

A Boeing 747 is nearly twice as heavy as the aircraft the power plants are designed to withstand, and a smaller aircraft carrying conventional explosives would probably penetrate a reactor containment structure. This approach to radiation release would, of course, be suicidal, but demonstrably there are terrorists fanatical enough to sacrifice their lives for what they believe to be a greater goal.

There are simpler ways for terrorists to effect a radiation release at a nuclear power plant. A former U.S. navy demolition specialist testified before Congress that

> . . . as one trained in special warfare and demolitions, I feel certain that I could pick three to five ex-underwater

16. "Reactor Safety Study: An Assessment of Accident in U.S. Commercial Nuclear Power Plants, Main Report" (Nuclear Regulatory Commission, WASH-1400, October 1975).

17. Cited in *Mike Gravel Newsletter*, 31 October 1973.

demolition Marine Reconnaissance, or Green Beret men at random and sabotage virtually any nuclear reactor in the country. It would not be essential for more than one of these men to have had such specialized training. . . . The engineered safeguards would be minimally effective and the amount of radioactivity released could be of catastrophic proportions.[18]

A 1974 Government Accounting Office (GAO) survey of security systems at nuclear plants drew attention to the vulnerability of the spent fuel storage pools located at reactor sites. In a letter to then AEC Chairman Dixy Lee Ray, a GAO official noted:

According to AEC and licensee officials, the used-fuel storage facility at a nuclear power plant is more accessible and vulnerable to sabotage than is the reactor core. Such a storage facility generally is an uncovered pool of water near the reactor. The highly radioactive used fuel does not have the same degree of physical protection as that provided to the reactor core by the reactor containment vessel.[19]

Terrorists might consider the spent fuel storage pool of a nuclear reactor as an inviting target. Dropping a waterproof bomb in this storage pool would probably result in high-level radioactive contamination of the power plant itself, making its evacuation necessary.

Nuclear power plants may justifiably be considered military equalizers. Locating a nuclear power plant near a metropolitan area gives terrorists or revolutionaries (or small enemy nations) a target which in effect can disrupt an entire city by radioactive contamination, necessitating precipitate evacuation. This concept of military equalizer is one which, to the best of my knowledge, no national department of defense has yet recognized. The GAO study referred to above also pointed out that at U.S. nuclear facilities "there has been no specific coordination with other Federal Agencies, such as the Department of Defense and the Federal Bureau of Investigation, to protect against or respond to attacks by paramilitary groups."[20] Moreover, federal regulations specifically exempt the nuclear industry from responsibility for defending against sophisticated attacks on nuclear plants.[21]

Other areas of the nuclear fuel cycle could conceivably be targets for terrorist attack as well. These would include spent fuels being transported by rail or truck, and waste storage sites. In either case, a terrorist attack would involve the penetration of the transport cask with explosives and the consequent release of radioactive materials into the environment. This clearly would not be a strategy for terrorists or revolutionaries desirous of impressing a local population with their benevolence. Conceivably, though, the terrorists could perceive themselves as benevolent if they believed their action to be the only way to stop a dangerous technology (such

18. B. L. Welch, Statement before the Joint Committee on Atomic Energy, 28 March 1974.

19. Henry Eschwege, letter to AEC Chairman Dixy Lee Ray, 16 October 1974, p. 2.

20. Ibid., p. 3.

21. IOCFR 50.13: "An applicant for a license to construct and operate a production or utilization facility, or for an amendment to such license, is not required to provide for design features or other measures for the specific purpose of protection against the effects of (a) attacks and destructive acts, including sabotage, directed against the facility by an enemy of the United States, whether a foreign government or other person, or (b) use or deployment of weapons incident to U.S. defense activities."

as nuclear power) before industrial societies became too dependent upon it.

In the United States, between April 1969 and July 1976, there were 235 threats of violence or acts of violence toward nuclear facilities, and the frequency of such actions is increasing—there were 55 just in the first eight months of 1976.[22] As far as is known, none has yet succeeded in the loss of nuclear material or in causing damage to nuclear equipment or the general public, but the likelihood that one will soon succeed is not trivial.

BRIEF SCENARIOS FOR U.S. POLICY-MAKERS

To give some idea of the difficulties which policy-makers may face in the future, let us consider the following brief scenarios.

—A U.S. army base is destroyed without warning by a low yield nuclear weapon with no clues as to who is responsible.
—The U.S. embassy in India is destroyed in the same manner.
—A cadre of revolutionaries, including a nuclear engineer, take over a nuclear power plant and threaten to initiate a core meltdown if their demands for policy change are not met.
—An American-owned factory in France is discovered to have been saturated with plutonium oxide, and threats are received that the same will happen to other American corporations if certain government policy changes are not made.
—Japanese extremists divebomb an American nuclear reactor causing a core meltdown.
—A German terrorist group threatens the nuclear bombing of an unspecified U.S. target in Europe unless the Netherlands releases certain political prisoners.
—A multinational terrorist group, in possession of plutonium oxide, begins contaminating U.S. targets in Latin America and Asia, each time reiterating a demand for the United States to withdraw its nuclear weapons from Europe.

CONCLUSIONS

—Nuclear or radiological weapons in the hands of terrorists or revolutionaries could provide a significant threat to any society, particularly urban and industrial societies.
—Terrorists or revolutionaries can use nuclear or radiological weapons to extort money or extract political concessions from a government.
—Once a nuclear or radiological weapon is used by a terrorist or revolutionary group, other such groups will be more likely to threaten this approach and also more likely to be successful in having their demands met.
—Since retaliation will be difficult if not impossible against possibly unlocatable and even unidentifiable terrorists or revolutionaries, it will be necessary to prevent any diversion of nuclear weapons or special nuclear materials anywhere in the world. As yet, no criteria have been established as to how nuclear safeguards can be assured for the present, let alone for a conceivable future with many more nuclear weapon and nuclear power states.
—The threat of nuclear terrorism could precipitate restrictions on

22. A complete listing of threats and acts of violence to licensed and unlicensed nuclear facilities may be obtained from the Energy Resources Division Administration and/or the Nuclear Regulatory Commission.

civil liberties. Policy-makers of the future will have to make some hard decisions in this area, particularly if nuclear power continues to expand as an energy source.

—It is not inconceivable that nuclear terrorism could intensify international tensions and catalyze international wars, particularly if the terrorists are not identifiable or are misidentified.

—The serious nature of the potential consequences of nuclear terrorism demands equally serious policy decisions by current government policy-makers. A starting point is an evaluation of the consequences of continued development and exportation of nuclear technology and a realistic assessment of how effective nuclear safeguards can be expected to be on a worldwide basis.

—The solution to the problem of potential nuclear violence by terrorists or revolutionaries must be founded in a broad international context if it is to be effective.

Safeguards against Diversion of Nuclear Material: An Overview

By RYUKICHI IMAI

ABSTRACT: Non-proliferation is basically a political objective, which because of the technical nature of the problem and because the world is faced with the likelihood of the rapid spread of nuclear technology, requires technical means of implementation. It should be obvious that technology as such cannot solve what is essentially an issue of international politics, but the two have to complement each other. This point has not been well understood by the world's arms control community. International safeguards, as currently administered by the International Atomic Energy Agency, have a number of definite—and expected—technical limitations. Moreover, if the system of safeguards is to be effective, answers will have to be found for a number of political questions, such as "What is a meaningful level of nuclear armament for a country?" or "What international sanctions would be available in the event of the diversion of nuclear material?" At the same time, unlike other verification measures in various arms control agreements, the system of nuclear safeguards has special features which make it uniquely feasible if applied under correct circumstances. Safeguards can be a meaningful and powerful tool of an international non-proliferation regime if combined with political and other considerations and properly orchestrated.

Ryukichi Imai received his M.S. from the University of Tokyo, an M.A. from the Fletcher School of Law and Diplomacy, an A.M. from Harvard University, and a Ph.D. in nuclear engineering from the University of Tokyo. He has been active in journalism, in government-related work, and in the field, as well as being a practicing engineer. His current positions include: General Manager of Engineering, Japan Atomic Power Company; Special Assistant to the Minister of Foreign Affairs; and member of the Standing Advisory Group on Safeguards Implementation, IAEA. He has written extensively on science policy, nuclear power, Japanese defense, and non-proliferation, among other subjects.

THERE are definite limitations to the capabilities of the International Atomic Energy Agency (IAEA) safeguards in preventing proliferation of nuclear weapons. Those of us who participated in the original formulation of the safeguards system had known it from the outset, and have been saying so, long before the U.S. Congress and the U.S. Nuclear Regulatory Commission (NRC) rediscovered it recently. In fact, many people had the impression that U.S. official interpretation had consistently rejected this point of view. Many of the limitations come from technical, legal, or institutional reasons. On the other hand, there are factors which make nuclear safeguards uniquely feasible compared to other technological innovations, for which the separation of potential risks from benefits through international control pose increasingly difficult problems.

Although originated by the spread of nuclear technology,[1] proliferation is essentially a political issue and safeguards are no more than technical means which contribute to its solution; they are not substitutes for a political solution. If this point is accepted, the combination of IAEA safeguards with other political and economic tools will effectively reduce the risk of further proliferation of nuclear weapons to an acceptable level. In such an exercise, it is important to weigh properly the comparative risks arising from the expansion of peaceful nuclear technology to the Third World, the somewhat related problem of terrorists' access to plutonium, and the real danger involved in the existing arsenal of weapons of mass destruction in the hands of the superpowers.

ROLE OF POLITICS AND ROLE OF TECHNOLOGY

Non-proliferation is a political objective, whereas safeguards are technical means to help achieve it. For any political objective, detailed and precise definition is not easy because the changing political climate tends to render definitions obsolete over time. On the other hand, a technical system cannot effectively function unless boundary conditions are set in unmistakable technical language. The major cause of difficulties in the application of international safeguards has been that only a handful of people paid any attention to the job of interpreting vague and general political requirements of non-proliferation into precise definitions of technical boundary conditions. The technical community regarded the job as primarily in the political domain and went ahead with a set of fairly conventional assumptions which happened to suit their technical capabilities, whereas the politicians did not even realize that the problem existed and simply assumed that the technical people must have eased their headaches. Communication between technical and political worlds has not improved very much.

A technical system which aims at the direct prevention of proliferation differs from one whose objective is to detect early indications of proliferation. The former involves police type direct intervention both for prevention before the fact and for pursuit and recovery after the fact. The latter is a network of surveillance which can detect anomalies in industrial activities of peaceful nuclear application. Roughly speaking, the two systems reflect

1. For expected growth of nuclear power and its implications, see, for example, the Atlantic Council of the United States, "Nuclear Fuels Policy" (Washington, D.C., 1976).

the difference between "physical protection" and "international safeguards," a difference whose legal implications are clear. Under the normal understanding of international law, only the latter system can be imposed on sovereign states, with their consent, while physical protection is primarily a sovereign act.

"Indication of proliferation" is difficult to define in an objective manner. The following are some examples of how it may be defined:

a. diversion of nuclear material from a peaceful nuclear fuel cycle in an amount sufficient to produce one fission bomb (But over what period of time?)

b. unexplainable disappearance of 20 or 30 bombs' worth of nuclear material from peaceful fuel cycle (including normal operating loss and measurement inaccuracies)

c. unusual activities within a country's industrial or research facilities which traditionally would be regarded as weapons-oriented (What if a country invented an unusual route to nuclear weapons?)

d. signs of inexplicable irregularities in or deviations from normal industrial activities (In addition to the difficulties of defining what is normal, novel research and development projects almost always involve off-normal activities.)

The necessary and sufficient indication of weapons proliferation will also be governed by such other considerations as:

1. How does one actually go about manufacturing a bomb? (There are a number of popular theories regarding this technical know-how.)[2]

2. What are a country's industrial and technical capabilities for the manufacture of nuclear warheads or their delivery systems? (This involves an assessment of combined capabilities either with or without assumptions concerning facilities unknown to the inspectorate.)

3. Type and degree of nuclear armament which serves national interest best. (This might range from a crude fission bomb to a sophisticated combination of very complicated warheads and long-range precision delivery systems.)

Item one is the essential ingredient of safeguards, yet it is one of the closest-held secrets in the world. Item two is a matter of technical judgment, whereas the third item involves essentially a subjective judgment regarding military and political trade-offs between the costs and benefits of nuclear armaments, as well as of the policy intent of the country. It is difficult to find a formulation which is universally applicable to all the cases.

EVOLUTION OF IAEA SAFEGUARDS

The current IAEA safeguards (which are outlined in document INFCIRC/153) represent a major revision from past practices, in order to accommodate the requirements of Article III of the Non-Proliferation Treaty (NPT).[3] Its basic logic may be described as follows:

a. it provides for *timely detection* capabilities

2. Mason Willrich and Theodore Taylor, "Nuclear Theft, Risks and Safeguards" (Cambridge, Mass.: Ballinger Publishing Company, 1974), is an example of such popular theory but without technical justification or persuasion.

3. For general discussion of the INFCIRC/153 system, see, for example, Ryukichi Imai, "Nuclear Safeguards" (Adelphi Paper no. 86, the International Institute for Strategic Studies, London, March 1972), and Benjamin Sanders, "Safeguards against Nuclear Proliferation," Stockholm International Peace Research Institute, 1975.

b. of *diversion* from *peaceful nuclear fuel cycles*

c. of *significant quantities* of *nuclear material*

d. so that such capabilities will serve as a *deterrent* against

e. nuclear *proliferation*, because either

f. detection leads to international *sanction* or

g. lack of detection means *verification* of no diversion.

From the time the term "safeguards" was initially used in the General Assembly resolution establishing the United Nations Atomic Energy Committee back in 1945, it has come a very long way. Throughout the initial period, it was nothing very much more than a vague idea to prevent the military use of atomic power, as originally proposed in the Acheson/Lilienthal report regarding international control and monopoly of atomic energy. Very little had been known or understood in the international community about the technology of atomic power itself or its possible implications.

When the International Atomic Energy Agency was established in 1957, its statute stated that the agency should "ensure so far as able, that assistance provided by it or at its request or under its supervision or control is not used in such a way as to further any military purposes" (Article II). The provision that the agency may administer safeguards on a non-agency project if so requested by member states (NPT safeguards fall into this category) was almost an afterthought at the time. From its later history, it is amusing to realize that it was Japan who insisted that safeguards should be internationally administered and inserted in her Agreement for Cooperation with the United States of 1958 a provision that bilateral safeguards be transferred to IAEA as soon as possible (Article II).

The first document by the agency which spelled out safeguard procedures was prepared in 1961 and dealt with reactors with less than 100 megawatts thermal output. By 1965, after extensive discussion among international experts, the agency adopted a more generalized safeguards system known as INFCIRC/66/ Rev 2. Although this was a well-organized first attempt, INFCIRC/66 contained two controversial points:

1. a provision which allowed IAEA inspectors to have access at all times to all places within the national fuel cycle in most of the cases;
2. lack of specific technical criteria to determine whether there has or has not been diversion.

The first point was related to the protection of commercial secrets from misuse by IAEA inspectors, as well as to the undue disturbance of commercial operations. The second item meant an open-ended system which left the final determination of diversion to subjective judgment by individual inspectors. The implications of charges of diversion are too serious to be based on a single individual's opinion. Because of the failure to weigh properly implications of the safeguards within the fuel cycle for IAEA resources, it tended to be inefficient and the number of inspectors estimated for the year 1980 was in the thousands, which is clearly unrealistic in view of the other IAEA activities.

After considerable discussions both at IAEA and among the member states, what emerged as a major modification was the document

INFCIRC/153, the so-called Model Agreement under NPT. It has been worked out at the IAEA's Safeguards Committee of 1970, which lasted almost for a year and in which representatives of 48 states participated. What was presented at the outset of this section embodying the logical chain from (*a*) to (*g*) is a shorthand description of the new system, which is much more satisfying as an objective technical system. As long as the words in italics can be clearly defined, the system does not require any more subjective judgment. Furthermore, a technical tool was provided in the form of a theory of statistical sampling, which limits the inspectors' access requirements to minimum predetermined locations in the fuel cycle, and which, through predetermined calculations of sample size and other factors, allows IAEA to come out with objective statements such as "we have verified that there has [not] been a diversion of more than X kg of nuclear material within the past six months and the probability that this statement is correct [confidence level] is 95%."[4]

One may note that as far as the technical system is concerned diversion, not proliferation, becomes the central theme, and safeguards are no longer concerned with whether the diverted material is immediately turned into bombs or simply stored away somewhere or may even reflect an accounting error in nuclear material management.

4. For technical discussion of the system as well as its evolution, see, for example, Wolfgang Häfele, "Systems Analysis in Safeguards of Nuclear Material," Fourth United Nations International Conference on Peaceful Uses of Atomic Energy, A/CONC/49/P771, 1971.

LIMITATIONS OF THE SYSTEM

Referring to the issue of diversion threshold criteria, it would seem a lot simpler if one could adopt "the amount of nuclear material needed for a fission bomb" as an alarm level for the system. This will evidently cover any other possible definition of the criteria and will be the most thoroughgoing. Unfortunately, this cannot be accepted for two reasons.

As of the end of 1975, IAEA had 84 safeguards agreements covering 133 facilities. The agency's safeguards-related staff numbered 116, of whom 75 were professionals. Diversion criteria in use for that year were less stringent than those required to detect the loss of materials which could produce one bomb per year for any one country, yet, even on that basis, of the amount of inspection works which the agency had been authorized to carry out in 1975, it could fulfill only about one-third of the load with the existing staff.[5] Practically, this means that the most stringent, and therefore most thoroughgoing, diversion criteria could not be adopted, and it will become increasingly so with the expansion of the world's nuclear power program.

A more fundamental reason for inadequacy of the one bomb criterion is technical. In today's technology, the highest degree of accuracy currently possible in the measurement of the amount of plutonium in a reprocessing plant is plus or minus 1 percent. A typical commercial fuel reprocessing plant will handle 1,000 tons of fuel a year, which would contain six to seven tons of fissile pluto-

5. From an internal IAEA document.

nium. It is then easy to see that 1 percent of this is about 10 times the requirement of a single fission bomb. In other words, measurement error alone will exceed a one bomb threshold without anyone attempting to divert plutonium intentionally. In a somewhat simplistic presentation, diversion criteria for a country with a reprocessing plant handling 1,000 tons of fuel a year has to be at least 10 bombs worth.

Instead of rushing to the hasty conclusion that nobody should be allowed to operate a fuel reprocessing plant, let us examine other intrinsic limitations contained in the current safeguards system.

a. Safeguards systems can only function as effective deterrents if international sanctions against unauthorized diversion are spelled out in advance. This, unfortunately, is not the case and the reaction of the major powers to the Indian test of 1974, although India may not have violated any written pact, was nevertheless a frustrating experience for those genuinely concerned about proliferation. Even if the international community could agree on measures of sanction, it would then face difficult legal questions such as "Can one exercise sanction on the basis of a probablistic statement which may be 95 percent right but 5 percent wrong?" or "Why should a country be punished for the diversion of 10 bombs worth of nuclear material when it may be at perfect liberty to divert nine?"

b. Another important question relates to the definition of the national fuel cycle. Nations are obliged at the start of IAEA safeguards application to declare the entire nuclear facilities and nuclear materials within the country, to be updated every time changes take place. In the application of safeguards, should one assume the existence of a clandestine fuel reprocessing plant? If not, for a country without a declared reprocessing facility, monitoring plutonium presents a relatively easy problem because the country cannot extract plutonium from spent reactor fuel. If one has to assume the existence of a processing plant, the problem becomes infinitely more complicated, because then the system has to deal with unknown and unspecified elements and this means that detailed control on low enriched uranium will be required as a starting point for plutonium production. In general, there is a "cops-and-robbers" game played between imaginative adversaries unless IAEA can limit the extent of exotic diversion scenarios beforehand. (Permanent stationing of inspectors at nuclear facilities will not solve the problem, because one can easily create a technically consistent scenario which beats any defense even under that condition.)

c. Between NPT safeguards and previous IAEA practice, there is a definite discrepancy in definitions as to what it is that constitutes proliferation. A good example is a peaceful nuclear explosion (PNE), which is prohibited under the NPT because it is an explosion, but not prohibited under the previous system because it is peaceful. On the other hand, a naval propulsion reactor is allowed under NPT because it is not explosive but has been prohibited under bilateral agreements (and therefore under IAEA safeguards based on transfer agreements) because it is military. In the actual safeguards applications, what is at issue is only diversion. Incompatibility in definitions may be further illustrated if one imagines an IAEA inspector who is looking at a laboratory in which metallic plutonium is worked on, appearing very much like weapons development but without a weapons assembly line. All the nuclear material is correctly reported and there is no diversion. The work is explained as development of a new plutonium fuel concept for fast breeder reactors. Under NPT, states are free to conduct research and development for peaceful purposes. The most the inspector can do is to write a footnote in his inspection report, and the agency in Vienna might have to wonder whether the incident should be reported to the board of governors and, if so, under which provision of the safeguards agreement.

The problem of diversion thresholds, and the three additional examples mentioned here, make it clear that safeguards cannot be a mechanical process either technically or legally and that combinations of worst-case-assumptions will only lead to impossible situations. If one assumes a country possesses the technical capabilities to convert plutonium nitrate into a fission bomb within 90 days, then to require that the safeguards system detect diversion more than 90 days before the bomb production is an absurdity. What the current system under INFCIRC/153 does is to identify the logical relationship among the proliferation problems and to separate technical and political components so that the system can function effectively within the well-identified limits.

IMPLICATIONS FOR THE FUTURE

The technical effectiveness of IAEA safeguards has been taken up for discussion on a number of occasions recently, including the latest meeting of the IAEA's Standing Advisory Group for Safeguards Implementation, an international committee of experts to advise the Secretary General. Taken at the cops-and-robbers game level, one can imagine several cases in which IAEA would not have detected diversion if nations followed very complicated and prohibitively expensive diversion schemes. On the other hand, U.S. Secretary of State Kissinger has argued that "since the inception of safeguards, we know of no nation that has acquired nuclear weapons through any diversion of nuclear material subject to either bilateral or IAEA safeguards."[6] (India's CIRUS reactor is not under safeguards.)

Both of the above are true, and it becomes a matter of judgment as to which one of the two points of view one would like to adopt. This, in turn, is governed by one's conception of the mechanism for proliferation as well as the incentives to proliferation. What is more important than an assessment of past performance is the evaluation of the effectiveness of safeguards in the future, especially with rapid expansion of the world's nuclear capacities and the seeming desire of many LDCs to acquire this technology for energy generation. It is also important to look at the broader significance of the role of safeguards, for a good deal of misunderstanding and confusion today seems to come from a simplistic approach which regards safeguards as an instrument for the prevention of nuclear proliferation.

6. Statement by Henry Kissinger to the Senate Committee on Government Operations, 9 March 1976.

Any major technology has good and evil sides, and this is particularly true in the case of nuclear power. On the one hand, generation of electricity and heat through nuclear fission promises a practically unlimited supply of energy, especially when the era of fast breeder reactors materializes. The oil crisis of 1973 highlighted in many people's minds the basic problems of too heavy a reliance on oil. Since the higher oil prices made the relative economic position of nuclear power favorable, there are many countries that would like to increase the nuclear portion of their national energy supply. This is particularly true as the intrinsic limitations in other energy alternatives become clear and people have come to realize that the wide-scale utilization of solar power or fusion energy will have to wait at least until the next century. The negative side of nuclear power includes the spread of artificial radiation, the proliferation of nuclear weapons, and a possible increase in unrest due to concern about increasing amounts of plutonium. (This precisely would be the case in the days of fast-breeder reactors.)

For some time, attempts had been made to resolve this dilemma through the application of risk/benefit analysis until it was discovered that finding a common measuring unit for the risk of proliferation as against the benefit from energy supply is virtually impossible. People are discovering that they live in a multiple-value society in which some regard a continued supply of energy as the most important thing while others consider increased consumption of energy and further economic growth as the most undesirable. If nuclear proliferation is to be prevented at any cost, then the solution is simply to stop having any more nuclear power. It is a philosophical issue beyond reprocessing or safeguards, on which, however, it will be very difficult to arrive at a universal consensus. Like the problem of nuclear safety, the safest reactor is no reactor, because technology cannot assure absolute safety under any circumstances. A technology is safe when the probability of large-consequence accident is very low. Similarly, in whatever formulation it may be presented, the safeguards system is also an exercise in probability which, by definition, cannot give absolute assurance against proliferation. At best, it represents a reasonable compromise which tries to derive as much benefit as may be practicable from the novel and large technology called nuclear power, while at the same time it tries to hold the undesirable risk from the same technology to the minimum acceptable.

MORE THAN MEANS OF VERIFICATION

In this regard, nuclear safeguards are very different from other means of verification accompanying international agreements on arms control and disarmament. Conceptual application of safeguards technology may be found in such things as pollution control on a worldwide scale. (There are already attempts in the technical community to extend the basic concepts of IAEA safeguards to international control of air and ocean pollution.)[7]

Differences from other cases of verification may be examined in the following way. The verification pro-

7. Some of the works by the International Institute for Applied Systems Analysis, Luxemburg, are related to this subject.

vision in the Strategic Arms Limitation Talks (SALT) I Agreement refers to satellite observation of ICBM silos or the construction of new SLBM launchers. Procedures as well as objects of surveillance are very well defined. It is a process of counting numbers of existing weapons and of assuring that the number does not increase beyond the threshold. It is clear that in the current conception of the technology there is no such thing as a peaceful ICBM or peaceful SLBM, so that any unauthorized increase is a violation of the SALT Agreement. The same is true with nuclear test ban treaties, except for the case of peaceful nuclear explosions. The United States and USSR had to go to the trouble of drawing up a separate PNE treaty to accompany the underground test ban treaty of 1974 (TTBT) with a long and complicated protocol which spells out the definition of PNEs. PNE, however, is a great deal easier to regulate because such explosives are still far from becoming practical engineering tools, and in any event the technology is held only by the nuclear weapon states.

The verification of the existence of chemical weapons is, in many ways, similar to nuclear safeguards. As far as the technological base is concerned, chemical engineering serves both peaceful and military purposes, with the peaceful portion dominating. As the participants in the CCD are discovering, meaningful verification has to start with a definition of the chemical agents to be placed under surveillance, then they must be located among the vast industrial activities of the nations concerned. With due respect to the efforts being displayed in Geneva, such an exercise is an extremely difficult one, to say the least.

What has made nuclear safeguards feasible is a lucky combination of two situations. One is the fact that people started talking about safeguards long before nuclear power became an industrial reality, so that there has been sufficient time for planning. Another important element is that there are only two ingredients in the nuclear fuel cycle, namely uranium and plutonium. Both give off various kinds (and levels) of nuclear radiation, which requires the two materials to be handled in isolation from other industrial activities. Also, radiation-emitting substances are so easy to find even in a very minute quantity that they are often employed as tracers in chemical, physical, or biological analysis.

Without the two characteristics mentioned here, nuclear safeguards would have been very difficult. At the same time, one needs to be reminded of the fact that nuclear energy as a whole is suffering from excessive and much too detailed technology assessment before it has ever had an opportunity to prove itself industrially. It is often said that if the same approach to any other technology had been adopted, and all the possible adverse effects had been brought to social attention in advance, the world would never have seen wide-scale utilization of electricity, motorcars, or airplanes. There is some similarity to this in the way nuclear safeguards are being discussed today, not as actual experience or likely expectation but in anticipation of exotic diversion schemes.

COMPROMISE AMONG CONFLICTING FACTORS

From the foregoing discussion, it is clear that nuclear safeguards cannot be ends in themselves. They play a role in conjunction with other political and technical tools to reduce the probability of nuclear weapons proliferation. A number of important factors need to be considered in this regard.

a. Instead of applying uniform procedures to all the countries of the world, there will have to be an optimum deployment of available safeguards resources according to the different requirements. Technically advanced countries usually cannot expect to enhance their national security by manufacturing a couple of fission bombs. At the same time, the very large volume of nuclear material handled annually in their fuel cycles makes low diversion detection threshold unrealistic. Either a much higher threshold should be adopted, or, instead of an inspection program based on nuclear material accountancy control, IAEA should choose other and more elaborate technical means and keep the level and pattern of national nuclear activities under constant surveillance.

b. Less developed countries, which claim an interest in nuclear power, may be in a totally different situation. On the other hand, the starting scale of their nuclear activities will be small and thus amenable to somewhat detailed inspection schemes without requiring too much in the way of resources. (In spite of popular reactions, it will take quite some time before the nuclear programs of Brazil or Iran would build up to a large scale.)[8] On the other hand, it is argued that the LDC's prevailing interest in changing the status quo of the world's political, military, or economic order may provide opportunities for a small number of crude nuclear weapons to serve what may be their definitions of national interest. However, these countries will have to rely on the outside industrial centers for the supply of nuclear technology and major nuclear components as well as for various necessary services. Thus, it may make practical sense to apply different approaches and different standards of diversion detection in the case of LDCs. One possible way to solve the problems (*a*) and (*b*) simultaneously would be to adopt a diversion detection threshold which is proportional to the annual throughput of nuclear material within the national fuel cycle.

c. For quite some time to come, an indigenous commercial fuel reprocessing plant in countries with, say, less than 30 nuclear power stations, would not make economic sense. Some people argue, on the basis of the estimated reserve of available uranium resources and of the economics of the fuel cycle, that fuel reprocessing and subsequent transition into a plutonium-fueled energy system can only promise a very uncertain future. Although it is premature to base long-term policy on today's understanding of technology and economics, internationally controlled spent fuel storage or fuel reprocessing may make sense under certain conditions. Some of the features that would make such a proposition attractive may include, in not necessarily mutually consistent fashion, the provision of construction capital which is compatible with the technological and commercial risk of reprocessing, the provision of technology with some performance guarantee, or making a much needed plant site available with radioactive waste handling capabilities. Without tak-

8. Norman Gall, "Atoms for Brazil, Danger for All," *Bulletin of the Atomic Scientists*, June 1976.

ing any of these steps, insistence on the concept of regional reprocessing merely on the merit of its safeguards will not convince the world's nuclear community. To deny reprocessing (thereby denying chances of plutonium fuel) without providing for uranium resources and uranium enrichment service, and yet at the same time to vigorously market nuclear reactors, will only invite the world's antagonism. One cannot place safeguards above nuclear power and still pay lip-service to the world energy problem.

d. Nuclear industry requires very large investment and very long lead time both for the development of technology and of manufacturing capabilities. This fact together with the somewhat restricted geographic concentration of major uranium reserves make international trade in nuclear power inevitable. Even the United States is finding out that she cannot support the complete industry with her domestic demands alone. The need for overseas markets is much more acute for European countries and Japan. To discourage nuclear trade as leading to proliferation would be neither wise nor practical.[9] The supplying countries' agreement worked out by seven nations through the secret London meeting of 1975 seems to be a promising first step toward striking a proper balance between the need for promoting trade and the requirement for protecting technology against weapons proliferation.[10]

e. There seems to be an exaggerated fear of terrorists' use of nuclear material, either for the manufacture of bombs or for the contamination of the environment. Although the importance of correct physical security measures cannot be overemphasized, this exaggeration can only do harm. It is difficult to assume that terrorists would find the nuclear route to be the optimum way of applying threats to society and thereby publicizing their respective causes.[11] Because one can never deny the possibility of complete social madness, and because measures for physical security are a useful supplement to effective safeguards by providing necessary containment and surveillance over nuclear material of critical nature, a physical protection program needs encouragement. At the same time it should be always kept in mind that physical protection by definition is a sovereign act for the maintenance of domestic social order, whereas safeguards are administered within sovereign states by international organizations. As important as the physical protection of nuclear material is the positive step of assurance by nuclear weapons states to the rest of the world that weapons in their possession will neither be stolen nor misused.

f. It seems very clear as far as the amount of risk is concerned that one should be more afraid of the tens of thousands of megatons that already exist in the hands of the superpowers than of the yet nonexistent potential bomb in the hands of unidentified states. Unless this is kept in proper perspective, and unless the basic under-

9. Donald Avery and Ryukichi Imai, "The International Nuclear Fuel Cycle Market," American Nuclear Society/European Nuclear Society meeting, November 1976.

10. Not much has been published regarding this secret accord. See, for instance, "Strategic Survey, 1975," the International Institute for Strategic Studies, London, 1976.

11. Roberta Wohlstetter, "Terror on a Grand Scale," reprinted in *Survival* (The International Institute for Strategic Studies, May/June 1976).

taking for nuclear arms control and eventual disarmament is faithfully pursued, insistence on non-proliferation alone would invite the charge that those so doing are displaying the arrogance of self-appointed God's custodians of nuclear technology. It is also very important to realize that the non-proliferation situation of the past years did not arise merely from general acceptance of the superpowers' concern over nuclear weapons, but much more from the lack of need and incentives. If the Indian test increased the needs and incentives of some emerging powers for the acquisition of nuclear weapons, political measures to remove or reduce such incentives should precede any amount of technical safeguards.

Reducing the Incentives to Proliferation

By GEORGE H. QUESTER

ABSTRACT: There are two very different kinds of incentives to nuclear proliferation. We are used to seeing nations deter potential enemies and win political concessions with such weapons. A newer, very different, kind of incentive stems from the economic overlap between peaceful electric power reactors and the production of weapons-grade plutonium or enriched uranium; there may now be an economic cost to steering away from the bomb, rather than a cost to making it. Reducing the political-military incentives to proliferation will require a case-by-case approach. Some of these incentives can be decreased by extending the American nuclear umbrella, as for Europe and Japan. But a serious problem can then emerge in preventing proliferation by such "outlaw states" as South Africa, Israel, and Taiwan. For much of the world, moreover, the bomb will be more of a political-prestige item than a military tool, so that a superpower nuclear umbrella would be redundant or counter-productive. Reducing the economic incentives will also require a case-by-case approach. This cannot be achieved by simply cutting off technological assistance in the nuclear field. Rather, it must be done by using such assistance as a subtle "carrot" or "stick," to persuade the leaders of countries like Brazil and Japan to stay away from bombs.

George H. Quester, Professor of Government at Cornell University, is currently serving as Chairman of the Government Department and as Associate Director of the Cornell Peace Studies Program. He was educated at Columbia and Harvard Universities and has authored several books, including The Politics of Nuclear Proliferation *(Johns Hopkins Press, 1973).*

WHY indeed are there any incentives to nuclear proliferation? Given all the hardships and hostility that may be produced by a move to nuclear weapons, shouldn't it be apparent to one and all that the existing nuclear club is large enough?

Students of traditional international politics and realpolitik would respond all too quickly here that the incentives are obvious, for an additional weapon gives additional power, and power pays off in this anarchic world. A nation possessing nuclear weapons may be able to compel other nations to make concessions. At the least, a nation possessing such weapons can very plausibly deter the most objectionable actions of another state. Would the Russians have invaded Czechoslovakia in 1968 if the Czechs had possessed nuclear weapons? The elementary logic of mutual deterrence suggests that they would not.[1]

Apart from incentives based on such straightforward military considerations, one could also see some indirect advantages and incentives at the level of political prestige. Hasn't the world taken Britain and France more seriously because of their nuclear stockpiles? Wouldn't the world have lost interest in China after the internal tumult of the Great Cultural Revolution, except for the fact that China had detonated an A-bomb and an H-bomb? Even when the possession of nuclear weapons cannot be translated into any meaningful military scenarios, it hovers in the background as a symbol of national power, changing the way prestige and status are distributed by the public opinions of the world, changing the way political negotiations may be settled.

A second kind of incentive may be more surprising, for it comes in the realm of economics. Most of us have expected nuclear weapons to be expensive, and are thus appalled that India could waste millions on such a bomb or that Iran could be contemplating squandering its oil riches in copying India. Yet the economic factor here is more subtle and perverse, such that bombs could become very cheap, such that avoiding nuclear weapons could even be expensive.[2]

We are all quite justified in distrusting spin-off arguments as they are used to justify most military programs. We are told civilian goods are developed as a nice by-product of military research programs, such that we should not be so critical of the high costs of the military programs; yet this is often misleading propaganda, for the same civilian goods could be developed at far lower costs if they were pursued directly, rather than as the supposed spin-off by-product of a weapons program.

The difficulty in the nuclear case is that the spin-off phenomenon works in exactly the opposite direction and may not be bogus at all. To produce electricity by means of nuclear reactors may make perfect sense today, after the price of oil has risen so much. Yet the operation of such reactors quite naturally will put countries into contact with plutonium and enriched uranium, the materials needed for atomic bombs. Staying away from the bomb

1. For a classic statement of this kind of analysis, see Pierre Gallois, *The Balance of Terror: Strategy for the Nuclear Age* (Boston: Houghton Mifflin Company, 1961).

2. See Mason Willrich, ed., *International Safeguards and Nuclear Industry* (Baltimore: Johns Hopkins Press, 1973).

might thus be optimal for arms control and neighborly understanding among the countries involved, but staying away from the bomb might require staying away from the most cost-effective source of energy. Alas, therefore, one has thus found another powerful incentive or drive toward nuclear weapons proliferation.

What can one then hope to do to decouple such incentives, to prevent the spread of nuclear weapons from going on and on?[3] There is indeed hope that proliferation can yet be contained. The hope in part is based on some "lucky breaks" in the political and economic environment that may partially compensate for the bad luck we have described above. The hope must additionally be based, however, on some important policy choices which will confront all of us in the future. If these choices are handled wisely, proliferation will be easier to stop; if they are handled badly, our troubles may increase.

DECOUPLING MILITARY INCENTIVES

To turn first to the military incentives to proliferation, how does one shape policy to deemphasize these? Some analysts have predicted that the halting of nuclear proliferation will require the United States to play the role of "world policeman" again, extending its own nuclear umbrella to provide protection comparable to what any erstwhile proliferator would find in a national nuclear weapons program.[4] Much has been written to contend, however, that the existing nuclear-weapons states, or most especially the United States and USSR (the two superpowers), must now greatly limit their own possession, deployment, and brandishment of nuclear weapons, to avoid setting up the irritation between have and have-not that could make Nth countries look for an "equalizer."[5]

The first prediction seems strategically sound; the second would seem to make moral and symbolic sense. Examples can be found to support either prognosis. Denmark is a nation that shows no signs of feeling an incentive to proliferation, even though it wishes very much not to be liberated by the Soviet army; the counter-threat that the United States would escalate to the use of its own nuclear forces has since 1945 been an important reassurance to Danes and to many other West Europeans that they will not be thus "liberated." Brazilians, by contrast, may become furious at the implication that Moscow and

3. For basic treatments of the shape of the nuclear proliferation problem, see Richard N. Rosecrance, ed., *The Dispersion of Nuclear Weapons* (New York: Columbia University Press, 1963); Johan Jorgen Holst, ed., *Security, Order, and the Bomb* (Oslo: Universitetsforlaget, 1972); Robert M. Lawrence and Joel Larus, eds., *Nuclear Proliferation: Phase II* (Lawrence: University of Kansas Press, 1974); and Ciro Zoppo, *Trends in Nuclear Proliferation and U.S. Security* (Santa Monica: California Seminar on Arms Control and Foreign Policy, 1975).

4. For a well-balanced statement of these kinds of positions, see William B. Bader, *The United States and the Spread of Nuclear Weapons* (New York: Pegasus, 1968), pp. 110–19.

5. For examples, see William Epstein, "The Proliferation of Nuclear Weapons," *Scientific American*, April 1975, pp. 18–33; and Elizabeth Young, *The Control of Proliferation: The 1968 Treaty in Hindsight and Forecast*, Adelphi Papers no. 56 (London: Institute for Strategic Studies, 1969). A balanced overview of the two kinds of position can be found in Joseph I. Coffey, "Nuclear Guarantees and Nonproliferation," *International Organization*, vol. 25 (Autumn 1971), pp. 836–44.

Washington can be trusted with the latest in nuclear weapons while Brasilia can not.

What follows will be an attempt to sort out these conflicting arguments for the categories of situations to which they appropriately apply. There is indeed a zone of the world covered by the American nuclear umbrella where nothing much should be changed. For Western Europe and for Japan, the likely American escalation to the use of nuclear weapons has been an important stabilizing factor in the background, and this explains Bonn's and Tokyo's adherence to the Non-Proliferation Treaty (NPT). There is no point to having the United States "brandish nuclear weapons less" for these cases. Indeed, to begin any well-publicized American withdrawal of tactical nuclear weapons from Europe, or to open any extended discussion of "nuclear free zones" for these areas, risks upsetting the balance of feelings which have so nicely negated the incentive to proliferation here. For Europe and Japan, in summary, proliferation is not a problem, and peace is not a problem, precisely because the United States is remaining around as a nuclear policeman.

There is another category of countries for which the military impact of a nuclear weapons program is real, but where the American commitment has not so comfortably been settled into place and where proliferation will be more of a problem. These basically are the "outlaw" states of the 1970s, insufficiently covered by the American nuclear umbrella, where a more obtrusive American presence would be welcome but may not be available, where proliferation may thus occur as the regimes in question hunt for alternatives. The list here includes Israel, South Africa, and Taiwan, all states in the bad graces of world opinion as expressed in the United Nations General Assembly; over time it could also come to include South Korea and perhaps even Iran. Each of such states may tend to see an indigenous nuclear weapons option as the necessary ultimate veto, in the face of hostile states that would like to put the regime or state in question out of existence.

However one feels about the regime in Taipei or Pretoria or Seoul, it cannot be denied that a greater American commitment to the status quo here would ease rather than worsen the proliferation problem. If an American guarantee to Israel or Iran could be made airtight, it might simultaneously end the military incentive for a move toward nuclear weapons by these states.

Yet the world does not consist only of regimes like Copenhagen and like Pretoria. There is indeed a third category of countries for which the military possibilities of nuclear escalation or nuclear deterrence play much less of a role, and here the diminution suggested for the visible presence of superpowers may indeed make sense. Happily enough, this is the bulk of the world. Unhappily, proliferation among the short list of threatened nations above may upset the equanimity of these other states as well.

One can dismiss most of the military cases preferred by bomb advocates and professional military officers in this kind of Nth country. The bomb is in truth more of a political symbol here than an operational tool. The major issue for the future of proliferation here will thus not concern scenarios for battle situations and deterrence crises.

Nor will non-proliferation be heavily dependent on substantial disarmament by the two superpowers. There are many grounds for being critical of the way the United States and Soviet Union have conducted the Strategic Arms Limitation Talks (SALT). Yet one does not need to worry that bad handling of the talks threatens the world with a World War III. However much or however little SALT now accomplishes in heading off new rounds of the Soviet-American arms race, it is not likely to undo the stability resulting from previous rounds of that race. The atmosphere of SALT moreover is at least so stage-managed as to suggest to the world that Russians and Americans are not contemplating making nuclear war against each other. All of this, thus, reinforces a pattern that can only be categorized as world boredom with bombs, as the publics of the world have become uninterested in keeping count of numbers of missiles and numbers of nuclear powers and have become resentful of anyone boorish enough to force them to dwell on the subject again.

A substantively more ambitious SALT negotiation may be very desirable in its own right, but it may not have an greater impact for discouraging further proliferation than what is already underway. At the worst, if the more ambitious negotiations led to a great deal of discourse on the details of missile postures and first-strike scenarios, it could be counter-productive to the intention of taking away the glamor and incentive of going nuclear.

DOWNGRADING POLITICAL INCENTIVES

A most appropriate yardstick for anti-proliferation policy with reference to this third category of countries might simply be to "keep nuclears out of the news." SALT and other arms control discussions should be managed so as to maintain the impression that weapons cannot make any crucial difference anymore, that there are no "revolutionary weapons breakthroughs" coming over the horizon, that serious problems and serious solutions are to be found elsewhere, far removed from the possibilities of nuclear weapons.

Part of the goal here is of course to remove whatever glamor is attached to the possession of nuclear weapons. Another part is to remove any invidious feelings or irritation that might occur because states like the United States and Soviet Union get to keep their nuclear arsenals. If image and prestige are the bulk of what the proliferation problem is about for this third class of nations, the problem may have to be managed more in terms of political image than substantive arms control.

Similar ambivalence must, thus, be expressed about the desirability of supporting nuclear no-first-use policies or nuclear free zones as a way of reducing the incentives to nuclear proliferation. As elsewhere, an excessively abstract analysis can be a problem here rather than a help.

On a quiet, de facto basis, the United States has indeed indicated that it will not be brandishing or deploying nuclear weapons in much of the world. There is, in effect, a no-first-use policy for Southeast Asia and for other regions of the underdeveloped world, regions where the conventional force advantage of the Soviet Union has never frightened the publics that matter. Whether this quiet, de facto approach should be upgraded to explicit statements and treaty signatures is another matter. When the countries of a region put together something like the new Latin American Nuclear Free Zone, it might indeed be well for the United States to avoid quibbling with it and opposing it.[6] The tougher overall problem will come in keeping the logic of nuclear free zones and no-first-use from casting into question the American commitments to nuclear escalation in defense of Western Europe and Japan.

There are some other political policy steps which the United States might consider to further the deglamorization of nuclear weapons. A termination of underground nuclear testing by the two superpowers would surely have a beneficial impact, as long as it was not achieved through an overly visible and tortured and litigated negotiation process. A deemphasis of earlier talk of "peaceful nuclear expositions" would be similarly beneficial, again if the projects can be dropped quietly. As suggested above, any achievement of the substance of SALT, without amplifying the procedural visibility of SALT, would be altogether beneficial.

However, compared to the possible signals to be extracted from a more meaningful SALT negotiation, or even a nuclear free zone, a far greater impact to halting proliferation in this third zone can be achieved by keeping nations in the second group above—the seriously-threatened nations—from actually moving to detonate a bomb.

Israel may supply the model here, generally thought to be in possession of such weapons but never quite punctuating this assumption by detonating such a bomb. South Africa now seems to be pursuing a parallel policy. In each case, one gets repeated official denials, typically worded so as to be less than categorical. In each case, one also gets rumors and off-the-cuff remarks hinting that a nuclear weapons stockpile is being collected.

The states pursuing such a policy clearly obtain some of the gains of outright proliferation, while avoiding some of the costs for themselves and for the world. Subliminally or otherwise, the message must be reaching Arab leaders that they can not hope anymore to attain their dream of pushing Zionist Israel into the sea. Even if victory could be won on the conventional battlefield, Israel would presumably destroy Cairo and Damascus and Mecca as part of its last-gasp retaliation, and Arabs must know this now. Knowing it over time will produce what nothing else could produce, the acceptance of something called Israel. South African leaders can aspire to something similar, erasing the hope of black African leaders that somehow all the whites can be forced to leave.

At the same time, the posture of asymptotically approaching the bomb, of never openly announcing possession, and never test-detonating it, markedly reduces outside public arousal about proliferation. In a funny and illogical way, the world only counts what has been detonated. India is rated inside the club while Israel is rated out. If proliferation to Argentina and Brazil and Japan and Australia is to some extent causally linked by what the publics sense about the prior extent of proliferation, keeping the detonation from occurring in Israel or South Africa will be terribly important.

6. For basic material on Latin America, see John R. Redick, *The Military Potential of Latin American Nuclear Energy Programs* (Beverly Hills, Calif.: Sage Publications, 1972).

RESPONDING TO ECONOMIC OPPORTUNITY

We must now turn to the other of our initial list of kinds of incentives, the economic overlap between peaceful programs and military programs, with the discouraging wave of suspicions and tensions it creates. Will economic considerations in the net spell the undoing of the effort to halt proliferation? Or are there some helpful breaks from nature, and astute policies, that can be harnessed here as well?

One form of economic problem was widely forecast eight years ago, and has not materialized, specifically the simple economic cost of the inspection safeguards of the International Atomic Energy Agency (IAEA), safeguards which will be required by terms of the Non-Proliferation Treaty or are required otherwise under the bilateral contracts negotiated between seller and purchaser of nuclear reactors.[7] Significant breakthroughs have been made in introducing techniques of automation and in conceptually redesigning the future reactor complexes, to make possible inspection systems of higher reliability and lower cost. The fears expressed that the International Atomic Energy Agency would have difficulty in finding competent personnel to serve as inspectors has thus far not materialized. While the agency has been behind schedule in developing the inspectorate required, the growth of power reactors has also been continually behind schedule, so that the two are basically in phase. The fears often voiced in the past of incipient commercial espionage have also been substantially quieted.

A related form of economic problem stemmed from the fact that countries already having nuclear weapons would not logically come under inspection under the NPT system, thus perhaps allowing them an unfair advantage in escaping the costs of such inspection. Much of the steam has also now gone out of this issue.

As a public relations gesture of sorts, the United States and Britain in 1968 voluntarily offered to place their civilian nuclear facilities under IAEA inspection, thus to equalize the impression of economic burdens and of risks of commercial espionage. Skeptics here were quick to note that the IAEA was certainly not likely to waste its time and manpower on inspecting the United States as thoroughly as West Germany or Japan or Libya. The United States already had the bomb, why would it want to produce a clandestine bomb in some reactor system as well?

Yet the apparent logic of this difference has also now been muffled by the growing fear of theft of plutonium by criminal or terrorist groups.[8] For reasons having little or nothing to do with Nth-country proliferation, the United States and Britain are now also going to have to subject their peaceful nuclear power industries to the costs and rigors of tighter safeguards against theft and inversion. The periodic visits of IAEA inspectors, originally seen as a publicity stunt, may now even be welcome in functional terms for keeping the local inspectorate

7. See Lawrence Scheinman, "Safeguarding Nuclear Materials," *Bulletin of the Atomic Scientists*, vol. 30, no. 4 (April 1974), pp. 34–6.

8. See Mason Willrich and Theodore B. Taylor, *Nuclear Theft: Risks and Safeguards* (Cambridge, Mass.: Ballinger Publishing Company, 1974).

on its toes. Some of the risks of commercial espionage will now be run as much by General Electric as by Siemens; the inspector from the International Atomic Energy Agency may be no more prone to secretly conducting such espionage for Westinghouse than would be the inspector for the U.S. Nuclear Regulatory Commission.

The major economic problem for the halting of proliferation is thus not one of inequity of burdens, although the anti-NPT propaganda voiced in 1968 at times made it seem that way. The major problem is, instead, as stated above: that innocent pursuit of peaceful economic advantages will still pull countries like West Germany and Australia and Iran and South Korea perilously close to the bomb. What if reactors and uranium enrichment plants and plutonium reprocessing plants all prove to be cost-effective in civilian terms for such countries, now that the price of energy has gone so high? It will be more difficult to question the motives of the countries involved, and more difficult to deny them the equipment they seek.

The margin for safety in such a world will be thin, and one might thus very much wish that the entire dilemma could somehow be headed off. But even here a policy of subtlety will be in order. We will, with good reason, remain uncertain for some time further into the future whether nuclear electric power production will really be as cost-effective as its proponents claim. If it is not, much of the arms control problem would be eased, for there would be no reason for Nth nations to come "innocently" so close to the bomb. The United States, thus, should certainly not be in the position of subsidizing and pushing nuclear power ahead of other less dangerous possibilities, for example, ahead of solar energy. The United States, in supporting nuclear technology, should moreover consider the relative monitorability of alternative reactor designs and uranium enrichment processes, perhaps in the end subsidizing one and trying to stifle another, so that the IAEA's safeguards task will at least be made easier. Active support might be given to multinational facilities ahead of the purely national, and the United States might offer to maintain the most sensitive plutonium reprocessing facilities on its own territory.

Yet again, all this should be offered in a soft-sell manner, lest someone in an Nth country be handed a demagogic argument that U.S. desire for a nuclear weapons oligopoly has vetoed something of great economic benefit to the poorer nations of the world. If nuclear power production is to be rejected for ecological and safety reasons, for example, it would be far better if Sweden and France and Australia were allowed the lead in reaching this conclusion. Most of the worrisome power reactors will not go into operation as early as scheduled, and some may never go into operation at all. The cause of halting proliferation will be made far easier politically if it, however, does not appear that such slowdowns and cancellations were the result of pressure from Washington.

The Role of Sanctions

But what then if technology nonetheless breaks in the wrong way, so that national nuclear programs involving the entire fuel cycle turn out to be economically desirable for a great number of countries?

The remaining options for United States non-proliferation policy sometimes get discussed in terms of sanctions and other times more broadly in terms of disincentives. If there is a difference between the two concepts, it is probably only in that the latter list can be broader, including carrots withheld as well as sticks brought to bear. Sanctions smell of threats, threats which may be difficult to execute. Sanctions may, thus, have to be declared openly to be effective, with all the irritation this produces. What follows is a typology of disincentives which the United States and other anti-proliferation states can apply, including a few deliberate sanctions:

a. simple political condemnation—that is, the minimum implied in statements that the United States or any other state would view a move toward the bomb with the "utmost seriousness"

b. the denial of any additional nuclear equipment in the future

c. the withdrawal of all trained American personnel

d. the denial of all forms of economic assistance—including even the non-nuclear

e. the termination of military alliance support

f. the forcible removal of any nuclear facilities which have been diverted from their promised peaceful purposes to the production of explosives

g. the outright use of military force against the state which is moving to the bomb, or has made the bomb.

We are all tempted to snicker at option (*a*), the simple condemnation of another act of proliferation at the political level. Yet this should not be discounted too totally. For many nations in the world, prestige and outside admiration will be the only reason to reach for the bomb. If attitudes have changed, so that condemnation rather than admiration can be directed at the Nth nuclear power, U.S. policy will have something to work with here.

Leaping ahead to matters of military policy and military action, each of the last three options, (*e*), (*f*), and (*g*), are also plagued with credibility problems. How much can one threaten to terminate alliances because of a move to nuclears? After the debacle of Vietnam, who would propose to send in the marines to try to recover an American reactor or a French plutonium separation plant, simply because the recipient nation had announced its withdrawal from the Nuclear Non-Proliferation Treaty, or its abrogation of the solemn contracts by which such facilities had been purchased in the first place? More particularly, if the offending state has already got a few rudimentary nuclear weapons into its arsenal, who will be in the mood to begin a war about this?

None of these threats lack all punch, of course. The threat that leaves something to chance can still be very useful in international politics. For example, we do not know exactly what we will do if the USSR invades Western Europe; but because Moscow does not know exactly what we will do, it remains deterred from starting such an invasion in the first place. We do not know exactly what we will do if a state violates its commitments and manufactures a nuclear weapon. But if that state does not know what we will do, it may still be deterred from making the move.

Yet much of the credibility and punch of what the United States can do will stem from the economic portion of the array, just as much of the proliferation problem begins here. Option (*b*), the denial of additional nuclear equipment in the future, might look like "locking the barn door after the horse has been stolen," but this is misleading, for most of the worrisome countries we are considering will feel a continual need for further expansion, further improvement and renovation, and so forth, all of which will depend on new inputs of American technology. Countries like Brazil have a bomb lobby and an industrial-expansion lobby. The essence of U.S. policy here must, thus, be to use the second to defeat the first.

Option (*c*) will have particular impact in countries like Iran, which have economic-expansion programs running far ahead of the supply of trained manpower. American and French and German nuclear engineers will be essential to the Iranian program for decades into the future, and for the programs of many other countries. It should not be impossible for the United States and its fellow nuclear suppliers to pass laws forbidding their nationals to work for nuclear programs which are producing explosives, just as they pass laws forbidding their citizens to fight in foreign armed forces. A nation defying the NPT or its contracts could, of course, try to hold foreign engineers in the country as captive labor, but the entire prospect is cumbersome enough to suggest a disincentive to a bomb decision.

Option (*d*) is a more farfetched and difficult response to apply. Cutting off economic aid in general, not just nuclear assistance, might have been impossible in the Indian case, if only because the newspapers of the world within a week would have shown photographs of starving babies. Where the Nth country is a little less hard-pressed economically, however—for example Brazil or Iran—this may be a much more credible sanction or disincentive. The United States and many other countries may quite naturally want to terminate economic cooperation with anyone who upsets the tranquility of a region by acquiring atomic bombs.

In the application of economic pressures, the recommendation, as before, will again have to be for a policy which does not advertise its logical clarity, which does not try to treat all countries the same way, which is subtle and low-key.

As noted, many of the Nth countries we are so concerned about will have a continuing need for American and other technological imports, as part of a continuing appetite for additional energy and additional technology. Many of such states will, thus, be ready to accommodate to the halting of weapons proliferation in various ways, as long as it seems that this is required to speed or maintain the availability of such American inputs. Perhaps they will be willing to sign and ratify the Nuclear Non-Proliferation Treaty; Japan's ratification of the NPT is an example of this.[9] Other states perhaps will be willing to do more, or to do other things, to reassure the outside world that bombs are not being made, for example by submitting to IAEA safe-

9. For a comprehensive overview of Japanese attitudes on nuclear proliferation, see Daniel I. Okimoto, "Japan's Non-Nuclear Policy: The Problem of the NPT," *Asian Survey*, vol. 15 (April 1975), pp. 313–27.

guards even if the NPT is not signed, or by making unilateral declarations that nuclear technology will not be used for weapons manufacture.

The leverage here will be derived directly from these nations' dependence on the advanced technology of the United States and of five or six supplier states. The linkages should not ever be stated too baldly or explicitly, however, for this would run the risk of enraging the public opinions of the less-developed Nth-countries involved. As an analogous model, one might note the treatment one is subjected to at airline check-in stations, where ticketed-passengers get to move right through while the unticketed may be asked to "please step aside for a moment"—with all the traumas of missed flights this implies. The airlines never threaten, but they make one very cooperative nonetheless.

Economic considerations are powerful. In large part this is why we have a nuclear proliferation problem. In countries like Japan and Brazil and Australia and Iran, such powerful considerations may, however, outweigh the whims of anyone who wanted a bomb option just for "the fun of it," just for the national stature it would produce. If the United States can win the cooperation of the ministries of economics and commerce and industry in each of such nations, some powerful leverage indeed will be at hand.

The organization of the Nuclear Supplier's Conference in 1975 and 1976 fits this model of policy very well. The periodic bursts of outrage about the threat of proliferation in the U.S. Congress, on the other hand, may be far too unsubtle.

SOME OPTIMISM ABOUT AN APPROACH

The overall drift of the argument here has been that the halting of nuclear proliferation will require a low-key and subtle approach, masking what some would see as internal inconsistencies but perhaps nonetheless succeeding in containing the spread of nuclear weapons. The desirable political message for Germany may, thus, differ from the optimal one for Brazil. The correct economic approach for Iran may differ from that for Japan. How can the United States and other states opposed to proliferation expect to get away with this?

The approach is made possible by the lowered visibility of nuclear matters around the world. As the world pays less attention to nuclear matters, its inherent desire for weapons is decreased, and its irritation with alleged great-power inconsistencies is decreased. A subtle approach can maintain this kind of low visibility. Excessive abstraction and clarity can lose it.

Excessive abstraction also sometimes produces needless pessimism about whether anything can be done about nuclear proliferation, making the halting of the spread of such weapons seem a once-and-for-all question. Nothing in this paper should be taken to read that proliferation is overstated as a problem; but it can easily be misstated as a problem.

Nuclear proliferation is somewhat comparable to population growth, in that only half of the rate projected by the alarmist commentators still may produce an unacceptable crowding, even if this crowding comes a little later. Populations, moreover, can go down if the birth rate simply falls below the replacement rate, as indeed may happen in some industrialized countries. On the nuclear side, however, no real tendency toward deproliferation seems in evidence. British fervor for opting out of the nuclear club seems to have cooled, and the merger of British and French nuclear forces into a single nuclear-weapons entity (defined, that is, as an entity whereby a single veto on all nuclear firings from the unit was established in either Paris or London) also seems unlikely.

Yet the analogy between population bomb and nuclear proliferation also suggests some reassurance. No one can claim to be content with endless growth in either category, and thus some action has to be taken. Yet panic on either front can be outflanked by saying that a freeze as of 1985 is just as acceptable as a freeze as of 1965. If India and Israel and one other country make it into the nuclear club by then, this is not yet a world in which everyone has the bomb.

ANNALS, AAPSS, 430, March 1977

Part II Introduction: . . . and Where We May Go

By JOSEPH I. COFFEY

It is, of course, possible that the reluctance of many states to "go nuclear" may mean that another decade will elapse before a seventh country does so. The likelihood of this outcome may be increased if the nuclear powers combine stronger controls over the transfer of technology with measures to improve security guarantees and to reduce their own armaments. It might be further increased if they and the other industrially-advanced states accelerate the flow of capital to the underdeveloped countries, improve their terms of trade, and otherwise give indications that these countries need neither fear continuing exploitation nor rely on their own resources to achieve their social and economic objectives. Thus, it is conceivable that this dangerous world may be only a little more dangerous 10 years hence—at least so far as nuclear proliferation contributes to danger.

However, we can count neither upon the wisdom of statesmen nor upon the effectiveness of the policies they adopt and must recognize that, under certain circumstances, the world may become a more dangerous place. If India goes beyond the detonation of a single nuclear device to the creation of a nuclear force, Pakistan may be even more inclined to develop a countervailing capability then she now is. If Israel, facing defeat or dismemberment, actually uses the atomic bombs she allegedly possesses, then potential proliferators among the Arab states may push ahead with nuclear weapons of their own. Or if other states, though not directly threatened, continue to believe that prestige, influence, and even power, can be enhanced through the acquisition of nuclear weapons, they, too, may produce them, with consequent impact on nations still hesitant to go nuclear. Hence, it is by no means unlikely that we may have, by the middle of the next decade, 10 or 12 nuclear powers rather than six and a half, as is now the case.

In the longer run, the prospect is even gloomier, in that many more nuclear reactors will be in operation, and much more fissionable material available for weapons; innovations in nuclear technology will make it easier to produce that material and fabricate those weapons; and the "multiplier effect" already noted may intensify other pressures to go nuclear. In fact, barring a radical transformation in the international system which will reduce threats to security and minimize the importance of power as a means of attaining national objectives, it is conceivable that we may, in the words of the late President Kennedy, see a world "in which 15 or 20 or 25 nations may have these [nuclear] weapons . . . [a situation of] the greatest possible danger and hazard."[1]

1. *The New York Times*, 23 May 1963.

Even if a world of 10 nuclear powers, or 20, were unlikely, it might be worth examining its implications—if only to persuade ourselves of the desirability of taking steps to prevent its emergence. As it is, we cannot say with assurance that such a world *is* unlikely: the incentives to proliferation outlined above are very strong and the disincentives both difficult to apply and far-reaching in their consequences. Accordingly, we will, in the second part of this volume, look first of all at "The Nth Powers of the Future" and at the structure of the international system and the characteristics of the actors in a world of (many more) nuclear powers. Next, we will consider a number of issues which might arise in such a world, as with respect to arms control policy, to the role of international organizations, and to the process and nature of decision making.

Finally, since this journal is addressed primarily to an American audience, we will sketch some policies which might commend themselves to an administration taking office, say, on January 20, 1989. To this, let us proceed.

ANNALS, AAPSS, 430, March 1977

Nth Powers of the Future

By ASHOK KAPUR

ABSTRACT: Acceptance of the NPT by a majority of states after 1968 created an impression that the danger of further proliferation beyond the five nuclear weapon states (US, USSR, China, UK, and France) had been put to rest. India's "peaceful nuclear explosion" shattered this impression and pointed up the danger of proliferating nuclear options, if not nuclear weapons. The list of potential proliferators has changed from the 1950s to the 1970s and may continue to change in the 1980s. Israel and, by some views, India are on the list, but others like Japan, Australia, South Africa, Brazil, South Korea, Taiwan, and Argentina are being added. This paper asserts that proliferation, while unstoppable, is slow, not because the NPT is necessarily working, but because the military and economic security perceptions of potential proliferators do not dictate a faster rate of proliferation. Yet the possible deterioration of the strategic environment in the 1980s may induce faster proliferation. The new stress may not be on the acquisition of nuclear arms but, because nuclear arms are becoming militarily less useful, it may be on development of nuclear options coupled with a strategy of their nonuse or nonconversion into weapons.

Dr. Ashok Kapur is Assistant Professor in Political Science at the University of Waterloo, Ontario, Canada. He is author of India's Nuclear Option: Atomic Diplomacy and Decision Making *(New York: Praeger Special Studies, 1976). He has written extensively about Indian foreign policy, Asian political affairs, and arms control and disarmament in scholarly and professional journals.*

PREDICTING proliferation trends is a hazardous activity because national intelligence estimates of capabilities and particularly of intentions are imprecise, our conceptions and images[1] are culture-bound, and ambiguities not only characterize the world order but, furthermore, are deliberately fostered in the negotiating behavior of the major military powers. Still the exercise must be undertaken if the margin of uncertainty is to be reduced and if realistic solutions are to be found which appeal both to the major military powers and to potential Nth powers.

Incentives and disincentives to "go nuclear" vary from one state to another. For our purpose, incentives to explode a device or to possess one in an untested form could be any of the following: to achieve a deterrent against a potential nuclear enemy; to neutralize the conventional military superiority of an enemy; to gain international, regional, or domestic prestige; to participate in international or regional security policy making; to reduce dependence on a great power; to stay abreast of modern technology so that scientific-technological dependence on great powers is avoided or minimized; to create ambiguity in an enemy's calculations; to induce the enemy of a potential proliferator not to force the latter to decide in favor of making nuclear weapons; to experiment with the potential economic prospects of peaceful nuclear explosions; and so on.[2]

Disincentives against going nuclear (defined as developing and deploying nuclear weapons systems) could be any of the following: premature decisions to produce and deploy nuclear weapons could increase regional and international tension and could interfere with normalization of relations; there are budgetary and political advantages in the noncommitment implied in continuing nuclear research and development without moving toward weapons production; if nuclear weapons are becoming less useful militarily, weapons with long lead-times may be obsolescence-prone and costly for national development and yet may not add to national security; threats to proliferate can aid negotiations of conventional arms transfers; and so on. This paper assumes that security assurances by great powers are worthless in the perceptions of Nth powers. The prospects of nuclear disarmament (defined as zero level of arms) are nonexistent at present and perhaps even undesirable in contemporary international relations. Finally, morality has practically no role in a highly nuclearized, militarized, and commercialized world.

Overall, at present the incentives to go nuclear exceed the disincentives. The message of the paper is that no one is really interested in negotiating disarmament because states, even the developed ones, continue to be dissatisfied, politically, militarily, and economically. While militarily powerful states want to negotiate arms control (meaning stable military relations with no necessary reduction of arms), to regulate the dangers of unlimited competition rather than to reduce their arsenals, many of the Nth powers want to improve their bargaining position vis-à-vis their

1. Images are loosely defined to mean one's view of the other side's expected behavior and its expected consequences. Included also in the definition is one's self-image: what we are, what we want, what we can do, and what the likely effects of our actions are.

2. For a further discussion of incentives and disincentives, see William Epstein, "Why States Go—And Don't Go—Nuclear."

competitors by altering the structure of contemporary international society. This means a desire to diffuse further the distribution of power and influence in the world today. So long as nuclear power is an element of power and influence, its growth will continue to be motivated by political and security considerations, irrespective of how the growth is rationalized. It may or may not be important for the evolution of world order that many of the Nth powers are located, or are likely to be located, in the southern half of the globe.

In a sense then, the problem of slowing proliferation in the less satisfied states in the Third World requires a prior understanding of the policy perceptions in these societies and the effects of the behavior of the industrialized and westernized societies in the Third World. The problem is not merely one of educating or reeducating Third World elites. It is also one of expanding the range of public education and reeducating the elites in the developed societies. Conceptualizing the relationship between horizontal and vertical proliferation using detailed case studies is, therefore, a desired underpinning of scholarly and policy activities. It is not our point that Nth powers will seek nuclear explosives capacity just because five states have nuclear weapons. It is our point that, if nuclear weapons remain useful as military and diplomatic instruments for five nuclear weapon states, the nuclear factor may enter the in-house bureaucratic debates of Nth powers in a big way in the 1980s. Many societies share the goal of slowing vertical and horizontal proliferation, but how one negotiates desired outcomes depends in part on how one perceives the issues.

SCENARIOS OF THE FUTURE

As indicated previously, the future will be shaped by a number of factors, many of which are unrelated to nuclear proliferation. Even in that context, not all relevant factors may be desirable, and those that are may have diverse and sometimes contradictory impacts; for example, a normalization of relations between the USSR and the PRC may make strategic arms limitations (and hence acceptance of curbs on proliferation) more likely, but it may also arouse fears among the Japanese which could induce them to seek nuclear weapons. Nevertheless, it is possible both to define active trends which could slow proliferation and, in the light of these, to assess the likelihood of proliferation, just as it is possible to assess that likelihood under other and less favorable circumstances. To this task, then, we will proceed.

AN OPTIMISTIC SCENARIO

The central lesson about proliferation to be learnt from a study of French, Chinese, and Indian behavior is that proud and powerful societies are unwilling to exempt themselves from the opportunities and obligations of power politics. This motive has the potentiality of creating stability or instability, depending on whether the superpowers are willing to share their prerogatives or whether their policy is to exclude other major military powers from the decision-making process in strategic affairs, for example, in SALT (Strategic Arms Limitation Talks) and the CCD (Conference of the Committee on Disarmament). A primary assumption underlying this optimistic scenario is, therefore, that the global powers begin to recognize the implications for proliferation of their efforts to duopolize power and to determine outcomes by virtue of that power. If so, it may be that potential Nth powers will decide to slow or to abandon attempts to acquire a nuclear option, on the grounds that they can obtain the political benefits of proliferation without incurring the political (and other) costs.

Another (and equally debatable) assumption underlying the optimistic scenario is that China is brought into closer and more beneficial contact with the rest of the world. At least one superpower now recognizes the importance of bringing China into the Strategic Arms Limitation Talks. Thus, L. I. Brezhnev states the following:

> Certainly the time will inevitably come when the question of associating other nuclear powers with the process of strategic arms limitation will come up on the agenda. Any powers that refuse to join would be assuming a grave responsibility before the peoples.[3]

If this statement is seriously intended, one implication is that the future of SALT depends on Chinese participation. Another implication is that eventually both superpowers may desire Chinese participation in the SALT dialogue and thereby pave the way toward involvement of the major military powers. This may even lead to a merger of the SALT dialogue and the work of the Conference of the Committee on Disarmament at Geneva in the 1980s. This scenario assumes that some sort of normalization between Moscow and Peking may occur, and if the frontier dispute is bypassed, if Sino-Soviet trade and military ties are restored to an extent, China may become willing and able to participate constructively first in the UN Special Session on Disarmament in 1978 and then in the SALT dialogue in the 1980s.

If Moscow and Peking can mediate their rivalry through bilateral means, the normalization process (according to this optimistic view) is likely to aid normalization in regions neighboring the USSR and China, particularly in South Asia. Thus, if Sino-Soviet normalization occurs, if it leads to (or is preceded by) Sino-Indian and Indo-Pakistani normalization, some of the incentives to go nuclear (beyond exploding a nuclear device) are reduced. Here, the nexus of China-India-Pakistan normalization is held to account for slow and controlled proliferation of nuclear options in South Asia, with the implication that complete normalization (an ideal state) could conceivably lead to no proliferation. Likewise, the prospect of China's active participation in the disarmament dialogue at the UN Special Session in 1978 could result in arms reductions by the great powers, and thereby improve the climate for further slowing of proliferation among at least some of the Nth powers. Overall, in this scenario, once China's entry into the superpowers' nuclear dialogue has been arranged, a momentum toward arms reduction may grow because the underlying security issues, or at least some of these, will have been resolved. A spillover effect of this dramatic change will be to induce other major military powers to avoid complicating the international security agenda by continuing pro-

3. Leonid I. Brezhnev, *Report of the CPSU Central Committee and the Party's Immediate Objectives in Domestic and Foreign Policy* (25th Congress of the CPSU, 24 February 1976).

grams for the acquisition of nuclear weapons.

Another factor in the optimistic scenario is the expectation that France can be induced to alter its present position on the Non-Proliferation Treaty (NPT) and its present policy of promoting nuclear sales of reprocessing plants and other sensitive technology to potential proliferators in the Third World. Because of the French position in the London Agreement (1976), three issues are at stake: first, to explore the prospects of upgrading the safeguards requirements with a view to moving toward full scope safeguards which apply to the entire peaceful nuclear industry of states which are not presently nuclear weapon powers; second, to question the political wisdom of sales of sensitive items like reprocessing plants; third, inasmuch as the Federal Republic of Germany (FRG) is held to be hiding behind the French position, a shift in the latter could conceivably induce a shift in the former as well, so that there is no repeat of the FRG-Brazil nuclear deal. This scenario is optimistic inasmuch as there is a hope, if not an expectation, that the French position has evolved and may continue to evolve to an extent that it coincides with policies of the United States and Canada. Optimism is warranted inasmuch as further technological barriers can be realistically created against the Nth powers in current and future nuclear sales.

A fourth factor is rooted in the view that select Third World societies may be credited with innovative strategic thought and behavior. This scenario suggests that analytically it is possible to differentiate among three types of nuclear strategies for states to follow. The first type, as practiced by the superpowers, is to engage in constant arms racing on the assumption that incremental change in the adversaries' capacities has the potential of shifting the balance or of increasing the uncertainties. The second type may be the one China appears to follow: namely, to avoid arms racing, to seek a minimum deterrent but not to endeavor (deliberately or inadvertently) to bridge the gap in capabilities because bridging is difficult and/or unnecessary. The third type, which India is probably practicing, is to engage in nonconversion of its nuclear option into a weapons system. If the first type expresses a preference for non-use of nuclear weapons, the third type expresses a preference for nonconversion of an option into deployable weapons.

A fifth factor is the perception that select Nth powers are beginning to tone down their enthusiasm for nuclear proliferation and have become receptive to some extent to Western discussions about the dangers of proliferation. Whether this shift in attitudes will continue depends in part on these countries' continuing efforts to educate, coupled with efforts to create more technological and political barriers against sensitive nuclear exports. Thus, the impact of this factor on proliferation, like that of others, is dependent on deliberate policy choices by both existing and potential nuclear powers.

REGIONAL OUTCOMES UNDER AN OPTIMISTIC SCENARIO

If proliferation is seen as a process rather than a terminal condition, five regions bear scrutiny: South and Southwest Asia, Northeast Asia, the Middle East, Southern Africa, and Latin America. Because the range of inquiry is vast and each society has its own set of perceptions and circumstances, what follows is a rash attempt to paint a picture in bold brushes. Our task is to provide a sense of the future and to leave detailed case studies for future research.

South and Southwest Asia

India is a useful starting point, not because it is actually the sixth proliferator in the world, but because it appears so to many observers. Proliferation in Pakistan will validate the theory of nuclear chains. Western thinking is somewhat as follows: Just because India tested one peaceful nuclear explosion (PNE), this will induce Pakistan to copy India. It is noted that Pakistan reacted in many ways to India's test: (*a*) by developing its indigenous nuclear option; (*b*) by seeking external guarantees against nuclear threat or aggression; (*c*) by seeking conventional arms as a trade-off to a threat to go nuclear, and so on. But the implications of alternative strategies are not spelled out in these analyses. Secondly, India tested a nuclear device to demonstrate its political will. Its purpose was not achieved and hence India will need more nuclear tests. Hence Pakistan will need to continue to copy India until Pakistan and India have a mutual deterrent. It is assumed that, given technological momentum, Indian PNEs will gradually and eventually become nuclear weapons, if they already are not so at present.

There are problems with the foregoing. If "action-reaction" is central to explaining Indo-Pakistan nuclear relations, why was Pakistan's nuclear development stifled or slowed during 1958–72 when Pakistan's diplomats actively argued about the dangers of Indian proliferation? Plainly, President Ayub Khan was more interested in Pakistan's economic and military development. Thus, the domestic-political barriers to proliferation must be noted in the case of Pakistan up to 1972, if not later. True, Mr. Bhutto may want to be innovative by renouncing Ayub Khan's policies, and thereby to impress public opinion. But surely today someone in Pakistan is arguing about the utility of having more rigs to tap oil versus having more nuclear reactors.

Admittedly, Pakistan's atomic energy talent is now first rate. With the French sale of a nuclear reprocessing plant, and/or if Pakistan is able to secure a reprocessing laboratory from a West European source, or if Pakistan gains through clandestine contacts with South Africa (which South Africans deny), Pakistan can be assumed to have by 1980–81 a capacity to explode a device. Yet someone in Islamabad may be arguing today that it is sufficient to have a capacity to explode a device but not to use it, since Pakistan, unlike India, does not distinguish between peaceful and military explosions; that leaking information about that capacity through the pages of *Pakistan Times* will be sufficient to induce Indian restraint; since the reprocessing capability will be heavily safeguarded by the International Atomic Energy Association (IAEA), the burden and the opportunity for violating the safeguards should rest on Indian action which threatens Pakistan's national security, for instance, an Indian invasion of Pakistan. In other words, it may make sense for Pakistan to follow Israel's example rather than India's.

There is also a problem with

those who argue that Pakistan will need to go nuclear because India will continue to test, because India's first test failed in its primary goal—to impress the major powers who needed impressing. But who is to say that the test was not an exercise in political signaling? Instead of arguing that a nuclear test by a poor country devalues the impact of a test, perhaps the reasoning should be as follows: India's test proves that an unevenly developed society, with food-population problems but with a first-rate scientific establishment and a fine diplomatic machinery, can explode a device. Testing a device still requires much political commitment and scientific/technological prowess. India's test proves that the major powers were impressed with the fact that India would dare to flout their prescriptions in such a subtle and yet explicit fashion, and damage the NPT.

In other words, if the message was sent and received, the acknowledgment implies two things. First, India is not going to be in a hurry to keep exploding nuclear devices unnecessarily. Secondly, if the message is converted into action by the receiver, the result is a search for normalizing subcontinental relations. The question at present is not if there will be normalization, or if there is normalization. Rather it is about its speed, scope, and permanence. In Indian thinking, the sense is strong that protecting Pakistan as a strategic buffer is in India's self-interest and India has no wish to seek common borders with the Soviet Union and Iran, a sentiment which Iranians probably share. As such, advocates of nuclear explosions in Islamabad will need to carefully assess the foreign policy implications. This does not mean that India is against Pakistani proliferation. It means that India prefers a pace of proliferation in Pakistan which is slow, as is India's, and predictable, as it should be, so that South Asia's constituents abroad have a chance to fully comprehend the geo-strategic realities and to adjust their sanctimonious perceptions to realities.

If the Indo-Pakistan nuclear chain is at best a slow process, the addition of Iran to this chain is even more difficult to assess. Iran has adhered to the NPT. This means little, since the Shah of Iran has already declared the possibility of changing the policy should circumstances change. Iran has a modest atomic energy program, and it imports nuclear items from the United States, France, and West Germany, among others. Neither India nor Iran can benefit from the disintegration of Pakistan, but Iranian nuclear arms (or an option) could relate to two contingencies: to deter a troublesome Soviet presence in the Persian Gulf, and/or to catch up with India and Pakistan if these countries acquire a nuclear weapons status. The Shah's plan to make Iran the world's fifth great power could be a motive.

However, both motives are not real at present. Given anti-Soviet fears in Iran, its conventional capacities are better means to police the Persian Gulf. The role of status is important if the Shah perceives India as the emerging dominant power in the region. Yet, this is not an issue now. The Shah's concern with India's nuclear status, however, may become meaningful if the Indo-Iranian détente fails and if the two regional powers come to disagree about the future of the Indian Ocean.

But if Iran, unlike India and Pakistan, is still at the prenuclear option stage, it nevertheless has strong nuclear concerns. At present, these are expressed in its disarmament diplomacy. If they are not clarified, they could conceivably enter the Iranian bureaucratic debate in a big way, as they could in debates in select Arab societies during the 1980s. At present, Iran does not need PNEs. But at the same time, it does not want its hands to be tied with extensive rules. Israel's nuclear bombs do not bother Iran. Still it prefers a Middle Eastern nuclear weapon free zone (NWFZ) to become a steppingstone toward the NPT, with a view to induce Israel to join the NWFZ.

Talk about an Indian-Pakistani-Iranian nuclear chain is considered highly speculative at this stage. Instead, the Iranian stress is to get the nuclear weapon states (NWS) to accept in principle a willingness to discuss security guarantees. The exact details, or sequence of moves, or the eventual outcome of moves is imprecise. For instance, what are the geographical limits of a Middle East NWFZ? Does it include North Africa and South Asia? Conceivably, Iran's NWFZ diplomacy implies probing on Pakistan's behalf also, and a linkage is implied between a quest for NWS's security guarantees and the definitions in an NWFZ. The arguments about NWFZ are directed to the nuclear superpowers but also to bureaucratic debates in Middle Eastern societies. If the United States could come out with a stand that it will provide a strategic umbrella, this would neutralize the advocates of nuclear weapons.

Instead, the superpowers' attitude is to stonewall. While the United States appears to be more forthcoming than the USSR, neither is prepared to play the game on any other terms than its own. While paying lip service to the idea of an NWFZ, neither superpower is really willing to let an NWFZ hinder its freedom of action. At least the superpowers are not sure that an NWFZ will not hinder that freedom. For instance, until Sino-Soviet relations improve, the USSR is not even willing to consider a no-threat pledge.

Given such tendencies, Iranians conclude as follows: The whole exercise of finding NWFZs in the Middle East and South Asia may be too late and India, Israel, and Egypt remain suspicious. Still, the disarmament process is a long one, and quick progress should not be expected, even if some progress is made that may be worthwhile. Moreover, at present for Iran there is no real alternative except to talk about disarmament. The superpowers may come to a point that having an NWFZ could serve their strategic purpose. But until that happens, Iran needs to resist U.S. pressure to seek more control through proposals such as regional reprocessing plants.

The Pacific region

The foregoing scenario suggests that slow proliferation is tied to an expectation of a slow normalization in Sino-Soviet affairs, accompanied by Sino-Indian and Indo-Pakistan-Iran normalization. This process can buy time, just as the implementation of safeguards under the London Agreement can buy time. Buying time is useful if the time is to be put to constructive use to educate elites in developed and developing societies. The strategy of talking about non-proliferation should be discarded because posturing produces counterposturing. A more constructive strategy might be to stop talking about non-proliferation publicly but quietly stressing, for instance, the economic and technical problems of buying and selling reprocessing plants. Or better still, the odium of discrimination can be removed if all nuclear exports are similarly safeguarded, irrespective of the status of the buyer in terms of the NPT.

If a strategy of buying time makes sense for South Asia, normalization in Central Asian relations may have adverse implications for Japan in the 1980s. At present, Japanese views stress the following: Seoul does not face a nuclear threat from North Korea. If Seoul acquires nuclear weapons, they would look provocative to North Korea and Japan. Seoul is not likely to acquire nuclear weapons and, if it has nuclear ambitions, Washington is likely to check these. Nuclear weapons for Taiwan is not a probability even though Taiwan, more than Seoul, can develop these. According to Japan, there is no speedy solution for disarmament; it is still trying to create an atmosphere for disarmament.

Japan is clearly the key to proliferation in the Pacific area, not because it is more influential than China but because it is more unpredictable. True, Japan participates in the London Agreement. Still, its position should be noted. The positions of Canada, the USSR, the UK, and the US are similar (though the United States has a greater recognition of obstacles). They seek safeguards on the entire fuel cycle, and if possible, on all peaceful nuclear industry of a recipient state. France and West Germany seek only safeguards on their supplies, and this represents the supplier's consensus. Japan is somewhere in between these positions. It has traditionally mistrusted standards unless these apply to all their competitors. This may change after Japan's ratification of the NPT.

Several circumstances make Japan's nuclear abstention chancy in the 1980s. The logic and argument against nuclear proliferation are not really clearcut. As NPT safeguards requirements are constantly upgraded, the NPT safeguards will be used increasingly to interpret the work of the IAEA. This may increase resentment among IAEA members who resent IAEA/NPT safeguards. So far, the NPT regime has barely survived despite the superpowers' effort to insulate the IAEA and the NPT from criticism in the NPT Review Conference. If nothing tangible happens in the field of disarmament by the early 1980s, the NPT regime could collapse. Some states have already threatened withdrawal. In such a tenuous setting, a trend toward Sino-Soviet normalization could create doubts about Japan's future, about the credibility of the U.S commitments in the Pacific region, and about the effect of a shift of the Asian balance in favor of the Communist states. Furthermore, the prospect of Sino-Soviet normalization could conceivably induce the USSR to take a harder line against the United States. In such circumstances, it may make sense for the Japanese to make their nuclear option visible, with or without tacit U.S. concurrence. And if Japan defects from the U.S. alliance, Australia may find itself preparing its nuclear option, if it already does not have one at present.

Latin America and South Africa

The national circumstances of Brazil/Argentina and South Africa vary with regard to proliferation. South Africa's future in Africa is bedeviled by the pressure of black Africa. Argentina and Brazil carry no such burden of racism. Still, there is merit in examining these societies collectively. South Africa and Brazil are economic giants among pygmies. Brazil and Argentina are most active in disarmament diplomacy. Brazil and Argentina adhere to the Treaty of Tlatelolco (with reservations) but not to the NPT; South Africa rejects the NPT at present but officially is keeping the matter of adherence under review. All three have positions on the NPT similar to India's, and Brazil and Argentina have expressed themselves in favor of the PNEs. South Africa has first-rate enriched uranium technology but not reprocessing technology, whereas Brazil has gained access to German jet nozzle technology. South Africa participated in the Zangger Committee discussions but is not a party to the London Agreement.

The real impact of these societies lies not in the probability that they will develop nuclear weapons, but rather in their revisionist views about nuclear safeguards and their impact on the disarmament debate. The FRG-Brazil nuclear deal is not viewed in Argentina as the first step toward a Brazilian bomb. Neither are South African nuclear bombs of much use against fanatical black guerrillas. The real point about Brazil and Argentina (and Mexico) is that they think the superpowers are playing a double game: to consolidate their hold on the structure of power in the world and to express phony concerns about horizontal proliferation. That is, the great powers agree on marginal disarmament issues or issues which can be safely ignored but not on issues which threaten the present structure of power. It is argued by Latin Americans that if NWFZs are to be promoted, there should be common treatment for all such zones; the rights and obligations should be identical or equivalent. The Tlatelolco Treaty is a useful model, but it is not *the* model. Even this treaty shows how the NWFZ concept cannot really be implemented until the views and interests of all involved parties are taken into account.[4]

A PESSIMISTIC SCENARIO

Even under the optimistic scenario, we might see eight or ten nuclear powers a decade hence rather than the five (or six) now extant. The pessimistic scenario does not envision a rapid and uncontrollable increase in the number of proliferators, partly because the Third World societies most likely to proliferate have paid constant and careful attention to the external environment. It does, however, recognize that because these countries are relatively immune to Western pleading about the dangers or proliferation, there are likely to be considerable difficulties in negotiating non-proliferation in a complex international environment.

If, therefore, Sino-Soviet-Indo-Pakistani normalization fails to establish interdependencies in the political, security, trade, commercial, and cultural areas, if intergovernmental and intersocial habits of cooperation and interdependency fail to emerge within 5 to 10 years, the weaker parties are likely to make visible their need to seek security through conventional and nuclear means, that is, to practice self-reliance and to seek minimal dependency on external partners. In this case, there may be controlled proliferation among continental (or sub-

4. John R. Redick, "Regional Nuclear Arms Control in Latin America," *International Organisation*, vol. 29, no. 2 (Spring 1975), p. 438.

continental) Asian societies while the process is less pronounced or marginal in insular Asian countries, including Australia.

Even if normalization succeeds in Sino-Soviet, Sino-Indian, and Indo-Pakistani relations (that is, among continental Asian states) this does not mean an end to proliferation. If these countries are able to negotiate and moderate their rivalries in a decade or so, given the long lead-time for nuclear weapons development, will U.S. allies (namely, Japan, Australia, Iran, and perhaps even the Federal Republic of Germany) find themselves constrained to rethink their nuclear options? As a corollary, will Taiwan and South Korea be tempted to make their nuclear options visible, either to follow the lead of the other U.S. allies or to strengthen their negotiating stance vis-à-vis the United States? In short, will proliferation among the U.S. allies be a function of normalization between two Communist states and India?

Even if it is not, one may see a trend toward a multi-polar world, because the danger of superpower nuclear conflict has lessened and because new centers of regional and international power and influence have emerged. From a Third World and a third party perspective, this is a desirable and an inevitable trend. However, the superpowers' loss of political and economic control over third parties means also a loss of control over their decisions to create nuclear options or to build nuclear weapons. Hence, while some incentives to proliferation may diminish, so will some disincentives, and one may, for a variety of reasons, see the emergence of 10 or 20 new nuclear powers, if not during the eighties, at least in the nineties.

IMPLICATIONS FOR THE SUPERPOWERS

A firm conclusion about the outcome of the relationship between slow, controlled proliferation and non-proliferation processes cannot be offered because future foreign policy alignments are unpredictable. Still, superpowers' reactions to the optimistic and pessimistic scenarios may be briefly noted as well as policies which they might follow to bring about what each power may regard as an optimistic future for itself.

To date, non-proliferation has been regarded as a goal shared by the superpowers since at least the mid-1960s. There are doubts over whether the superpowers' commitment is real or bilateral and regional priorities signal a limited defection from non-proliferation and arms control. Thus, the USSR could not, and did not, complain too much about India's test because the USSR still needs India against China. Likewise, the United States, unlike Canada, chose not to terminate its nuclear supply relationship with India because that would mean a loss of leverage and of political and technological intelligence. It is debatable whether unwillingness to punish India reflects a superpower preference to tacitly support India or a recognition that punishment would serve no use. Overall, superpowers' reactions are seemingly guided by a joint concern to slow proliferation. This identity of views exists at the level of rhetoric and, to an extent, in the Nuclear Suppliers' Club meetings. But the identity is not total. The USSR believes in, and adheres to, a policy of "full scope" safeguards in its supply policy. The United States believes in safeguards for items supplied, that is, the end use of those items must be according to the supply contract but the entire nuclear industry of the recipient is not safeguarded. Therefore, Soviet safeguards are more demanding than U.S. ones. Aside from this, if Sino-Soviet relations do not improve, the superpowers are likely to continue to defend the NPT, to seek improvements in the IAEA, to stress the need to safeguard or prevent the export of sensitive technology, and so on.

However, a real question exists of whether or not the USSR would abandon its commitment to nonproliferation and arms control if the bait was the prospect of Sino-Soviet normalization in the 1980s, where both the USSR and China adopted a give-and-take policy. In such a hypothetical situation, the joint anti-proliferation strategy of the superpowers could change. The USSR, China, and France could begin to pave the way for a merger of the SALT and the CCD dialogues. And such an optimistic situation for the USSR and its partners can only be pessimistic for the United States and its allies, if this meant a reduced emphasis on superpower détente, that is, keeping China out of SALT.

The policy implications for the United States are troublesome for the 1980s. To encourage a slowdown of proliferation, for example in South and Southwest Asia, the United States ought to encourage the Sino-Soviet-India-Pakistan normalization process. But normalization and nonproliferation in South Asia are marginal to U.S. security, whereas Sino-Soviet normalization is central to U.S. security. Consequently, it makes sense for the United States to tolerate South and Southwest Asian nuclear proliferation as well as proliferation elsewhere, except perhaps among allies whose assistance and dependence is needed to promote U.S. interests. It may make sense for the United States to debate publicly the underlying interests rather than to harp endlessly on a goal which may, in select circumstances, be counter to U.S. interests.

Finally, it should be recognized that issues deemed to have been solved or shelved could appear actively on the agenda again in the 1980s. It must never be forgotten that détente is a highly tenuous activity in terms of what is sought and what is achieved. Neither must it be forgotten that there is a constant interaction between Europe and Central and East Asia in the foreign strategies of the major powers.[5] The NPT emerged in the context of a superpower concern to keep the lid on Bonn's nuclear aspirations and to keep Germany divided. Whether or not the concerns are justified is beside the point. If Sino-Soviet normalization takes root, the German-Soviet Ostpolitik may become unhinged, with or without the tacit approval of the United States. In such circumstances in Europe and in Asia, global and continental relations rather than regional or local ones will have radicalized the shifts toward proliferation on a scale much larger, and with many ominous implications, compared to the effects of a controlled Indian test.

5. Lionel Gelber, *Crisis in the West: American Leadership and the Global Balance* (London: The Macmillan Company, 1975), p. 118.

ANNALS, AAPSS, **430**, March 1977

Nuclear Proliferation and World Politics

By LEWIS A. DUNN

ABSTRACT: Varying technical deficiencies are likely to characterize the nuclear forces of many new proliferators. Regional interactions within a proliferated world probably would include increased nuclear arms racing, inadvertant or calculated nuclear-weapon use, and outside involvement in domestic nuclear coups d'état. In turn, the possible global repercussions of local proliferation are likely to include: a partial erosion of existing alliances, or, to the degree that present superpower ties remain unchanged, the risk of escalating conflict; growing nuclear "black and gray marketeering"; the spread of nuclear terrorism; a corrosion of political authority and legitimacy; and, ultimately, even growing global anarchy. Whether or not this initial assessment proves accurate will depend upon the difficulties of designing and implementing a proliferation-management strategy. Such a strategy might attempt, on the one hand, to affect which proliferated world emerged and, on the other, to influence Nth countries' nuclear postures, contribute to regional stability, and circumscribe the global repercussions of local proliferation. The gap between the gravity of a proliferated world's varied threats and the probable effectiveness of politically acceptable policy responses supports the fear that the initial depiction may be more than a nightmare scenario.

Lewis A. Dunn, on partial leave from the Hudson Institute, is writing a book on nuclear proliferation for the Twentieth Century Fund. At the Hudson Institute, he was the principal author and coordinator of Hudson's recent study, "Trends in Nuclear Proliferation, 1975–1995," and has played a role in other studies of nuclear proliferation. Before joining the Hudson staff, he taught courses in international politics and arms control at Kenyon College. He received his Ph.D. degree from the University of Chicago (1973).

WITHIN the coming decades, a growing number of countries could decide to acquire nuclear weapons.[1] Should such a second wave of proliferation occur, among its distinguishing features would be the spread of nuclear weapons to less developed, politically unstable Third World countries, the nuclearization of existing regional confrontations, and eventual access to nuclear weapons by subnational groups. Some observers regard the possibility of more widespread nuclear proliferation with relative equanimity. They argue either that present Western fears of proliferation are based upon an erroneous, if not racist, charge of Third World irresponsibility[2] or that the diffusion of nuclear weapons would contribute in some cases to increased regional stability.[3] Several of these persons go so far as to contend that widespread proliferation could result in the outlawing of large-scale violence.[4] On the contrary, a proliferated world is likely to be a nasty and dangerous place, entailing threats to the security and domestic well-being of virtually all nations and posing a serious possibility of a longer-term decay of global political order. To see why this may be so, it is necessary first to consider briefly the varied meanings of "going nuclear."

1. See Lewis A. Dunn and Herman Kahn, *Trends in Nuclear Proliferation*, Report prepared for the U.S. Arms Control and Disarmament Agency (Croton-on-Hudson, N.Y.: Hudson Institute, HI-2336/3-RR, 15 May 1976), pts. I and II.

2. See K. Subrahmanyam, "India's Nuclear Policy," in Onkar Marwah and Ann Schulz, eds., *Nuclear Proliferation and the Near-Nuclear Countries* (Cambridge, Mass.: Ballinger Publishing Company, 1975), p. 131.

3. In addition to the chapter by Fred Thayer in this volume, see, for example, Steven Rosen, "Nuclearization and Stability in the Middle East," in Marwah and Schulz, *Nuclear Proliferation*, p. 157.

4. See Pierre M. Gallois, *The Balance of Terror: Strategy for the Nuclear Age* (Boston: Houghton Mifflin Company, 1961), p. 113. For a more recent version, emphasizing proliferation of low-yield battlefield nuclear capabilities, see R. Robert Sandoval, "Consider the Porcupine: Another View of Nuclear Proliferation," *Bulletin of the Atomic Scientists*, May 1976, p. 19.

GOING NUCLEAR

The often-used characterization "going nuclear" telescopes a range of important proliferation choices and outcomes. But depending upon the specific characteristics of possible future Nth country nuclear weapon programs and postures, the distinguishing features and risks of a proliferated world would vary. For our present purposes, it suffices to note the following probable critical characteristics.[5]

"In the business" v. "serious but technically deficient" programs

At least initially, some future proliferators are likely to seek only "in the business" nuclear-weapon capabilities, that is, their purpose would be to demonstrate that they, too, could detonate a nuclear explosive device. Perhaps motivated by prestige considerations, or at a latter stage of proliferation by fashion, these countries would not seek a militarily operational nuclear force.

A greater number of prospective proliferators, however, could be expected to do otherwise. They are likely instead to attempt to develop serious nuclear forces, combining a growing stockpile of nuclear weapons; delivery systems; command, control, and communica-

5. For elaboration, see Dunn and Kahn, *Trends in Nuclear Proliferation*, pt. III.

tion procedures; protection against surprise attack; and strategic doctrine. In many of these cases, the resultant nuclear force may be characterized by significant technical deficiencies.

Although development of relatively well-packaged fission weapons, deliverable by a range of readily accessible weapon systems, should not pose a major problem for nearly all potential proliferators, their early-generation nuclear warheads might lack adequate safety design mechanisms. Moreover, if insufficient attention is paid to the risk of a nuclear-weapon accident, even later-generation weapons could be accident prone.[6]

Comparable concern about possibly inadequate provisions for control against unauthorized seizure and use of nuclear weapons by a dissident domestic group, a cabal of officers, or even an isolated military man also is warranted. Within existing nuclear-weapon states, such as the United States and the Soviet Union, development of sophisticated electronic permissive action link (PAL) systems has permitted them to purchase tight control without sacrificing operational readiness or accepting an increased vulnerability to surprise attack. Conversely, taken together, fear of surprise attack by a local nuclear rival and limited technological sophistication could force even such coup-vulnerable prospective proliferators as, for example, Iraq, Egypt, Syria, South Korea, Pakistan, Argentina, and Brazil *not* to follow their likely initial preference for tight control of their nuclear arsenal. More generally, development of a reliable and survivable command, control, and communication network may exceed the capabilities of the many low-to-medium technology prospective proliferators.

As for protection against an opponent's surprise disarming attack, crude mutual survivability should not be presumed to be the expected outcome of nuclearizing regional confrontations. Depending upon the specific opponents, the stage of proliferation, and their prior technical choices, reciprocal vulnerability, survivability against each other but not against a superpower, or unilateral vulnerability are as likely to be the resultant strategic balances. Moreover, in some cases whatever survivability does exist is likely to have been purchased by reliance upon a hair trigger, launch-on-warning (LOW) mode of protecting the nuclear force. These are yet additional reasons for skepticism about the technical characteristics of many new nuclear forces, for believing that not infrequently such forces probably would be characterized by what once was termed a high "propensity for war."[7]

Doctrinal perceptions of nuclear weapons' utility

The mainstream of Western strategic studies increasingly has argued that the sole purpose of nuclear weapons should be to deter the use or threatened use of other nuclear weapons. It would be false to presume, however, that the initial strategic thinking of all future proliferators would honor this conception of nuclear weapons' pur-

6. Current American weapons can be dropped accidently without producing a nuclear yield and can survive the heat and impact of air crashes. Achieving this degree of safety, however, necessitated a considerable expenditure of money and thought in the early to mid-1950s.

7. Thomas C. Schelling, *Arms and Influence* (New Haven: Yale University Press, 1966), p. 234.

poses and utility. On the contrary, some possible proliferators, especially where geography serves to provide natural invasion corridors, as in the case of Taiwan, South Korea, and perhaps Iran, appear more likely to look upon nuclear weapons as potentially useful battlefield weapons. Others must be expected to consider seriously these weapons' possible limited and coercive use or threatened use, either within a war-fighting defensive strategy or in support of expansionist, non-status quo oriented objectives. An Israel contemplating responses to a breakdown of its conventional defenses in a sixth Arab-Israeli war could contemplate the former; a nuclear-armed Iran seeking hegemony in the Persian Gulf in the early 1990s the latter.

Longer-term doctrinal development and perceptions of nuclear weapons' utility probably would be influenced heavily by the specific characteristics and consequences of the first use of nuclear weapons since Nagasaki. Successful use or threatened use by a new proliferator would erode the nuclear taboo and encourage others to reappraise upward their assessment of the military utility of nuclear weapons. Conversely, unsuccessful use, accidental use, or unauthorized use—perhaps during an internal political struggle—would have the opposite effect. Thus, the first nuclear use clearly would be a proliferation turning point. And, as the next section indicates, the probability that that will occur has to be evaluated as high.

REGIONAL INTERACTION IN A PROLIFERATED WORLD

If efforts to control proliferation prove inadequate, a world of 30 or more nuclear-weapon states, many locked in hostile confrontations, could emerge by the late 1980s–early 1990s. Even though in isolated cases such nuclearization of regional confrontations could prove locally stabilizing,[8] most frequently the outcome would be increased political and military competitiveness, confrontation, and probably conflict. Moreover, the destructiveness of future small-power nuclear wars would be significantly greater than that of either past local wars or manmade or natural disasters.

Patterns of regional nuclear arms racing

Nuclear proliferation is likely to be accompanied frequently, at least initially, by fairly intense qualitative and quantitative nuclear arms races. There is no reason to believe that the major countries in the Middle East, South Asia, and the Persian Gulf, for example, would acquiesce readily to second-class non-nuclear status or to a position of marked nuclear inferiority vis-à-vis their regional opponents.

Such regional nuclear arms racing would be fueled by several factors. Regional insecurity, competition for regional status, and traditional hostility all would play a part. In addition, in those arms races where each side's decisions were highly sensitive to estimates of the opponent's capabilities and intentions, for example, in the Middle East and South Asia, limited intelligence

8. Possible future Taiwanese acquisition might facilitate the emergence of more stable relations between Taiwan and the People's Republic of China by precluding invasion and strengthening domestic morale on Taiwan. Against that positive effect, nonetheless, would have to be balanced the adverse impact upon proliferation momentum and pressures for proliferation in Asia that probably would follow Taiwan's emergence as a nuclear-weapon state. Thus, it may not be possible to pick and choose which proliferation to oppose.

on those factors might intensify initial arms "spurts." Fears, and in some cases the reality, of the opponent acquiring a first-strike capability also would exacerbate arms race pressures. Finally, if nuclear weapons were used successfully in any region, that too would stimulate arms race efforts.

Nonetheless, it must be added that in some regional strategic situations, resource availability could become a serious constraint once such arms racing began. In South Asia, for example, Pakistan without outside assistance might find itself unable to keep up with India in a nuclear arms race. Thus, some regional nuclear arms races might begin, spurt, and then end with the weaker side reluctantly accepting an inferior position. In fact, where prior recent history of intense political and military conflict is absent, a combination of resource-constraint and a limited sense of threat could foster at the outset a more leisurely arms-race pattern. A possible future Argentinian-Brazilian nuclear arms race could be a case in point, although even here competition for regional influence and mutual uncertainty might result in more active arms racing.

Thus, a mixture of arms racing effects, skewed at least initially toward more intense regional competition, should be expected. Such nuclear arms racing would entail a costly diversion of scarce technical, economic, and organizational resources. Moreover, in regions that already are or could become arenas of politico-military conflict, existing hostility probably would be exacerbated and efforts to achieve a regional modus vivendi hindered. Further, in the ensuing political climate, the risk of inadvertent nuclear war, as discussed next, would be magnified commensurately.

Small power nuclear wars

Inherent to the nuclearization of existing confrontations in the Middle East, South Asia, and the Persian Gulf in all probability would be a high risk of inadvertent or calculated nuclear weapon use. Either or both governmental or nongovernmental action might be involved.[9]

To begin, given the likely technical deficiencies of many Nth country nuclear forces, discussed earlier, unintended nuclear exchanges erupting out of an intense crisis or low-level conventional conflict could occur. For example, if reciprocal vulnerability to surprise nuclear attack characterizes, as it may, the initial stages of nuclear strategic interaction between India and Pakistan and Israel and Egypt, strong preemptive pressures and growing reciprocal fears of surprise attack can be expected. Moreover, within such a strategic situation, the occurrence of a nuclear weapon accident, an unauthorized launch by a cabal of lower-level officers, anonymous nuclear detonation by a PLO-type group, or a warning system malfunction—any of which, for reasons already noted, would be possible—might trigger that inadvertent nuclear exchange.

However, concern about the outbreak of small-power nuclear wars is not based solely on an assessment of the potential propensity to war of particular Nth country nuclear forces. Some countries, to

9. "Local Munichs" and nuclear blackmail, involving threatened use of nuclear weapons, also can be expected to occur.

repeat, are likely to be attracted to nuclear weapons because of their possible military uses and consciously could decide to escalate to the employment of nuclear weapons rather than accept a conventional military defeat. Pakistani tactical use of nuclear weapons against invading Indian military formations in a hypothetical late-1980s conflict would be one possibility; Israeli coercive nuclear attacks against Arab military targets and high-value Egyptian targets such as the Aswan Dam, in response to an Arab breakthrough on the battlefield, would be another.

Another case of a conscious and calculated use of nuclear weapons would be an attempt by one new proliferator—or, following their unauthorized access to nuclear weapons, by members of its military—to trigger a nuclear exchange between two other hostile Nth countries. The risk of such a catalytic nuclear war erupting out of an intense crisis or low-level conflict in the early stages of Middle East nuclearization has to be taken seriously.

Nor can the risk of local anonymous use of nuclear weapons be dismissed. To illustrate, again with reference to a nuclearized Middle East, a more radical Arab government might conclude that a successful anonymous attack against Israel in the midst of serious peace negotiations was the only way to ensure those negotiations' collapse. It probably would succeed, if only because Israeli public opinion could be expected to preclude the government making any political-military concessions in the wake of such an Arab action. And, given the prospect of unauthorized access to nuclear weapons, the perpetrators here, too, could be a cabal of middle-ranking, fanatic officers.

The danger of preemptive nuclear wars also exists. Should proliferation occur, some countries are likely already to have deployed rudimentary nuclear forces by the time their opponents begin to do so, for example, Iran versus Iraq or Saudi Arabia or India versus Pakistan. To these earlier entrants, a preemptive attack against a potentially dangerous budding rival may not be unattractive. Or, assuming that nuclear use were thought too dangerous—perhaps for fear of a superpower response—a preemptive attack against the opponent's nuclear facilities using precision-guided conventional weapons still might be contemplated.

Even though the level of destruction in such small-power nuclear wars would vary with the specific case, the spread of nuclear weapons would bring an upward leap in the expected consequences of regional military conflicts. To illustrate, detonation of a single nominal-yield nuclear weapon in a Middle Eastern city might kill upwards of 100,000 people, while a counter-city exchange between small Indian and Pakistani nuclear forces could cause 10 million fatalities on each side. In contrast, the death toll in past Arab-Israeli wars has been counted in the thousands, while approximately 1 million persons, virtually all civilians, lost their lives in the 1971 Pakistani civil war. As for natural disasters, their death toll has only rarely been counted in the hundreds of thousands, let alone the potential millions of a local nuclear war.[10]

10. This estimate assumes the use of relatively low-yield fission weapons; the ad-

The regional consequences of nuclear coups d'état

Widespread nuclear proliferation is likely to be accompanied not only by increased competitiveness and more destructive regional clashes, but also by intensified domestic political conflict. In the many politically unstable future proliferators with their previous histories of military intervention in domestic politics, nuclear coups d'état may occur. Two aspects of this phenomenon, as well as its implications for regional stability, warrant brief attention.[11]

On the one hand, just as denying the government access to the radio station and neutralizing pro-government military formations outside of the capital have been critical elements of successful past coups, future Nth-country coup-makers may have to deny the government access to its nuclear force. Failure to do so might permit a leader who had survived the initial assault to use his access to nuclear weapons to rally his supporters and demoralize his opponents and their potential civilian allies; to threaten civil war; and, in essence, to change the situation from a military clash to a confrontation marked by coercive bargaining.

On the other hand, efforts by military factions within future coup-vulnerable proliferators to seize control of nuclear weapons also can be expected. By doing so, such a faction could hope to trigger a more widespread uprising, to force a loyal military leadership to meet its demands, to deter the use of force against them, or otherwise to use the threat of nuclear conflict to support their own coup. And, of greater significance, their access to nuclear weapons probably would make the difference between success and failure for some future factional coup-makers.

The implications for regional stability of such nuclear coups d'état should not be missed. Buttressed by their possession of nuclear weapons, more radical and romantic military men than might have been able previously to do so could gain power. And, once in full control of their country's nuclear arsenal, manifold opportunities for nuclear mischief would become evident to them. Alternatively, fearing that eventual control of nuclear weapons by more radical and romantic coup-makers, neighboring countries might intervene militarily. If time permitted, such intervention could involve support for the existing government. Or, to keep that country's nuclear weapons from falling into the "wrong hands," a disarming attack against its nuclear force and stockpile might be launched. For this reason, as well, continuing nuclear proliferation probably would result in increased and intensified local instability.

GLOBAL REPERCUSSIONS OF LOCAL PROLIFERATION

The longer-run consequences for global political life of widespread proliferation could be equally serious. Local proliferation might contribute to the emergence of disruptive new transnational forces and set in motion long-term trends, both of which could culminate in a cor-

vent of fusion weapons could result in an additional upward leap in expected destructiveness.

11. For elaboration, see Lewis A. Dunn, "Military Politics, Nuclear Proliferation, and the 'Nuclear Coup d'État,'" (Croton-on-Hudson, N.Y.: Hudson Institute, HI-2392/2-P, 20 April 1976).

rosion of domestic political authority and legitimacy and growing global anarchy.

An erosion of existing alliances?

If existing patterns of Soviet and American global involvement continue, most future confrontations between hostile proliferators would be characterized at least initially by some degree of superpower entanglement. Depending upon the specific situation, either superpower could be a reluctant guarantor, a committed ally, a partly disengaged ally, a patron, or an aspiring suitor of one of the hostile parties. More important, in many cases the two superpowers might find themselves involved on opposite sides of a hostile local confrontation. Inherent to that situation is the risk of a direct Soviet-American confrontation, high-level crisis, and even outright military conflict.

But, because of that risk of conflict, initial superpower entanglement gradually might give way to efforts to put political distance between themselves and at least some new nuclear-weapon states.[12] That is, both superpowers would be likely to reassess carefully their vital interests, those warranting continued acceptance of the risk of confrontation. In the United States, strong pressures to disengage might emerge, for example, if Taiwan and South Korea or perhaps even Israel and Iran overtly acquired nuclear weapons.[13] And, even where traditional vital American interests were seen to exist—as in the case of West Germany and Japan—if sufficient influence over these countries' nuclear postures were unobtainable, such pressures could grow.

An erosion or breakup of existing alliances, should it occur, would remove one important source of postwar order. To begin, in light of the earlier discussion of regional interaction, the stability of such a loosely structured global system may be questioned. Moreover, in some regions—both halves of Europe come to mind—superpower involvement may have served to prevent the recrudescence of past hostilities and tensions. And, at least in Western Europe, the American alliance structure by doing so has provided a necessary framework for regional political and economic cooperation. Further, dependence upon outside allied support has required at least some countries to moderate their regional behavior and could be expected to have a comparable future restraining impact.

Thus, local proliferation could trigger superpower disengagement and the partial erosion of existing alliances. That, in turn, would contribute to growing global disorder. Conversely, to the extent that present patterns of superpower entanglement remained unchanged, the risk of spreading conflict from small-power nuclear confrontations and wars cannot be discounted.

Nuclear "black and gray marketeering"

Much recent attention has focused upon the possible emergence of

12. The not necessarily negligible risk of nuclear attack or retaliation by a local proliferator also might increase pressures for reduced superpower involvement in unstable newly nuclearized regions.

13. Particularly in the cases of Taiwan and South Korea, partial American disengagement probably would have preceded these countries' decisions to acquire nuclear weapons. It would be a question, therefore, of undoing residual, though perhaps not insignificant, American ties.

nuclear black marketeering, entailing the sale of stolen fissile material or nuclear weapons themselves.[14] An equally disruptive potential global repercussion of increasing local proliferation would be the growth of nuclear "gray marketeering." A spectrum of transactions and activities might be involved. These range from covert government to government transfer of critical technical assistance for a nuclear weapon program to the actual sale or barter of nuclear weapons or their critical components. Also encompassed would be the ready availability of nuclear mercenaries willing to sell their knowledge and services to countries attempting to develop nuclear weapons.

Various economic, political, and ideological pressures might foster such gray marketeering. Selling technical assistance, or even the weapons themselves or their components, would be one way for a new nuclear-weapon state to reduce the financial burden of its own nuclear weapon program. Or, under certain conditions, a country might come to regard its nuclear weapon expertise as a service good to be bartered in exchange for needed vital raw materials or oil. Such economic motivations clearly would be an important factor in the hiring of nuclear mercenaries. As for ad hoc political pressures, to a possible future nuclear-armed Pakistan, provision of technical assistance or the transfer of special nuclear material and design information could appear an attractive way to acquire or solidify Arab or Iranian political support or at least to persuade them not to support its Indian opponent. Finally, broader ideological and political perspectives also might contribute to these activities' emergence. To illustrate, Israel, South Africa, and Taiwan are likely to be increasingly isolated in world politics as time passes. They might come to comprise a "pariah international," among whose activities could include nuclear weapon cooperation. An eventual Muslim nuclear weapon cooperative would be another, though less likely, example.

The growth of black and gray marketeering would change the characteristics of a future proliferated world. Not only would an expanding number of countries be able to develop nuclear weapons and to do so sooner; but, in particular, both very-low technology countries and nongovernmental organizations that otherwise would have been unable to do so increasingly would be able to acquire rudimentary nuclear-weapon capabilities.[15] Consequently, the problems of managing in a proliferated world would become more intractable, further heightening the risk of growing disorder.

Spreading nuclear terrorism

Further contributing to the erosion of global order would be the spreading of nuclear terrorism. Not only would widespread local proliferation increase the likelihood of terrorist acquisition of nuclear weapons, but it cannot be assumed that future terrorists would have no rational motive for using or threatening to use nuclear weapons.

A terrorist group might obtain a

14. See Mason Willrich and Theodore B. Taylor, *Nuclear Theft: Risks and Safeguards* (Cambridge, Mass.: Ballinger Publishing Company, 1974), pp. 107–20.

15. For elaboration, see Lewis A. Dunn, "Nuclear 'Gray Marketeering,'" *International Security* (forthcoming).

nuclear weapon in several ways. If plutonium recycling is practiced widely in the 1980s, physical security measures might not suffice to prevent the theft of fissile material with which they might fabricate their own device. Alternatively, the opportunities for stealing a nuclear weapon would be increased by widespread local proliferation. Furthermore, a radical government or an alienated military faction might arrange for a terrorist group to steal one of its nuclear weapons, thinking that its own purposes would be served by resultant terrorist use with a lessened risk of suffering the consequences of that action. Finally, if a black market emerges, the sale of special nuclear materials or of the weapons themselves would provide an additional source.

Possession of one or more nuclear weapons could be especially valuable for a terrorist group. To illustrate, consider a future successor group to the Palestine Liberation Organization (PLO). Such a group might threaten local action as a means of deterring hostile military action against it and of establishing a protected sanctuary for its activities. Intranation deterrence could be pursued, that is, against future equivalents of "Black September" in Jordan and current Syrian intervention in Lebanon. Actual use of a nuclear weapon by such a hypothetical successor to the PLO also could occur. Assuming movement in the late 1980s toward an Arab-Israeli peace settlement damaging to Palestinian interests, anonymous detonation of a nuclear weapon in Israel might be regarded as the only way to block such a settlement.

Moreover, the target of future terrorist use need not be local. Such a prospective radical Arab terrorist group could threaten anonymously, for example, to detonate clandestinely-inserted nuclear devices within American cities unless the United States stopped shipping arms to Israel. If the United States failed to heed this warning, then a device could be exploded. Or the target could be a West European ally of the United States whose ports were being used to ship NATO military stocks to Israel during a sixth Arab-Israeli war. Alternatively, for a future terrorist group whose objective was bringing down Western bourgeois society—just as the Japanese Red Army and the Baader-Meinhof Gang now propose—use of an externally procured nuclear weapon might be regarded as an appropriate means.

This prospect of spreading nuclear terrorism is a cause for concern partly because of its direct consequences. To note one, a single terrorist nuclear detonation within a Middle Eastern, American, or West European city probably would kill upwards of 100,000 persons. However, of equal concern is the danger that spreading nuclear terrorism would contribute to that corrosion of governmental authority and legitimacy discussed next.[16]

Corrosion of political authority and legitimacy

The initial result of attempts to manage both the specific problems of a proliferated world and the pressures inherent in living in a world of 30 or more nuclear-weapon states could be a global authoritarian political shift. Two sources of that authoritarian shift should be noted.

16. For a more complete discussion of terrorism's other possible implications, see the paper by David Krieger in this volume.

On the one hand, controlling against nuclear theft, nuclear terrorism, and other proliferation threats could be seen within existing democratic societies to require and justify the adoption of measures inconsistent with liberal values and procedural norms. For example, restrictions over government power in such civil liberties areas as search and seizure, arrest and questioning of suspects, surveillance methods, individual privacy, and the collection and computer storage of dossiers all might be eroded. Similarly, restrictions on movement in and out of these countries as well as on internal movement could increase markedly. At the same time, the leadership within more authoritarian societies probably would find in these specific threats a useful pretext for even more extensive domestic repression and control. That is, just as President Park of South Korea has used the threat of a North Korean invasion to crack down on domestic dissidents, future leaders within similar countries could use similarly the threat of anonymous or terrorist nuclear attack.

On the other hand, the increased insecurity, hostility, and competitiveness of a world with upwards of 30 nuclear-weapon states probably in itself would create pressures for increased political authoritarianism. A siege mentality, fueled by a perception of the world as a much more dangerous and inhospitable environment and by political leaders' efforts to cope as best as possible with the manifold threats of that world might emerge. That siege mentality could manifest itself in a growing insularity, an intolerance of others, and in a national paranoia, all of which probably would have domestic counterparts.

Such an intensification of political authoritarianism might be, however, only a temporary phenomenon. If governments, even after adopting more authoritarian measures, proved unable to ensure national security, they might lose their authority and legitimacy. Popular and elite opinion, believing that governments were not meeting their obligations to "provide for the common defense," no longer would support them. Managing even domestic concerns could become increasingly difficult. Particularly in Western democracies, compromises, ambiguities, and partial solutions previously accepted as a matter of course in democratic political life might no longer be tolerated in the general climate of insecurity and reduced confidence in governmental capacity.

Moreover, even though such a loss of legitimacy and crisis of confidence might be more pronounced in industrialized countries, governmental legitimacy in the eyes of the elite probably would be eroded within less developed ones as well. In both cases, the outcome could be a growing inability to govern and perhaps the rise of new chiliastic mass movements within which individuals would seek a restored sense of security.

Growing global anarchy?

A world of several dozen nuclear-weapon states, therefore, would in all probability be a nasty and dangerous place, variously threatening the national security and domestic political well-being of virtually all nations. Should it prove impossible to defuse these varied threats, the resultant regional and global disorder could lead to purposive national efforts on the part of the strong to pull inward, reducing contacts with an increasingly anarchic environment. Over the long-term, a renewed insularity and domestic authoritarianism partly could replace today's interdependence. However, many weaker, politically unstable less developed nations not only might be unable to seal themselves off from a hostile world, but are also likely to confront growing threats to their domestic political integrity. Their viability as sovereign political entities could become even more tenuous as subnational groups and military factions gained access to nuclear weapons.[17] Thus, increasingly isolated bastions of authoritarian stability might well exist in the midst of recurring small-power nuclear wars; terrorist threats; "local Munichs"; and nuclear coups d'état, separatist struggles, and civil wars.

MANAGING IN A PROLIFERATED WORLD

But is the preceding not simply an implausible nightmare scenario? Is it not likely to become a self-denying prophecy, one proved false by future efforts to manage and reduce those very dangers it depicts? Much would depend upon the difficulties of designing and implementing a strategy for managing in a proliferated world. Although space precludes a thorough discussion of that here, the main dimensions of a proliferation-management strategy at least should be noted.[18]

Which proliferated world?

Notwithstanding preceding references to *a* proliferated world, different proliferated worlds, distinguished by the number of states that had gone nuclear and the types of nuclear-weapon programs pursued, are theoretically possible. That is, a prospective 1990s' proliferated world could have anywhere from several to several dozen overt new nuclear-weapon states. Concomitantly, these countries' nuclear weapon programs might range from a small "in the business" detonation of a nuclear explosive device to acquisition of reliable, stable second-strike forces, with many, however, clustered at the "serious but technically deficient" rung of the nuclear-weapon-program ladder. The problems and dangers of proliferation would be more or less severe from world to world. Put simply, to the extent that there are fewer new nuclear-weapon states and more of these remain at the lower rungs of the nuclear-weapon-program ladder, the burden upon other proliferation-management policies would be reduced.

Two policy implications of this proposition—particularly given occasional statements that the time has come to begin thinking about living with proliferation—should be made explicit. First, even assuming that a growing number of states decide to go nuclear, non-proliferation measures definitely would

17. See, also, George H. Quester, "The Politics of Twenty Nuclear Powers," in Richard Rosecrance, ed., *The Future of the International Strategic System* (San Francisco: Chandler Publishing Company, 1972), pp. 67–70. Quester's analysis, however, underestimates the impact of widespread proliferation upon interstate, as opposed to intrastate, relations.

18. For elaboration, see Lewis A. Dunn, "Managing in a Proliferated World" (Aspen Workshop in Arms Control, forthcoming), pp. 24–38.

remain necessary.[19] Given the importance of influencing which proliferated world emerges, such measures would comprise the most critical near-term management tactic. Second, should proliferation occur, measures to pressure or persuade countries to stay at the lower rungs of the nuclear-weapon-program ladder would be required.

Some specific approaches

One approach, even for different proliferated worlds, might seek to influence Nth countries' nuclear postures. On the one hand, given the likely technical deficiencies—and their potential consequences—of some, if not many, such forces, prudence at some point might require assisting future proliferators to develop more stable and controllable nuclear forces, such as by transferring PAL systems. On the other, proliferation-management strategy might attempt to influence the strategic doctrine of new proliferators. Notwithstanding the obstacles involved—for example, determining what desirable doctrine is—attempts to establish suitable institutional mechanisms (such as regional equivalents of the NATO Nuclear Planning Group) within which to influence at the margin doctrinal debate within new proliferators and to encourage them to think through the varied implications of their new status and reflect upon whatever "nuclear learning" has occurred in the past decades still might be valuable.

Pursuit of a code of nuclear behavior and support for regional nuclear arms control agreements could comprise key elements of a second approach, efforts to enhance regional stability in a proliferated world. One proposed code would proscribe the first use of nuclear weapons regardless of how grave the provocation. Based upon the principle of lex talionis, it would be enforced ultimately by the threat of equal and proportional nuclear retaliation by one or both superpowers against the first user. Before concluding that agreement upon and implementation of any such code would be a priori implausible, the possible impact upon superpower policies of a dramatic systemic shock, such as one or more local nuclear exchanges, should not be overlooked. As for possible arms control measures in certain regional situations, both verifiable force-size agreements and the establishment of mini hotlines usefully could be pursued. Furthermore, the possible strategic education role of local arms control talks should not be overlooked.

A third broad category of management strategy would entail measures to circumscribe the possible global repercussions of local proliferation. Thus, circumscribing the continuing risk of Soviet-American confrontation might require superpower agreement upon rules of engagement in local nuclear confrontations. Here, too, the possible impact of a future dramatic shock in fostering such agreements should be considered. Also, from the perspectives of both superpowers the adoption of measures such as improvements in damage-limiting systems, which could reduce the direct military threat to them that future proliferators might pose, could be seen as a necessary management tactic. Finally, policies to check the grow-

19. For suggestions to this end, see George Quester, "Reducing the Incentives to Proliferation," and Michael Nacht, "The United States in a World of Nuclear Powers," elsewhere in this volume.

ing risk of nuclear terrorism also would be required. In addition to efforts to reduce the chances of successful terrorist access to fissile material or nuclear weapons, a readiness both to hold other governments responsible for nuclear terrorists operating from their territories and to engage in "black activities" against the nuclear terrorists themselves could be warranted.

A nightmare scenario?

Taken together, the preceding sets of measures—along with efforts to influence which proliferated world might emerge—could comprise the basic components of a strategy for managing in a proliferated world. But adoption of many of the most important measures, such as agreement upon a code of nuclear behavior or upon superpower rules of engagement, would presuppose at the least a changed global political climate and other than a business-as-usual approach. And even after a dramatic systemic shock, agreement upon such fundamental reforms still might not be politically feasible. Conversely, those more readily politically feasible measures, such as providing limited technical assistance to Nth countries or supporting regional arms control, might be only palliatives. That is, there would appear to be a gap between the gravity of the likely threats within a proliferated world and the probable effectiveness of politically acceptable responses to them. Ultimately, it is this tension which most causes concern about the long-term character of world politics in a future world of widespread proliferation and lends support to the fear that this discussion's initial depiction of life in such a world is not merely an implausible nightmare scenario.

ANNALS, AAPSS, 430, March 1977

Arms Control in a Nuclear Armed World?

By COLIN GRAY

ABSTRACT: Beyond a continuing effort to inhibit further nuclear proliferation, the proper shape and direction of arms control policies for a nuclear-armed world are not at all apparent. Many of the more popular arms control ideas that are discussed in the hypothetical context of a nuclear-armed world do not fare well under close critical examination. Specifically, the arms control value of attempts by well-established nuclear-weapon states at nuclear deemphasis, of issuing broad nuclear guarantees of the security of non-nuclear states, and of proffering advanced conventional weaponry in lieu of nuclear weapons are not viable save under very restricted conditions. Probably the most challenging arms control question for a nuclear-armed world will pertain to the area of nuclear weapon safety. Technical assistance to new nuclear-weapon states could greatly reduce the risks of accident or the anxieties that must attend recognized first-strike vulnerabilities, but such assistance would also, unfortunately, remove an important argument discouraging proliferation and render a crude capability more ready—for a wide variety of possible policy ends. The arms control challenge in a nuclear-armed world will be a need to accommodate some nuclear use and a readiness to exploit the reactions to such use for the end of greater international stability.

Colin Gray is a member of the professional staff of the Hudson Institute. In 1974–75 he was an Assistant Director of the International Institute for Strategic Studies. He is the author of The Soviet-American Arms Race *(published by D.C. Heath in 1976) and of various articles on strategic weaponry and on arms control.*

THE MANDATE for this article presumes a nuclear-armed world. Such a world must contain many nuclear powers; the precise number is not important, what matters is the appreciation that this is a world considerably different from that of 1976, in that 20-plus states have acquired nuclear weapons and the (minimal, at least) means of delivery.

A major difficulty attendant upon an exercise directed toward the identification of the role of arms control in a nuclear-armed world is the near-impossibility of separating the effect of nuclear proliferation from other trends. More likely than not, trends will function synergistically. For an obvious example, it is not excessively pessimistic to foresee a vast increase in the population of less-industrialized countries, a substantial shrinkage in the amount of food available for export from such a critical food-producing area as North America (because of the growth of the indigenous population and a highly probable deterioration in climate), and—in part, therefore—a rapid increase in the number of nuclear-weapon states. In the twenty-first century a prime motivation pushing a state toward a nuclear weapon capability may not be a quest for status or even security (understood in its standard politico-military context), but rather a laudable desire to increase its international leverage toward the end of ensuring an adequate supply of calories for a swollen population.

The food question was cited above simply as illustration of the point that our comprehension of the nature of a nuclear-armed world almost certainly is inhibited as much by the fact that this world does lie 20, 30 years or more into the future as by the unfamiliar complexity of an international system encompassing 20-plus nuclear-weapon states.

Despite this, it is necessary to specify some minimal assumptions concerning the nature of a nuclear-armed world. As working hypotheses, the following premises are persuasive to this author:

1. Power and authority will be more fragmented in the international system than is the case in the 1970s. But, as rival poles of influence and security provision, the United States and the Soviet Union will continue to far outdistance any challengers.

2. In military terms, the current superpowers will far outshadow all rivals. There are no shortcuts to equal military status—not a nuclear strike capability per se, not precision-guided munitions (PGMs), and certainly not access to American cruise-missile technology.[1]

3. Because of their continuing contest for influence, the superpowers will impose a minimum of order (as often as not through the latent threat of the use of force) in regions long deemed vital to their interests.

4. But the proliferation of new nuclear-weapon states (NNWS)[2] will cause each superpower to examine

1. See Alexander R. Vershbow, "The Cruise Missile: The End of Arms Control?" *Foreign Affairs*, vol. 55 (October 1976), pp. 141–42.

2. NNWS is employed in the text with reference to those states which acquire nuclear weapons after the time of writing (October 1976). NNWS is intended to imply possession of a nuclear striking force that is very unsophisticated by comparison with the superpowers (and even the British and the French). As a catchall category, NNWS does, of course, blur distinctions that could be very important. Where important distinctions exist, they are made—elsewhere, NNWS was found to be useful.

very critically the character of its interests in each particular foreign security connection.

5. Notwithstanding the continuing primacy of East-West competitive interests over nuclear proliferation questions for the superpowers, there will be general recognition of a dictum of state policy which has, thus far, not received very explicit expression. Precisely, no state should be expected to accept responsibility for the nuclear actions taken by another—unless very close prior consultation has occurred (and even then some distance might be sought).[3] The case of an Israel facing defeat employing nuclear weapons is one possible exception.

OF RISKS AND COMMITMENTS

It is improbable that a nuclear-armed world will differ dramatically from that of the 1970s. The superpowers should not be expected to eschew alliance with all nuclear-armed states, and a general atomization of what occasionally is termed international society seems unlikely. However, there is a strong probability that a heavily nuclear-armed world will be subject to some nuclear terrorism and will witness (but not generally participate in) the conduct of nuclear warfare both between and within states—on a local level.

Because of the enhanced nuclear risks that the superpowers will run as a consequence of distant security connections, one should anticipate (1) the attenuation and abrogation of the more marginal ties; (2) some tacit agreement, or at least protracted discussion, among the major nuclear powers on the subject of nuclear rules of engagement. Both of these processes will be affected by the continuing competition of the superpowers, by the order in which proliferation occurs, and by the uses (or presumed uses) to which Nth countries will put their newly-developed nuclear forces.

The ways in which these forces are used could be affected by the technical characteristics of NNWS' nuclear strike capabilities. In other words, while the local presence of locally controlled nuclear forces should serve to revise upward official definitions of war-worthy provocations, both sides to a dispute could be acutely aware of the proposition that "he who does not fire first, probably does not fire at all."[4] Following a nuclear first-strike that was intelligently executed, many countries would not be in a good position even to wage sustained conventional combat.

Under these circumstances, many Western arms control notions will not transfer well, if at all, to the intellectual frameworks of the officials of some NNWS, who may not be overly-concerned with what Americans and Western Europeans mean by order and stability. Indeed, one can envisage countries perceiving a nuclear arsenal as an instrument for the effecting of change—for the ends of gain or justice (among a host of possibilities). The extraordinary qualities of nuclear weapons that have caused the officials of the nuclear-weapon states, thus far, to see those weapons as offering use options only of last resort, may be precisely the qual-

3. This dictum falls well short of the now long-standing French proposition that a nuclear-armed world means the end of alliances.

4. In terms of theory, the definitive statement remains "The Reciprocal Fear of Surprise Attack," in Thomas C. Shelling, *The Strategy of Conflict* (New York: Oxford University Press, 1963, 1960), ch. 9.

ities that officials in some NNWS would feel they could exploit in order to extort beneficial changes in their environments. The central question for this article is how, if at all, arms control instrumentalities might function (*a*) to reduce the risk of the occurrence of war, and (*b*) (scarcely less important in the context of this discussion) to reduce the likely damage should war occur.

SOME TECHNICAL STABILITY ISSUES

It may be argued that wars tend to occur, when they do, for political rather than military-technical reasons[5] and that measures enhancing the technical stability of the strategic environment are not all that helpful in reducing the risk of war. Nevertheless, arms controllers have, perhaps for "lack of a better hoss," paid considerable attention to them.

Nuclear disarmament, a special case of arms control, is unlikely to have a widespread appeal intended to restore stability to a precariously balanced world. The nuclear genie could not be put back in the bottle: disarmament would merely replace fears of immediate hostile nuclear use in a crisis with fears of hostile nuclear use following a period of nuclear mobilization (not to mention the suspicion that would be prevalent concerning concealed weapons).

The acceptability to NNWS of many of the arms control measures aimed at improving stability which are voiced by Western (and Soviet) commentators and officials would be a function of technical competence and economic strength rather than intellectual absorption. Almost regardless of the blend of motives that moved a state into the column of nuclear-weapon powers, there is unlikely to be much local opposition to the ideas that (*a*) secure second-strike forces are preferable to vulnerable first-strike (only) forces; (*b*) a flexible war plan is preferable to an inflexible one; or that (*c*) nuclear weapons should be protected against seizure by unauthorized groups. The problem for the transnational arms control community is less one of education than one of ensuring technical feasibility. The first purpose of arms control, to reduce the risk of war, might be served were NNWS to be granted access to the technology that diminishes vulnerability to a first strike.

Unfortunately, NNWS that achieved a security in second-strike potential would, almost by definition, pose a far more serious latent threat to the interests of major nuclear-weapon states than would NNWS that did not. But even if major powers did not ease NNWS acquisition of launch vehicles that could be protected by hardening or mobility, they could certainly vastly improve strategic and tactical warning time of attack. The provision of data from satellites and high-altitude aircraft overflights would be a conveniently private way in which the quantity and quality of the strategic response of an NNWS could be upgraded. However, any NNWS that came to rely upon Soviet or American intelligence of this kind would have slipped (back) into a form of strategic dependence—and the superpowers themselves might deem such technical assistance to be too committing.

Scarcely less important to many NNWS than the problem of ensuring some second-strike capability will

5. See Colin S. Gray, "New Weapons and the Resort to Force," *International Journal*, vol. 30 (Spring 1975), pp. 238–58.

be the need to protect nuclear weapons against unauthorized seizure and use. Nuclear weapon safety is probably the least controversial, and arguably is the most important, field for arms control effort in a nuclear-armed world. Whereas most arms control subjects (force level reductions, qualitative constraints, rules of engagement) will be thwarted, substantially, by the operation of the arms control paradox—the political hostility that makes arms control necessary, also makes it very difficult to accomplish—questions of weapons' safety are virtually (but not totally) nonpolitical. If NNWS do not avail themselves of the technical knowledge and experience available from some existing nuclear-weapon states, they will face an unpleasant dilemma.

Force survival must rest upon an instant readiness to strike—there will be little prospect of riding out a surprise attack. But, instant readiness implies that nuclear weapons are co-located, fully assembled, with their means of delivery. For countries with a stable domestic order and, possibly, a long (or, at least, very firm) tradition of apolitical armed forces, there is no problem. But a nuclear-armed world is going to see the emergence of nuclear-weapon states wherein the chief executives will believe, probably with good reason, that the only safe place for their countries' nuclear weapons is in the basements of their presidential palaces.[6] Consideration of deterrent efficacy and protection against seizure will be severely at odds.

TECHNICAL ASSISTANCE AND STRATEGIC COMPETENCE

It should be apparent from the above discussion that the transfer of technical data on, for example, permissive action link (PAL) technology, need not be an unmitigated blessing for the international community. In the absence of PAL-type safety systems, an NNWS might be compelled to keep its nuclear weapon components well separated and disassembled—for fear of unauthorized military or terrorist seizure. Similarly, though more generally, it is not self-evident that the major nuclear powers should look with favor upon technically stable local nuclear-weapon balances (heretical though this thought may appear at first glance). Vulnerable first-strike nuclear forces are likely to be scarcely less vulnerable to conventional than to nuclear surprise attack. Both local damage and the probability of the involvement of outside nuclear-armed powers would likely be greater, were each side to possess secure second-strike forces.[7] With a technically unstable balance between first-strike forces, it is much more likely than not that (*a*) one side will win a clear victory in a brief span of time, and (*b*) if nuclear weapons are used at all, their principal targets will be of a military character. Naturally, no military force has inherently first- or second-strike characteristics: those characteristics derive from an assessment of the probable weight and quality of the threat.

If a potential NNWS was confident that, following construction of a

6. See Lewis A. Dunn, *Military Politics, Nuclear Proliferation, and the Nuclear Coup d'État* (Croton-on-Hudson, N.Y.: Hudson Institute, HI-2392/2-P, 20 April 1976).

7. But, and it is a substantial but, countries with secure second-strike forces should not wage nuclear war against each other.

fairly minimal nuclear strike force, one or more well-established nuclear-weapon states would provide technical assistance of many varieties designed both to ensure weapon safety and to ease the path to a secure second-strike capability, the attractions of nuclear-weapon status should be more difficult to resist. The policy dilemma for a country such as the United States is clearly predictable. A very general policy of technical assistance, widely appreciated to be in force, would be folly. Some potential NNWS may seek nuclear weapons quite regardless of the fact that they would have to choose between maintaining a ready force and a force secure against illegal domestic seizure. Nonetheless, it is not difficult to anticipate contexts wherein many potential NNWS see some strong (external) security reason for acquiring nuclear weapons, but are strongly discouraged by the thought that dissident generals might seize them or that their first-strike character would impose a very unattractive rigidity upon policy in time of crisis.

The considerations raised and argued above may seem to have an air of unreality about them, in 1976, but in a nuclear-armed world they would be of major importance. Most of the nuclear strike forces in the column of 20-plus nuclear-weapon states would be small, prone to unauthorized seizure and use, and vulnerable to surprise attack. To render nuclear use less likely, a primary aim of arms control, the major nuclear powers should consider very selective technical assistance. But, unless that assistance is very selective and is hedged about with as many restrictions as feasible (given the assistance-providing power's interest in retaining its freedom of action in the event of local hostilities), transition to a world of 30-plus nuclear-weapon states would be encouraged.

The design of intrinsically worthy arms control regimes for the safer regulation of a nuclear-armed world is not that difficult an assignment. What is difficult is to specify just how each particular system of order is to be introduced and maintained. For a world wherein no power, or set of powers, is prepared to act as a self-appointed guardian of the status quo, arms control can aspire to little more than the registration and implicit endorsement of (very mixed) state intentions. A comprehensive ban on nuclear tests might be useful to reduce the confidence felt by governments in the military efficacy of their nuclear arsenals. But, in the absence of fairly painful sanctions, those countries most vulnerable to the potential impact of such a ban could simply, possibly with public regret, decline to accede.

NUCLEAR DELIVERY VEHICLES AND ARMS LIMITATIONS AGREEMENTS

The International Institute for Strategic Studies (IISS) has pointed to the fact that a very large number of nuclear-capable jet aircraft (*a*) have been supplied to potential NNWS, and (*b*) will become surplus in major air forces over the next decade.[8] However, it would be an error to presume that the availability of systems such as the F-104 or the F-4 means that serious nuclear delivery problems for some NNWS would not arise. While F-104s and F-4s, Mirage IIIs and (for a later generation) Mirage F-1s can deliver

8. *Strategic Survey*, 1974 (London: 11SS, 1975), pp. 37–8.

a single standard NATO nuclear weapon (of 1960s' vintage), they certainly would not be appropriate for the delivery of first-generation NNWS nuclear weapons (weighing 6,000 pounds and more). It is relevant to note that out of the IISS list of 13 "nuclear-capable aircraft deployed by threshold states," only one—the Canberra—has the kind of bomb-bay and load carrying potential that would be needed to deliver a first-generation atomic weapon. Major nuclear-weapon states cannot deny NNWS access to nuclear-capable delivery vehicles, but they can retard (for a few years, at most) the acquisition of delivery vehicles that match the "state of the art" of NNWS nuclear weapons design.

Two conclusions are appropriate concerning the merits of an attempt to help manage the risks in a nuclear-armed world by means of impeding access to nuclear-capable delivery vehicles. First, with respect to the ability to deliver 2,000–3,000 pound reasonably advanced weapons, any arms control effort is too late (even as of 1976, let alone 1986 or 1996 or beyond). However, by their own unaided efforts—which may be an unrealistic assumption—countries such as Libya, Pakistan, Iran, South Korea, Taiwan, Argentina, and so forth will not find it easy to design weapons that could be carried by F-4s, F-5s, F-104s, or MIG-21s. Second, given strong political determination, even countries with little technical infrastructure for a nuclear weapons program should be able to design nuclear weapons in the 1,000–2,000 pound range within a five-year period. Overall, there would not appear, at present, to be any very promising arms control action that might be taken with respect to nuclear-capable delivery vehicles.

In principle, the proliferation of SALT-like fora and SALT (Strategic Arms Limitation Talks) agreements involving NNWS could make constructive contributions to political and military stability in regions that are enduring the early stages of local nuclear arms competition. Candidates for nuclear arms limitation attention would be the nuclear strike forces of regional rivals—when neither party, really, wishes to achieve more than a demonstrated nuclear-weapon capacity, and a capability perceived to be not inferior to that of the other. It is possible that political ambitions may grow as a nuclear force takes shape, but the economic attractions of an arms limitation pact conveniently might interdict such a process. Arms limitations, essentially to freeze strictly nominal capabilities, should be eminently negotiable—given the absence of military anxieties pointed out above. However, it is not difficult to see how arms limitation agreements could be of negative utility between many hostile pairs of NNWS. Arms limitation agreements of substance would, in all probability, tend to freeze the deficiencies of immature nuclear strike forces. If strategic offensive forces were frozen at low levels of delivery vehicles (or warheads), then the premium upon cheating would be fairly high. In other words, the attractions and value of SALT-type agreements between NNWS would depend critically upon the purposes the individual NNWS saw as being served by their nuclear forces. For states seeking serious military capabilities in their nuclear weapon programs, arms limitation agreements of a non-cosmetic variety would probably be both non-negotiable (for roughly the same set of reasons that the Soviet-American SALT exercise has failed to cut deeply into capabilities or program intentions), and undesirable (in that continued unrestricted competition should lead the contestants into technically more survivable postures).

If arms limitation agreements between NNWS were to be verifiable, the contracting parties probably would have to have recourse to the good offices of those very few powers that maintained surveillance satellites. As with the provision of potential early warning data, such dependence would be both demeaning to the local powers concerned and entangling for the providers of the verification data. To cross the boundary of this article's mandate, it is worth noting the point that a large number of potential NNWS probably will not acquire nuclear strike forces on the model (though much scaled-down) of the superpowers, or of Britain, France, and China. Instead, with or without nuclear testing, many NNWS will let it be known—in very low key—that they are in the column of nuclear-weapons states, with the weapons being accumulated in disassembled forms (probably after the pattern of Israeli practice in the 1970s). In this way, states may benefit from whatever advantages flow from nuclear-weapons status, without actually having gone nuclear or deployed nuclear strike forces in ways which might maximally encourage emulation by neighbors. This tactic—of letting the world know that one is, say, probably two days away from an operational nuclear weapon capability—would have local arms race implications that have, as yet, been unplumbed by social scientists. To be politically useful, such a capability would have to be advertised (discreetly), while the secrecy as to the size and character of the stockpile should fuel worst (or bad)-case analysis on the part of rivals; but that very secrecy should also serve to dampen the force of arguments for matching responses on the part of neighbors.

By way of summary, a somewhat agnostic stance would seem to be appropriate on the subject of arms limitation agreements between NNWS. For states seeking simply to be recognized as nuclear-weapon powers, and as being not inferior to their regional rivals, such agreements could well be attractive and might offer ample excuse for the eschewal of familiar arms race tactics. But for states whose political cultures and/or security situations impose critical military duties upon emerging nuclear strike forces, arms limitation agreements might prove to be a dangerous irrelevance.

NUCLEAR DEEMPHASIS AND NON-NUCLEAR ARMS

Among the alternative means likely to be available for the promotion of arms control in a nuclear-armed world, policies of nuclear deemphasis by major nuclear-weapon states are probably the least likely to succeed. An American no-first-use doctrine would not find easy acceptance on the part of putative adversaries (how could they be certain?) while it probably would serve to promote much greater interest in nationally-owned and -controlled nuclear weapons on the part of allies. In short, one probably would suffer the worst of both worlds. The prospective utility of a no-first-use declaration upon incentives to proliferate, to threaten nuclear use, and actually to engage in nuclear warfare is not encouraging. It is difficult to see the moral force behind such a declaration when it would be offered by a country with an arsenal of nuclear weapons probably in excess of 20,000, and which still saw great utility in their deterrent (and even defensive) potential. However, American adoption of a no-first-use doctrine could be interpreted as evidence of a secondary concern (proliferation) dominating a primary one (the security of vital allies). No-first-use might well rest upon many worthy motives, but allies could be excused for interpreting it as meaning that the United States (for example) would rather they were overrun than that a single nuclear weapon be used. A policy more likely to encourage nuclear proliferation among allies and friends would be difficult to devise.

Although nuclear proliferation should, with few if any exceptions, be discouraged, it is reasonably certain that an attempt by the existing nuclear-weapon states to deemphasize the roles of nuclear weapons in their strategies is not a profitable path to follow. The whole world knows that nuclear weapons are important and different, and fairly cosmetic attempts to demonstrate the contrary are unlikely to find a receptive and credulous audience. The limited utility of nuclear weapons in day-by-day diplomacy is really beside the point. Some countries may feel that in their regional security contexts, a nuclear capability would forward their political ambitions. Also, since the U.S. cavalry may not arrive to the rescue in time (or, more likely, may not even be dispatched), some countries will feel that there is no close substitute for the locally-controlled nuclear weapon as a credible policy instrument of last resort (for example, Israel, Taiwan, Pakistan, South Korea—perhaps Yugoslavia).

To discourage proliferation on the part of those relatively few states which do genuinely face (what they see as) total threats to their national security, the United States needs to emphasize the reliability of its nuclear guarantee—even in the face of non-nuclear invasion. This, admittedly, is not easy to accomplish. As minimal policy advice, nuclear weapons should not be deployed where there is no robust intention to use them, in extremis. Simple, or even overly simple, as it may sound, the most effective way to enhance credibility in international politics is to say what one means, to mean what one says, and to have the capability to act. Credibility is not, and can never be, an either/or quality. An American president could state, firmly and without elaboration (or qualification), that, "if necessary," he would resort to nuclear weapons to defend (say) South Korea. Skeptics might question the sincerity of such a statement, but the statement, supported by the known presence of nuclear weapons in South Korea, would almost certainly be taken at face value by potential aggressors against South Korea. However, the credibility of this American commitment could be weakened by domestic debate in the United States.

As an arms control device, the flow of sophisticated conventional weapons might be employed as a lever for the discouragement of nuclear proliferation. This idea has already attained policy status in a very inchoate form, but its limitations are very severe. First, while a truly magnificent non-nuclear defense should indeed diminish local interest in the uncertain benefits of a national nuclear weapons program, such a defense should greatly increase the interest of more (and more vulnerable) neighbors in nuclear weapons. Second, unless the flow of conventional weapons is monitored very carefully, there is a very real danger that one would be providing the vital military infrastructure—not to mention the delivery vehicles—for a nuclear weapons program. In the unacknowledged name of nuclear non-proliferation, the supplier countries of non-nuclear weapons might innocently (or knowingly—with resignation) provide a diverse arsenal of eminently nuclear-capable systems. Third, to supply advanced conventional weapons essentially as a bribe designed to appease the proliferation impulse is to leave oneself open to blackmail. While the United States, inter alia, does not favor nuclear proliferation, neither does it (nor would it) accord non-proliferation so high a policy priority that it will fuel regional non-nuclear arms races around the globe at a pace determined by the credibility of threats to go nuclear on the part of local powers. The possibility of judiciously supplying conventional military equipment to selected countries, with a mind to dampening local enthusiasm for nuclear weapons, should not totally be dismissed. However, as a major arms control instrument, it would appear to be fraught with so many hazards that it should not be pursued (the cure might prove no less harmful than the disease).

ARMS CONTROL POLICY—A SENSE OF PROPORTION

It may appear unkind to say so, given the humane motives involved, but the beginning of wisdom with respect to thinking about arms control for a nuclear-armed world is to recognize that very little can be done that would be politically acceptable. So unacceptable is the prospect of proliferation that proliferators, the issuers of nuclear threats, and certainly the perpetrators of nuclear use should be punished according to the severity of their offense—so the argument goes. International society, an optimistic fiction, will be in no position to restrain, let alone punish, the users of nuclear weapons in a nuclear-armed world. The dominant motive should be expected to be sauve qui peut. Because of the risks involved, and because of the diversity of interests that are predictable, behavior in a nuclear-armed world will not be restrained in anticipation of the operation of a primitive nuclear collective security system. Collective security does not work in a politically-divided world—and would not work even in the event of nuclear use by a minor power.[9]

The first instance of nuclear use in war since 1945 will undoubtedly have an effect upon international behavior—but that effect will probably amount in sum to an acceleration of trends that were already clearly in evidence. It is appealing to speculate that a nuclear war confined to the Middle East or South Asia would function as did the light on the road to Damascus, whereafter all things become possible; but a more somber prediction is in order. It is more likely than not that a local nuclear war would be won by the initiator of nuclear use. Despite the near-universal disapproval that would follow actual nuclear use,

9. See the discussion in Colin S. Gray, *Strategic Doctrine for a Proliferated World* (Croton-on-Hudson, N.Y.: Hudson Institute, HI-2490-DP, 23 August 1976).

such use by a state, if it were in extremis, would be justifiable and would not lack for apologists abroad. After all, the NATO countries plan on employing nuclear weapons if they deem such use necessary—so why not South Korea, Israel, Taiwan, Pakistan, and others? In the event, it is predictable that official condemnations of nuclear use would be very closely associated with state political interests.

A quasi-arms control device which periodically attracts interest with respect to behavior in a nuclear-armed world, is the nuclear guarantee. Although much of this article has been phrased in a rather tentative way, hedged about with qualifications, on the subject of nuclear guarantees a more categorical form of expression is called for. Just as no state will accept responsibility for the genuinely independent nuclear decisions of another, so no state will accept responsibility for the defense of another that is threatened with nuclear use, unless vital national interests are believed to be at stake. Moreover, in a nuclear-armed world, the scope of vital (that is, worth fighting for) national interests is likely to shrink quite noticeably. Certainly no state will stand as nuclear guarantor on behalf of non-nuclear states threatened by nuclear-armed-neighbors—on a point of principle or in defense of a general rule of order for a proliferated world.

CONCLUDING THOUGHTS: MAINLY SHADOWS, SOME LIGHT

Arms control in a nuclear-armed world is a vast and fortunately totally speculative field of inquiry. By way of a terse conclusion and as one set of pointers to debate and future research, the following brief statements are offered:

1. Even in a nuclear-armed world, it will still be worthwhile to attempt to interdict putative nuclear proliferation chains.

2. Nuclear disarmament will not be of interest to NNWS, just as measures of substantial arms reduction lack appeal to American, NATO-European, and Soviet officials in the contexts of SALT and Mutual Balanced Force Reductions (MBFR).

3. Nuclear weapons safety must be a matter of major international arms control concern. But the arguments for improving the safety features of the nuclear weapons of NNWS will be offset, in minor key, by the considerations that the ready provision of technical assistance in this area may (*a*) render existing nuclear forces more immediately usable, and (*b*) remove an important argument in some candidate NNWS against nuclear proliferation.

4. To attempt to preempt regional nuclear arms competition by means of fueling regional conventional arms competition will be a policy of very, very restricted utility.

5. Attempts at nuclear deemphasis through the careful manipulation of declaratory policy will not work: if anything, such endeavors will encourage rather than discourage proliferation.

6. General nuclear guarantees offered in defense of any and all non-nuclear states threatened by nuclear-armed neighbors would be lacking in credibility, for excellent reasons.

7. Regional nuclear wars almost certainly will occur. For reasons of

prudence, fear, and plain selfishness (that is, one does not take needless risks on behalf of others), such wars need not, and should not, mean the end of human history.

8. Attempts to discourage further proliferation, or to limit the utility of nuclear weapon stockpiles, by means of restricting access to nuclear-capable delivery vehicles are very likely to fail. There has been, and will be much further, a democratization in understanding of nuclear weapons design, such that NNWS should progress from nominal weapons weighing 6,000 pounds and more down to weapons of 1,000–2,000 pounds in a very few years of development.

9. The mere fact of a nuclear-armed world will not prompt drastic changes in international behavior, any more than it will in the forms of political organization. However, the evidence of the consequences of nuclear use could be a very different matter. Sad to predict, the first genuine opportunity for a nonmarginal change for the better in the ways in which human beings provide for their security will occur not as a consequence of the emergence of a nuclear-armed world, but rather as a consequence of nuclear war.

The United Nations, the Superpowers, and Proliferation

By ABRAHAM BARGMAN

ABSTRACT: Although nuclear weapons are likely to spread to small and medium powers, the main problem for international security will be the effect of proliferation on the avoidance of nuclear war between the superpowers. It is therefore from their vantage point that this essay assesses the role of international organizations in a nuclear-armed world. A new class of disputes caused by violations of IAEA safeguards and permissible withdrawals from the NPT is destined to be placed on the Security Council agenda. These disputes, moreover, may provide the superpowers with the opportunity to cement their common interests in controlling the effects of proliferation. Further periodic Soviet-American confrontations of nuclear-crisis proportions are to be expected, albeit in a new political context complicated by proliferation. The UN can help resolve these, as it has past crises, by providing an organ of last resort, registering, implementing particular provisions of these agreements, and above all capitalizing on them to advance new resources for the promotion of international security. All of these roles could be better played if the UN established an International Nuclear Security Planning Group, to devise, plan for, and supervise the execution of measures which command great support—and superpower agreement. Anything more radical, unfortunately, would require a significant upsurge of insecurity which could only result from a boundary event such as the first use of nuclear weapons.

Abraham Bargman, Professor of Political Science at City University of New York (Brooklyn College), received his undergraduate education at the City College of New York and graduate degrees from New York University and the London School of Economics. In 1952, he joined the United Nations Secretariat's Section on Peaceful Settlement and from 1956 served as a Political Affairs Officer in the Disarmament Affairs Division. Since joining the CUNY faculty in 1967, he has published articles on international organization, as well as on arms control.

THE NEW phase of nuclear proliferation has awakened a concern about the danger of nuclear war and the use of nuclear weapons. It has done so, however, at a time when there is a deeply implanted conventional wisdom which holds that a nuclear war between the United States and the Soviet Union is virtually impossible. This sense of international security is attributed not to the United Nations, and certainly not to UN disarmament deliberations; rather it is associated with the sanction inherent in the stockpiles of nuclear weapons on each side. There also seems to exist a profound faith in the ability of the national security managers to cope with periodic superpower confrontations. This public faith places a great burden on "supermen," who are always playing the world's game with the expectation of pulling back from the nuclear brink. This will be possible, they think, because in the moment of crisis international security values, and in particular those exemplified by and reflected in the United Nations, provide rationalizations for withdrawal. They are neither too big nor too proud to avail themselves of UN mechanisms in such circumstances.

The supreme responsibility for international security from nuclear war still remains theirs, notwithstanding the democratization of nuclear power through proliferation and other tendencies in the international system which have distributed influence (if not power) over a larger area and among a greater number of states than was true during the heyday of the Cold War. The granting of this special responsibility to the United States and USSR in an age of proliferation is not so much a compliment as a critical reflection of the fact that they are and will continue to be in the dual position of arsonists and firefighters; their forceful competition for control of key areas of the world can be expected to continue notwithstanding proliferation and notwithstanding détente.

As an international peace and security mechanism, the UN no longer has the field to itself; bilateral relationships, regional organizations, and permanent conferences of ideologically kindred states now also represent the interests of its members. It has also become fashionable in some quarters to become disenchanted with, if not hostile to, the United Nations. Nevertheless, all problems still seem to end up at the East River, especially when they directly affect the superpowers, who alone have the resources and potential influence to make the maintenance of nuclear peace and security a reality.

Despite this, it is unrealistic to anticipate substantial change in the UN's authority at this time. In fundamental matters, UN members appear to prize their freedom from collective decisions, in other words, their independence. That the UN is what the environment and its members allow it to be is a truism; the dynamic interaction between its political process and the debates which take place within major governments on the meaning of national interest and international responsibility is not as well understood.

The contributions of the UN and of other peace and security organizations will depend in part on the intrinsic ability of these organizations to function under the circumstances noted above and in part on the problems governments place before them. Three problems seem to be likely to surface in an age of proliferation. A new type of dispute between states centered on nuclear rights and obligations which could test the traditional peaceful settlement practices of the UN is a most likely problem. The second problem goes beyond nuclear disputes and even nuclear tensions; it reaches the point of nuclear crisis. Direct or indirect confrontation between superpowers or other states with nuclear weapons constitute a severely threatening problem, because in nuclear crises the nuclear weapons are placed on alert and, as in Cuba in 1962, the world stands immobilized as the governments involved try to defuse the critical threat to nuclear peace. The third problem will arise from proposals to reform existing international institutions as the best—if not the sole—means of assuring international security in the midst of proliferation.

NUCLEAR DISPUTES AND TENSIONS

The UN Charter assumes that it is the responsibility of the parties to a dispute to find a way out of their difficulty without jeopardizing the peace and that disuasion in the form of sanctions is called for only when the Security Council determines that a threat to or an actual breach of the peace exists. In the UN system, as we can see, there are few foolish expectations regarding third-party influence on sovereign states. The UN's procedures provide for fact-finding, conciliation, and even the recommendation of terms of settlement, but it was never expected that all disputes must or would be settled, only that they would not be allowed to develop into threats to international peace and security. This is the institutional context within which potential nuclear disputes and problems will have to be considered.

The Non-Proliferation Treaty (NPT) constitutes an attempt to supersede the "laws" of power politics through international law. In the past, the periodic elevation of a great power into the ranks of the nuclear powers had been met by a fatalistic attitude based on the assumption that governments have a right, if not a moral obligation, to provide for their nations' security. Non-proliferation diplomacy, however, is based on an opposing element introduced by the NPT, that further additions to the nuclear club are not legitimate and are expressly prohibited to its parties. Even a non-party such as India may have been influenced by the new element, since it has not proudly avowed that the main purpose of the nuclear explosion carried out in 1974 was a military one.

Further proliferation will nonetheless create tense situations and international disputes. Among the potential nuclear disputes and tensions which are likely to come before international organizations are (1) violations of treaty obligations; (2) legal withdrawals from a treaty; (3) disputes and tensions stemming from specific nuclear activity; and (4) the development of new laws and general principles to deal with new problems, such as nuclear terrorism.

When disputes arise, it is one thing for an international organization and its members to live with the disputes rather than to attempt the difficult task of imposing solutions; it is quite a different matter when a treaty whose continuance depends on sanctions being applied is at issue in the dispute. Non-nuclear NPT states must now permit International Atomic Energy Agency (IAEA) inspection of all their nuclear facilities. In the future, certain non-parties will probably have to accept the same conditions as the price for nuclear imports. Should an agency inspector suspect or detect a violation, a report is filed with the IAEA Governing Board which, in turn, can take provisional measures through the IAEA. Serious cases of diversion of nuclear materials would be reported to the Security Council as the organ of last resort after the provisional measures and fact-finding procedures of the agency had been completed.

Should the agency fail to report the matter to the Security Council, it is likely that another party to the NPT would do so because it would feel sufficiently concerned about potential pressures on its own policy process. The matter would be reported by the member nation just as any other dispute or situation the continuation of which might endanger peace would be reported. In any event, the problem would be one of how to apply sanctions rather than whether to apply sanctions. This seems to have been the spirit in which Henry Kissinger addressed the thirty-first session of the General Assembly: "Any violation of IAEA safeguards must face immediate and drastic penalties."[1] Although past experience with Security Council sanctions points out the difficulty in getting unanimity among the great powers and, beyond that, the almost impossible task of bringing about actual sacrifice of political and commercial interests for the sake of the collective decision, in the case of such a violation the superpowers would at least share a common interest in the application of unilateral and multilateral measures.

For example, following the 1974 Indian explosion, the United States awakened from one of its periodic proliferation slumbers to create the ad hoc conference of nuclear suppliers. While what is known about this secret institution of some 15 countries does not suggest a rush on the part of all suppliers to impose "immediate and drastic penalties," the conference is a mechanism through which the United States, either alone or in combination with the Soviet Union, could attempt to coordinate sanctions against violators of IAEA safeguards. Whereas in ordinary disputes the superpowers may drag their heels along with the rest, in this case they have so much to gain from keeping the proliferation tendencies under control that there is a good chance of joint action with or without the legitimation of the Security Council or the Suppliers Conference.

A different issue would arise if a state party to the NPT should decide to withdraw from the treaty. To balance the discriminatory nature of the treaty, the superpowers agreed to include in Article X the right of a party to withdraw provided it gives three months notice to the Security Council and submits "a statement of the extraordinary events it regards as having jeopardized its supreme interests." The fact that withdrawal is permitted does not affect the political consequences for neighboring states and perhaps for the regime as a whole. The three months could serve as a cooling-off period if the action results from dissatisfaction over some other issue; the period might be used for intensive bargain-

1. Address by Secretary of State Kissinger before the 31st Session of the United Nations General Assembly, 30 September 1976, Press Release USUN—109(76).

ing between the party and the superpowers, particularly the United States, assuming that they define their common interest in opposition to the state attempting to withdraw.

Security Council deliberations may serve ancillary purposes, such as offering remaining parties new assurances if they feel that their security is jeopardized as a result of the withdrawal. Despite the legality of withdrawal, all the measures canvassed in relation to violations of the IAEA may be appropriate from a political standpoint in the case of withdrawal, but the legitimacy of any such measures would be enhanced by UN action. Finally, when a case of withdrawal does come before the Security Council, the statement explaining how the country's supreme interests have been jeopardized could lead to both a legal and political consideration of what is meant by the term "supreme interests"—one that is found in almost every arms control agreement. On the political side, the council would probably have to debate the significance of the extraordinary events. The deliberations might serve to clarify the tensions between, on the one hand, the undeniable sovereign right of the party to withdraw and, on the other hand, the supreme interest of the community in the avoidance of nuclear war. If time-honored vital interests have been inflated into supreme interests owing to the nuclear threat, the charter's concern for international security should also be given a higher priority for the same reason.

Speaking of legal approaches—something that went out of fashion along with the League Covenant or perhaps with the Hague Conventions of the turn of the century—there is a precedent for bringing nuclear disputes to the International Court of Justice (ICJ) even in cases in which a country is not a party to the relevant treaty. The reference is to the complaints brought by Australia and New Zealand against France in 1974 because of its atmospheric nuclear tests. Since France is not a party to the Partial Test Ban Treaty of 1963, the two countries relied on the 1928 General Act for the Pacific Settlement of International Disputes, from which France withdrew as a result of this case. What is of interest here is not only the fact that the ICJ presents another mechanism for dealing with nuclear disputes, but also that such action could have a political impact on the policy discussions within the government.[2]

As a result of a wave of proliferation, the Security Council is likely to be confronted with tensions inherent in the deployment of nuclear weapons. In the arms control literature, this phenomenon is referred to as the reciprocal fear of surprise attack.[3] Proliferation opens up new sources not only of disputes but of tensions as well, tensions being deeply implanted, long-lived "unformulated conflicts of power."[4] Take the case, for example, that was placed before the Security Council in 1958 by the Soviet Union charging that the flights of American bombers armed with nuclear weapons con-

2. See Thomas M. Franck, "Word Made Law: The Decision of the International Court of Justice in the Nuclear Test Cases," *American Journal of International Law*, vol. 69 (July 1975), p. 612.

3. See Thomas Schelling, *Strategy of Conflict* (Cambridge, Mass.: Harvard University Press, 1960), ch. 4.

4. For the distinction between disputes and tensions, see Hans J. Morgenthau, *Politics among Nations*, 5th ed. (New York: Alfred A. Knopf, Inc., 1972), ch. 25.

stituted a potential threat to the peace.[5] Although the council could do little more than air the complaint, discuss the problems of surprise attack and miscalculations, and encourage other members and the Secretary General to implore the parties to agree to partial measures designed to relax tensions, the effect on internal debates within the respective governments was probably salubrious. Not long after the council debate, the parties agreed to convene a conference on surprise attack which, despite its failure, laid the first foundation stone for Stategic Arms Limitation Talks (SALT). The point here is that nuclear disputes embedded in tensions created by asymmetrical nuclear deployments may require of the Security Council, not the usual combination of pressures for peaceful settlements and sanctions, but rather support for arms control measures.

Finally, we have the General Assembly's responsibility for general principles and new international law. There is, for instance, considerable interest in the problem of nuclear terrorism, but most governments have no official reason to address this potential source of domestic as well as international tension. This situation would change if the issue were brought to the General Assembly in the same way that West Germany isolated the issue of the taking of innocent hostages and requested the legal committee of the thirty-first assembly to draft a convention outlawing this particular form of terrorism. Although the problem of terrorism is usually anathema to the leaders of the Third World because it focuses on symptoms rather than on what they consider to be root causes, the problem of nuclear terrorism might command enough interest and support to win the approval of the majority. At the very least, an initiative would compel governments to address the issue and perhaps thereby raise everyone's consciousness.

It is, thus, possible to anticipate that a new group of disputes and tensions will appear on the agendas of international organizations as a result of nuclear proliferation and of the superpowers' desire to maintain the non-proliferation regime or at least to prevent breaches of the nuclear peace. Even in the absence of effective persuasion backed by sanctions, the fact that a state will have the opportunity of going to the Security Council or some other body already provides the dovish forces within the government with arguments against the worst case assumptions. From the standpoint of the responsibility of the superpowers, such submissions will be a test of the degree of their common interest in non-proliferation. One can assume that the superpowers will be particularly concerned with those nuclear disputes and tensions that could lead to their embroilment in a nuclear crisis.

NUCLEAR CRISES

A nuclear crisis is a confrontation in which nuclear forces are placed on alert status and miscalculation leading to the actual use of nuclear weapons is therefore a distinct possibility. The dynamics of a nuclear crisis have been demonstrated first in the Cuban Missile Crisis of 1962 and less menacingly during the Middle East War of 1973. Although the superpowers prudently managed to resolve the confrontation

5. See in particular Security Council *Official Records*, 815th meeting, 29 April 1958.

between them in these two cases, in a world of many nuclear powers this responsibility will most probably have to be shared.

From the standpoint of international organizations, the two examples of nuclear crisis can be compared in relation to three factors: (1) tension background, (2) management of crisis, and (3) implementation of mutual concessions.

The Cuban Crisis developed in a context marked by severe Cold War tensions while the Middle East War broke out after the European status quo had been legitimated, several arms control agreements had been achieved, and the two powers had signed the "Agreement on the Prevention of Nuclear War" of June 22, 1973.[6] In 1962 the UN was fully integrated into superpower relations, especially on issues affecting nuclear arms control. The 1973 agreement, as illustrated below, formalized the increasingly separate relationship that had developed with the aid of the Hot Line and SALT and relegated the UN to an afterthought: "Each Party shall be free to inform the Security Council of the United Nations, the Secretary-General of the United Nations . . . of the progress and outcome of consultations . . ." (Article V).

If one conceives of the UN in terms of its principles and purposes rather than as a practical instrument of diplomacy, then the 1973 agreement reflects the parties' recognition that "the danger of nuclear war and of the use of nuclear weapons" (Article I) places their responsibility for "the maintenance or restoration of international peace and security" (Article VI) in a very special context. Moreover, the 1973 agreement did not mean that tensions between the superpowers had been relaxed to the point where they were no longer a concern. On the contrary, the agreement reflected acute apprehension that their alliances could lead to nuclear crises "if relations between countries not parties to this Agreement appear to involve the risk of nuclear war . . ." (Article IV). In any event, the Agreement on the Prevention of Nuclear War reflected a radically changed perception of the role of the United Nations in the relationship between the superpowers; nonetheless, the United States and the USSR found the UN to be indispensable in October 1973.

Agreements such as this one are easily faulted in view of what happened in October 1973, but their worth should not be judged solely in terms of unenforceable declarations of good intentions. Rather, one must keep in mind that they provide the process whereby nuclear adversaries can arrive at a reinterpretation of their particular and special responsibility to the overarching charter purpose, namely, the avoidance of war among the great powers. All states with whom the superpowers are oppositely entangled should undergo the same process.

When we come to the actual management of nuclear crises, the role of the UN or of regional organizations is conditioned by whether the superpowers are directly or indirectly engaged and whether it is an issue which has previously been resolved collectively through the UN. In the 1962 "eyeball-to-eyeball" confrontation, the crisis was grounded in a nuclear dispute—whether the Soviet Union could deploy nuclear weapon systems in Cuba, albeit under Russian control. Crisis management involved a carefully gradu-

6. For complete text of Agreement on the Prevention of Nuclear War, see *American Journal of International Law*, vol. 67 (October 1973), p. 833.

ated show of force in the form of a quarantine and intensive, if not always coordinated, bilateral negotiations. The Security Council's function was simply to receive mutually exclusive resolutions from the parties, to publicize the dramatic facts, and, because of the status of the disputants, to discourage third-party meddling. The fact that the General Assembly happened to be in session apparently led the nonaligned diplomats to encourage the Secretary General to propose a freeze on actions by both sides, a measure which was finessed because a cooling-off period would have neutralized American pressure for the removal of the missiles.[7]

Were a similar situation to arise between two less powerful nuclear states, and provided that the superpowers were not taking opposite sides, the Security Council might not be as passive as it was forced to be in the Cuban case. In such cases, should China, France, or Britain wish to prevent action which the superpowers favor, the latter will have their aforementioned agreement on the prevention of nuclear war as a basis for enforcing a return to the status quo ante. In cases where the superpowers are on opposite sides, the situation will be similar to that of the Middle East War, with the significant exception that the local disputants might then also be nuclear powers.

The Organization of American States (OAS) was a key institution in the management of the Cuban Missile Crisis. Although it, along with the Organization of African Unity (OAU) and the Arab League, has authority to settle disputes between members, and therefore a third-party function, in this crisis it served to legitimate the quarantine. This is particularly noteworthy because one can imagine circumstances in a proliferated world in which regional organizations might, instead, legitimate the dissemination of nuclear weapons (when a majority of its members are in a confrontation with a hostile nuclear power). In 1973 the dispute was not a nuclear one, although the involvement gradually escalated to the point where both sides apparently unsheathed their nuclear weapons.[8] This crisis developed out of an act of war for which a cease-fire arrangement would normally be worked out in the Security Council. The dispute involved the superpowers as the chief negotiators since the local parties could not even meet bilaterally at the UN because the question of direct negotiations was itself a matter in dispute. Thus, the Security Council became little more than a mechanism for registering the cease-fire agreements reached in bilateral negotiations, which in turn reflected the fortunes on the battlefields. But the execution of the cease-fires, as this case dramatically illustrated, is not easily accomplished without the combination of great-power pressure and some third-party presence to symbolize the accord, which brings in the third factor—the implementation of mutual concessions.

In the Middle East Crisis of 1973, the UN peacekeeping force was in part a response to a Soviet threat to intervene to enforce the cease-fire. For the first time, the possibility of reliance on a Soviet-American

7. This account is based on Abram Chayes, *The Cuban Missile Crisis* (New York: Oxford University Press, 1974).

8. This account is based mainly on Marvin Kalb and Bernard Kalb, *Kissinger* (New York: Dell Publishing, 1975), chs. 16–19.

peacekeeping force, with or without UN blessing, was considered. While this was unacceptable to the United States at the time, it is an idea that might surface again in future nuclear crises, especially if other permanent members should not be willing to support a UN force.

In 1962, both the United States and the Soviet Union agreed that the UN should carry out on-site inspection to verify the removal of Soviet missiles. But Cuba refused to permit UN inspection and the United States instead relied on unilateral means of verifying compliance. There are two noteworthy aspects to this abortive role. One is the fact that, in the heat of the crisis, Khrushchev proposed on-site inspection and that the Office of the Secretary General should carry it out; both had previously been denounced by the Russians on ideological grounds. When the chances of miscalculation are great and the time for military decision is compressed into hours, the problem for powers caught up in a nuclear crisis is how to communicate signals that can be expected to register without much analysis. The fact that such key phrases as "on-site inspection" and "the Secretary General" had been well worked over in acrimonious debates made them particularly useful signals. By analogy, new nuclear powers should be encouraged to engage in seemingly fruitless arms control negotiations so that they, too, may have signals with similar potential effect should they be forced to rely on their own means for resolving a nuclear crisis.

The second aspect that is relevant for a proliferated world is the subsequent unwillingness of Cuba to accept UN on-site inspection which had been agreed to by the superpowers. One has only to imagine a situation in which other nuclear powers are involved to appreciate the kind of resistance the UN and the great powers are likely to encounter.

In both crises the superpowers had full command of crisis diplomacy; that may not be possible once proliferation takes place. This is what concerned William Jordan of the UN Secretariat as he reflected on the significance for the UN of the Cuban Missile Crisis:

> Should further nuclear powers emerge, and should therefore the bilateral dialogue in moments of crisis be replaced by a confused exchange of views between the sundry wielders of nuclear power, the likelihood of an outcome without resort to the actual use of nuclear weapons would seem diminished.[9]

In the Agreement on the Prevention of Nuclear War, the superpowers distinguish between nuclear war and the use of nuclear weapons. It may well be that as nuclear proliferation evolves, they will adapt their crisis management practices to include the likelihood that sooner or later nuclear weapons will be used. As in the past, the UN role is destined to be whatever is required to implement the superpowers' arrangement. In the event of the use of nuclear weapons, this might range from disaster relief to supervising the enforced dismantling of a nuclear weapon system. Perhaps this is a matter which could be studied

9. Quoted from an unpublished memorandum, "Nuclear Crises and the United Nations," written during the Cuban Missile Crisis by the late Dr. Jordan when he was director of the UN's Political Affairs Division.

within the UN Secretariat in anticipation of nuclear proliferation.

A nuclear crisis can also be viewed as an opportunity camouflaged by pervasive insecurity. One of the positive consequences of the Cuban Missile Crisis was the movement to prevent the further proliferation and dissemination of nuclear weapons. The first achievement was the Partial Test Ban of 1963; several years later, a nuclear free zone was created with its own Organization for the Prevention of Nuclear Weapons in Latin America (OPANAL). Though the general Non-Proliferation Treaty of 1968 left the nuclear powers free to engage in dissemination, it did inhibit the acquisition of nuclear weapons by states not then possessing them. The point is that a nuclear crisis can lead to some substantial positive achievement, with the assistance of the UN. Although the parallel consequence of the Middle East Crisis of 1973 has still to emerge, one can detect a pronounced shift from a total reliance on UN peacekeeping to a strong movement for a political settlement.

INSTITUTIONAL REFORM

The experience of the superpowers has some limited value as the only guide to future nuclear crises in a world of many nuclear-armed states. However, the democratization of power relations that is taking place means that fewer governments will accept the hierarchical notion of superpower supremacy and the premise that the avoidance of nuclear war between them is the supreme interest of all countries. Moreover, in the present nationalistic environment, the superpowers cannot expect states with a nuclear potential to sacrifice their own conception of national security on the altar of the high ideal of common security without concrete evidence of sacrifices.

The fact is, however, that in recent years the superpowers have not supported, nor have they been under great pressure at the UN to support, measures which would denuclearize world politics. They have, instead, learned to satisfy public opinion with limited arms control measures. That each General Assembly devotes most of its political agenda to disarmament items is a tribute to customary practice rather than to the commitment to arms control of the majority of states. Third World countries have so far not made denuclearization an integral part of their new world order. Since they control the General Assembly, which in the past has been the main mechanism for maintaining pressure on the superpowers, it will be they who will decide whether denuclearization measures will be incorporated into their negotiations with the industrialized world.

Although the superpowers are already committed by the NPT to embark upon denuclearization, they are fearful of tampering with a security structure that has at least enforced prudence even as it has created tensions and nuclear crises. Given their fear and the absence of effective Third-World leadership, it is difficult to envisage circumstances in which they might entertain Richard Falk's demand that denuclearization replace nonproliferation as the UN objective as part of a movement for "structural change by which is meant a fundamental rearrangement of institutional arrangements and authority patterns that currently give shape to international relations."[10]

The reforms of Leonard Beaton, on the other hand, would continue to place the primary responsibility for international security upon the superpowers. Starting with the premise that a stabilized posture of nuclear deterrence would be advantageous in a proliferated world, Beaton proposes to diffuse among all nuclear states the kind of "cognisance" that has developed between the superpowers.[11] My own view is that, unfortunately, governments are likely to follow this path rather than that of denuclearization.

Nevertheless, in this context, the UN might well adapt some of Beaton's ideas for institutional reform and, in particular, establish an International Nuclear Security Planning Group. The aim of this group, which might have the same relationship to the Security Council as the moribund Military Staff Committee, would be to anticipate and study the disputes and tensions that will arise as additional states acquire nuclear weapons. Another function would be to carry out, on a temporary basis, emergency measures for dampening a crisis, such as the special inspection or supervision of nuclear facilities or the monitoring of nuclear force deployments; the group would be a kind of nuclear peacekeeping cadre. A third function would be to help leaders of new nuclear states to understand the tensions associated with their new status and ways of ameliorating them. Finally, the group might also be responsible for planning and evaluating measures for partial denuclearization, such as the establishment of nuclear free zones.

Hopefully, these nuclear peacekeepers would be encouraged by the superpowers to persist in their specialized work in the midst of proliferation and active disputes on other issues. Given the interest of the superpowers in a stable nuclear environment, they might wish to use the group as the vehicle for the dissemination of procedures and technology designed to minimize the chances of miscalculation and nuclear accidents. Is it not high time for governments spending more than $300 billion each year on military power and security to permit a few citizens to serve exclusively an institution concerned only with the international implications of nuclear disputes, tensions, and crises?

More radical reforms of a supranational nature which would enhance the operational authority of international organizations are not likely to prove acceptable in the absence of deep and pervasive insecurity. Had it not been for two general wars which left the world emotionally and physically crippled, the League of Nations and the United Nations would probably not have been created. Perhaps only another boundary event—the first use of nuclear weapons—could tap the latent supranational impulses of some 150 governments. Until then, leaders must heed the imperative of proliferation: the international security symbols and mechanisms of the United Nations must be protected because all people and governments have a supreme interest in the avoidance of nuclear war.

10. Richard Falk, "A World Order Analysis of Nuclear Proliferation," *Forum for Correspondence and Contact*, vol. 8, no. 2 (October 1976), p. 111.

11. Leonard Beaton, *The Reform of Power* (New York: The Viking Press, 1972); see, also, the proposals for reform in William Epstein, *The Last Chance* (New York: The Free Press, 1976).

ANNALS, AAPSS, **430**, March 1977

Proliferation and the Future: Destruction or Transformation?

By FREDERICK C. THAYER

ABSTRACT: We must recognize that proliferation includes both nuclear power plants and nuclear weapons, the latter being only a follow-on to the former. The first step toward coping with proliferation is to accept that nuclear weapons are essentially political weapons of terror, not military weapons, even if we have convinced ourselves otherwise. For the near term, proliferation can enhance international stability if it occurs in balanced, rather than unbalanced, fashion. Over the long term, the issues are different. The critical global problem is finite limits to natural resources. Nuclear weapons are becoming both the cheapest and the only way of waging war. This faces us with a stark choice between alternative futures: (1) A world of iron or totalitarian governments, in which each state blackmails others so as to acquire scarce resources. The continuing shortages lead to rigid internal management and unending nuclear war. (2) A world in which shortages are recognized and we develop global agreements for resource distribution. The concept of sharing replaces property (both individual and state), social hierarchies (including the state) are transformed into other social systems we cannot yet describe in detail, and the social institution of war has no meaning. If we choose the first, there is no future. If we choose the second, we must soon begin a program of balanced deproliferation, in which we abandon both nuclear energy and nuclear weapons.

Frederick C. Thayer, Associate Professor of Public Administration and International Affairs, Graduate School of Public and International Affairs, University of Pittsburgh, is author of An End to Hierarchy! An End to Competition! Organizing the Politics and Economics of Survival *(New York: Franklin Watts, 1973) and of numerous pieces on organization theory, on policy formulation, and on defense policy.*

WE LIVE in an era of galloping nuclear proliferation, an era in which the spread of nuclear weapons is tied closely to the spread of nuclear power plants; many nation-states see nuclear energy as the only feasible near-term replacement for petroleum, which, before the end of the century, will be either largely depleted everywhere or well past the point of peak production. The connection between nuclear weapons and nuclear energy gives us an exciting opportunity to take the broadest possible approach to issues of proliferation. If we can transcend the narrowly military way in which we, especially in the United States, have dealt with these issues in the past, perhaps we can provide a basis for meaningful speculation about future political and economic relationships on a global scale. With that in mind, this essay first explores two general themes, each of them generally in disagreement with those of my colleagues in this volume; I then turn to a brief exposition of two possible world futures, our major task (as I see it) being to consciously choose between them.

As to the general themes:

1. Nuclear proliferation already has reached a point where it is long past the time to dispel most of the mythology with which we have surrounded nuclear questions. In particular, we must recognize that nuclear weapons remain the weapons of terror they were when we first used them. They transform all warfare into the immediate destruction of civilian populations, and it is nonsense to continue to pretend otherwise.

2. For the very near term, accelerated proliferation seems inevitable. For practical purposes, we cannot discourage proliferation without insisting that other countries give up not only the idea of arming themselves with nuclear weapons, but also expansion of their energy production for peaceful purposes. This being immediately impossible, we have no choice but to seek forms of proliferation which might retard the expansion of instability if not actually produce greater stability. It makes no sense to cling to a stance which simply condemns all proliferation as bad.

Each of the two likely world futures is based on a premise which, despite its increasing prominence, is less influential than it should be. The world's natural resources are finite, and we fast approach the limits to those resources, in particular those that are nonrenewable. We face an apocalyptic choice, each course frightening—if for different reasons:

1. Some now predict that recognition of the finite limits to resources will lead to ever more authoritarian control of all social activity by "iron governments" which will struggle bitterly against each other for possession of whatever is left. The primary use of nuclear weapons, whether in the hands of governments or terrorist groups, will be to blackmail others to hand over the resources in their possession or, alternatively, to protect one's own resources from blackmail. Almost inevitably, this will lead to some form of nuclear holocaust.

2. Others predict that a profound and peaceful social transformation is possible, the first of such magnitude since the shift from hunting to agricultural societies approximately 5,000 years ago. The transformation will include the demise of social hierarchies and economic market systems and the development of

global networks for reaching agreement as to how and to whom available resources will be distributed. Once we recognize that resources are limited, the moral justification for property (individual or national) will vanish, sharing will be the only possible mode of existence, and such social institutions as war will have no legitimacy.

I shall attempt to make a plausible argument that we have some reason for optimism. It turns out, for example, that even if we consciously proceed in accordance with the pessimistic scenario (1), the policy decisions we take will actively, if inadvertently, lead to the realization of the optimistic scenario. Before getting to these scenarios, however, I turn to a reassessment of the immediate past.

THE DEMYTHOLOGIZING OF NUCLEAR WEAPONS

While the nuclear superpowers are reluctant to admit as much, the expansion of nuclear capability to very small states, and to terrorist groups as well, will lead over time to a profound and necessary demythologizing of nuclear weapons. The United States and the USSR have attempted, and attempt now, to maintain the fiction that nuclear weapons are fundamentally military, not political, weapons. We have gone to great lengths to avoid admitting what we demonstrated at Hiroshima and Nagasaki; nuclear weapons (like fire bombs) are most effective when they are used against civilian population centers. It is worth recalling some of the scenarios we have developed in a forlorn attempt to conceal the obvious.

—We developed doctrines of rational war, including the assumption that any first strike would make sense only if directed against an opponent's weapons, even though we included the phrase "bonus effect" to describe the substantial damage any such strike would do to nearby population centers. From the standpoint of justifying military budgets, this was a useful doctrine, because a very large number of missiles are needed if one seeks to ensure he will be able to destroy an enemy's entire missile force. In outlining these doctrines, which had to assume rationality on both sides, we conveniently overlooked a basic internal contradiction; a rational war could be conducted only if each side had two or three times as many missiles as the other, a bit unlikely to say the least.[1] In pursuing the doctrine, we even planned at one time to locate all missile complexes in very isolated areas so as to ensure our civilian population would not be damaged in a rational first strike. This proved logistically unmanageable, but we retained the imagery anyway.

—We developed some of the silliest civil defense theories imaginable. One prominent strategic theorist argued that if the Soviets misbehaved, we should evacuate our urban populations to the countryside, issue the Soviets an ultimatum, launch a first strike against Soviet missiles if they disobeyed, accept whatever insignificant second strike they could launch against our cities, wait until the fallout had subsided,

1. Only now, when MIRV (Multiple Independent Targetable Re-Entry Vehicles) enable each side to deploy more warheads than the other side has launched vehicles is such a war conceivable—and even then, disarming strikes could not reach important elements of the strategic nuclear forces, such as missile submarines at sea.

and then repopulate the cities. This approach to rational war seemingly justified a U.S. first strike, the book in which it appeared became an all-time best seller, but the theorist conveniently ignored the elaborate evidence put together within the government as to the utter impossibility of total evacuation of the cities.

The government itself, in the early 1960s, adopted an opposite approach, one based upon a Soviet first strike (a bit more morally comforting). Because the Soviets would (rationally) attack only missiles, not cities, we designated downtown buildings as suitable for fallout shelters and urged other citizens to install them in their backyards. While also a neat budgetary trick (blast shelters would be prohibitively expensive in cities), this program had both tragic and amusing side effects:

1. At one press conference during which he urged citizens to add fallout shelters to their homes (a business which underwent a fast cycle of boom and bust), then Secretary of Defense McNamara was asked why he had not installed such a shelter in his home. His response? "I rent a home in Washington; I do not own it."

2. Assuming an imbalance of fallout capability in nonwork hours (most of the space was located in downtown areas), the government developed the "freight-car" concept. Many citizens were expected to travel toward the center city so as to make the shelters closest to their homes available to those living still farther away from the downtown areas. This assumed a willingness on everyone's part to ignore the shelter closest to him, and it also assumed a massive traffic jam. At one legislative hearing, a congresswoman from Michigan was incredulous; the policy, she said, meant that if Soviet missiles arrived at night, only the pimps, prostitutes, and drunks of downtown Detroit would be saved.

3. Quite a few citizens, among those who installed residential fallout shelters, prepared to shoot neighbors who demanded access to those shelters. If a shelter were overcrowded, its occupants might have to exit before the fallout had subsided, hence shooting one's neighbor seemed morally justifiable. The national discussion of this issue was at best ugly.

When civil defense was a major item on the public agenda, the fundamentally contradictory nature of the first strike and second strike theories was never made clear, principally, I think, because those advocating first strike approaches did not wish to be too forthright in their advocacy. Both sides, however, deluded all of us by implying that fallout would be the only substantial problem of a U.S.-USSR nuclear exchange.

—We developed various theories about "clean" and "dirty" missiles, arguing that, if both sides would only agree to refrain from developing dirty ones, relatively clean and undamaging nuclear wars could be fought.

—We emphasized the need for a wide range of tactical nuclear weapons. These would give us, so we heard, a "spectrum of capabilities," and it would easily be possible to conduct "sanitary" strikes against very small targets (bridges, for example), thus further ensuring no damage to nearby civilian populations (as in Europe).

—We developed a fascination

with "blue water deterrents," the notion that if the United States would rely on missile-carrying submarines, any Soviet first strike would completely avoid the United States. Some carried this further, suggesting that if both sides relied on submarines, there might be no damage to civil societies at all.

Given our policy-makers insistence that our nuclear stockpile was military, not political, in nature, an unresolvable debate was inevitable. Those who understood the basically terroristic character of nuclear weapons shouted "Overkill!"; but those justifying the weapons saw only a continuing need to stockpile enough missiles to knock out enemy missiles (and there could never be enough). As the stockpiles on both sides grew and grew to levels none of us can comprehend even now, we tried to tell ourselves that we could maintain those old distinctions between combatant and noncombatant, military and civilian, thus protecting the nonmilitary parts of society from destruction. We even denied our own experience, in that we conveniently chose not to remember that during World War II, we increasingly had turned to the terror (fire) bombing of cities even as we continued to speak vaguely of precision bombing.

Once in a great while, the press of events compelled us to admit (if only implicitly) that our strategic doctrines, taken together, amounted to nonsense. This was especially the case during the Cuban Missile Crisis of 1962, when the president undertook to explain on national television the precise nature of the Soviet threat. His position was that the Soviets had placed offensive missiles in Cuba, but he then described the threat in terms of the precise distances between those Soviet missiles and a number of American cities. In the doctrine of rational war, of course, offensive missiles would be aimed at American missiles, not cities, but few noticed that in a time of real crisis, the first casualty was the doctrine of rational war. The missiles were, simply stated, a clear notice from the Soviets that any further U.S. attempt to overthrow Castro would bring the Soviets to his defense, and the notice was heeded when the United States guaranteed to protect Castro.

This criticism of the way we have handled nuclear issues cannot be confined to policy-makers. Throughout the 1950s and 1960s, for example, there emerged in the United States a substantial academic community devoted to full-time teaching and research on issues of national security. Doctrines of rational war provided a basis for endless treatises about "throw weight," "CEPs," and "risk calculus." Given the underlying premises, the larger political and moral issues hardly were addressed at all and, to this day, many attempt to hold the line against the introduction of such issues. Almost instinctively, they reject what might be called "the French view," which argues in effect that nuclear weapons are basically political, or terrorist, in nature, hence a modest nuclear force can be highly effective. To that, our policy-makers and defense intellectuals respond that a small force cannot be effective precisely because it is too small to be militarily effective.

The result of all this is that many approaches to the issue of proliferation, including some in this volume, seem inherently contradictory. If the issue is a serious enough one to warrant publication of this volume, it can only be because the

French view is fundamentally correct. Were the long-term U.S. approach to be taken as valid, the acquisition of modest nuclear capabilities by many countries would not be significant enough militarily to worry about. Clearly, we are worried about proliferation, even as we generally continue to avoid discussing the associated political and moral issues. This makes most of the arguments against proliferation largely irrelevant to the countries to which we address them, and it generally blinds us to the possibility that in the world as now constituted, proliferation may not always be politically destabilizing. To that question I now turn.

BALANCED PROLIFERATION: A SHORT-TERM HOPE

The present trend toward proliferation should demonstrate once and for all that the Non-Proliferation Treaty (NPT) was never anything but a pious hope based upon illogical premises. Two such premises never received the attention they deserved: one was the concept of nuclear umbrellas supposedly erected by nuclear superpowers, the other was the nature of the NPT as something of a military alliance.

Inherent to the NPT was the notion that the United States and USSR would separately guarantee to protect their allies, friends, or client states from nuclear blackmail or attack by the other. Many states that were non-nuclear at the time, whether or not they joined the NPT, had little faith in such guarantees, and it was foolish to expect otherwise. The umbrella concept depended, of course, upon the fallacious nuclear doctrines outlined above. To clearly recognize nuclear weapons as fundamentally terroristic and most effective when used against civilian populations is to see the absurdity in attempts to convince a U.S. ally that we would make our civilian population the hostages of that ally's foreign policy. Further, the umbrella approach ignored the old dictum that nation-states may have permanent interests but not permanent allies. An umbrella concept logically requires that nuclear guarantees be extended or withdrawn as various countries change sides. Suppose, for example, that China had sought the protection of an umbrella; could the United States logically have been expected, in recent years, to guarantee reprisal against the Soviets if they attacked China?

Also inherent to the NPT was the implicit premise that the nuclear superpowers should jointly undertake to destroy, by direct attack if necessary, any other country's attempt to develop nuclear weapons. I do not suggest that immediate destruction of an emerging nuclear capability is the only possible sanction or disincentive that can be used in any given situation, but I do suggest that the logic of the NPT required such joint action if the superpowers were serious about preventing proliferation and if nothing else worked. The general absurdity of such joint U.S.-USSR action led me to label the NPT as an impossible alliance which could never be implemented.

Even if alliance always has been impossible, however, U.S. and USSR nuclear capabilities have led to positive developments, indeed to an important form of global stability. The nuclear superpowers have developed, over more than a decade, elaborate rituals and detailed precautions designed to avoid direct confrontation between them.

These have included the now-famous hotline, explicit signals and personal reassurances about the meanings of specific foreign policy actions, a formal agreement to avoid war, and even a willingness to virtually ignore any action that might lead to direct confrontation. We were careful to avoid any action when the Soviets erected the Berlin Wall, we rejected the alternative (favored by some) of destroying Soviet missile emplacements in Cuba (which would have led to the deaths of many Soviet technicians), and the Soviets were quiet when we mined the harbors of North Vietnam. In many other crises, both sides have dispatched both explicit and implicit signals to reassure each other. All these activities, of course, demonstrated the poverty of our strategic doctrines. Leaders understood, if they did not announce, that any U.S.-Soviet engagement would lead immediately to all-out nuclear exchange, with no pauses along the way. Few would argue now that a conventional war involving the nuclear superpowers could be managed so as to avoid nuclear exchange.

There is something to be said, then, for balanced proliferation as an improvement over unbalanced proliferation. Whatever the United States might like to believe about its own peaceful intentions in international politics, it is plausible to argue that relationships between the United States and USSR are more stable than they would have been if the latter never had acquired nuclear weapons. Given any situation involving more or less continuous high tension within a group of nation-states, as in the case of Israel and other countries in the Middle East, the acquisition of nuclear weapons by only one of these states may be more destabilizing than acquisition by all. If, as some evidence indicates, the Israelis have gone nuclear, a case can be made that the superpowers have an interest in encouraging, or at least not discouraging, the acquisition of nuclear weapons by Israeli opponents.

The United States cannot effectively pursue a policy of balanced proliferation by itself. At the minimum, specific implementation on a case-by-case basis would have to be jointly worked out with the Soviets, and perhaps with others as well. This is because an important part of the policy would have to be the specific withdrawal of all implicit or explicit understandings concerning umbrella protection. If it makes sense, for example, for the United States and the Soviets to promote balanced proliferation in the Middle East, or in the case of India and Pakistan, it makes just as much sense to make clear to the proliferating countries that they cannot expect any further military support from the superpowers. Balanced proliferation, in other words, would turn out to be a form of disengagement of the superpowers from regional conflicts.

It follows that a concept of balanced proliferation depends upon complete acceptance of the arguments proliferating countries have made against the NPT and the nuclear superpowers, just as it also depends upon the experience the superpowers have acquired. Other countries have discounted the usefulness of umbrellas, so they cannot have it both ways. Once a country acquires a nuclear military capability, it must admit it cannot expect a nuclear superpower to provide an unwilling umbrella. The long experience of the United States and the Soviets in managing nuclear weaponry can only be interpreted as a mutual understanding that all direct military action against each other must be avoided if nuclear war is to be avoided. This experience suggests, some commentators notwithstanding, that limited wars between nuclear-armed countries are impossible.

I do not suggest for a moment that balanced proliferation can be expected to delay proliferation, but the premises underlying this policy would not include an assumption that a slowdown in proliferation is always preferable to a speed-up, the general assumption of most authors in this symposium. Indeed, the logic of balanced proliferation suggests that once proliferation is seen to be inevitable, little is gained by attempting to retard it. Hence, balanced proliferation would be a policy of conscious acceleration of proliferation, and this just might work over the short term.

This is a less startling assertion than it seems at first glance. Our present approach to proliferation disguises a great deal of proliferation by labeling it as peaceful in nature. We engage in nuclear proliferation when we export the technology for building nuclear power plants, and it is foolish to pretend otherwise. A policy of balanced proliferation would merely recognize this phenomenon for what it is and carry it to its logical conclusion.

It follows that balanced proliferation would have a profound effect upon the international system. The withdrawal by the superpowers of all nuclear guarantees to proliferating countries would have the effect of terminating alliances as we have come to know them. Each nuclear state would have to fend for itself in a world of nuclear states, knowing that its friends could not afford to risk their own populations as the price of maintaining that friendship. I suggest this already is widely understood, because it is the most logical explanation for the attempts that are made to keep secret the acquisition of nuclear weapons. We should not conspire to keep proliferation a secret; we should openly recognize it every time it occurs, and make clear at the time of the announcement that we can no longer lend our support to the proliferating country.

Balanced proliferation would not be an ideal policy, nor even a good policy in any moral sense, only a better policy than the ones usually advocated. At its best, it could provide only an incremental improvement in stability over a more unbalanced form of proliferation. Over the long term, of course, we cannot sensibly define as stable any world in which many countries have terror weapons at their disposal, let alone a world in which terrorist groups also are able to acquire terror weapons. But it is equally foolish to pretend that even a world in which only the United States and the Soviets had such weapons could be forever stable, yet that has been, and remains, both the central thrust of our nuclear policy and the central thrust of most analyses of that policy.

For the short term, then, it is time to abandon the notion that those now possessing nuclear weapons are somehow more sane, trustworthy, or rational than other countries likely to acquire such weapons. We can make no plausible argument in behalf of this notion, and we never have been prepared to implement it by destroying new nuclear capabilities. So it becomes necessary to speculate about longer-term trends. What are the possibilities?

PROLIFERATION AND THE FUTURE: TWO SCENARIOS

In a 1976 speech to the United Nations, former Secretary of State Kissinger emphasized a major paradox of the times. Nationalism, as he put it, had become a more powerful force in the world than ever before. (As I have argued above, nuclear proliferation contributes to this by making alliances decreasingly effective or even credible, thus transforming the international system into the most atomistic system imaginable.) Kissinger also noted that even as nationalism had become more significant, there was increasing recognition of interdependence within the international system. He implied that acknowledgement of interdependence would require, sooner or later, substantial modifications to our definitions of sovereignty and independence, the hallmarks of nationalism. An example from the recent past can be used to highlight the possibilities.

The British Broadcasting Corporation produced a few years ago a series of documentaries on "The Energy Crunch" and, in the documentary concerning petroleum reserves, introduced a startling speculation. As the BBC put it, an important reason for the withdrawal of the United States from Vietnam may have been the increasing realization that large-scale conventional warfare, especially aerial bombing, could no longer be sustained because of oil shortages. While this factor never was mentioned by U.S. policy-makers, it is interesting to ask what might have occurred in the United States if, at the time of the OPEC oil embargo, we had been conducting large-scale bombing raids on North Vietnam. U.S. citizens might not have been content to wait two hours or more to purchase $3 worth of automobile gasoline, knowing that large amounts of petroleum were being refined into aviation fuel to keep the bombers in the air.

As I suggested at the outset, the fast approaching depletion of petroleum resources is a major cause of the peaceful nuclear proliferation now underway. It is not yet widely acknowledged that we already are in an era where nuclear war is not only the cheapest but perhaps the only form of warfare available to any state. The superpowers continue to maintain huge conventional forces, and they continue to supply their client states with all sorts of petroleum-powered equipment (land and air), but there is little likelihood this equipment can be used on a sustained basis. As I also suggested in an earlier section, nuclear war is, in virtually all cases, likely to be terroristic, city-busting attacks on civilian populations. Generally speaking, it is likely to be impossible for any state to protect itself against all such attacks. As one scholar suggested quite a few years ago, reliance on nuclear weapons implies a mutual inability on the part of all states to preserve their territoriality, the further implication being that the nation-state was approaching its demise.

This becomes more of a possibility now than it was at the time he first predicted this demise, primarily because of the increasing inability to fight conventional wars. In both of the scenarios I briefly outline here, I assume to begin with that not only are we fast running out of oil, but also of many other natural resources which, taken together, have sustained the social institution of war within manageable economic parameters. I believe the evidence is overwhelming on this score, but it is not my purpose to convince doubters. I suggest only that proliferation would be less an issue than it is if economical substitutes for nuclear energy were easily available. Given this fundamental assumption, pessimistic and optimistic scenarios seem possible.

A pessimistic scenario

We already are partly the prisoners of a pessimistic scenario, beginning with the embargo levied against the United States by the petroleum exporting countries (OPEC) in 1973. Shortly thereafter, the president and the secretary of state announced that if at any time in the future a further OPEC embargo or excessive price rise threatened the United States with "economic strangulation," the United States would seriously consider taking military action. Serious students of foreign policy suggested that it was both possible and desirable for the United States to capture the largest pool of remaining oil (in Saudi Arabia) and then set fair prices for its sale. During the presidential campaign of 1976, the successful candidate announced that he would consider any future OPEC oil embargo the equivalent of an economic declaration of war on the United States and would respond accordingly.

In a world of fast-diminishing resources, with each state attempting to secure as much as it can of the available supply of each resource, and with conventional warfare increasingly ruled out because of the lack of resources to support it, nuclear weapons become increasingly attractive for the purposes of (1) protecting one's natural resources from blackmail threats by other nuclear states or terrorist groups; (2) making such threats credible when they must be used to secure resources from other states possessing them; and (3) generally protecting national security in the only way left to any state to do so.

In this scenario, each state is committed to the maximum possible economic growth, and the achievements of society as a whole and all the organizations and individuals within it are measured on that basis. Growth in the Gross National Product and per capita income are considered extremely important, and long-term doubts are usually resolved in favor of maximum growth. Where some might argue against continued reliance on nuclear energy because of the possibility of nuclear accidents or because of the difficulties in isolating nuclear wastes from the environment for hundreds, or perhaps thousands, of years, these arguments are cast aside on grounds that they are overstated or, alternatively, that technology will enable us to overcome any problems in the long run.

While the national actors in this scenario pay some attention to such problems as overpopulation, they seek technical solutions. One, already widely proposed, is the colonization of outer space. Perceived as only the newest of many frontiers conquered heretofore, outer space seems to offer great possibilities for building new communities in the form of space stations. These might be capable of absorbing a good deal of the world's overpopulation, and it is thus assumed that growth need not be limited to the planet Earth.

In this atomistic world of nuclear-armed states, each state turns more and more to "iron government" (the phrase used by one serious analyst of the future) to maintain rigid discipline within its borders and organize the defense of its national fortress—beset by the possibility of nuclear threat and/or attack from any and all directions. An iron government in the United States, for example, might have to respond to a demand (tied to a nuclear threat) for food needed to feed starving populations. To sustain a suitable defense posture over the long term, each state is compelled to substantially restructure the national map.

A highly developed society such as the United States is an intricate web of networks, transactions, and interactions. Were any major U.S. city to be destroyed today by a nuclear missile, that destruction would have an immediate effect upon much of the rest of the country. Were our cities more self-sufficient, and at the same time more decentralized, the loss of any one city or several of them would have much less effect. It follows that a policy of national defense against nuclear attack requires an intensive long-term program of self-sufficiency, community by community, plus a program of extensive relocation so as to minimize the damage from nuclear attack. People must live within walking distance of their work, the distance between the production and consumption of goods must be reduced to the absolute minimum, and even cities must grow as much of their own food supplies as humanly possible.

Having forcibly reconstructed the national society into a group of more or less self-sufficient, modular communities, the function of national iron government becomes the management of international bargaining in a world of many iron governments (and iron terrorist groups). Depending upon the precise nature of the threats being exchanged, a government (in the United States or elsewhere) would have to decide whether to deprive some of its communities of resources so as to respond to a nuclear threat, whether to accept the nuclear destruction of one or more communities as the best bargain that could be struck, and so forth. The scenario simply continues in this vein until all the actors are no longer able to continue. Nation-states, existing in a Hobbesean state of nature, fight each other to the bitter end for the control of the remaining resources.

An optimistic scenario

Once recognized, finite limits to resources lead all states to conclude that they can no longer assume that their resources are their possessions, to be distributed as they (individually) see fit. To recognize finite limits to resources, in other words, is to remove the moral justification for property, especially as we have defined it in the West. We have justified property largely on the premise that natural resources are generally available to all on the basis of hard work. Once it is understood that this is impossible, property becomes the equivalent of theft.

The acceptance of the notion of finite limits to resources makes it possible to give an operational and concrete meaning to interdependence. All resources become everyone's resources, to be shared, distributed, allocated on some agreed basis, and "might makes right" cannot be the basis of decision making.

Oddly enough, recognition of limits to resources leads to the same sort of societal restructuring as does the pessimistic scenario outlined above. Those who argue for social change on the basis of limits to growth predict and urge development of self-sustaining communities, even neighborhoods. One distinguished group of British scientists suggests that the building block of this social redesign (on a global scale) should be communites of some 500 citizens. These communities, while as self-sustaining as possible, are then linked together in decision-making networks which allow for global management (without central authority) of such things as food production and distribution, population control, energy production and consumption, allocation of seabed resources, and the like.

As we are already partly into the pessimistic scenario, so are we partly into its optimistic counterpart. In recent conferences seeking to resolve the law of the sea, especially in the context of deep seabed mining of minerals, developing countries insisted upon an international regime that could distribute profits around the world. Industrialized countries, especially the United States, argue for a more free-enterprise approach, but deeper issues came increasingly close to the surface. It seemed implicitly understood, for example, that any organizational design which allows for any international regulation of deep seabed mining will lead, almost automatically, to international regulation of all such mineral production. If country A, for example, has the market for one of its primary resources threatened by the exploitation of that same resource in the seabed, then the international community must protect country A's economy by either direct subsidy to country A or by restricting the mining of that resource in the sea. We are getting close, that is to say, to comprehensive global management of production and distribution.

In the optimistic scenario, long-term survival of the planet and its inhabitants takes precedence over economic growth. Doubts about the effects of particular actions are resolved in favor of long-term, not short-term, considerations. This leads to abandonment of nuclear energy on grounds that the long-term dangers surrounding its use may even exceed the dangers associated with nuclear weapons. There being no way to assure political, organizational, and geological stability in the long-term management of nuclear waste materials, the world adjusts the operation of economic systems on that basis.

Given the assumptions of this scenario, the social institution of war becomes impossible to sustain, not only because we cannot afford to waste resources in that manner but also because once the concept of interdependence is operationalized, sovereignty and independence can have no meaning. While I label this scenario optimistic, the degree of social change needed to realize it is painful and frightening to most of us. Global agreements on the distribution of resources are likely to require a lowering of material living standards in the most industrialized countries. The management and, perhaps, reduction in world population is likely to profoundly alter, even possibly remove, the family as a basic social institution, in that the central function of procreation would be denied many families. The disappearance of the conventional definition of property seems, at first glance, to remove the most fundamental motivation for an individual to work, but, as some argue, the same phenomenon might enable us to experience work as something we do because we wish to do it, not merely because we must do it to survive. And, of course, the separation of work from income and the distribution of resources according to agreement leads to a major diminution in the functions of social hierarchies.

If the pessimistic scenario leads to some form of socialism, much more authoritarian than democratic, the optimistic scenario transcends all known forms of capitalist market systems and socialist planning systems. There is no way to suggest in detail how the political and organizational systems in such a world actually would function, beyond the impressionistic outline already attempted. The extent of the change can only be imagined, as by speculating on the nature of a presidential election campaign in which both candidates (assuming the conventional two-party U.S. system) were pledged to reduce the Gross National Product for the sake of planetary survival. It remains only to briefly summarize the likelihood of realizing each scenario.

THE APOCALYPTIC CHOICE

The combination of nuclear issues and limits to resources provides us with a choice between stark alternatives. The present international system, as extrapolated in the pessimistic scenario above, seems to lead inexorably to something approaching global destruction; if not from nuclear war, destruction may occur from thermal pollution, for example, as everyone pursues unlimited economic growth. The change inherent in the optimistic scenario, conversely, would be the first social transformation of such magnitude since the shift from hunting to agricultural societies (and the rise of urbanism) some 5,000 years ago. Even if the optimistic scenario is assumed the most desirable of the two, there remains the question of whether it can be achieved through relatively comfortable means or only after profound crisis and perhaps total destruction of the system we know.

Perhaps it is typical of the apocalyptic choice we face that the two scenarios share at least one major factor—the shift to modular, self-sufficient communities—and perhaps some associated implications are worth further exploration. It seems likely that self-sufficient communities, even if they remain attached to conventional nation-states, will not consent to being used as bargaining chips in international confrontations between their parent states and other states. By the same token, a largely self-sufficient community (we might even call it a "city-state") would have a decreasing need to blackmail any other community in an attempt to capture its resources. If a community did feel the need to ensure its own survival, it seems likely the community would insist on having its nuclear weapons under its control.

I conclude that whether one takes a pessimistic or an optimistic approach, we are fast approaching the demise of the nation-state as we know it. This leads me to suggest, perhaps only as a form of wishful thinking, that the optimistic scenario is the more likely outcome. The legitimation of interstate violence has been legitimized or constitutionalized only within our various approaches to international law, and these doctrines are vastly different from what many of us accept within a nation-state. It might require a massive constitutional change to legitimize the use of any weapons, in particular nuclear weapons, in what might be called "intercity war." Until the demise of the nation-state is widely recognized, therefore, it is likely to retain its status as the only social actor with legitimate authority to wage war on its contemporaries. By the time the demise is recognized, we may be sensible enough to avoid legitimizing the acquisition of nuclear weapons by individual communities.

If, over the short term, balanced proliferation seems preferable to what is happening now, balanced deproliferation seems even more important if the planet is to survive. Deproliferation is an issue that cannot be approached solely from a military perspective, in that it is just as important—perhaps even more important—to abandon nuclear energy as to abandon nuclear weapons. Balanced deproliferation requires, then, that groups of countries in direct conflict with each other must reach agreements to phase out both nuclear power plants and nuclear weapons. This is nowhere more important than in the case of the United States and USSR which, if the world is to survive, must soon move well beyond such relatively meaningless issues as strategic arms limitation.

Serious students of public policy have, for the most part, been trained to expect and prefer evolutionary, even incremental, approaches to policy-making. They often resent and reject any argument which seems based on apocalyptic choices, and they dislike agreeing with any proposal requiring a quantum leap into an uncharted future. Given that understandable reaction, it is enough to suggest for now only that we accept the complete intertwining of all nuclear issues. If we are serious about proliferation, surely we must recognize that we cannot deal separately with weapons and power plants. We are at a point where we cannot affort to permit the march of modern science to continue simply because we know the next step. If we cannot begin to reverse the trend, at least within the next decade, there can be little hope over the long term.

ANNALS, AAPSS, 430, March 1977

Decision Making in a Nuclear-Armed World

By MICHAEL BRENNER

ABSTRACT: Strategic analysis for the next generation promises to be preoccupied with the permutations and combinations of multi-player nuclear games. The spread of nuclear arms to several new states will appreciably complicate the efforts of the two superpowers to maintain a high level of stability in their bilateral relationship, while posing further challenges to military planning and crisis management. The new strategic environment will place an unprecedented burden on the capacity of the U.S. government to integrate the several facets of national security policy; to execute it in a consistent, coordinated manner; and to take swift, informed action in crisis situations. This is the case whether one speaks of programming force options to assure presidential control over operational use; making necessary reconciliations between Soviet-oriented military planning and the requirements for addressing third•country nuclear threats; or institutionalizing a closer cooperation with allies on such diverse issues as export regulations and concerted contingency plans. There are three key ingredients to any plan for achieving a greater degree of coordination in making and implementing strategic policy: technical competence must be combined with decisional authority; senior national security officials should share a fund of ideas about the preferred direction of policy and the effective means for conducting it; an interagency committee of principals is needed that serves as the prime instrument for making executive departments effective contributors to, and executors of, policy.

Michael Brenner is Associate Professor in the Graduate School of Public and International Affairs at the University of Pittsburgh. He presently is conducting a study, under a grant from the Ford Foundation, of United States government policy-making on issues of nuclear proliferation. His writings on national security and arms control include articles in World Politics, International Affairs, The Bulletin of Atomic Scientists, *and the* International Studies Quarterly.

SPECULATION about national security decision making in a world where nuclear arms have become common military currency can begin with two presuppositions. First, American policy will experience a profound failure—due in large measure to the weaknesses and inadequacies of a disjointed, segmental policy process. Second, thinking about nuclear strategy, military planning, and governmental procedures for formulating and conducting foreign policy will have to be significantly revised. Past tolerance of laissez-faire attitudes within the Executive branch would underscore the crucial need for a renovation of policy-making formats under the new, proliferated conditions that former practices have permitted. A further assumption is that those acculturated to the old system will resist reform of either the process or substance of U.S. national security policy in a nuclear-armed world.

The advent of nuclear weapons forced dramatic changes in conventional military doctrine, the statecraft that employs them as instruments of national power, and the means for their control. They have imparted a very special by-play to the normal procedures for managing weaponry—placing premiums on centralized command and instilling deeply conservative attitudes about crisis management and the operational utility of armaments. The terms of the bilateral strategic relationship between the United States and the Soviet Union, as it came to express the logic of nuclear stalemate and common interest, has been the principal concern of officials and analysts for a quarter-century.[1] Strategic analysis for the next generation promises to be preoccupied with the permutations and combinations of multi-player nuclear games and the exacerbated problems of achieving an equivalent level of nuclear stability.

An analytic excursion into the futuristic realm of nuclear decision making among 12, 15, or 20 nations runs the danger of being overwhelmed by the multitude of new considerations that will enter into the calculations of governments and by the complications of devising national strategies in an international environment populated by new military powers that transform political alliances and security systems. It is unavoidable that this brief article concentrates on a few of the issues raised by proliferation. The discussion will deal primarily with problems of military planning and crisis-management for the U.S. government at some unspecified date in the future when, as is conjectured, most of today's prospective powers would have acquired some substantial nuclear capability. The intensity of the effects noted, and the saliency of the policy questions presented, will

1. The adaptation of military doctrine and national security planning to the nuclear realities of a world with five powers is a necessary background to the discussion of decision making in a proliferated global environment.

Among the several works recounting the post-war nuclear diplomacy of the U.S. and USSR, two deserve special mention. George Quester, *Nuclear Diplomacy: The First Twenty-Five Years* (New York: Dunellen, 1970); Jerome Kahan, *Security in the Nuclear Age: Developing U.S. Strategic Arms Policy* (Washington, D.C.: The Brookings Institution, 1975).

There have been a number of perceptive accounts of modern strategy in the nuclear age. They include: *Problems of Modern Strategy, Part I* (IISS, Adelphi Paper No. 54, February 1969), contributions by Raymond Aron and Michael Howard; Richard Rosecrance, *Strategic Deterrence Reconsidered* (Adelphi Paper No. 116, spring 1975).

vary according to the scope and pace of proliferation. Other major powers will face analagous problems arising out of the new military and diplomatic circumstance, although they will be cast somewhat differently for each, and the range of available responses will also differ.

DECISION-MAKING ADAPTATIONS IN THE NEW ENVIRONMENT

Protecting deterrent stability

The overriding purpose of American and Soviet nuclear policy is, in Raymond Aron's words, "not in ruling together over the world . . . but in not destroying each other."[2] Tomorrow a principal concern will be to avoid being involved in a nuclear war not of their own making. Each makes enormous expenditures of fortune, technical skill, and diplomatic effort to safeguard itself against nuclear attack. Together, they have taken practical steps to reduce the hazards of misperceived intent or faulty communication. Their first priority in a world of proliferated nuclear arms will be devising measures to protect their common stake in nuclear stability against new menaces. Above all, that will entail: (1) reinforcing command and control mechanisms and (2) refining communications between the leadership of the two leading nuclear powers. The threat of attack from unforeseen, or unforeseeable directions, perhaps with no diplomatic or military forewarning, underscores the common need for precautionary action.

The impact on strategic decision making probably will take several forms:

Means will be sought to improve strategic intelligence and to monitor the origin and scope of any hypothetical attack on one of the superpowers or its allies—whether launched by missile, aircraft, or otherwise, the Defense Department already has given public indication that future threats beyond that posed by the Soviet Union warrant improvement in U.S. surveillance capabilities. As Secretary of Defense Donald Rumsfeld wrote in the *Annual Defense Department Report* (FY 1977), "the future threat posed by third countries, whether the Chinese or an emerging nuclear nation, requires a continued emphasis on surveillance and warning, together with R & D on light area defense."[3] Among the projects noted were the light CONUS bomber air defense, extension of the AWACS airborne surveillance system to allies abroad, as well as exploration of new interception techniques.

The appearance of nuclear threats from new sources is likely to give renewed impetus to research and development of an effective Ballistic Missile System. One of the arguments made by early advocates of BMD was the protection it could afford against a crude attack from a reckless government in possession of a rudimentary nuclear force. Of course, any proposal for deployment would run up against the prohibitions written into the Strategic Arms Limitation Talks (SALT) records and would require Soviet-American agreement on its revision—with the accompanying reopening of the debate over ABM's potential for destabilizing the stra-

2. Raymond Aron, *Peace and War* (New York: Doubleday & Company, 1966), p. 11.

3. Secretary of Defense, Donald H. Rumsfeld, *Annual Defense Department Report FY 1977* (Washington, D.C.: Government Printing Office, 1976), p. 59.

tegic balance between the superpowers.

The fear of an unprovoked attack by a reckless government or imperfectly controlled military establishment (undeterred by the retaliatory threat) might well also revive the idea of "launch on warning"—that is, programming U.S. ICBMs so that they could be launched upon receipt of signal from satellite surveillance or forward radar nets reporting what appears to be an incoming missile or salvo of missiles. The distaste that policy-makers have always felt about installing hair-trigger response mechanisms is due to its irrevocability—the fear that an unretrievable missile might be launched on inaccurate or incomplete information, or that the response was out of proportion to the actual attack. Launch-on-warning arrangements qualitatively change decision making in a fundamental way, insofar as they deny political authorities some portion of their discretionary authority to determine the character and magnitude of response to an attack. It introduces that element of automatism, the "Doomsday effect," that national leaders so deeply wish to avoid. Logically, there would be an interest in reconciling the desire for quick response with some measure of insurance against the loss of control—and, hence, incentives created for technical investigation of systems that would extend the time after launch during which an ICBM might be destroyed in flight.

As a practical matter, the logic of launch-on-warning itself might well be less pursuasive than some commentaries on the consequences of proliferation suggest. The principal problems raised by the existence of several possible attackers are:

1. how effectively to deter a host of variously motivated potential enemies under a variety of circumstances;
2. how to inform oneself of the source of an attack.

The capability to retaliate would seem to be the least vulnerable factor in the equation. It is knowing whom to retaliate against and preparing a response proportional to the threat (which might be a relatively small one) that are the truly vexing questions.

Whether or not serious thought is given launch-on-warning techniques, proliferation almost surely will provide a new spur to Soviet-American efforts at facilitating safe management of nuclear weapons. Accustomed to the relative security that gradually has come to characterize their bilateral nuclear dealings, they can only look with dread on the arrival of potentially disruptive new nuclear players. The paramount need will be to maintain crisis stability. More extensive and routine use of special communications links, the hotline, certainly would seem in order—with the necessary technical and administrative steps taken to ensure unimpaired communication. One innovation could involve installation of secondary lines between strategic command headquarters, to speed up the transfer and exchange of information that might indicate the source of an attack of uncertain origin.

A more far-reaching and radical innovation would be the creation of formal or quasi-formal arrangements for the pooling of intelligence in nonemergency as well as emergency situations. While each country surely will continue to conduct satellite surveillance and use other methods for collecting as much data as it could about the operational capabilities and strategic plans of third-nation nuclear forces (as no doubt both now do with regard to China, and the Soviets with regard to the United Kingdom and France), confidence would be increased to some immeasurable degree by the availability of corroborating or supplementary data. Moreover, a perceived threat from unofficial, terrorist groups liable to use unconventional means of delivery would create a strong incentive for pooling political intelligence—although here there might be appreciable differences in the weight accorded the problem by the two governments.

Agreement to coordinate intelligence activities, while exceptional, does follow the logic of earlier joint efforts at corking the nuclear genie. Making the necessary adjustments in organizational procedures, intra-governmentally, could prove a more formidable obstacle. All bureaucracies guard their unique mission and are jealous of sharing their privileged information. Government intelligence agencies feel most strongly on this score. It probably would require a clear presidential mandate firmly stating the U.S. national interest of treating with the enemy on those sensitive matters, assiduously enforced, to set the process in motion. Equally strenuous follow-up by representatives of the White House staff or Foreign Intelligence Board would probably be in order to assure active compliance with the directive. This innovation, as with most of the decision-making changes called for by the new condition of generalized proliferation, would place premiums on the interagency coordination and highlight the importance of devising the means for coherent, logically consistent policy making.

Strain conflicts

Certain aspects of proliferation emphasize the parallelism of Soviet and American interests and point toward a further concertation of their nuclear policies. Others will place strains on superpower condominium that could jeopardize the stability of their carefully nurtured strategic modus vivendi. Probably the most disruptive consequences would flow from the perceived need to plan for multiple contingencies against an array of possible opponents. In particular, impetus will be given to programs for improving the accuracy of delivery systems and enhancing their targeting flexibility.

Secretary Schlesinger's public announcement in January 1974 of plans to revise the United States' Single Integrated Operations Plan (SIOP) "to ensure that American policy-makers had [options] for the discriminate and controlled use of nuclear weapons" is accompanied by the revival of counterforce doctrines that envisage nuclear exchanges with the USSR of varying scope, intensity, and duration.[4] All these scenarios share the conceptual premise that it is possible and in some instances is desirable for the United States to prepare to fight a nuclear war to determine a victor and loser. The direction of present official thinking and policies is summarized in the following paragraph from the 1977 Posture Statement.

4. Paraphrased by Lynn Etheridge Davis in *Limited Nuclear Options, Deterrence and the New American Doctrine* (London: IISS, Adelphi Paper No. 122, winter 1975/76), p. 1.

The most explicit statement of Dr. Schles-

> At the same time, selected portions of our offensive forces are acquiring the flexibility to respond to more discriminating attacks. Not only is our inventory of preplanned options increasing; we are acquiring the retargeting and command-control capabilities to respond rapidly to unforeseen events. No hostile and reckless power can assume that our hands will be tied because our only choices in response to a limited nuclear attack are inactivity or the holocaust. More appropriate options now exist. We propose to go on refining them—and making systems improvements such as increased accuracy—so as to ensure that any attack can be met by a deliberate and credible response.[5]

Arguments for developing a more diverse array of more accurate weapons, programmed to cover a wide range of readily adjustable targets, gain new credence in a nuclearized world. The number of potential targets increases markedly as those in new nuclear countries are added to sites in the Soviet Union and China accorded some measure of priority. Accuracy, prized because it allows enemy military targets (especially ICBM silos) to be attacked with negligible civilian damage, thus presumably lowering the odds on a massive retaliation, acquires a new attraction since it permits (*a*) a preemptive attack against the nuclear forces of a minor power that gives indication of preparing a first strike; or (*b*) retaliation in honor of a pledge, unilaterally or jointly given, to a non-nuclear nation (for example, as in exchange for adherence to the Non-Proliferation Treaty) that then becomes the victim of a nuclear attack or threat by a belligerent neighbor. Flexibility in targeting, of course, simplifies the task of shifting available forces from one mission to another.

A commitment to achieving higher levels of accuracy, flexibility, and diversity implies specific policies on weapons development and deployment, strategic doctrine, and approaches to extending limitations on offensive weapons in phase two of SALT with the USSR. This is not the place to tackle the controversial and very significant issues that have been introduced by the renewed emphasis in American policy on counterforce concepts and weaponry.

The point to be emphasized with reference to proliferation is that, with the arrival on the nuclear stage of new actors, the decision-making process within the U.S. government will be biased in favor of proceeding with those programs and policies keyed to counterforce objectives. This holds true on weapon systems: MARV (Maneuverable Re-entry Vehicle), the new generation of ICBM (the "MX"); on doctrine: the emphasis on targeting military sites in a counterforce mode; and on arms control bargaining strategies, that is, fighting shy of any restrictions on qualitative improvements, ascribing military virtues to cruise missiles, resisting a lowering of the threshold on underground nuclear tests. In sum, the proliferation factor could well shift the burden of proof in intramural debates strongly against the arms-control advocates, making the success of their position all the more dependent on active political

---

inger's own views, which now permeate much of the U.S. defense establishment, is in J. R. Schlesinger, "US-USSR Strategic Policies," hearing before the Subcommittee on Arms Control, International Law and Organization of the Committee on Foreign Relations, U.S. Senate, 4 March 1974 (Washington, D.C.: Government Printing Office, 1974), pp. 1–17.

5. Rumsfeld, *Annual Defense Department Report*, p. 14.

intervention by the White House. (We should also be reminded that a not dissimilar process probably will be occurring within the Kremlin, hardening positions on their side.)

Projecting strategic images

A collateral result of orienting contingency plans toward minor nuclear powers in an inherently unstable strategic environment would be to give new prominence, and support, to war fighting scenarios—with possibly unfortunate side-effects on Soviet-American perceptions of threat and deterrent credibility. The two spheres of strategic planning cannot readily be kept in idea-tight intellectual compartments.

The projection of strategic images is not so refined an art, nor statesman so adept practitioners of it, for there to be a realistic hope that thinking and preparation for preemptive and/or counterforce attacks by the United States or USSR against a minor nuclear power would not color attitudes about the possible uses to which their nuclear forces might be put against each other. To a very substantial degree, nuclear doctrines and plans are guided by a desire to project certain conceptions, attitudes, ideas—about objectives, capabilities, and tolerances—and expectations. If two quite different and perhaps divergent sets of images are being conveyed, there are the ever-present dangers of (*a*) tangled communications, and (*b*) introducing force structures and procedures that are appropriate in one case, but seriously disruptive in the other.

Calculated image manipulation, always a skill whose subtlety tends to elude governments, demands truly virtuoso talent under these new conditions. To those governments who are wavering on the nuclear brink, the United States will emphasize the inutility of the weapon and the formidable technical and economic costs of establishing a credible deterrent. Yet to the government that has built a relatively small number of weapons, and has an unsophisticated delivery system, the preferred message is just the opposite: that is, what you have is enough for your purposes (especially where there is no obvious, nuclear-armed antagonist in mind with a disproportionately larger force—the unstable asymmetrical relationship); nuclear status is not a function of numbers; deterrence is a flexible concept and countries will be inhibited about attacking any nuclear-armed state—however elementary its retaliatory forces. The risk is that counsel intended for the ears of country B will be overheard by country A.

Somewhere along the way, a loss of doctrinal credibility is unavoidable. Public action and statements will either have to be drawn from a clearer pool of strategic concepts—with a resulting loss of diplomatic flexibility—or a truly diabolical cunning achieved in the recondite art of confecting and manipulating ideas about the ends and means of nuclear military power.

Targeting and force planning

The accentuated interest in nuclear war fighting, along with the imperative to scrutinize all facets of strategic doctrine and force planning, will increase the pressure on the president and his appointed deputies to become directly involved in drawing nuclear options and in SIOP's (and tactical nuclear weapon) programming. One of the more slowly emerging truths about American nuclear strategy since World War II is that actual control over targeting and the design of operational plans has lain with the military services. To put the matter bluntly, the orientation and format of the system produced has been largely impervious to shifts and turns in the official doctrines promulgated by presidents and secretaries of defense. Operational planning and weapons technology have moved along one set of tracks, political-military strategy along another—at times parallel, at times divergent, and only on rare occasions in tandem. There are three fundamental organizational and policy problems that will have to be confronted in an attempt to make targeting decisions and contingency plans more in tune with centrally conceived diplomatic and military strategy. (The proposals we make for reform of decision-making structures in the next section will address the issues they highlight.)

1. The competence for formulating realistic scenarios encompassing the several possible uses of nuclear weapons is dispersed in bureaus and departments throughout government. Yet to bring their opinions to bear on targeting and operational planning decisions means opening up an ultrasensitive area that has been an exclusive military preserve. Just to suggest such an innovation raises a host of security problems, not to speak of questions of bureaucratic prerogative or the challenge of fashioning an efficient, manageable arrangement for giving civilians a say in, if not ultimate control over, nuclear options.[6]

2. Targeting and planning issues are inseparable from (*a*) the military research and development program; and (*b*) deployment decisions. A more active role for the president and his civilian advisers in the former field would have two far-reaching consequences. First, it would place a burden on the White House staff and Pentagon civilians that they never have borne successfully in the past—requiring that knowledgeable, intelligent judgments be made at far earlier stages in the process of technical innovation and exploitation than they are now. Second, it would vastly increase their leverage on the entire process wherein the need, desirability, design, and cost-effectiveness of new weapons systems are largely determined.

3. Procedures for crisis management of nuclear weapons will also be complicated in a world where nuclear weapons are widely proliferated. Present formats and communication systems were designed with a certain picture in mind of what the situation would be like. The enemy would be the USSR (conceivably China); the circumstances a grave international crisis; the constellation of forces well understood; the options relatively limited. By contrast, a crisis involving a minor nuclear power, or powers, with numerous and not easily separable ramifications for the Soviet-American or Sino-American nuclear connection, creates a definitely more ambiguous and fluid situation where the chances of miscalculations and mistakes are commensurately greater. What setup would make most effective use of

6. The practical problems of reforming the present military-controlled procedures for SIOP's programming are given informed, perceptive analysis by Davis, *Limited Nuclear Options*, pp. 17–18.

the specialists in nuclear planning, the country or regime experts, as well as cabinet officials, the joint chiefs, and presidential advisers? How do you reasonably prepare for so many contingencies while avoiding both over-formalized planning and ad hoc crisis consultation?

DECISION-MAKING STRUCTURES

There has been one recurrent theme in our sketch of the medley of policy problems created for U.S. government decision-makers by the proliferation of nuclear weapons—the unprecedented challenge to our capacity to plan coherent policies; to execute them in a consistent, coordinated manner; and to take swift, informed action in crisis situations. Conditions in a nuclearized world will be less forgiving of policy disjunction than in the past whether one speaks of programming nuclear options and assuring presidential control over operational use; making the necessary reconciliations between Soviet-oriented military planning (and arms control objectives), and the requirements for addressing third-country nuclear threats; synchronizing regulations (unilateral or multilateral) governing the export of nuclear and related technologies with diplomatic strategies; or institutionalizing a closer cooperation with allies on issues ranging from crisis management to commercial policies. Certainly, the erratic performance of government agencies in recent years while the genie of nuclear proliferation elusively slipped through the groping fingers of policy-makers underscores the dangers of segmental policy making. It calls for an overhaul of existing procedures, such as they are, for interdepartmental coordination.

At the risk of gross oversimplification, there appear four basic functions for which the present organizational setup is inadequate:[7]

1. to integrate systematically the several facets of strategic policy arising from the complex interplay among major and minor nuclear powers;
2. to bring political considerations to bear more directly on military planning and weapons development programs;
3. to manage crises that hold the potential for nuclear exchanges;
4. to coordinate diplomatic strategies and military planning with allies in NATO (and with Japan).

The case for policy integration and consistent implementation is as easy to make as reform is difficult. Getting on top of the foreign and defense bureaucracies has been the elusive goal of every post-war administration; success, where achieved, has been episodic or ephemeral.

The most conscientious and successful attempt has been the national security system installed by Henry Kissinger under President Nixon. The Kissinger format has had worthy objectives and many virtues that should be incorporated into any structural arrangements designed to favor coherent policy making based on a well-defined set of ideas. It created pressures on the bureaucracies to focus on issues as stated and formu-

7. This is an exercise in speculative assessment of decision making in a hypothetical future that already has seen widespread diffusion of nuclear weapons. If we were writing about today's world, the main emphasis would be on what has to be done to contain proliferation, especially the wedding of economic policies and technology transfer to political purposes.

lated by the president and his chief foreign policy assistant; it effectively centralized decision making; and it sought to establish the connection between immediate problems and longer-term considerations. Its weaknesses have been equally manifest, and much commented upon:

1. The task of policy planning has been gradually squeezed out by a deepening involvement in operational matters.
2. The secretariat function of developing options and structuring choices has been in conflict with the National Security Advisor's role as advocate, and later principal formulator, of policy.
3. It failed to devise a strategy for making the bureaucracy a willing and effective instrument for implementing foreign and defense policy.[8]

Whatever one's personal scorecard of the National Security Council's (NSC) performance under Dr. Kissinger, some version of the NSC format is the most suitable model for organizing the decision-making process in the future, whether the deliberation is in the council itself or elsewhere. What follows are a few ideas on how it might be adapted to perform the four functions listed above.

A. I begin with the conviction that a high level of centralization is necessary, desirable, and possible. Alternative arrangements that stress decentralization and overlapping jurisdictions have in the past demonstrated glaring deficiencies that would be all too apparent, and dangerous, in the more demanding environment of a nuclearized world. Compartmentalization of responsibility and specialization of role, as with the military's independent determination of targeting objectives and force programming, would be unacceptable to a president and cabinet who want to integrate military plans with the diplomacy of nuclear crisis management. Policy making as an interminable group-grope—where ends as well as means are in a constant state of negotiation among bureaucratic baronies—is as unavailing of intelligent policy as it is inefficient in performance.

B. The trick is to achieve a coherent design and coordinated effort, on the one hand, while, on the other, benefiting in the shaping of policy from wide participation by agencies with specialized competences, a participation that both encourages a hearing for diverse views and favors informed, flexible implementation. Execution of centrally-plotted policy certainly would suffer if there were no prior consultation with area experts who could best evaluate approaches aimed at influencing the national and personal sensitivities of a government considering use of its small nuclear arsenal or if Washington denied itself well-prepared communication with officials on the spot during such a crisis.

C. At first look, the NSC seems the proper forum through which to prepare major policy choices, to deliberate on them, and to draw the guidelines for policy. It stands closest to the president and is relatively unencumbered by the rigid organizational structures and entrenched preferences of the State

8. Among the more insightful critiques of Kissinger's NSC system are: I. M. Destler, *Pesidents, Bureaucrats and Foreign Policy* (Princeton, N.J.: Princeton University Press, 1972). Also, John P. Leacacos, "The Nixon NSC: Kissinger's Apparat," *Foreign Policy*, no. 5 (1971).

Department, Pentagon, CIA, and the other foreign policy bureaucracies. Successive post-war presidents have found it a convenient instrument for exercising a measure of control over national security policy and programs and leverage on intramural policy debates.

The NSC approach, though, has been perhaps too convenient. Reliance on a personal national security advisor—and his small, loyal staff—has served as an avoidance device that releases the chief executive from his responsibility to get a handle on recalcitrant agencies whose outlook and performance were often self-serving and inefficient. The effort to expedite communication and improve coordination between the White House and the departments of government has reduced the incentive for department heads to make their agencies effective contributors to, and executors of, policy. The failure to build organizational strength down through the executive departments limits the capacity of the United States to attend to several major issues simultaneously, leaves important sources of competence and expertise untapped, and makes the successful conduct of policy and its coordination excessively dependent on the stamina and virtuosity of a few individuals.

Without pretending to offer a blueprint for recasting the U.S. national security apparatus, or specifying exact formats, a number of conditions can be identified that must be met if we are to have the capacity to fulfill the policy obligations discussed above:

First, the technical competence of central policy-making bodies must be enhanced. Under Dr. Kissinger, the NSC did not have the expertise to pass judgment on such matters as the dissemination of nuclear reactor and fuel processing technology. In other spheres, it had to fight strenuously to pry out of the Pentagon critical data about weapons performance and targeting. Technical information, and the competence to evaluate it, must be brought to where the decisional responsibility is.

Second, it is essential that there be a clarification and delineation of responsibilities between the national security adviser and department secretaries. The NSC is best suited to serve two key roles. First, it must act as the agent of the president in structuring the policy debate (and, in exceptional instances, mediating conflicting agency views—especially at the implementation stage). Second, it could do the intellectual side of the planning function, that is, projecting current analyses, plotting linkages, mapping strategies. The former task is a natural for the NSC as part of the executive office of the president. The latter might well be passed to the State Department's renascent Policy Planning Office, which has been instrumental in forcing attention onto the connections between exports of nuclear facilities and fuels and arms control considerations. Most important, the NSC should be relieved of operational responsibilities and the diplomatic action left to others.

Third, organizational structure per se makes little difference unless there is the conviction to make it work. Policy coherence ultimately depends on high-level officials, backed and inspired by the president, who share a fund of ideas about the preferred direction of policy and the effective means for conducting it. Diverse perspective and multiple advocacy have their virtues. But clashes over fundamentals and failure to settle basic disputes over policy premises and objectives extract a high price in internal dissonance.[9]

It is hard to see how anything remotely resembling a coherent policy could emanate from an administration where basic conflicts would exist between the secretaries of state and defense over whether, for example, it was in the American interest for country X on the Soviet border to acquire a Y-level nuclear capability. On the other hand, it is easy to see how circuits could be crossed (as they are today) so that approval is given for the export of a sophisticated nuclear or launcher technology contrary to the preferences of the State Department.

From 1974 through 1976, the Working Group on Proliferation of the NSC's Verification Panel served as the clearinghouse for the administration's preparations on the NPT Review Conference and subsequent matters pertaining to the spread of nuclear weapons generally. In the view of many participants, though, its performance has been inconsistent and it never has succeeded in establishing itself as the vehicle for making and overseeing execution of administration policy.[10]

Reconstituted as a cabinet committee, however, and retitled to indicate a wider range of responsibility (Committee on Nuclear Programs is one properly innocuous name), such a body could serve as the president's steering committee on principal matters nuclear. Chaired personally by the president, or in his absence by the national security adviser (accorded cabinet rank to obey diplomatic etiquette), its membership would be composed of the heads of the major departments and agencies. The committee should be backstopped by a Committee of Deputies (under and deputy secretaries) to provide for administrative follow-through. Staff of the National Security Council would provide the secretariat services of scheduling, agenda preparation, and coordinating interagency communication.

The committee would be the instrument through which: (*a*) senior officials would join in drawing the outline of national policies on strategic needs, military planning, and political initiatives; (*b*) issues of current importance would be brought to decision; and, periodically, (*c*) the execution of agreed policies and programs would be critically evaluated. Thus, the responsibility for substantive policy direction would shift from the national security adviser to the department secretaries and agency directors acting collectively under presidential direction.

It follows logically that the com-

9. The cost of disjunction is high. The Nixon-Ford administration's inability to decide, and make stick, its judgment as to whether the logic of rough equivalence (as expressed in SALT) or more subtle counterforce conceptions were to serve as reference for U.S. defense planning has produced contradictory policies and has frustrated the completion of a second round agreement.

10. In good part, the VP-WGP's activities were supplanted by an informal network of younger, middle-level officials in ERDA, Policy Planning and Political Military Affairs in State, and elsewhere. The shortcomings of devolving policy planning and instigation onto such an unstructured group are obvious: its lack of decision-making authority, its impermanency, and its inadequacy as a vehicle for implementation when it succeeds in winning approval for any collective proposal emanating from it.

mittee also should be the prime mechanism for decision making in crisis situations—being best qualified to provide the president with pertinent information and to appraise contingency plans. Policy direction and crisis-management are, though, two distinct if not separable activities. For both, expert staff support is critical, our fourth condition of effective reform of nuclear policy-making institutions.

Particular attention should be given to creating a staff planning group for the proposed Committee on Nuclear Programs (located for convenience within the NSC apparatus), whose prime task would be to prepare contingency plans for all emergency situations involving the use or threatened use of nuclear weapons—whether the protagonists be hostile or friendly, major or minor nuclear states. A Cabinet Committee on Terrorism, chaired by an assistant to the secretary of state, already is in existence. Its jurisdiction covers actions by unofficial groups involving nuclear or non-nuclear threats. Planning analyses could be conducted, under the administrative direction of the national security adviser, by a select group of council officials combining technical, political, and communications talents. It is preferable that they should be selected from agencies such as the State Department's Bureau of Political-Military Affairs; the Secretary of Defense's Offices of Atomic Energy Intelligence, International Security Affairs, and Net Assessments; the Program Analyses Office of the NSC; Arms Control and Disarmament Agency's (ACDA) Non-Proliferation and Advanced Technology Bureau; and the CIA. The advantage of having a high-powered staff drawn from, but organizationally separate from, the executive departments is that it could not be identified with any one agency and its status jeopardized by the shifting currents of bureaucratic politics and the personal fortunes of that body's director.

Two points regarding the staff's work should be emphasized: (1) there should be absolutely no restriction on their access to military or diplomatic information; (2) their plans should be periodically discussed and assessed by the parent working group, to ensure that the work does not degenerate into sterile paper exercises and that the agencies are in an informed position to meet the requirements for implementing the plans that are drafted.

Clearly, a principal aspect of the planning group's work will be to elaborate scenarios for the use of nuclear weapons under a variety of circumstances. For their analyses to be of practical utility, they should be done in conjunction with the targeting planning of the joint chiefs of staff and incorporated in the SIOP. It is to be expected that the military will fight any proposal to relinquish their control over the actual programming—for reasons of both organizational integrity and concern for secrecy. A president convinced of the value of the organizational reform, as outlined here, can take two tacks to assuage the military's anxieties. First, he can affirm his prerogative as commander-in-chief and declare the essential importance of bringing political judgments to bear on military plans that directly affect his power to provide for the national security in a crisis. Second, he can address the secrecy problem and the valid concern that the process for making targeting decisions may get out of hand by stressing the smallness of the special NSC group and by exercising scrupulous care in choosing people of the greatest probity and highest caliber.

D. Innovations would also be called for in present arrangements for consultation and collaboration with allies. The multiple uncertainties attendant upon nuclear proliferation, the greater plausibility given war-fighting scenarios, the reviving of doubts about the credibility of the American deterrent and defense pledges, and joint participation in what, hopefully, will be a permanent Suppliers Club to utilize whatever control remains on the dissemination of nuclear technologies—all will place strains on the U.S. alliance with Western Europe and Japan.

Many of the problems that arise can best be dealt with through bilateral diplomacy, informal discussions, and quiet understandings, for example, common political strategies to be taken vis-à-vis a prospective nuclear power, and how to dampen the interest in nuclear weapons shown by a non-nuclear member of the alliance. Others appropriately should be considered and acted on in established regional and international forums, for example, the Suppliers Club's implementing guidelines governing the provision of nuclear fuels, the technology presumably having already been widely diffused, and the possibility that the International Atomic Energy Agency might monitor multilateral arms control agreements which restrict weapons deployments. However, a category of issues remains to be handled within the alliance, and it requires a regular consultative mechanism.

Two types of problems stand out. The first concerns the sorts of targeting and contingency planning questions we discussed in the American policy context. They will also pose dilemmas for intra-alliance coordination. The Nuclear Planning Group (NPG) now exists for the explicit purpose of assuring that our allies have a voice in military planning, in coordinating the deployment and possible use of the three national nuclear forces, and in providing easy communication in crisis situations. What will be in order in the future is a thorough review of the present arrangement, with a critical look at the effectiveness of NPG procedures and plans for the contingencies of a post-proliferation world. Serious thought also should be given to the creation of an analogous consultative body with the Japanese.

The alliance is less well prepared to address the political and diplomatic challenge of managing the volatile affairs of an international system in which nuclear arms have become widely distributed. Influencing the spread of weapons, moderating regional conflicts in adjacent areas between new nuclear powers, shaping imaginative arms control proposals, the several tasks aimed at preventing a lowering of nuclear thresholds around the world, would be the common responsibility of all the alliance members and cannot be effectively dispensed by the United States alone. We assume that the strains of a proliferated world will not produce a siege mentality and inward-looking American policies. Certainly, success in handling these problems is impossible when allies act at cross-purposes, intentionally or inadvertently.

The need is for a political counterpart to the NPG, a Political Policy Group (PPG). It would be a permanent body, capable of sustained effort, one that does not smack of a political directorate, and one that has the expressed mandate to handle the politico-military problems arising from nuclear proliferation. The model might well be the NPG, with a different mix of competences, with greater stress on the coordination of active diplomatic strategies. A Political Policy Group, unlikely in itself to create unity out of diverse interests and opinions or to resolve the problems that will be placed in its care, nonetheless would be an essential means of extending into the alliance the hoped for logic and coherence of U.S. decision making that will be a requisite for survival in the future.

ANNALS, AAPSS, 430, March 1977

The United States in a World of Nuclear Powers

By MICHAEL NACHT

ABSTRACT: There is little consistency in American policy toward those states that have obtained independent nuclear weapons capabilities. Bilateral relations between the United States and the new nuclear state prior to weapons acquisition have proven to be far more accurate indicators of future trends in U.S. policy than the acquisition by the state of nuclear weapons per se. In the future, five basic options confront the United States: malign neglect, nuclear realignment, confrontation politics, equality promotion, and adaptive continuity. The last option, which involves the implementation of a variety of political-military and energy-related strategies, is the most likely one to be adopted. Major shocks to the international system, however, will drive the United States toward greater use of sanctions against the new nuclear states.

Dr. Michael Nacht is Assistant Director of the Program for Science and International Affairs and Lecturer on Government at Harvard University. He is also co-editor of the quarterly journal International Security *and is a continuing consultant to the Ford Foundation in international security affairs and arms control. His research interests include Soviet-American relations, the role of nuclear weapons in world politics, and the broad security objectives of American foreign policy, and his articles on these subjects have appeared in* Foreign Affairs, Foreign Policy, *and other professional journals.*

WHAT courses are open to the United States as nuclear weapons spread? Which strategies will be adopted to try to control this spread? What will be the effect of nuclear proliferation on alliance relationships and on United States policy toward potential adversaries? These questions are not new, for concern about the spread of nuclear weapons to other nations has been strongly evident in America since the end of World War II. While the intensity of this concern has grown appreciably since the Indian explosion of May 1974, over the years it has varied considerably with circumstances and has led to the adoption of markedly different policies.

The acquisition of the bomb by the Soviet Union confirmed the view that Soviet military power posed the greatest threat to America's well-being in the postwar period, validated the policy of containment that had been operational for more than two years, and stimulated an already substantial nuclear weapons program in the United States. Efforts by two of America's traditional allies—Britain and France—to acquire nuclear weapons produced quite different reactions. In the case of Great Britain, American nuclear assistance, which had been provided since the late 1940s and was stepped up with amendments to the McMahon Act in 1954, subsequently included classified information on bomb development and fabrication and a complete nuclear submarine propulsion plant with sufficient enriched uranium to fuel the plant for 10 years. This assistance was crucial to the development of the British nuclear force. By contrast, the United States attempted to persuade the French to forgo the nuclear option, refused to provide assistance to their nuclear weapons program, and later failed to co-opt the French nuclear force into the military framework of the North Atlantic Treaty Organization (NATO).

The spread of nuclear weapons to Asia has only marginally affected American policy toward the nuclear states in the region. China's acquisition of nuclear weapons led the United States to overestimate temporarily the military strength and technological sophistication of the People's Republic, and it was the potential of the Chinese to deliver nuclear warheads at intercontinental ranges that was used as a rationale by the Johnson administration to support the case for the deployment of the Sentinel anti-ballistic missile system. But, by and large, the American policy toward China that was formulated immediately after Mao's revolutionary victory did not change with the Chinese nuclear detonation in October 1964, and the subsequent opening to China that did come under President Nixon cannot be interpreted as having been strongly influenced by Chinese nuclear capability.

With respect to India, American influence declined precipitously after the United States sided with Pakistan in the 1971 India-Pakistan war. The Indian detonation of a peaceful nuclear explosion left this situation virtually unchanged, although it did prompt Secretary of State Kissinger to make his first official visit to New Delhi in an attempt to improve relations. But the United States has neither achieved this objective nor taken the opposite stance of adopting economic or political sanctions against India, as Canada has done, to punish the Indians for their nuclear transgression.

In sum, there is little consistency in American policy toward those states that have obtained independent nuclear weapons capabilities. Bilateral relations between the United States and the new nuclear state prior to weapons acquisition, which were in turn based upon a complex set of political, economic, military, and historical considerations, have proven to be far more accurate indicators of future trends in U.S. policy than the acquisition by the state of nuclear weapons per se.

Will this pattern continue if a large number of new nuclear states emerge, or will nuclear proliferation on a wide scale so transform the international system as to invalidate any inferences drawn from the past about U.S. policy that are applied to the future? No one knows with certainty. But it seems that as the pressures for and the actuality of nuclear proliferation increase, the United States will be forced to choose among a number of basic options in adapting to a world of nuclear powers.

THE BASIC OPTIONS

One option open to the United States is that of malign neglect. America could permit nuclear proliferation to proceed without attempting to use its considerable political and economic influence to slow the process. It could, to a very great extent, withdraw from the international arena, passively witness the dissolution of its structure of alliances, and remain deliberately aloof from nuclear and non-nuclear conflicts among other nations. It could turn inward, concentrating instead on the maintenance of its massive military arsenal for deterrence purposes while building an elaborate array of air and ballistic-missile defenses to protect itself as well as possible from a nuclear attack on its continental homeland.

There is virtually no prospect of this option being adopted, however. Despite the extraordinarily painful experience in Vietnam, the United States—its government and its people—has remained fundamentally internationalist, though perhaps no longer interventionist, in its approach to world affairs. The sense of the United States as a superpower continues to be the dominant perception, not only of the vast majority of Americans, but of most of the peoples and governments around the globe as well. With this perception of America's status, there is, at least implicitly, a set of concomitant rights and responsibilities which the United States is expected to exercise. As the most powerful military nation of the Western democracies, it is looked upon as the principal counterweight to the expansion of Soviet influence. The strength of the American domestic economy, its extraordinary technological sophistication, and its pervasive international reach necessarily involve the United States in a web of interdependent political and economic relationships with scores of nations whose governments, their rhetoric notwithstanding, seek such relationships. And even states that have often viewed themselves as potential adversaries of the United States—China, some of the socialist states of Eastern Europe, a number of Arab nations—have, in their own national interests, argued against American retrenchment and sought American diplomatic assistance. Consequently, there are no significant voices in the United States or abroad which are likely to persuade America to adopt the option of malign neglect.

A second option for the United States would be to promote nuclear realignment. This would involve a conscious and overt American effort to scrap its existing security arrangements in favor of creating a ruling elite composed of the nuclear-weapons states. Since it is already the case that every permanent member of the United Nations Security Council is a nuclear "have" nation, there is precedent for such an approach. The aim of this realignment would be to formalize what is an implicit fact in world affairs: nuclear weapons are significant and they automatically elevate the status of those states that possess them. By accentuating the differences between the nuclear haves and the nuclear have nots, a commonality of interests would be fostered among the nuclear nations, thereby reducing the likelihood of interstate conflict among the nuclear powers. Indeed, since its nuclear explosion, India has at times conveyed the impression that it was due certain privileges now that it had entered the nuclear club. By granting such privileges and underscoring the nuclear/non-nuclear distinction, the United States could promote the idea that the nuclear badge had become the lone symbol of the powerful in international politics. Over time this condition could, ironically, impose order on rather than create chaos within the international system.[1]

This option, however, has little to recommend it. As a consequence of the deep political divisions among the nuclear powers, a compact among them would be extremely fragile at best, and they would be almost certainly incapable of adopting a coordinated policy to halt the spread of nuclear weapons. On the contrary, promoting the status of nuclear weapons in this way would surely encourage nuclear proliferation rather than deter it, placing in many hands the ability to initiate nuclear war. The result would be large numbers of vulnerable forces with inadequate command and control systems, subject to seizure by national and subnational groups. Preemptive strikes would be more likely. An increase in regional conflicts initiated by nuclear powers against non-nuclear neighbors could be anticipated. And because the superpower rivalry would not be muted, there would be a substantial probability that in regional conflict situations the Soviet Union and the United States would support opposing parties, thereby running the risk of frequent nuclear confrontations. American security interests would therefore not be at all well served by a realignment of nations that underscored the primacy of nuclear weapons.

A third option is to adopt a policy of confrontation politics. In many ways, this would be the opposite of the second option. Rather than

1. This notion of nuclear realignment providing international stability is a variation of the concept of a unit veto system in which it was hypothesized that the possession of nuclear weapons by all nations would promote a condition in which each state could successfully deter an attack upon its homeland initiated by any other state. See Morton Kaplan, *System and Process in International Politics* (New York: John Wiley and Sons, Inc., 1957), pp. 50–2, and his more recent thoughts on the subject, Morton Kaplan, "The Unit Veto System Reconsidered," in Richard Rosecrance, ed., *The Future of the International Strategic System* (San Francisco: Chandler Publishing Company, 1972), pp. 49–55.

promoting the elite status of the nuclear states, and thereby encouraging proliferation and instability, the United States, acting either alone or in concert with the Soviet Union, could behave as a nuclear bully, imposing or threatening to impose severe sanctions against any state that either appeared intent on acquiring nuclear weapons or had in fact done so. The range of sanctions could be quite extensive: the severing of diplomatic relations, the cancellation of trade and assistance agreements, the provision of nuclear weapons to the regional rivals of new nuclear states, and "surgical strikes" against the new nuclear facilities and associated delivery vehicles. This option would amount to the overt use of United States political, economic, and military power to prevent near-nuclear states from crossing the nuclear threshold.

The likelihood that this approach will be adopted, except in rare instances, is remote. The will of the Executive branch to utilize confrontation politics and perhaps military force in order to stem nuclear proliferation in regions distant from those areas widely regarded as bearing quite directly on U.S. national security interests (that is, Western Europe, Israel, and Japan) is not very great. The Vietnam experience, applicable or not, would likely be invoked, and the support for such actions in Congress and among the American electorate is unlikely to be forthcoming; opposition and denunciation is the far more probable reaction. Moreover, threats of coercion, if proved not to be credible, would be counterproductive in that they would reveal the weakness of U.S. non-proliferation policy. There is, in addition, the problem of applying the policy in a consistent and even-handed way. Would the United States be willing to implement the same sanctions against both a nuclear Israel that felt threatened with annihilation and a nuclear Iran that had acquired these weapons as part of an overall policy to seek hegemonial control over the Persian Gulf states? Hardly. To determine a set of sanctions that would be appropriate in all cases to the perceived threat while commanding both domestic and international support would be enormously difficult. As a consequence, this option is unlikely to be the principal path taken by the United States to cope with nuclear proliferation.[2]

A fourth option might be termed equality promotion. Many students of the nuclear proliferation problem believe that its underlying cause rests in the fundamental inequality among states—inequality in economic, political, and military terms particularly between the rich states of the north and the poor states of the south. This much-discussed gap between north and south must be narrowed, it is argued, if the incentives to acquire nuclear weapons are to diminish. To tackle the problem from this vantage point would place great demands on the United States. As the world's foremost economic power, the United States

2. This is not to imply that sanctions would have no place in American non-proliferation policy. The ability of the United States to pressure South Korea in 1976 to terminate its contract with France for a chemical reprocessing plant indicates that confrontation politics can be applied and can be successful. This is particularly true in situations in which the United States has substantial economic and military investments that it could credibly threaten to withdraw. But the thrust of the argument is that such situations are not numerous and that, consequently, confrontation politics cannot dominate U.S. policy.

would be called upon to lead the way in redressing the imbalance between north and south. This might mean a return to the massive American foreign aid programs of the 1950s and 1960s, transfers of whole industrial plants, infusion of high-technology products including advanced digital computers, the establishment of management training programs and other educational curricula from preschool through graduate studies—all this to scores of nations in an effort to stimulate economic and social development in much of the Third World.

These efforts would need to be supplemented, in many instances, by military assistance. A large number of nations would seek to obtain modern, sophisticated conventional arms of the quantity and quality that, in recent years, the United States has sold to Iran and Israel, and they would not have the funds to pay for them. At the same time, the United States would have to reduce significantly its nuclear arsenal, either unilaterally or through joint negotiations with the Soviet Union. Reductions in the number of delivery vehicles and nuclear warheads and a substantial slowing of the pace of weapons modernization would all have to be clearly demonstrated before many of the nuclear threshold nations would feel that north-south inequality had been narrowed sufficiently to warrant their forgoing the nuclear option. Failure to take these steps would only confirm the view currently held in many Third-World states that the acquisition of nuclear weapons is the only option available to them to equalize the power imbalance between the rich and the poor.

This path, like the others, is unlikely to be taken, and for a number of reasons. Inequality has been an inherent characteristic of both human affairs and international affairs throughout the ages. Except in the rarest of circumstances, the rich have never willingly taken great strides to equalize material imbalances. Rather, the poor have remained poor, or they have grown rich through their own efforts, through good fortune, or because they used force to obtain wealth from the rich. It is extremely unlikely that the rich nations generally or the United States in particular will deviate from this pattern. Moreover, it is not at all clear that, if such inequality gaps were bridged, the effect on nuclear non-proliferation would be favorable. For it is becoming increasingly apparent that the term "north-south conflict" is exceedingly imprecise as an explanation of the forces stimulating nuclear proliferation. The south, in fact, is composed of a highly heterogeneous group of nations that differ markedly in all measures of national wealth. And for most nations of the south, it is a neighboring member of the same region that is its principal rival and its principal threat. Surely Argentina seeks a nuclear capability far more because Brazil may soon acquire nuclear weapons than as a consequence of the fact that Britain and France already have them.

To be sure, the United States can be expected to take a leading role in the years ahead to ameliorate north-south relations and to contribute to some fundamental restructuring of the international economic order. But this will fall far short of achieving a condition of equality among nations. The view is strongly held in U.S. policy-making circles that the incentives for nuclear proliferation rest more with issues of national prestige and regional conflicts than with matters of economic and military inequality. America is, therefore, not about to embark on an enormously costly program of economic and military assistance nor to initiate substantial unilateral reductions in its nuclear arsenal that might provide the Soviet Union with political or perhaps even military advantages.

A fifth option that might be termed adaptive continuity is the likely approach that the United States will follow in coping with a world of nuclear powers. This option involves utilizing a mix of strategies tailored to specific aspects of the nuclear proliferation problem and adapting, as most governments do, pragmatically and incrementally to changing circumstances as they unfold.

ADAPTIVE CONTINUITY

As has already become evident in the debates in the United States on nuclear non-proliferation policy since the Indian detonation of 1974, attempts to control the spread of nuclear weapons will move along essentially two lines: political-military strategies and energy-related strategies.[3] These strategies may be summarized as follows.

Political-military strategies

Strengthen the Non-Proliferation Treaty (NPT). The NPT remains the principal international legal instrument for retarding nuclear proliferation. Unless or until its legitimacy collapses in the face of a large number of states violating or withdrawing from it, the United States will do what it can to see that it is retained and that its effectiveness is improved. Indeed, the fact that a number of important states have recently ratified the treaty (notably the Federal Republic of Germany in 1975 and Japan in 1976) testifies to its continued legitimacy within the international community. The treaty will therefore receive overt and high-level support from the United States, which will continue to attempt to induce nonmembers to ratify it.

At this stage the NPT is a necessary but not a sufficient condition for nuclear proliferation to be controlled. It is of great symbolic significance, and its collapse would signal that the effort to control proliferation had failed, thereby further stimulating the nuclear spread. The United States is likely to move in the direction of attempting to create incentives for nonmembers to join the treaty, such as making the transfer of U.S. nuclear technology conditional on the recipient nation being an NPT member and accepting full safeguards as specified in the treaty. It is unlikely, however, that the United States will move so far as to offer amendments to the treaty for fear that the amendment procedures could open the way for some states to withdraw.

Press for Soviet-American strategic arms control. The United States will move ahead in seeking to reach agreements with the Soviet Union in the control of strategic arms, not only because of the utility of the agreements in their own right,

3. The following discussion draws heavily on the author's "Strategies to Slow Nuclear Proliferation: A Propositional Inventory," an unpublished discussion paper prepared for the Aspen Arms Control Workshop on Nuclear Proliferation, 2–6 August 1976, sponsored by the Aspen Institute for Humanistic Studies and the arms control research centers of Harvard, Cornell, and Stanford Universities and the Massachusetts Institute of Technology.

but also because of the linkage made between lack of progress at the Strategic Arms Limitation Talks (SALT) and the prospects of nuclear proliferation. Whether this linkage is legitimate or contrived, progress in SALT will positively affect the perceptions of some have nots toward the haves and should influence the domestic debate in threshold countries in favor of restraint. While it is probably correct that nuclear proliferation will be a by-product of regional conflicts, the great power aspirations of some threshold countries, and a number of domestic political considerations that vary from state to state, progress in strategic arms control will at worst have no effect and at best have some positive effect on curbing proliferation.[4]

Adopt pledges of non-use of nuclear weapons against non-nuclear weapons states. There is the prospect, although it is not very great, that the United States will consider some form of pledge concerning the non-use of nuclear weapons. Great caution must be exercised in this area because such pledges could create serious doubt about the credibility of American security guarantees to its allies in Europe and East Asia. It is possible that a non-use pledge could be formulated with the provision that it would not apply to non-nuclear states that assist one or more nuclear weapons states in aggressive actions against other nuclear weapons states or their allies. Indeed, it could be accompanied by explicit assurances to the Federal Republic of Germany and Korea concerning American intentions. If such a pledge proved satisfactory to America's allies and were endorsed by the other nuclear powers as well, it might reduce the likelihood of nuclear weapon use, it would be an indication of the diminishing political utility of nuclear weapons in the foreign policies of the major powers, and it would be significantly reassuring to non-nuclear states.

Adopt a comprehensive test ban treaty. The United States should be expected to pressure the Soviet Union to become party to a comprehensive test ban treaty (CTBT) that would prohibit any further testing of nuclear weapons for any reason whatever, thereby excluding both underground tests and peaceful nuclear explosions (PNEs). A CTBT would have the effect of diminishing the importance of nuclear weapons in world politics, would testify that the nuclear powers are serious in adhering to the provisions of the NPT, and would make it more difficult politically for a near-nuclear state to take the PNE path to an independent nuclear weapons capability. These advantages far outweigh the claims of opponents that a CTBT would slow needed progress in advanced weapons development, reduce the reliability of existing weapons and thereby weaken the credibility of the nuclear deterrent, lower the guard against technological breakthroughs by potential adversaries, be difficult to verify, and accelerate the flow of highly skilled manpower away from weapons research and development work.

As nuclear proliferation continues, it will be increasingly important that a CTBT enter into force but progressively less likely that it will. At present, the position of both

4. A detailed view of the relationship between arms control and nuclear proliferation is presented by Colin Gray elsewhere in this volume.

Soviet and American officials is predicated on an all-or-nothing approach, cognizant that France and China will not sign. As new states enter the nuclear club with weaponry at varying levels of technological development, their proclivity to conduct weapons tests will virtually guarantee that no universal CTBT could be ratified.

Establish nuclear free zones. There remains enormous difficulty in establishing nuclear free zones, as evidenced by the Treaty of Tlatelolco, and it is precisely in those areas of the most intense regional conflicts—the Middle East, the Indian subcontinent, Korea—that the inevitable variations in military potential among the protagonists make the chances for reaching such agreements least likely. Moreover, the nuclear free zone approach will become hopelessly utopian as nuclear weapons spread. The best the United States could hope to do would be to assist where feasible in the settlement of regional disputes among non-nuclear powers, thereby diminishing the need for these states to acquire nuclear weapons.

Maintain and enhance security guarantees. It can be anticipated that the principal stimulants to nuclear proliferation will continue to be threats to the security of non-nuclear states. By maintaining and enhancing security guarantees, the United States could both constrain the options of the non-nuclear states and provide assurances to them that would diminish the incentives for these states to develop independent nuclear weapons capabilities. Whether the United States will be able to establish and preserve new guarantees is difficult to assess. At present, long-standing commitments involving the United States are being increasingly (not decreasingly) questioned, and the prospect of extending these arrangements in a credible fashion to other threshold countries appears to be quite slim. Moreover, in cases where the establishment of security guarantees might be possible, the conditions demanded by the non-nuclear states in terms of economic and military aid may prove to be unacceptable to the United States. Nonetheless, as nuclear weapons continue to spread, the maintenance of security guarantees is a most logical course for the United States to pursue.

Impose sanctions against new nuclear states. Because of the lack of support both at home and abroad for U.S. armed intervention, except where its vital interests are concerned, there is little prospect that the use of military sanctions will be a significant U.S. tool in coping with nuclear proliferation. Political and economic pressures and sweeteners are likely to be applied, however, to persuade non-nuclear allies to remain non-nuclear. Should one or two nations cross the threshold, the United States may well try to deter others by heavily penalizing the new nuclear states. But these penalties will be country-specific, limited in scope and duration, and unlikely to include military instrumentalities.

Other approaches. Two other techniques might be attempted by the United States in future efforts to contain the spread of nuclear weapons. The first concerns the intentional downgrading of the utility of nuclear weapons in American foreign policy, and, hopefully, in world politics generally. This approach has little promise of succeeding, because the status of nuclear weapons possession, once gained by a state, is difficult to relinquish.[5] While it may well be the case that more cautious use of language concerning the employment of nuclear weapons would be of some help, the overall impact of the acquisition of nuclear weapons on otherwise weak military states should not be underestimated.

A second technique would be for the United States to provide precision-guided weapons and other sophisticated conventional arms to threshold states in lieu of these states acquiring indigenous nuclear capabilities. Here again, the likelihood of success is low. Conventional weapons, no matter how sophisticated, have neither the deterrent value of nuclear weapons nor their prestige. This tactic could buy time, but in the long run it would not satisfy a state that sought nuclear weapons for either prestige or deterrence purposes.

Energy-related strategies

Establish supplier agreements to regulate the transfer of nuclear technology. Nuclear proliferation can be constrained by minimizing the opportunities for national governments to acquire weapons-grade material. This fact will be as true in a world of many nuclear powers as it is today. The United States, by reaching agreement with the other nuclear supplier nations not to sell or assist in the development of fuel reprocessing plants or uranium enrichment facilities, could impede further nuclear proliferation, no matter what its level, at any point in time. By agreeing to provide and subsidize fuel cycle services at substantial economic advantage to recipient states (compared to those states having their own facilities), the United States could seek to enter into agreements which guarantee the security of supply of energy resources to these recipients. In cases where nuclear facilities are provided, assurances must be obtained that the spent fuel will be returned to the supplier. There are considerable difficulties inherent to this strategy in terms of managing alliance relationships and coping with the instabilities of a nuclear cartel. But the benefits to be derived are worth the effort. This approach should continue to be an effective non-proliferation strategy in the future.

Exercise unilateral restraint in nuclear energy programs. It will remain highly desirable for many years to come that the United States refrain from taking steps with respect to its own nuclear energy programs that would increase the likelihood of the spread of weapons-grade material. Delaying both permission for plutonium recycling and the decision to produce fast-breeder reactors is consistent with this objective. Should the United States move ahead with both these developments, weapons-grade material would spread extremely rapidly and the battle to retard nuclear proliferation would be lost. Those who support plutonium recycling and the production and sale of fast-breeder reactors point to unproven economic arguments to substantiate their case. Unless and until extraordinarily compelling eco-

5. Great Britain may, however, be a counter-example. Should Britain's political and economic decline continue, serious consideration may be given to the relinquishment of the British nuclear force, most probably through a strategy of planned obsolescence. The likelihood of this eventuality is exceedingly low, however.

nomic arguments can be made in support of these programs, there is every reason to delay them.

Establish multinational nuclear facilities. In the years ahead, the United States may well take the lead in establishing multinational nuclear facilities as alternatives to national facilities. These facilities could perform fuel cycle operations from uranium enrichment to waste disposal and could vary in organizational structure from a bilateral supplier-recipient arrangement serving the fuel cycle needs of only one nation to a system of multiple ownership and management serving an entire region. The establishment of such facilities would increase the economic and political costs of acquiring national nuclear facilities and would increase the effectiveness of safeguards against diversion of materials, since each of the participating nations would serve as a monitor against diversion by others. Although multinational facilities run the risk of stimulating reprocessing activities and serving as agents for the transfer of technological know-how, these risks are worth taking. Serious consideration by the United States of converting one or more of its national facilities into a multinational facility is a likely prospect in the years ahead.

Increase financial support to the IAEA. To prevent the diversion or theft of materials from national facilities, the safeguards program of the International Atomic Energy Agency (IAEA) will undoubtedly require expansion, and increased efforts will need to be made to provide physical protection of these facilities. In effect, such measures can only be achieved with substantial technical and financial assistance from the United States. While care should be taken to ensure that American assistance does not so dominate the agency that it comes to be perceived as a tool of U.S. policy, sufficient aid must be provided to generate an effective IAEA safeguards program. This program is a necessary, although not a sufficient, condition to control nuclear proliferation in the years ahead.

Reduce interest in nuclear energy by adopting alternative energy sources. If the United States were to turn away from nuclear energy, the prospects of nuclear proliferation might well decline. This step would not be an easy one, however. It can be accomplished by imposing a significant energy conservation program and by expending large resources on alternative energy sources—particularly solar energy. On balance, it is likely that the social and economic costs of a major conservation program are simply too high to make it politically feasible in the United States. Moreover, solar energy, if well developed, will probably be economically attractive only on a small scale. It would appear, therefore, that there are, in fact, no alternatives to increased reliance on nuclear energy. Only three events could alter this conclusion: insufficient capital to finance nuclear facilities; a major nuclear accident (resulting from a system failure, not sabotage), creating fear about the reliability of nuclear facilities and turning public opinion away from nuclear energy; or a technological breakthrough that provides a new and inexpensive source of energy.

Each of these political-military and energy-related strategies requires considerable elaboration and argumentation that cannot be presented in a paper of this length.[6] They have been cited to indicate the range and complexity of the efforts that the United States can be expected to undertake in coping with nuclear proliferation. They vary greatly in difficulty and in level of effort; for example, reaching Soviet-American strategic arms control agreements that would influence some threshold states to remain nonnuclear would clearly be far more difficult than increasing financial support for the IAEA. But a set of parallel approaches is undoubtedly what is called for.

This conclusion reflects the judgment that non-proliferation policies will continue to be implemented in a world of many nuclear powers. In the face of the Nth power acquiring nuclear weapons, the United States will act to prevent the N+1 power from taking the same step.

There is, however, one significant caveat with respect to the option of adaptive continuity, and this concerns the pace of the nuclear spread. The United States has, until now, been able to adjust to nuclear proliferation because its pace has been gradual and the spread has been largely restricted to the major powers who have exercised extreme caution in their handling of the weapons. Should proliferation accelerate, technical deficiencies in the new nuclear forces and the prospect that some national leaders might act irresponsibly will make the world a far more dangerous place and will adversely affect American security interests.[7] A major shock to the system—for example, the sale of a nuclear weapon, the use of a nuclear weapon in anger, or the widespread availability of laser isotope separation technology and expertise permitting off-the-shelf bombs to be acquired by many states within a one-year period—would so suddenly and dramatically alter the nature of international political relationships that it is highly improbable that the United States, under such circumstances, would retain an incremental and cautiously pragmatic approach to the problem.

Should a shock to the system materialize, the United States is likely to move aggressively to halt further nuclear proliferation, using coercive and military measures where necessary. The building of specialized offensive and defensive forces tailored to meet the threat posed by small nuclear-armed states would be encouraged. In some instances, the United States might share its technological expertise with new nuclear states to improve their command, control, and communication systems so as to minimize the likelihood of accidental or unauthorized use of nuclear weapons. While a fundamental rethinking of defense policy and alliance relationships might well be stimulated, it is highly probable that sanctions

6. Some of these approaches are addressed elsewhere in this volume. See, particularly, the papers by George Quester, Lewis Dunn, and Michael Brenner. On energy-related strategies, consult *Nuclear Energy and National Security*, A Statement by the Research and Policy Committee of the Committee for Economic Development, September 1976. The case against fuel recycling is best made in Henry S. Rowen and Gregory Jones, *Influencing the Nuclear Technology Choices of Other Countries: The Key Role of Fuel Recycling in the U.S.* (Pan Heuristics, August 1976).

7. Although some Third-World spokesmen claim that this view is racist, the fact is that nations are not equally endowed with either technologically sophisticated delivery vehicles or political wisdom.

against new nuclear states would dominate the American reaction.

Whether U.S. security in a world of nuclear powers can be maintained utilizing any of the measures suggested above is an open question. Until the option of adaptive continuity is proven to be ineffective, however, it will constitute the American response.

GLOSSARY

Any specialized area has its jargon, and nuclear proliferation is no exception. This glossary defines those terms most frequently used in the various papers which may be new to readers, including both those which are highly technical (for which, see the papers by Drs. Barnaby and Imai) and those which are more or less commonly emphasized in debates in military policy.

Arms control—any measure limiting or reducing forces, regulating armaments, and/or restricting the deployment of troops or weapons which is intended to induce responsive behavior or which is taken pursuant to an understanding with another state or states.

Arms race—the competitive or cumulative improvement of weapons stocks (qualitatively or quantitatively) or the build-up of armed forces based on the conviction of two or more actors that only by trying to stay ahead in military power can they avoid falling behind.

Atomic bomb—a weapon based on the rapid fissioning of combinations of selected materials, thereby inducing an explosion (along with the emission of radiation).

Breeder reactors—reactors in which the process of fission enhances the concentrations of fissionable materials in the fuel or in a "jacket" covering the reactor, thereby producing more fuel than is used.

Coercion—the attempt to induce a change in behavior through actual punishment, supposedly applicable when compellance fails.

Compellance—the attempt to induce a change in behavior through threatening undesirable consequences in the event of refusal.

Deterrence—the prevention from action by fear of the consequences. Deterrence is a state of mind brought about by the existence of a credible threat of unacceptable counteraction.

Disarmament—the reduction of a military establishment to some level set by international agreement.

Fissile material (or fissionable material)—isotopes (variants) of certain elements, such as plutonium, thorium, and uranium, which emit neutrons in such large numbers that a sufficient concentration will be self-sustaining, that is, will continue to produce increasing numbers of neutrons until it is damped down, explodes, or the material is exhausted. (See Frank Barnaby, "How States Can Go Nuclear.")

Fusion—a process whereby the atoms of light, non-fissionable elements such as lithium are transformed under pressure, yielding helium and energy in the form of radiation.

General and complete disarmament—the total reduction of an actor's military establishment to the point where no military capability is present.

Going nuclear—the acquisition by an actor of a nuclear capability regardless of size; it may only be the possession and/or explosion of one nuclear bomb.

Horizontal proliferation—the spread of nuclear capabilities across states and/or nongovernmental actors.

IAEA (International Atomic Energy Agency)—an international organization charged, among other things, with monitoring the production and use of special fissionable materials.

Kiloton—one thousand tons (of TNT equivalent).

N + 1st power—that following an Nth power, that is, the next proliferator but one.

Nth powers—a reference to additions to the group of powers possessing nuclear weapons; the next country of a series to acquire nuclear powers.

Non-nuclear (weapons) state—one not possessing nuclear weapons.

Nuclear device—a nuclear explosive which may: (*a*) be intended for nonmilitary uses such as construction, hence peaceful nuclear explosive; (*b*) be too heavy and/or too cumbersome for delivery on military targets and hence useful only for test purposes.

Nuclear free zone—a stretch of territory from which all nuclear weapons are banned.

Nuclear materials—see Fissile materials.

Nuclear Non-Proliferation Treaty (NPT)—a treaty which, among other things, binds those non-nuclear countries adhering to it to forgo the acquisition or production of nuclear weapons and all signatories to abjure transfering such weapons to a non-nuclear state.

Nuclear option—the ability to go nuclear within a short period of time if one chooses.

Nuclear proliferation—the process by which one actor after another comes into possession of some form of nuclear weaponry, and with it the potential of launching a nuclear attack on other actors.

Nuclear reactor—a mechanism fueled by fissionable materials which give off neutrons, thereby inducing heat. Reactors are of three general types: (1) power reactors, in which the heat generated is transformed into power in the form of electricity; (2) production reactors, which are designed primarily to increase concentration of certain fissionable materials, such as plutonium, Pu-239; (3) research reactors, which are designed primarily to produce isotopes (variants) of some materials and/or to induce radioactivity in others, for applications in genetics, medicine, and so forth.

Nuclear reprocessing—the separation of radioactive waste (spent fuel) from a nuclear-powered plant into its fissile constituent materials. One such material is plutonium, which can then be used in the production of atomic bombs.

Nuclear safeguards—any number of ways to protect nuclear power or production reactors from accidental spillage of nuclear waste, from theft of nuclear materials, or from the diversion of these to unauthorized purposes, such as weapons production.

Nuclear terrorism—terrorism is the systematic use of terror as a means of coercion. Nuclear terrorism involves the use (or threatened use) of nuclear weapons or radioactive materials by an actor, state, or nongovernment.

Nuclear (weapons) state—one possessing nuclear weapons, whether fission, fusion, or both.

Permissive Action Links (PAL)—electronic systems for the control of nuclear warheads whereby these can be armed only if positive action to this end is taken by a duly constituted authority, such as the president of the United States or the supreme allied commander, Europe.

Plutonium recycling—a process whereby plutonium in the spent fuel of reactors is separated from other fissile materials and reused, either as reactor fuel (see Breeder reactors) or for atomic weapons.

Preemptive strike—an attack launched in the expectation that an attack by an adversary is imminent and designed to forstall that attack or to lessen its impact. Usually refers to a strike on an adversary's delivery vehicles, weapons stocks, and other components of nuclear forces.

Radioactive materials—those giving off Beta rays, Gamma rays, or other forms of radiation. Radioactive materials may or may not be fissionable.

SALT (Strategic Arms Limitation Talks)—the discussions between the United States and the USSR on the limitation of strategic armaments which have been under way since 1970. So far these have led to: (1) a treaty limiting the deployment of anti-ballistic missile (ABM) systems; (2) an agreement setting ceilings on intercontinental ballistic missiles (ICBMs) and submarine-launched ballistic missiles (SLBMs) for a five-year period; (3) the Vladivostok Accord, setting ceilings (*a*) on all strategic nuclear delivery systems (including heavy bombers) and (*b*) on MIRVs (multiple independently-targetable reentry vehicles).

Spent fuel—fuel which has been in use in a reactor for some time and which in consequence has changed composition and diminished in its ability to give off neutrons.

Supplier's Club—a name used in reference to those countries which have the ability to make nuclear reactors and other essential equipment and which have banded together to discuss policies for the sale of nuclear plants to other countries.

Targeting Doctrine—principles governing the selection of targets to be attacked in the event of war, the allocation of weapons to those targets, and the order in which they will be (or can be) attacked.

Vertical proliferation—the development and enlargement of an actor's nuclear capacity in terms of further refinement, accumulation, and deployment of nuclear weapons.

Book Department

INTERNATIONAL RELATIONS AND POLITICAL SCIENCE

CALVIN D. DAVIS. *The United States and the Second Hague Peace Conference: American Diplomacy and International Organization, 1899–1914*. Pp. 398. Durham, N.C.: Duke University Press, 1975. No price.

Idealists look primarily to international law and organization as the means through which the security-power dilemma among nation-states can be resolved. Leaving aside the numerous peace plans and grand designs from Kant to Woodrow Wilson, the world took its first major step in the long history of international organization with the First and Second Hague Peace Conferences of 1899 and 1907. No one has chronicled the events leading to and surrounding these conferences with greater historical insight and judgment than Professor Calvin D. Davis. Writing in 1962 of the First Conference, Davis concludes: ". . . The First Hague Peace Conference achieved little in the way of progress for humanity. . . . The conventions and declarations . . . and later agreements based upon those documents were paper achievements—masks concealing failure."

Looking back a decade later in his history of the Second Conference, Professor Davis found his own judgment too harsh, explaining that while the conference had overlooked the prime political problems of the era, it had laid the foundations for new approaches to arms limitation, international arbitration and the laws of warfare, especially the latter. The First Conference founded the Permanent Court of Arbitration with a list of names of arbiters and judges; the Second Conference drew up a convention for a world court failing only to agree on the means of appointing judges, a failure that was resolved when the Permanent Court of International Justice was inaugurated on February 15, 1922. Of four American members of the Permanent Court of Arbitration, only one, John Bassett Moore, accepted election by the Council and Assembly of the League, "notwithstanding that he had opposed American entry into the League" (p. 363).

From the outset, it was the forces of international politics and fear of other nations, coupled with the high costs of armaments, that inspired international initiatives however vocal and persistent the peace groups may have been. For example, the decision to call the Conference of 1899 originated within the Russian Finance Ministry as Russia and Austria sought to avoid the strains of matching France and Germany in an artillery buildup. Reactions to this reflected security-power concerns. Lord Salisbury warned that "arms were a serious deterrent to war." The Prince of Wales suspected the Russian ministers of intrigue. Kaiser Wilhelm II privately warned his foreign minister, Count von Bülow, that there could be a "bit of deviltry" in Russia's move. The French feared dire effects on their military position and the United States telegraphed acceptance but explained that the war with Spain made arms limitations below present levels impractical. Mahan pointed to Russian concern with American power as its motivation and Rudyard Kipling wrote the poem, "The Bear that Walks Like a Man."

Notwithstanding, the First Conference went forward in part because "all questions concerning the political relations of States . . . [were] absolutely excluded." Enthusiasm then and in the Second Conference centered less on armaments than on arbitration and the role of permanent international conferences. Writing of the Second Conference, Professor Davis notes that any student of international affairs "would have quickly decided that the appellation 'Peace Conference' meant little" (p. 137). "Proposals for limiting armaments had failed even before the Second . . . Conference opened" (p. 161). In all the notes and confidential talks in the year preceding the Conference, "none believed that his government threatened his neighbors, yet each feared his country's neighbors" (p. 161). It was this and not novel methods and procedures at the Hague that shaped national policies and brought on World War I. The thousands of documents and millions of words that passed among statesmen were less important than a mutual recognition of the security-power dilemma. Professor Davis dwells on this less than would a political realist but the lesson is clear from the historical account he so faithfully and lucidly provides. His is at least a minor classic.

KENNETH W. THOMPSON

University of Virginia
Charlottesville

EUGENE LINDEN. *The Alms Race: The Impact of American Voluntary Aid Abroad.* Pp. x, 275. New York: Random House, 1976. $10.00.

Linden's title, with its cuteness, is inaccurate: there is no account of a "race"; "voluntary aid" is really just CARE which he notes is largely public (that is, tax-financed) anyway; "abroad" is Lesotho, a most atypical country. The result is a much less general volume than the title suggests, especially with respect to its conclusions.

The conclusions appear in the latter third or so of the book in terms far more general than the bases of analyses should allow: charity has a self-serving role to play in the "consumer" economies; ridding ourselves of guilt through contributions to such agencies as CARE inevitably leads to the breakdown of traditional Third World institutions to the detriment of the recipients. This occurs as the economic "missionaries" seek to prepare traditional institutions for "free enterprise" in much the same way as religious missionaries proselyte. And as for their religious counterparts, enthusiasm in converting varies inversely with the degree of the "faith" of the individual.

This is the principal criticism of the book: the conclusions—valid or no—are essentially independent of the early parts of the work but on which they presumably rely. There is just too much dog here to be set into motion by the little tail.

The history of CARE through various stages—as a means of delivering assistance to specified individuals, as a general relief agency, and finally as a self-appointed development agency—is interesting. And the setting of Lesotho into which Linden takes us is also fascinating. He writes well. But literary skill is no substitute for analytic solidity. He deals mostly with short-term change, and he frequently gives the impression that demonstration of weakness in a particular project is tantamount to proving that the project was counterproductive. Abkhasia is painted in terms of extreme underdevelopment but also producing many who live past 120 years of age, with male potency well into the nineties. Almost any "development" to be offered by the West would damage this entirely enviable situation.

Possibly true, but this says very little to policy for the 90 or more percent of the Third World where life expectancy is far short of that in the "consumer world."

The New Guinea Maring tribe is for Linden a sort of model of the traditional. This tribe practices slash-and-burn. Each decade or so it has an enormous feast by killing off almost its entire swine herd, and then engages in bloody battle decimating the various clans. This behavior limiting animal and human population permits prolonged survival of the Marings in delicate ecological balance. Linden does *not* say that the traditional is better than any other conceivable arrangement, but he implies it is better than any alternative which can be expected from the West's charitable and/or developmental efforts.

This leaves the final problem: What to do? Is there a preferred pattern for charitable/development assistance? Is zero charity really better than a positive amount? Is the guilt *relieved* from giving to CARE really less than the guilt *acquired* (after reading Linden) from giving to it?

JOHN M. HUNTER
Michigan State University
East Lansing

MICHAEL OAKESHOTT. *On Human Conduct*. Pp. viii, 329. New York: Oxford University Press, 1975. $18.50.

The first question I ask of any writer "On Human Conduct" is whether a man is responsible for his actions or is a creature of his environment and/or the stars? This author answers,

> Understood in terms of its postulates, 'human conduct' is 'free' (that is, intelligent) agents disclosing and enacting themselves by responding to their understood contingent situations in chosen actions and utterances related to imagined and wished-for satisfactions sought in the responses of other such agents, while subscribing to the conditions and compunctions of a multitude of practices and in particular to those of a language of moral understanding and intercourse. A human relationship is not a 'process' made up of functionally or causally related components; it is an intelligent relationship enjoyed only in virtue of having been learned and understood or misunderstood. . . . *Civitas* is an engagement of human conduct; *cives* are not neurophysiological organisms, genetic characters, psychological egos of components of a 'social process', but 'free' agents whose responses to one another's actions and utterances is one of understanding; and civil association is not organic, evolutionary, teleological, functional, or syndromic relationship but an understood relationship of intelligent agents (p. 112).

The preceding is a summary of his first essay, defining terms and presuppositions of his concept of civil association, the 'state' as *societas* in which *socii* pursue their own interests under accepted conditions, and the state as *universitas*, a partnership which itself becomes a person. His third essay traces tensions of such ideas in the European 'state' or 'nation' of the past five centuries.

In this book the retired Fellow of Cambridge University shares a lifetime of reflection, seeking to "enlighten" rather than to "instruct". His political philosophy draws from many disciplines, for example, history, philosophy, political science, psychology, economics, sociology, jurisprudence, theology and current and classical literature in many languages. Vocabulary and sentence structures give a reading level of perhaps Grade 20, if there is such a Grade! For example,

> . . . Psychology . . . has emerged from the enterprise of theorizing such 'goings-on' as feeling, being interested, perceiving, being disposed, learning, remembering and forgetting, wanting, wishing, willing, believing, playing, acquiring habits, etc., etc., identified, not as states of consciousness or exhibitions of intelligence, but as observable processes; that is, understood in terms of theorems which denote regularities which are not themselves exhibitions of understanding and do not have to be learned in order to be operative . . . they have equipped this science with concepts (often borrowed from other sciences) in terms of which to formulate theorems about the postulates of these processes—faculty, instinct, drive, association, reflex, organic tension, function, valence, canalization, tolerance, conservation, latency, threshold, trace, reinforcement, *prägnaz*, deflection, sublima-

tion, repression, field of perception, configuration, etc., etc. . . (pp. 20–21).

Concern for the future rather than the past is suggested by Footnote 1 on page 313:

It is perhaps worth noting that notions of 'world peace' and 'world government' which in the eighteenth century were explored in terms of civil association have in this century become projects of 'world management' concerned with the distribution of substantive goods. The decisive change took place in the interval between the League of Nations and the United Nations.

What is a 'state', a 'nation'? The modern European state developed from 'feudal' backgrounds, seeking to bring together persons, communities and fragments of communities, strangers to one another, separated in respect of language, moral imagination, customs, aspirations, conditions of living, moved by local affections and animosities, exhibiting the differences of religious belief commonplace in Christendom since the twelfth century. Professor Oakeshott would like to see preserved in the modern state individual freedoms of citizens, seeing them threatened by political promises to give plush benefits if we will just turn over everything to the state. Shall we call it a "social service state', a 'Welfare state', 'social security', 'socialization', 'social ownership', 'nationalization', 'integration', 'cultural engineering', 'communism', 'collectivism', a state understood as a 'public service corporation'?

The teleocratic drift which two world wars imparted to all European governments (combatants and neutrals alike) and the techniques of control and integration devised in these circumstances have been reflected in an ever more confident belief in its appropriateness.

The notion of a state as an all-embracing, compulsory corporate association and of its government as the manager of an enterprise is then to be recognized as one of the most obtrusive of the strands which constitute the texture of modern European political reflection (p. 311).

How can the man limit such remarks to Europe? How different are any of our 'states'?

ROLFE L. HUNT

New Rochelle
New York

ALVIN Z. RUBINSTEIN, ed. *Soviet and Chinese Influence in the Third World.* Pp. v, 231. New York: Praeger Publishers, 1976. $17.50.

Alvin Z. Rubinstein has edited and written the introductory chapter to a very important volume on the foreign policy of the Soviet Union and China toward Third World nations. The book is a significant contribution in two senses: firstly, in that it deals with the highly essential, albeit difficult, concept of influence, and secondly, in that it examines substantively a variety of aspects of Soviet and Chinese policies. Among these aspects are the military assistance programs of the two communist powers, their economic links with developing countries, the diplomatic dimension, and so on.

By concentrating on the notion of influence, Rubinstein and his associates seem to reject the tendency of some political scientists to ignore this concept as too ambiguous and complex. If politics is the science of influence, then influence must be conceptually defined, operationally measured, and empirically assessed. The major contribution of the introductory chapter is in taking the first step toward a better conceptual understanding of influence. Unfortunately, however, Dr. Rubinstein conceives of influence as a product, not as a process—a conception which tends to ignore the dynamics of the phenomenon. The editor errs also by making the methodologically unsound distinction between explanation and prediction. If we can come to understand what causes influence, we can definitely predict it.

The eight substantive chapters deal with Soviet and Chinese influence over particular regions (the Persian Gulf, Black Africa, and Latin America), countries (India, Indonesia, Egypt, and Cuba), and the Palestinian guerrilla movement. The papers are usually the products of careful research, clear writing, and extensive documentary support (an exception, insofar as documentation is concerned, is Mr. Kerr's analysis of Soviet-Egyptian relations). A major problem with this set of papers, however, is that they are only loosely related to each other and to the theoretical framework set by the editor. Though some contributors occasionally refer to this framework, others write with a minimal awareness of it, and some depart totally from Rubinstein's scheme in order to develop their own conceptualizations. The papers of Maoz and Ginsburgs, for example, are of an a-theoretical nature, while the study of Legvold adopts an independent theoretical outlook. The result is conceptual disintegration, a problem so common to edited volumes.

Nevertheless, this book should wholeheartedly be recommended to those who are interested in the development of a theory of influence in international relations, as well as to those who are interested in Soviet and Chinese relationships with Third World countries.

ILAN PELEG

Lafayette College
Easton
Pennsylvania

WILLIAM SCHNEIDER. *Food, Foreign Policy and Raw Material Cartels*. Pp. vii, 122. New York: Crane, Russak & Co., 1976. $5.95. Paperbound, $2.95.

The OPEC-induced energy crisis has catapulted economic issues into the main arena of international politics. Combined with the post-Vietnam disenchantment of the U.S. toward the use of military force, oil embargo and other potential raw material cartels, the potential of economic weapons as instruments of foreign policy has received new attention. What William Schneider has done in this brief and readable book is to review the contemporary global economic situation map and postulate the utility of various economic strategies as foreign policy instruments.

Schneider stated his thesis succinctly in his introduction:

> Economic warfare may become the gunboat diplomacy of the backward nations of the world. Arab nations influencing the policies of the United States and its allies in the Middle East crisis are subject to at least some degree of emulation by other states or collection of states in certain circumstances.

In the second chapter, Schneider reviewed U.S. experience with economic warfare. He concluded that we had set too high expectations in both the World War II bombing of German industry and in abortive efforts to slow down Soviet economic-military developments. At the same time Schneider asserted that economic warfare could be a useful adjunct to an integrated foreign policy.

In disarming the possibility of agricultural exports as a component of economic warfare, Schneider contended that "The U.S. lead in agriculture is greater than Arab dominance of the petroleum market." This factor matched with the chronic inadequacies of Soviet agriculture and food deficiencies elsewhere, makes U.S. agricultural products "a very useful element in support of foreign policy."

In addition to oil, however, Schneider next demonstrates that the United States and its industrialized allies in Western Europe and Japan are increasingly dependent upon foreign sources for critical materials.

After examining both sides of the coin, Schneider advocates the creation of a U.S. government grain reserve for both humanitarian and political purposes. He suggests that few raw material cartels (oil aside) appear feasible in the long run.

The availability of a grain reserve, insulated from the U.S. domestic market, would "make possible the exercise of an economic warfare in agricultural products a routine component of U.S.

diplomacy." Even if this weapon might not be used with enthusiasm, "its mere existence could constitute a new force in the arsenal of American diplomacy."

Schneider's exploration of how the United States might take advantage of a major U.S. edge in dealing with the increasingly complex problems facing the United States in many areas of the world merits consideration by U.S. policy makers at the highest level.

WILLIAM R. KINTNER

Foreign Policy Research Institute
Philadelphia
Pennsylvania

ROBERT WARREN STEVENS. *Vain Hopes, Grim Realities: The Economic Consequences of the Vietnam War*. Pp. 229. New York: New Viewpoints, 1976. $5.95. Paperbound.

Citizens, politicians, and scholars do not wish to be reminded of the events and consequences of the Vietnam War, but this study is a classic review of the damage to the American economy in the last decade because of the economic policy decisions by the Johnson and Nixon administrations. The bungling of foreign policy in Vietnam sabotaged the noble experiment of achieving reasonably full employment without inflation and with significant social legislation that occurred from 1961 to 1966 in the brief tenure of the "age of the economist." The deception by LBJ of the escalation of war expenditures in 1965–66 with the economy near capacity without a reduction in private spending terminated the experiment in economic rationalism and generated the shocks to the economy that have yet to be stabilized.

The first part of the book is a brief review of the textbook tools of macroeconomic policy as applied from 1961 to 1966 and the textbook case of how not to use the tools in the past decade. The abuse and doubt of the role of economic policy-making by the public and even economists since 1966 was created because of the lack of information concerning the defense expenditures and the lack of broad public support of the "government's dirty little war." There never was a coordinated policy to finance the war once it escalated beyond that stage and the resulting political and policy debates were distorted by the ideological stances on the war.

The war on poverty was the first domestic casualty of the war. LBJ's attempt to have guns and butter was effectively jettisoned after 1965 due to the lack of political leadership and a lack of funds; however, the attempt to maintain the war on poverty and the political infeasibility of passing a tax increase to fight both wars led to the inflation that still persists. The real gains achieved in the 1960s due to social legislation were exceeded by the increased aspirations which led to disillusionment and defeatism.

The violent distortions in the economy and the destabilizing monetary and fiscal policies utilized because of a lack of a coordinated economic plan to finance the war have led to increased unemployment, inflation, balance of payment disequilibria, and an international financial crisis. A less obvious victim was the attack on the economic education of the polity and politicians. The balanced budget as an end and the return of the "old-time religion" of fiscal conservatism threaten to make economic stabilization policy even more difficult to implement through the political process. The Vietnam War is the classic example of how not to finance a war.

The attempt to save face while disentangling from the war, created additional costs and policy errors by the Nixon administration. The demand-pull inflation engineered by LBJ's deception in 1966 was vigorously attacked by the policies of Nixon in 1969–71 when the cause of inflation had already passed into the cost-push stage; hence, the restrictive policies were not effective and only generated more unemployment. The ideological position of the Republicans to balance the budget and reduce federal spending would have been justified by the economic conditions in

1964–68. The readiness of the Democrats to use fiscal stimulus and incomes policy from 1965–73 would have greatly reduced the economic consequences of the war; ironically the classic blunders of economic policy were due to the process of policy-making and not due to a lack of understanding of economic stabilization.

The quantification of budgetary cost of the war is based on James Clayton's testimony before the Joint Economic Committee and alternative estimates to allocate defense costs added by the Vietnam War. The Vietnam War was the second most costly that we have been engaged in and the cost yet to be paid in veteran benefits and interests will be at least double the original outlay of $110 billion. The full costs including future budgetary costs, opportunity cost of conscription, and the indirect cost of recession and inflation due to the war burdens are estimated to be about eight times the budgetary costs. The cost allocations are indeed crude estimates and alternate means of estimation by the defense department are given fair presentation by the author. This social accounting and economic debate may be somewhat confusing to the layman and still repetitious; but the lesson to be learned from this evaluation is vital if we are to avoid such massive errors in the future.

Professor Stevens has provided an interesting, readable account of the economic and political errors that have resulted from the "dirty little war." If the United States is to be involved in future wars or police actions, it can avoid the tremendous costs imposed by not protecting the civilian economy from disruptions due to war financing. The underlying theme of the book is the evils that are generated by policy made from an ideological position and the evils of secrecy in government. The problem of secrecy as practiced by Johnson and Nixon can be used to explain many of the political and economic problems of the past decade. If not, hope for the future will again be dashed by the grim realities of the consequences of war-related effects on the economy.

W. E. SPELLMAN

Coe College
Cedar Rapids
Iowa

TED TAPPER. *Political Education and Stability: Elite Responses to Political Conflict*. Pp. viii, 265. New York: John Wiley & Sons, 1976. $17.95.

Classical political theory assumed that the character of a citizen is a reflection of his regime. How political character is developed and the implications of that development has been a principal theme of the seminal works of political science. In the 1960s political science became almost wholly engrossed with the traditional problem of character development. However, the vocabulary of traditional analysis was changed. Concern for the character of a citizen was replaced by a preoccupation with his 'behavior,' and the processes which determined political behavior were referred to as 'socialization.'

As Tapper explains, "political socialization is both a process through which individuals acquire their political behavior and a framework within which some things are learnt rather than others" (p. 249). His work then is an analysis of these processes and a general survey of the primary socialization literature. Tapper concedes that an "obituary" for this literature might just as easily have been penned; but he takes the position that socialization research can be carried forward if the "crisis in political science" is properly addressed. Tapper's understanding of crisis follows from the central tenet of socialization studies—namely, that the function of political socialization as an input of the political system is to provide stability. If, given the postulation of system theorists that the political system seeks simply to maintain itself, and in light of the many socialization studies which revealed how efficiently the values of the state were imbibed by children, how is it to be explained that these same children later as graduate students raised havoc at Berkeley? Similarly, if the system was socializing citizens as effectively as the literature seemed to presume, how is it possible to account for the agitation of blacks, women and other dissident groups? Tapper suggests that to answer these questions it is necessary to recognize that while socialization and stability constitute the pre-eminent reality of politics, socialization is not a neatly coordinated and monolithic education for citizenship. Instead, the author states that while socialization may aim for consensus it also provides for role differentiation which may in fact be counter-productive to the requirements of stability. In five well-drawn case studies Tapper explains how socialization processes often work at cross purposes and occasionally produce tension and disharmony in the political system.

What is lacking from this critique of socialization theory is an appreciation of its more profound shortcomings. The greater problem is not that socialization may be dysfunctional and its theory unprepared to explain dissensus. More to the point, socialization theory has not identified the political and has simply failed to explain politics. This in no small way is due to the pronounced ideological biases of such theory made evident by the twin concepts of behavior and stability. But why should it be supposed that stability and behavior or conformism are the essence of politics? Tapper does note in passing criticism which in effect holds that socialization theory is a celebration of the status quo; yet he does not adequately rebut that charge. The author denies, for example, that class provides a useful perspective for understanding conflict, and then proceeds to case studies of conflict (Afro-Americans, Catholics and Protestants in Northern Ireland, working-class Tories, women and students), which if anything undercut that denial. The cardinal question however for an objective political science is not how these groups were socialized or whether their socialization in terms of the needed inputs of the system was useful or not. It is better to ask what are the reasons for such political action and whether the current political order ought to be preserved, modified or radically restructured.

In other words, dissensus and revolutionary action do not pose a crisis for political science, but only for theory based on the assumption that politics can and should be controlled. If political science suffers from a crisis, this is only because politics has been confused with public administration. This is not to say that socialization is an uninteresting subject; it is to suggest that the study might be extended, that someone ask how political scientists are socialized or inclined to think or not think about politics. Political theory has always recognized the need for the political education of the citizenry. But classical political theory was also cognizant that the political education of the good citizen did not necessarily make that citizen a good man.

PAUL L. ROSEN

Carleton University
Ottawa, Canada

W. ALLEN WALLIS. *An Overgoverned Society*. Pp. ix, 292. New York: The Free Press, 1976. $10.00.

Not only by the title of this book, but also by the answers given to the questions raised within, this volume cannot be viewed as an objective analysis of American political-economic society. All the answers go against government, mostly in this case the national government. To be sure, it is gaining more operating room, it is breaking down traditional constitutional barriers, it is becoming more and more collectivist. Free enterprise and the market economy are fighting for survival. The author follows Walter Lippman: "the sickness of an overgoverned society." Yet, while there is another side to the coin, in this book you don't get it.

Be that as it may, there is much to be said for this approach. But what can be done? How can this trend be constrained? Who will lead the way back? Professor Wallis picks out the intellec-

tuals, "the academic-journalistic complex." They are the ones, not creators of ideas, nor actually too sharp at analyzing them. Rather they are what Friedrich Hayek calls "intellectual middlemen," following the lead of top scholars and researchers. Over a long period of time, they will spread the good word around—the truth makes free. What the rest of us are going to do until this happens deponent saith not. We are on our own. Pretty thin gruel.

The author shows considerable economy savvy, but not too much on the political ball. Furthermore, the book is a heterogeneous package of essays and speeches, not at all geared for solid reading, not integrated into the conservative philosophy Professor Wallis strives for. He covers all manner of subjects: the draft, the price of steel, Watergate (who doesn't), business and government, unmet social needs, the consumer, the welfare explosion, political entrepreneurship, the power of the people, social security, modern communication, and so on. All very well, much of it is informative and knowledgeable, but without much readability. As a guide for thinking and acting conservatively, it just won't do. It is not a milestone in the battle with the Big State.

Are there enough scholars and researchers out in the open who are bending their talents for the free society, limited government, individualism, private property, the free market, and unfettered enterprise? Professor Wallis names some, and they have eminent qualifications, but they are all too few, and besides they lack charisma. Liberals—not conservatives—are the academic, literary and journalistic majority today.

HAROLD F. ALDERFER

Mechanicsburg
Pennsylvania

AFRICA, ASIA AND EUROPE

MICHAEL AVI-YONAH. *The Jews of Palestine: A Political History from the Bar Kokhba War to the Arab Conquest*. Pp. xviii, 278. New York: Schocken Books, 1976. $16.50.

This work, now happily made available in English, has long (1946) been a standard text for the given period among scholars with access to the Hebrew original (*In the Days of Rome and Byzantium*). The comprehensive analysis by Professor Avi-Yonah of the socio-political forces that shaped this largely neglected period should prove of great value to the larger scholarly community that will now be enabled to examine his tightly reasoned and broadly documented study.

The topics covered in this treatise are self-evidently significant—the disastrous Judean revolts against Rome; subsequent efforts at evolving a compromise modus vivendi between the Jews and Rome; the evolving relationships between Judaism and Christianity; the Church as the spokesman for Rome; the Byzantines and the Jews; the Persian invasion; and finally, the Arab conquest. The author clearly brings to bear a solid background in the elements centrally necessary for a proper understanding of the dynamics of this period—Roman political documents, Jewish traditional texts and the patristic literature of the Church; without any of these, this synthetic history could clearly not have been written.

Avi-Yonah chose his point of departure well—the end of the Bar Kokhba rebellion, and the grave challenges its failure placed before the Palestinian Jewish community. Professor Salo Baron, writing in Volume II of his monumental *Social and Religious History of the Jews*, put it this way:

> When the failure of the Bar Kocheba uprising put a stamp of finality on their loss of national independence and central sanctuary as well as on the total separation of Christianity, the Jews faced one of the greatest crises in their history. Although long accustomed to life in Exile amidst more or less hostile neighbors, they were now confronted with an internal foe who either denied or tried to arrogate to himself all those traditional doctrines which had made Jewish minority existence worth living (p. 170).

This newly militant Christianity, along with its main competitor, the newly revitalized pluralistic paganism, was to be the major challenge to Jewish loyalty and survival for the next several centuries.

In the course of his presentation, Avi-Yonah focuses appropriate attention on the political conflicts of the 2nd century, the economic upheavals of the 3rd, and the religious persecutions of the 4th century. He properly highlights the distinguished 500 year history of the Patriarchate, and the significant roles played by nationalism on the one hand, and messianism on the other, in maintaining Jewish autonomous aspirations throughout the period.

The work is appropriately subtitled a "political history," clarifying the absence of substantial bodies of available archeological and theological historical material. Similarly, although much documentary use is made of Talmudic texts, the climactic completion and sealing of the Palestinian Talmud is virtually glossed over in silence. These caveats quite aside, the volume is a most welcome addition to the library of materials now available on the history of this sensitive period, and as another major exemplar of the important works of scholarship Professor Avi-Yonah has made available to the English-reading public.

HERBERT ROSENBLUM
Hebrew College
Brookline
Massachusetts

WALTER BARROWS. *Grassroots Politics in an African State: Integration and Development in Sierra Leone*. Pp. iii, 265. New York: Holmes & Meier, 1976. $25.00.

THOMAS S. COX. *Civil-Military Relations in Sierra Leone*. Pp. viii, 271. Cambridge, Mass.: Harvard University Press, 1976. $14.00.

With interest in black Africa heightened by current events, the appearance of these two timely studies compels our attention. Although both focus on political development and decay in Sierra Leone, their conclusions contribute to an understanding of third world politics in general.

Walter Barrows, through a study of the role of the paramount chief, offers thought-provoking insights into the viability in the modern political setting of traditional institutions. He rejects the notion of a contradiction between traditional and modern institutions and questions whether the latter inevitably displace the former during political development. Instead, he offers a synthetic model of change. Barrows also questions a static view of pre-colonial society, urging the reader to see the fluidity and motion which existed in the traditional setting. Further, he notes that some aspects of traditional politics, such as the establishment of chiefly ruling families, were actually grafted onto native society by the colonial administration. It would have been interesting had he explored further why some innovations took hold and similar ones failed, as in the case of the Mammy Queens and rotating chiefs.

Barrows' case studies of grassroots politics are most instructive and his references to the activities of the Poro secret societies are particularly fascinating. The overall picture that emerges is one of intra-elite conflict and cleavage sparked by a utilitarian search for self-interest, rather than any sense of identity or ideological purpose.

Thomas S. Cox's study rejects the notion that the military establishment entered into Sierra Leone politics as a modernizing elite impatient with traditional forces and the slow pace of change. Although this motive has impelled other military takeovers elsewhere in the third world, Cox sees the *coups d'état* in Sierra Leone as part of intra-elite cleavages. He supports Barrows' view that the pursuit of individual self-interest and utility is a guiding principle in Sierra Leone politics.

Cox traces the origins of the military establishment, which as an arm of the colonial power, was designed primarily for internal security functions. Since it offered fewer opportunities for advancement and social status than did the civil service, it attracted second-rate candidates. Cox argues that only under the British administration did the army represent state-wide interests rather than private ones. He shows how independence produced a situation where opportunism prevailed and self-serving drives for power and prestige became commonplace. Once primordially inspired cliques emerged, ethnicity and tribal loyalties became a dominant factor in political life and in civil-military relations in Sierra Leone.

In discussing the role of the military throughout the third world, Cox makes some generalizations about Middle Eastern armies which an area specialist might question. For example, is there a "class orientation" of Middle Eastern armies, a pattern of "ideological polarization" and "interclass conflict" of civil-military relations in the area and a "North African tradition" in the armies of Egypt, Libya, Algeria and Morocco (see pp. 2–3, 12, 79–80)? His reference to Israeli assistance in training officers and in developing an intelligence service under the Lansana-Sir Albert Margai faction is disconcerting, particularly if Cox intended to imply Israel's involvement in Sierra Leone's domestic politics. Sir Albert's arrangements with Israel were not unique. In fact, during Sir Milton Margai's tenure, Israel had undertaken assistance projects in Sierra Leone in such non-military and apolitical areas as medicine and construction. Thus a cooperative relationship antedated Sir Albert's assumption of power and, in fact, was already established by 1961, when this reviewer served as Assistant Director of Information in the Israel Foreign Ministry's Department for International Cooperation.

Both the Cox and Barrows books are primarily for the specialist although of the two, Barrows is more readable. His theoretical chapters devoted to model-building are clear and concise. He offers excellent maps, tables and figures. Unfortunately the book is marred by the absence of an index and bibliography and, considering the price, by an inexcusable number of printing errors (for example, pp. 43, 53, 61, 69, 103, 121, 223, 234, 249, 257). Cox's study, on the other hand, reads like a doctoral dissertation, which indeed it was. There is no map, no glossary of terms and none of the useful background information on Sierra Leone which Barrows includes.

SYLVIA KOWITT CROSBIE
Immaculate Heart College
Los Angeles
California

JOHN F. COVERDALE. *Italian Intervention in the Spanish Civil War.* Pp. xxi, 455. Princeton, N.J.: Princeton University Press, 1975. $18.50.

In its origins, its prosecution, and its consequences, the civil war in Spain was basically a Spanish affair. But contemporaries, confronted with the evidence of foreign assistance to both sides, saw the war as an international conflict, a transcendent struggle between the forces of good and evil, variously defined. This interpretation did little to clarify the role of foreign intervention; on the contrary, the passions aroused by outside aid quickly distorted its extent, influence, and intent. Only in recent years have historians attempted to evaluate objectively the impact of foreign involvement on the outcome of the war. The present volume by Professor Coverdale of Princeton University makes possible a balanced assessment of Italian aid to the Nationalist forces of General Franco and its consequences for both Spain and Italy.

Based primarily on hitherto inaccessible Italian diplomatic sources, this study necessarily focuses on the formulation and implementation of policy in Italy by Mussolini, who made all major decisions with regard to Spain throughout the conflict. Coverdale demonstrates that especially in the opening stages of the war, Mussolini's strategy was more defensive than offensive; ideological and economic imperialism were secondary to the protection of traditional Italian interests in the Mediterranean, potentially endangered by the pro-French policies of the Second Republic. Subsequently, the commitment of 50,000 Italian troops, together with substantial material aid, made prestige an equally important motive for continued Italian intervention.

The author's analysis illuminates the pitfalls of foreign involvement in domestic conflicts. Mussolini's desire for a spectacular Italian victory (especially after the debacle at Guadalajara) and for a rapid conclusion to the war brought his officers into frequent disagreement with General Franco, whose principal concern was the effective occupation of conquered territory. Despite their contribution to the war effort, the Italians were forced to endure their frustration because only Franco seemed to hold out the possibility of ultimate victory. For the same reason, the Italians hesitated to offend Franco by insisting on a Fascist political orientation within the Nationalist zone. The formal similarities between the Nationalist regime and Italian Fascism were not the result of Italian pressure but of Franco's political opportunism.

Coverdale's sources also enable him to provide accurate information on the amount of Italian aid to reach the Nationalists during the war; he concludes that while Italian and German aid was not overwhelmingly superior to that provided the Republicans, it was nevertheless "an essential element in the Nationalist victory." Unfortunately but unavoidably missing from his otherwise comprehensive analysis is an examination of Nationalist policy vis-à-vis its foreign supporters. Until Spanish archives are opened to investigators, this study will stand as the best existing treatment of a highly controversial subject.

CAROLYN P. BOYD
University of Texas
Austin

DONALD K. EMMERSON. *Indonesia's Elite: Political Culture and Cultural Politics*. Pp. 303. Ithaca, N.Y.: Cornell University Press, 1976. $14.50.

In an effort to determine how various cultural, including religious, differences are reflected in "politically relevant orientations" Emmerson, during 1967–69, interviewed forty members of the then Indonesian political élite, twenty of them higher ranking bureaucrats in the central administration (drawn from a list of 651 senior officials of major government departments), and twenty from the 369 members of the Indonesian parliament. The size of this sample was governed, according to the author, by his consideration that a larger sample might entail the danger of "quick, artificial" interviews that would confirm the researcher's bias rather than reflect the position of the respondents. Three chapters, the heart of the book, deal with the results of Emmerson's interviews, and they are preceded by a brief historical chapter on the evolution of the bureaucracy and representative organs in Indonesia, and by a chapter detailing the life and career of two interview respondents, presumably characteristic of the two categories sampled. A concluding chapter essentially seeks to place the findings in a contemporary setting, and a "Postscript" describes Emmerson's re-interviews in 1974 and 1975 of the two respondents whose backgrounds he had presented earlier.

It is difficult to find anything of significance, either in the author's interview results (is this small a sample really an advantage?), or in his method of presentation. Among the general conclusions, for example, are (1) that cultural minorities are likely to be generally more defensive than "their counterpart majorities" and less inclined to tolerate alternate religious truths, and (2) that secularization, to the extent that it erodes religious or ethnic identity, may reduce "extreme views" and so contribute to a consensus. Neither of these two observations is likely to raise an eyebrow of a student of minority problems or of political modernization. As the majority of respondents were raised in the Dutch colonial period before the Second World War, with its long enduring bureaucratic-administrative traditions, it is not surprising to read that (1) the great majority of Emmerson's sample of bureaucrats had fathers who also were civil servants, and had a "colonial nostalgia," while (2), for those without such traditions in their own family lives, that is Emmerson's sample of members of parliament, the fathers were more likely to have had careers in the private sector.

Again, considering Emmerson's bureaucratic sample, in terms of its family background, it was to be expected that the majority in this sample were of Javanese origin. But then, considering the syncretic thoughtworld of the Javanese bureaucracy, pre-war and today, it is hardly remarkable that those in Emmerson's bureaucratic sample had a higher degree of "eclectic religious tolerance" (and, presumably, had "weak" Islamic religious identities) than his group of parliamentarians, some of whom, by virtue of their office, would likely be much more attuned to political parties with a definite religious commitment.

There have been only two general parliamentary elections in Indonesia, in 1955 and 1971, and one wonders about the representativeness of Emmerson's sample of legislators, as interviewed in 1967–69. Indeed, the presumably representative legislator introduced by Emmerson in his second chapter lost his parliamentary seat in the 1971 election; his values and political orientations no doubt remain felt in the Indonesian legislative sphere today, but one can only speculate in what representative degree.

There are other problems with Emmerson's methodological categories. Degrees of intensity in religious commitments are generally hard to establish with precision. For Emmerson, however, a "medium strength Muslim" (as opposed to a "strong" or "weak" Muslim) is one who, though keeping the fast, neither prays "regularly" nor refers "frequently" to his religion, yet is one for whom Islam is "not insignificant" as a "personal referent." What is meant by "regularly," or "frequently," or "not insignificant," or "personal referent," is unfortunately not disclosed. As for a "weakly religious" Muslim, Emmerson defines him as one "whose formal affiliation" only "minimally" affects behavior and "self-image" (of religiosity?)—surely a largely tautological definition. The reader is expected to take all this seriously, however, since Emmerson finds it "noteworthy," for example, that "among bureaucrats more than four-fifths of the weak Muslims had fathers in the public sector, whereas only half of the medium-strength Muslims did."

The book is not entirely without merit. It is good to see Emmerson make the point that the concepts of santri (orthodox Muslim) and abangan (referring to religiously more eclectic persons), concepts rediscovered and greatly overdrawn by some U.S. writers on Indonesia in recent years, may at least in some instances be inherently less antithetical than has been suggested, becoming polarized primarily in a partisan political context. Then, too, for those unfamiliar with the literature on Indonesian political institutional development, the bibliography cited in the notes of the introduction, and in the first chapter, and again at the end of the book, can, despite some selectivity, be quite helpful. On balance, however, the reader should not be misled by the title of this volume. Because of its narrow focus, the dated quality of the samples analyzed, and the questions that must be raised about its methodology, the insights of the book are as little representative of "Indonesia's élite" or of Indonesia's "political culture" as Pluto is representative of our planetary system.

JUSTUS M. VAN DER KROEF
University of Bridgeport
Connecticut

C. P. FITZGERALD. *Mao Tse-tung and China*. Pp. vi, 166. New York: Holmes & Meier Publishers, 1976. $9.50.

This study by a former Professor of Far Eastern history at Australian National University in Canberra is a eulogy of Mao which preceded his death by some three to four months. It is a brief, popularized version of Mao's life that leaves no doubt that the author considers Mao one of the greatest, if not the greatest, figure in the twentieth century, perhaps in history.

Against a background of contemporary developments, Fitzgerald traces Mao's life from a young scholar through the founding of the Chinese Communist Party, the war with Japan and the civil war, to the period of the Cultural Revolution and his conflict with Lin Piao. Unfortunately, the lack of objectivity which characterizes Fitzgerald's book does a disservice to Mao for it makes no differentiation between the earlier and later period of his career and glosses over the complexity of his struggle to gain control of the Chinese Communist Party (the Tsunyi Conference is mentioned only as electing Mao as Chairman), the subtlety of his strategy in dealing with the Japanese and Chiang Kai-skek, and the ebb and flow of his power between the fifties and seventies.

While it is recognized that in such a short study little space can be devoted to the contributions of Mao's colleagues, the result is a one-dimensional product. Fitzgerald also seems loath to admit the depth of the conflicts over policy within China. For example, in the 1958–59 conflict he tends to downgrade the Commune program, the Great Leap Forward, or relations with the Soviet Union as major issues. He prefers to depict the conflict as centering on personalities, on differences between Mao and Liu Shao-chi, on the role of the creative force of mass opinion versus hierarchy and discipline. This latter issue is also used to explain both the Cultural Revolution and the break with Lin Piao. The author suggests that Lin, like Liu, would have imposed a rigid hierarchical structure on China in contrast to Mao's reliance on his revolutionary instinct, disbelief in elite rule and faith in the masses. This oversimplification ignores the fact that the Lin Piao affair was a succession struggle fought over hard policy issues, particularly with regard to economic development and perhaps foreign affairs, and a struggle between Party and Army for control of China's political system. The political role of the military is minimized as is the widespread support that Lin had within the Army. Finally, this affects Fitzgerald's prognosis for the future where he nowhere mentions the key role the military may play in determining the nature of the succession to Mao.

ALICE LANGLEY HSIEH

Arlington
Virginia

TOM FORESTER. *The British Labour Party and the Working Class*. Pp. x, 166. New York: Holmes & Meier, 1976. $11.50.

Since World War I the British Labour Party has been able to provide alternative governments to the Conservative Party. After World War II the Labour Government of Clement Attlee nationalized major industries and greatly extended the social benefits of the welfare state. But in recent years the enthusiasm for socialist reform has abated. This decline has enabled the Marxian Socialists to contend that the Labour Party has lost its radical zeal and is being taken over by the middle classes. Tom Forester is quick to refute these criticisms and to deny that there is a permanent trend downward in the fortunes of the Labour Party. His book demonstrates clear continuities between the Party of today with the Labour Representation Committee of seventy-five years ago when the Labour Party was founded. The author further shows that the Labour Party, although dedicated to the interests of the working class, has never been able to win more than two-thirds of the electoral support of the working classes. He finds that working classes, like other people, cherish a multitude of values, both social and cultural, that divide them from one another and create enmity among neighbors in every community.

In this book the author carefully distinguishes between the Parliamentary Labour Party (PLP) and the Constituency Labour Parties (CLPs), and he is concerned primarily with the latter and not the former. The PLP comprises the MPs and the Ministers who form the Government when Labor is in office and the Shadow Government when the Conservatives have a majority. The PLP elects their own Leader who eventually becomes the Prime Minister. The CLPs are the local units of the Labour Party whose primary purpose is to maintain the electoral organization which turns out the vote at elections. The strength of the CLPs depends more on the economic and social conditions of local communities than on the quality of the national leadership. Most histories of the Labour Party have been written without much knowledge of the CLPs, but in recent years scores of studies have been made by social scientists of the Labour Party at the local level. Since this careful research has been embodied in scholarly books and articles not readily available to the general reader, Tom Forester has written his book to survey this literature and to show the relationship between the CLPs and the working class. This excellent introduction to the literature deserves a place on the shelves of all those teaching comparative politics, social stratification, and recent British history.

RAYMOND G. COWHERD
Lehigh University
Bethlehem
Pennsylvania

ARNOLD J. HEIDENHEIMER, HUGH HECLO AND CAROLYN TEICH ADAMS. *Comparative Public Policy: The Politics of Social Choice in Europe and America*. Pp. 296. New York: St. Martin's Press, 1975. $12.95. Paperbound, $5.95.

A growing number of universities in North America have recently been adding courses on comparative public policy. Useful articles have appeared in the journals investigating the content and purpose of a new approach to the traditional concerns of both comparative politics and public policy. The problem of teaching such courses to undergraduates and graduates in a coherent manner has received less attention. With the appearance of this informative and useful volume that problem will be at least temporarily eased. The authors have sought "to enable those interested in public policy and the social sciences to surmount disciplinary and national boundaries" (p. 1). They have generally succeeded in presenting comparative data and alternative explanations for the similarities and differences in the public policy experience of several Western industrial societies. Using the United States as their reference point, the authors have drawn most of their material from Britain, Sweden, and West Germany with briefer references to France, Holland, and Denmark.

In the first of three parts, the study focuses on three areas of social reform: health policy, secondary education, and housing policy. The first of these areas is a popular topic because not only does the United States remain the only advanced industrial society without a comprehensive health policy, but in most other cases the basic principle of universal access to medical treatment has not recently even been an area of real controversy. To be certain, costs and administration have been a challenge in both Sweden, Britain, and other states providing collectively financed health care. In housing policy the problem of coherence between means and ends is more universal. Secondary educational policy finds the United States providing the benchmark with Sweden pursuing similar goals, and West Germany sticking firmly to the traditional early "tracking" of youth into specialized secondary schools. The authors use the widely available quantitative data on number of students (percentage of age groups) attending secondary schools for varying numbers of years. There is, however, little consideration of qualitative differences between secondary education systems or within national systems over time. It is often claimed by opponents of comprehensive secondary schools in West Germany and Great Britain that American and Swedish comprehensive schools have often lowered the quality of education and that American students study longer but do not reach the same average levels of academic achievement as the students in the traditional European tracked secondary schools. Such qualitative questions are, of course, very difficult to address, but they are essential to the systematic comparison of national policies. Recent UNESCO studies of comparative secondary school achievement levels in science and mathematics may provide a clue.

Ensuing chapters consider issues of local-national governmental policy interaction with specific reference to urban, educational, and transportation policies. There is some overlap between the treatment of educational issues here and those already treated in Part I, but the focus is somewhat different. For instructional purposes the treatment of educational governance issues in a separate section probably makes sense. The last section looks at income distribution issues through both maintenance and taxation policies. These questions are the heart of current reappraisal of the welfare state, and the authors manage to present complex material in a form that is readily understandable by non-economists. These chapters are fairly complete, but one could wish that an effort to introduce the concept of "lifetime incomes" had been made. The impact of taxation and transfer payments and social services provided without charge (or at less than cost) to the user can be considerably different over an extended period than in a single year.

A concluding chapter on growth and reform potentials in Europe and America does a good job of tying the case studies together. It also raises several questions about the future of the "welfare state" in the light of current economic, social and political changes in Western industrial societies. Three broad variables are noted as explaining differences in national social policy: structure of the political system, ideologies dominant in national cultures, and social conditions that give priorities to specific programs. Although the authors indicate that the expansion of social policies has nowhere created a social utopia, America lags severely in most programs. The prevalent attitude in the United States that social programs do not work reminds one, in the face of the evidence presented here, of Mark Twain's quip about Christianity.

ERIC S. EINHORN

University of Massachusetts
Amherst

CHAE-JIN LEE. *Japan Faces China: Political and Economic Relations in the Postwar Era*. Pp. v, 242. Baltimore, Md.: The Johns Hopkins University Press, 1976. $12.50.

Based largely on Tokyo and Peking publications, this compact book deals essentially with the manner in which Japan's ruling Liberal Democratic Party and opposition Socialist Party reacted between 1949 and 1972 to the shifting policy of the People's Republic of China. The JSP, which generally supported the policies of the People's Republic, was powerless to influence the LDP, which followed the U.S. policy of maintaining diplomatic relations with Taiwan and containing mainland China. China's aim was to loosen Japan's ties with the U.S. and Taiwan, prevent Japan from rearming, and normalize Chinese-Japanese relations. Some progress was made by Prime Minister Hatoyama in improving relations between Japan and China, but his successors, Kishi, Ikeda, and Sato, conscious of the U.S. connection and of Japan's large and profitable trade with Taiwan, were repelled by such things as China's Great Leap Forward, Cultural Revolution, abortive military coup in Indonesia, diplomatic strains with certain African countries and Cuba, and self-isolation. Even JSP leaders found that their close identification with China was a serious political liability. Though retreating in 1969 from her past militant and xenophobic foreign policy, China bitterly denounced the Nixon-Sato communique that year on the reversion of Okinawa as signaling "Okinawanization" of Japan, revival of the Greater East Asia Co-Prosperity Sphere, and sabotage of Korea's unification. The Soviet Union welcomed Okinawa's reversion as a deterrent to the development of a unilateral strategic force by Japan and to China's regional military temptations. Sudden news of Nixon's visit to China in 1971 produced a profound shock throughout Japan. No less shocking was the UN General Assembly vote to seat the People's Republic of China. China's new spirit of cooperation was attributed to her concern over the Soviet threat. Despite strong resistance from the pro-Taiwan forces in the LDP and top Japanese business circles, Prime Minister Tanaka, responding to Japanese public opinion and softening Chinese demands, established diplomatic relations with China in 1972, laying the foundation for exchanging advanced Japanese technology for Chinese oil and coal. Thus, without weakening her vital security arrangements with the U.S., Japan broadened her participation in the international power game.

The three core chapters of the book are amplified by an introductory chapter and a closing chapter. The appendixes consist of six pertinent papers on the progress of negotiations between Japan and China. Numerous illustrations and tables fortify the author's main points. The index is adequate.

JUSTIN WILLIAMS, SR.
Washington, D.C.

LINCOLN LI. *The Japanese Army in North China, 1937–1941: Problems of Political and Economic Control*. Pp. 278. New York: Oxford University Press, 1975. $27.00.

This book furnishes another chapter in the slowly growing literature on Japanese-occupied Asia. Drawing extensively on Chinese and Japanese sources, particularly material from the archives of the Japanese Foreign Ministry and records of the North China Army, the author examines the policies by which the Japanese sought to consolidate their control over North China during the period between the renewal of hostilities in 1937 and the outbreak of the Pacific War.

Those familiar with Japanese policies in occupied areas elsewhere in Asia will recognize numerous similarities. There were conflicts not only between civilian and military components of the government, between Tokyo and local commands, but also between military units—for example, between the North China Army and the Kwantung Army, its neighbor to the north. Japanese distrust produced local, collaborationist administrations which were very decentralized, virtually unarmed, and without a significant measure of autonomy. Little attention was paid to education, except of a narrowly technical kind, so that the number of schools and students declined. The goal of economic self-sufficiency tended to discourage any attempt at reforms and, in a food deficit area, intensified friction with the local population. Japanese civilian economic and financial interests, even the Zaibatsu, played a distinctly subordinate role.

How did Japanese policies affect the history of the Chinese Communist Party? At the heart of Japan's problem in North China, Li asserts, was a shortage of manpower which made it impossible for them to control the whole territory and which produced a four-zone arrangement which included neutral as well as Communist-held areas. In the attempt to quell opposition, the Japanese resorted to terrorist measures such as the notorious Three-All policy which intensified Chinese hostility, provoked guerrilla warfare and provided the Communists with the opportunity to assert their leadership. The fact that the Japanese eliminated virtually all non-Communist military units in the region also worked to the advantage of the Communists. In the argument as to whether the basis of the Communist appeal lay in their role as nationalist leaders or as social and economic reformers, Li's position is that both were involved but that, in North China, the national leadership role did not emerge until after 1941.

Neither the Communists nor the Chinese population are the central actors in this book, however. The focus is on the Japanese, what they did and why. It is from this perspective that the book makes its contribution—an important one—to the study of a significant period in Asian, as well as Japanese, history.

WILLARD H. ELSBREE

Ohio University
Athens

ALAN P. L. LIU. *Political Culture & Group Conflict in Communist China*. Pp. 205. Santa Barbara, Calif.: ABC-Clio Press, 1976. $17.95. Paperbound, $5.75.

The temptation to apply analytical political theories to the study of Chinese politics is almost irresistible for political scientists with a behavioral orientation and a special interest in China. Alan P. L. Liu's book *Political Culture & Group Conflict in Communist China* is one of the examples attempting to "link Chinese studies with general social science concepts" (preface). This work examines group conflicts in China during the Cultural Revolution from 1966 to 1969. Liu's basic approach is to interpret the Red Guard Movement in a theoretical framework of group conflict. The book is divided into three parts dealing with the conflict process, conflicting groups and, conflict and order. It discusses the various aspects of group conflict during this period, such as political culture, mobilization, violence, the major groups involved, and conflict resolution.

The strength of this book is its comprehensive coverage of the theoretical concepts applicable to the Cultural Revolution. It views the Red Guard Movement with one single analytical focus—group conflict. Many of Liu's interpretations are based on general theories of group conflict and thus have gone beyond the descriptive analysis in historical narratives. Liu has done a thorough and meticulous job in gathering relevant theories.

The difficulty with this book is that in his preoccupation with fitting events in the Cultural Revolution for theoretical explanation, Liu has failed to pay sufficient attention to the larger perspective of the Red Guard Movement in the Chinese political system. The Cultural Revolution is conceived, initiated, promoted, directed and finally suspended by Mao Tse-tung and his close associates. Contrary to Liu's contention that the Cultural Revolution lacks a clear and identifiable goal (p. 174), Mao has definite and officially stated objectives in launching this movement. The Red Guard organization is one of the several instruments used by Mao to achieve his goals. Space does not permit elaboration on this point here. The rivalry among Red Guard groups is largely confined to lower levels. They are not spontaneous pressure groups as those in Western societies. They have never challenged Mao's precepts nor his authority, and they only attack people who are not protected by Mao. Their activities are constrained by the basic policies laid down by the Chairman. The break down of control over the Red Guards in some provinces cannot be construed as the total collapse of Mao's leadership over them. The dissolution of the Shen-wu-lien by the Central Cultural Revolution Group in January 1968 and the final crack down on radical Red Guards by the People's Liberation Army have convincingly demonstrated Mao's control over the course of the Cultural Revolution.

A more serious problem of this book is its extremely limited sources on Red Guards' personal experience which is the basis of most of Liu's theoretical conclusions. For this first hand observation, Liu relies chiefly on the account of two former high school Red Guards, Ken Ling and Dai Hsiao-ai, from Fukien and Kwangtung respectively. One of the frustrations for students of Communist China is the scarcity of reliable data. Fortunately, the study of the Cultural Revolution is a rare exception.

Many original documents and eyewitness reports including interviews with former Red Guards are available in Japan, Hong Kong, Taiwan and other countries. Liu does not appear to have consulted many of these sources. The heavy dependence on the experience of two high school students from the two southernmost provinces of China may not reflect the reality of the nationwide situation. Furthermore, the Red Guards are led by college students in Peking, not by high school students in the provinces.

Two minor matters ought to be pointed out also. The book includes too many unnecessary lengthy quotations. In a small book of only 205 pages, these quotations seem to be a waste of valuable space. The name K'ang Sheng, one of the top Chinese leaders who played an important role in the Cultural Revolution, is misspelled as Kang Shen throughout the book.

Liu's book has not shed any new light on our understanding of the Chinese Cultural Revolution, nor has his work added any new information on the subject. But Liu's commendable effort to apply general social science concepts and theories to the analysis of the Cultural Revolution has provided a significant example of the rewards and pitfalls in the theorization of Chinese studies. It is a useful book for students of political science, especially for those who are interested in comparative politics.

GEORGE P. JAN

The University of Toledo
Ohio

EDWARD J. SCHUMACHER. *Politics, Bureaucracy, and Rural Development in Senegal*. Pp. xxi, 279. Berkeley: University of California Press, 1975. $18.75.

While providing a general introduction to government in Senegal from 1957 to 1970, the particular value of this study lies in two areas. One is the exploration of the inner workings of Senegalese politics, which the author likens to a political machine. The other is an attempt to evaluate the ability of the governing elite to create and implement policy that is designed to modernize rural economic structures.

Senegal's political life is historically indebted to the institution of patron-clientage—a system that preceded colonial rule. Today its one-party state is sustained and nourished by an extended series of patron-client networks leading from local to national levels. In return for support, loyalty, or esteem, the leader offers material or status-oriented rewards. Politics is not centered on ideology or symbolic values, but is materially oriented. Jobs, contracts, licenses, loans, scholarships, and the like are the spoils, and the struggle to gain access to positions that control and mete out the rewards is intense.

In Schumacher's view politics of this type hinders administrative efforts to secure compliance with innovative development policies, and allows only for the perpetuation of the status quo. Modernization, too, is undermined by the fact that traditional leaders and structures in rural areas are more effective than representatives of the centralized bureaucracy. (This is a debatable point and I shall return to it.) On the whole this is the rationale the author develops in order to account for the fact that there have been more failures than successes in Senegal's rural development. Official response to failure has been to shape new strategies. Time-tables have been lengthened for attaining goals; individual (rather than ideological) rewards are emphasized; expectations and preferences of international funding agencies are being catered to.

But will this achieve the desired reforms and facilitate development? Schumacher thinks not. Others have suggested that increased development is dependent upon a more efficient and publicly accountable bureaucracy. For them the bureaucracy based on a Western model is appropriate to Africa, and Schumacher is in agreement. In fact he recommends Senegal's bureaucratic establishment be strengthened, although he is quick to warn that specific research on how to implement this is yet to be done.

In coming to this recommendation the author has relied heavily on previous prescriptions by his peers, whereas his own investigations have suggested alternative lines of action. For example Schumacher finds that traditional institutions, leaders, and values in rural areas are extremely resilient and adaptable. Yet this sector is glossed over as the author—and he is not alone in this regard—searches for ways to strengthen rural productivity.

Perhaps it is here and not at the bureaucratic level that it is appropriate to ask if the Western model of development has obscured a possible source of support. Suggestions that the bureaucracy be reinforced still overlook the practical issue of who is to oversee the implementation of policy, the introduction of innovative elements, and especially the securing of compliance on a day-to-day basis. Civil servants as a rule do not like to live and work in rural communities. Traditional leaders and notables do.

In their recently announced plans to restructure local government, Nigerian administrators indicate they will design units large enough to be development-oriented but flexible enough to utilize traditional authorities as leaders, advisors, and enforcement officials. Thus while development-oriented scholars continue to urge there be stronger bureaucracies, they miss a point that some administrators are themselves beginning to recognize: impersonal dealings with unknown civil servants do not necessarily produce compliance. Local leaders have well-established relationships, influence with their public, and a vested interest in the welfare of their communities. As conduits for development policy they may still offer one of the least tapped resources of the new nations.

Schumacher has not considered this possibility. Any shortcomings in his policy recommendations, however, are more than compensated for in other respects. He has provided an abundance of information on Senegal's bureaucratic and agricultural sectors. Interest in rural development in Africa is gaining momentum and therefore Schumacher's solid contribution comes at an appropriate time.

SANDRA T. BARNES
University of Pennsylvania
Philadelphia

RISHIKESH SHAHA. *Nepali Politics: Retrospect and Prospect*. Pp. viii, 208. New York: Oxford University Press, 1975. $7.50.

This excellent work constitutes an extremely informative, comprehensive, and up-to-date treatment of the government and politics of Nepal. It presents a balanced and objective analysis as well as a reasoned critical assessment of the Nepali political system. The analysis is complemented by selective and compact historical accounts of the evolution of principal institutions and political circumstances. Mr. Shaha is an experienced participant-observer who judiciously and skillfully combines the perspectives of political theorist, statesman, and social scientist. He is completely familiar with the major events and central figures in Nepali politics, and he brings to this study not only systematic scholarship but exceptional interpretative insight. While he has often been a candid but constructive critic of the current regime, he has played an important role in the government of Nepal and has served as a principal architect of the present constitution as well as ambassador to both the United States and the United Nations.

The book is divided into three parts which deal with political development, the Panchayat system of legislative representation, and international relations. The basic theme is the impact on politics of the tension between the indigenous culture and modernization. Mr. Shaha correctly perceives the paradox involved in a traditional Hindu monarchy embracing an ideology of development when most of the characteristics associated with the various dimensions of development and Westernization would tend to undermine the bases of traditional authority. His general recommendation seems to be for Nepal to pursue an active development program which, he believes, can best be facilitated by a relaxation of the tendency toward the centralization of power in the palace, a broadening of representation and the revival of party and opposition politics, and a realization of the more democratic principles of the constitution in order to increase political participation and social mobilization.

Mr. Shaha tends to accept too uncritically the views of American political scientists regarding the character and requirements of development and institution building. He also too easily accepts the Western image of politics as an ideal of democracy and a criterion of political development. Intellectuals in developing countries would do well to pay as much attention to recent critics of pluralism and interest group liberalism as they do to social scientific literature which implicitly equates political development with political culture and institutions. However, the deficiencies of this book are minor, and, after living for a year in Kathmandu, I judge it to be a thorough and lucid account of the politics of this Himalayan kingdom and the best general work on this subject that is available.

JOHN G. GUNNELL
State University of New York
Albany

ROBERT L. TIGNOR. *The Colonial Transformation of Kenya: Kamba, Kikuyu, and Maasai from 1900 to 1939.* Pp. 372. Princeton, N.J.: Princeton University Press, 1976. $25.00.

This is a very competent book. From the introductory passages one feared it might be just another diatribe against colonial exploitation, but in fact the author is both well-informed and dispassionately critical.

His examination of the pros and cons of the controversial system of indirect rule as practised in Kenya is excellent. His portrait of John Ainsworth as the type-figure of the administrator whose paternal concern for the welfare of his charges conflicted on occasion with their social and economic interests brings out more clearly than any general commentary could do the virtual impossibility of finding a satisfactory solution for the problems with which he was confronted.

Education and the Christian Missions; dispossession from tribal land; forced recruitment of labour for private as well as public service; alien legal institutions; these problems have arisen time and again all over the world ever since Columbus discovered America.

(Curiously enough, considering their record further south, the Spanish rulers of California seem to have solved them better, or perhaps avoided creating them more successfully, than most.)

They are considered here in great detail in their East African setting. It is ironical how often the most furious resentment was aroused not by punitive action, to which Africans were only too well accustomed, but by well-intentioned reforms. Such was the attempt to compel people to send children to school, and above all the interference with the barbarous but vital custom of female circumcision, which was destined to provide the major incentive to Mau Mau.

It is remarkable how public opinion has changed during the last fifty years. Up till late in the 19th century nobody seriously questioned the principle that a strong nation expanded at the expense of its neighbours. Sometimes the latter were exterminated, as happened in North America and Australia. Sometimes they were absorbed, as happened to the Picts in Scotland. Sometimes they were assimilated, as in the ancient Roman and modern French empires.

A remarkable manifestation of this expansionist ideology was the Anglo-Saxon dream of world domination, a tremendous pioneering force in its day. The half-hearted attempt after the '14–'18 war to create a white dominion in the highlands of Kenya was, apart from the creation of the state of Israel, which was sui generis, the last example of this attitude, though not, alas, of nationalist aggression.

Not the least important aspect of this book is its discussion of the reasons for the emergence of the Kikuyu as the dominant power in post-colonial Kenya. Like the Ibos in Nigeria, they seem to have a special capacity for adaptation to modern conditions, coupled with a quickness of wit and a general ability which leave their rivals far behind. Knowledgeable persons used to tip the Luo as their most likely rivals.

When you have finished reading this excellent book you may be interested in two others. One is Julian Huxley's *Africa View*, which strongly influenced British colonial policy in this area from 1931. The other is a novel by Nicholas Montserrat, called *The Tribe Which Lost Its Head*.

K. D. D. HENDERSON

Wittshire
England

LATIN AMERICA

COLIN G. CLARKE. *Kingston, Jamaica: Urban Growth and Social Change, 1692–1962*. Pp. xii, 270. Berkeley: University of California Press, 1976. $25.75.

In this, the first systematic study of a city in the English-speaking Caribbean, Colin G. Clarke (a geographer from the University of Liverpool) is essentially asking: how and why did Kingston develop so badly? This city, with more than 500,000 inhabitants in 1970, or one quarter of Jamaica's population, is of course the storm center of Jamaica's current political/economic/social crisis. Clarke blends geography, history, economics, sociology and demography in his analysis, with prime focus on the post-World War II period, especially the Kingston census returns for 1943 and 1960. His text is richly illustrated with 32 tables, 93 maps, and 32 photographs of the city.

Clarke tells a depressing story of a town that has never begun to fulfill its great practical and aesthetic potential. Kingston has a magnificent natural setting, facing a superb protected harbor, and is built on a spacious rising plain flanked by mountains. It was originally laid out on a generous gridiron plan, echoing William Penn's plan for Philadelphia ten years earlier, but this plan was sabotaged (as in Philadelphia) by the early inhabitants, who wanted to crowd along the harbor front and business center. The merchants who dominated the place in the eighteenth-century heyday of Jamaican sugar production spent little of their wealth on domestic architecture, and—as in all towns in English America—expended almost nothing on public buildings, parks or promenades. As large numbers of free coloureds, ex-slaves and fugitive slaves began to filter into Kingston to escape from labor on the sugar estates, the rich whites withdrew into northern suburbs above the city, where their successors remain today. Clarke shows how the city has always been so rigidly stratified along static geographic/economic/color lines that it is nearly pointless to debate whether race or class is the more important determinant. Up to the 1960s the small white (or European) sector has controlled Kingston. The far more numerous coloured (or Afro-European) sector—joined over time by Jews, Chinese and Syrians—has held low to median jobs and lived in the city center or inner suburbs. The Negroes (or Africans) and East Indians, the largest sector of the population by far, have consistently been relegated to the worst jobs or to permanent unemployment, and have long lived in overcrowded tenements and stockaded squatter camps in West Kingston. Though this city has been a magnet for two hundred years to peasants and plantation laborers, it has always lacked the industrial base for adequate working class employment. As Clarke demonstrates, throughout the colonial period the white island leaders did little or nothing to meet the economic and social problems of the Kingston poor. Since World War II the new black leaders have tried hard to promote industrialization and have instituted significant improvements in education and in housing for middle income Kingstonians, but so many poor and uneducated people have flooded into the city in the last generation that all plans have totally failed to meet their needs. Nearly 200,000 slum dwellers are now increasingly turning to murder and political violence as outlets for their frustration.

In assessing an interdisciplinary book such as Clarke's, it is easy to think of additional things the author might have done. Being an historian, I wish he had not relied on thin and antiquated secondary sources for his treatment of the eighteenth and nineteenth centuries: there is a wealth of unexploited data in the island archives, such as the thousands of inventories listing the possessions of colonial Kingstonians in the probate records. An architectural historian would wish for much fuller treatment of Kingston's consistently unimpressive experiments in tropical building. A city planner would like fuller discussion of the changing physical layout of the town, or perhaps some comparison with other Caribbean towns—for example, Port-of-Spain, Trinidad, which despite its crowded natural setting has devoted far more open space to parks and promenades than Kingston has. A sociologist could wish that Clarke had supplemented his excellent cartographic and tabular analysis of the 1943 and 1960 censuses with interviews of a cross-section of residents from key enumeration districts. A political scientist would want the story carried past 1962 so as to trace geographic/economic/color changes (if any) during the first decade of independence. But no one author can do everything, and Colin Clarke should be congratulated for accomplishing an innovative, imaginative and highly interesting analysis of a very important Caribbean city.

RICHARD S. DUNN
University of Pennsylvania
Philadelphia

SHEPARD FORMAN. *The Brazilian Peasantry*. Pp. viii, 319. New York: Columbia University Press, 1975. $13.50.

Shepard Forman is an anthropologist whose professional interest in, and human concern for the Brazilian Peasantry dates to the early 1960s. His latest work on the subject is a clearly-written, well-organized attempt to describe and explain the past and current condition of that important but oppressed segment of Brazilian society. The author approaches his subject in a direct and logical manner, beginning with the historical evolution of the Brazilian Peasantry, proceeding to the economic, social and political dimensions of the agrarian crisis, and concluding with peasant religion and movements of social protest.

The historical section is useful in that it provides evidence that, contrary to what many authorities believe, peasants are, and for centuries have been a very important element in the Brazilian socioeconomic system. Slaves, of course, were important during the colonial period and throughout most of the Empire; but, from the earliest times a free peasantry also existed and, indeed, played a crucial role in the economy. The relationship between peasants, patrons, and the land has always been subject to change, but, in the twentieth century, increased emphasis on commercialization has created a situation of severe crisis for the agrarian lower classes.

In describing the peasant's social position, the author sheds further light on a society which others have described as "patrimonial." "Hierarchy," says Forman, "is a fundamental tenet of Brazilian Social life" (p. 75.). Peasants are obliged to seek out "patron-dependancy" relationships in order to survive. The patron is often extremely harsh but the peasant rarely questions his authority since he sees it as basically legitimate. This, in part, explains why organized peasant reform movements are extremely rare in Brazil.

Forman's discussion of the economic

dimension is also quite useful. In it, the author maintains that recent increased emphasis on commercial export agriculture has threatened the peasant in two ways. First, it has increased the value of the land, therefore leading to the displacement of peasants through mechanization. Second, it has changed market relationships shifting the advantage from peasant vendors to middlemen who prefer to buy from large producers. What is more, various panaceas—such as group colonization and the creation of cooperatives—which have been proposed as ways of alleviating the economic insecurity of the peasants, do not seem to work very well when put into practice.

The political picture is no brighter. The peasant has never had much real political power. To this day he remains disenfranchized and unorganized while the agricultural elite—though now somewhat less influential in national politics—continues to dominate the rural scene.

The study concludes with a particularly poignant examination of peasant religion. Though nominally Catholic, Brazilian peasants, according to Forman, are manipulative and this-worldly in their approach to religion. Individuals enter into "contracts" with saints, groups from time to time cast their lot with latter-day Messiahs, all in an attempt to alter a world in which they are otherwise virtually helpless. Religion in this sense, is a pressure valve for peasant discontent.

Forman's study, then, is a welcome contribution to the literature. It is a well-written, well-documented treatment of an important subject. What is more, it provides a number of fresh insights which help the reader to understand and empathize with the plight of this "agglomerate of dispairing people, longing to be saved, still seeking the miracle, and still acquiescing to the will of God" (p. 245).

THOMAS W. WALKER

Ohio University
Athens

PETER D'A. JONES. *Since Columbus: Poverty and Pluralism in the History of the Americas*. Pp. vi, 282. Totowa, N.J.: Rowman and Littlefield, 1976. $12.50.

As an ostensible five-century history of some two dozen diverse cultures, this book is an unmitigated failure. There are only about 220 pages of text—260 less those used for maps and photographs. Not all historians, even if using a more suitable size of book, would want to analyze together both of the Americas, for essentially they are profoundly different. In spite of its faults and lacks, the United States has been an economic and social success; and one can therefore draw parallels with less favored countries only by emphasizing its every negative element and passing lightly over every positive one. The distortion is not incidental, in a tendentious detail here or there, but rather pervasive, comprising the framework of the entire content.

The substance of the book consists largely of lists of dates, names, places, more dates. Some of these facts are wrong (for example, Allende was not a lawyer but a physician). Some summarize complex social questions with a truly sophomoric assurance (for example, "FDR simply did not spend *enough* on public works and employment"). But most of these details, with no discernible context, are simply meaningless and thus unutterably dull.

Since one of the author's reiterated points is that in most of Latin America the "nation" has been a more or less artificial construct, the organization of the book's material by country is seldom successful. If the "revolution" by which Panama broke away from Colombia is put between quotation marks, should one then discuss the opinions and actions of "Panamanians"? If in Latin America the difference between "liberal" and "conservative" parties is often nominal, should one devote space in a too short book to contests between them?

In fact, then, the dimensions of the principal framework are several highly questionable concepts—"dependency," "neo-colonialism," "plural society," and the like. It is not merely that some of these reify political biases but, as Jones uses them, they change their meaning with the locale. As developed in Horace Kallen's analysis of the United States, "cultural pluralism" meant that immigrant groups should not be forced to adapt fully to established American norms. Such a policy recommendation differs fundamentally from French Canadians' demands for cultural or even quasipolitical independence, as well as from the economic-cultural-political denigration of Indians in Mexico, Brazil, or Bolivia. To cook up all these in one pot is to prepare a stew that no knowledgeable person will find palatable.

WILLIAM PETERSEN

Ohio State University
Columbus

ALEJANDRO PORTES and JOHN WALTON. *Urban Latin America: The Political Condition from Above and Below*. Pp. 217. Austin: University of Texas Press, 1976. $13.95.

In the midst of the publication explosion on urbanization and urban life in Latin America, Portes and Walton have written important interpretive and analytical essays. Using the extant literature, utilizing their own research, and unafraid to be conjectural, they have produced a book that is often exciting.

Other than the joint, brief Introduction and Conclusion, each author is represented by two long essays. In "Elites and the Politics of Urban Development," Walton compares the civic concern of the leaderships in Guadalajara, Monterrey, Cali and Medellín, and proceeds to seek the causes of the very different records. His "Structures of Power in Latin American Cities" is far more ambitious. With evidence from 26 studies (of which four are his own) he explores the validity of seven propositions that have been posited as to "the structural correlates and consequences of the distribution of power." *Inter alia* he finds that in the shift from rule by small, tightly interrelated elites there is neither a displacement of those elites nor a widening of effective political participation to incorporate groups outside the elites. Rather, there are merely new styles of elite domination:

> The emergence of new urban elites based on alliances among the class interests of landowners, industrialists, exporters, development-minded politicians, and foreign investors has at least perpetuated, if not exacerbated, earlier structures of inequality. Nowhere do we encounter evidence of a net gain in the power or privilege of the peasantry and the urban worker (p. 168).

Or, again: he finds no example, in the studies, of "a viable and representative pattern of political pluralism . . . Seldom do middle-class interests constitute an independent source of political power, and there are no cases of regularized lower-class access to policy-making circles (p. 164).

The fundamental sources of elite attitudes and of continued elite domination are succinctly plumbed by Portes. "The Economy and Ecology of Urban Poverty" traces the history of the Iberian cities on the continent; cities that served as loci for conquest and exploitation, for an elitist social order, in which the poor were tolerated while remaining "an object of total unconcern to the official and wealthy city, except perhaps as objects of Catholic charity." And, he argues, this character has survived to the present, absorbing into its value system later immigrants, migrants, and the socially mobile. The spatial shift of the social composition of the cities is delineated: the elite move from the center to the periphery with, often, their own neighborhoods geographically separated from the sprawling shanty towns by the middle and artisan sectors occupying the original core—with, of course, the soaring urban land market manipulated to the benefit of the elite landowners.

Best of all, in this reviewer's opinion, is Portes' "The Politics of Urban Poverty." The urban poor *do* feel frustrations, often severe ones, although there is an absence of "structural blame" for them. The poor *do* participate in collective political action when they believe it to be both necessary and possible in meeting needs: especially housing and landownership. Their political participation is rational: "Rational adaptation and instrumental organization to cope with the existing social order have been the trademarks of the politics of urban poverty in Latin America." The particular form of participation, including vote bargaining, petitions and land invasions, depends largely upon the dominant political conditions. And, being aware of political conditions and embroiled in the task of sheer survival, they will not throw their support to revolutionaries until victory is assured or achieved. These findings, and many more, are supported by wideranging evidence and specific case studies. Along the way, Portes also gives what one hopes is final interment to two common myths about the urban poor: that they are locked in a "subculture of poverty," and that they are a seething hotbed of fury and radicalism. Comfortably logical "continuums of political participation" receive justifiably rough handling.

In their Conclusion, the authors note that the explosive urban growth of Latin America (there are about 20,000 urban squatter settlements on the continent) is far from being a sign of progress. On the contrary, it lies at the center of the circle of excessive centralization, inequality, and stagnant agriculture.

A paperback edition would be most welcome.

DONALD HINDLEY
Brandeis University
Waltham
Massachusetts

FRANK SAFFORD. *The Ideal of the Practical: Colombia's Struggle to Form a Technical Elite*. Pp. xiii, 373. Austin: University of Texas Press, 1975. $15.00.

Can the leadership of a developing country foment economic growth by providing technical education and attempting to develop values oriented toward the technical? Very little, if the Colombian experience in the 19th century is to be our guide. Frank Safford argues here that, in Colombia at least, economic growth was itself the prerequisite necessary for the implantation of a technical orientation.

Continuing attempts in the 19th century by part of the upper class in this aristocratic Latin American nation to modify cultural values toward the technical and the practical are described in detail. Early nineteenth century Colombia which had a static agrarian economy and a large proportion of poor and uneducated alongside a tiny wealthy aristocracy who abhorred manual labor, early experimented with manual industrial training. A chapter follows on academic science for the upper classes. Science was not attractive because there were few career possibilities. The careers of upper class youth who were sent abroad for technical and scientific training are explored in a later chapter as are the origins of a Colombian engineering profession. An epilogue treats the twentieth century evolution of technical elites in Colombia.

We believe that Safford's thesis is generally correct for Colombia. His descriptions of the interplay between the various obstructions such as the aristocratic social values and a hierarchical social structure and barriers such as geographic and economic conditions are interesting to the reader who wishes to delve into the details of a case study. There are, however, problem areas in the monograph which detract from its value. Safford's thesis that "the early republican elite sought to direct the upper classes as well as the poor toward technology and economic enterprise" is inadequately documented. Nowhere do we find a discussion of the instruments by which the elite directed the upper class to this end. In fact, the government had neither the authority nor the resources to create incentives to do so. Upper class youth studied abroad with their own families' resources.

A second difficulty relates to the lack of background of the author in engineering. One example is his use of the word "road" instead of "trail." To engineers a road is a finished surface which accommodates wheels. But there were

no roads in Colombia until the twentieth century. He also fails to perceive that it has been geology rather than topography which has posed the major problem in the Colombian Andes in the construction of railroads, roads, and even trails.

The bibliography is extensive, but it contains some questionable entries (for example, *Manuela, novela de costumbres colombianas* by Diaz which is not referred to in the text). There are some nagging errors in spelling (even of Colombia, p. 235), some partly translated phrases (p. 359), and abbreviations unexplained (p. 332). Many of these could have been caught by more careful review. Others of content and interpretation could have been corrected had the author personally consulted with even several of the many engineers mentioned in the volume (Julio Carrizosa Valenzuela, Vicente Pizano Restrepo, among others highly knowledgeable and respected).

It will be a pity if this monograph is not translated into Spanish for, in our judgement, it would stir much more interest and discussion in Colombia than it is likely to have among social scientists and engineers in the United States. The main strength of the study is its historical detail and the telling of the story rather than in the validation of the thesis of development preceding the technical and the practical since there is no evidence that the effort in terms of organization and resources was ever very great in 19th century Colombia.

DONALD L. HUDDLE and
ALBERTO GOMEZ-RIVAS
Rice University
Houston
Texas

UNITED STATES HISTORY AND POLITICS

ALWYN BARR. *Black Texans: A History of Negroes in Texas, 1528–1971.* Negro Heritage Series, No. 12. Pp. xi, 259. Austin, Texas: Jenkins Publishing Company, 1973. $8.50.

Blacks occupy an integral place in Texas history. Alwyn Barr attempts to cover the multiplicity of black Texans' experiences from 1528 to 1971 in a single volume. His primary purpose is to provide general readers with "a summary of available information about Negroes in Texas" (p. viii). Barr also seeks to reinterpret certain aspects of black Texans' history and to provide high school and college instructors with a survey which in part will serve as a corrective for existing textbook treatment of Negroes. Primarily descriptive rather than analytical, his account basically relies upon information contained in secondary sources.

Barr's survey contains no central thesis, other than the general story of the problems, progress, and continued frustrations black Texans have faced at almost every turn. The book begins on an uneven note by attempting to cover from the time the Moorish slave Estevan journeyed with Cabeza de Vaca and his master to Texas shores in 1528 to the close of the Civil War in but two chapters or 38 pages. Coverage of the post-1865 era broadens to include black activities during Reconstruction, the heightening of black pride, and the current status of black families. Barr conveys a sense of the hardships facing black Texans when they sought better education, entry into the professions, and the acquisition of rights guaranteed to all Americans. Echoing the findings of recent historians, Barr notes the growth of segregation prior to the 1890s, the increased importance of black churches and social organizations when Negroes' political and economic positions were circumscribed, and the generally accelerated rate of progress for blacks in the post-1940 era.

Overall, Barr's account reads easily and contains much factual information. The text is free of footnotes, and the bibliographic essay reflects extensive reading in secondary sources, including unpublished dissertations, theses and papers. The book, however, is not without problems. Noticeable gaps and omissions plague Barr's narrative. Given the span attempted and the voids in existing scholarship, a synthesis like *Black Texans* is bound to slight some topics. Nevertheless, one is surprised to find such scant attention paid to events of the magnitude of the Civil War, World War I, the New Deal, and World War II, in the lives of Texas blacks. Indeed, such treatment will lead many scholars and teachers to question whether a study of this scope should have been attempted in a single, slender volume. Alwyn Barr's *Black Texans* offers general readers a compact survey, but historians and instructors will conclude that the volume attempts more than it can deliver.

PAUL W. BREWER

Albuquerque
New Mexico

STUART M. BLUMIN. *The Urban Threshold: Growth and Change in a Nineteenth-Century American Community*. Pp. xiv, 298. Chicago, Ill.: The University of Chicago Press, 1976. $16.50.

This study of Kingston, New York, between 1820 and 1860, is one of the first books in the growing field of urban history actually to examine the process of urban growth. Most recent works of the so-called "new urban history" have contented themselves with minute dissection of urban social structure. But Blumin is primarily interested in how country towns become transformed into cities and the effect of urbanization on community life. Hence both the choice of town and of time period are significant—Kingston was an old agricultural town which saw its economy and social life transformed in the antebellum period.

Blumin begins with an analysis of Kingston's economy and social structure in 1820, when most residents were farmers and descendants of the Dutch settlers. The paucity of sources for this period makes this the weakest part of the book, but it provides a backdrop for understanding the massive changes of the next forty years. Blumin next analyzes the major forces for change in Kingston: the opening of the canal in 1826, which linked this Hudson River town to eastern Pennsylvania coal fields; and the arrival of European immigrants and native migrants, permanently altering Kingston's social structure. Most of the book analyzes the results of these changes. The physical landscape changed; local political issues took on greater importance, as the town experienced local versions of national conflicts; and the organizational structure of the town became more complex. Using both sophisticated analysis of quantitative sources, along with newspapers and diaries, the author captures the subtle process of change in this town.

Community identification is the central concern underlying this examination of urban development. Blumin questions the common assumption that urbanization in the nineteenth century meant wrenching changes and a breakdown of tightly-knit communities. He argues quite the contrary: that there was very little sense of "community" in the pre-1820 town, whereas the increasingly complex organizational structure which accompanied urbanization intensified residents' awareness of, and attachment to, Kingston as a community. He stresses the ways that the changes brought by urbanization heightened Kingstonians' sense of community. Local political issues did not capture much attention before 1820, but urbanization created local issues of sufficient importance to command the attention and energy of a sizeable proportion of residents. Before 1820, most residents knew everyone else in town, but Blumin finds no evidence that they identified with Kingston as a community per se. The voluntary organizations of the 1850s, however, generated strong loyalties, which Blumin equates with community attachment. Provocative as this argument may be, however, it remains unproven. Despite the scarcity of evidence on pre-1820 Kingston, Blumin dismisses the possibility that Kingstonians may not have written about community awareness because they took it for granted. Their attachment to various organizations in the 1850s might indicate loyalty to specific groups, rather than to the whole community. But reservations about his thesis cannot obscure the high quality of this book. In analyzing the process of urbanization and its consequences for political and social organization, Blumin has helped set the pace for future work in this field.

LYNNE E. WITHEY
University of Iowa
Iowa City

RALPH ADAMS BROWN. *The Presidency of John Adams*. American Presidency Series. Pp. x, 248. Lawrence: The University Press of Kansas, 1975. $12.00.

Time was when hardly anyone had a kind word for John Adams. In the past three decades, however, scholars have done much to resurrect the image of the New Englander. Ralph Adams Brown's volume probably represents the most laudatory treatment of Adams to date. The author attempts to show that Adams' critics and opponents were incorrect in their assessment and that Adams' administration "was marked by wise and unselfish decisions. . ." (p. ix).

While not presenting much new material, Brown's discussions cover many important aspects of Adams' tenure. Foreign affairs, the focus around which virtually all other issues revolved during the late 1790s, receive the most attention. Adams is pictured as a president contending with a potentially explosive national temper and political opposition within and outside his party as the country moved into an undeclared war with France. The author concurs with Adams' assessment that the achievement of peace with France was the greatest accomplishment of his career.

Few would quarrel with Brown's assessment of the centrality of foreign affairs, but many readers will take issue with the degree to which the author slights other areas. Brown shows, for instance, that Adams preferred peace over his own political advancement, but leaves the reader puzzled over Adams' views on the importance of the election of 1800 or the role of political parties. The organization of the book adds to the imbalance. Only after carrying the diplomatic story down through the fall of 1799 does the author return in any detail to the Alien and Sedition controversy and other earlier, often related domestic developments. The result is a choppy, fragmented story. There also is a problem of perspective. If the study of a public figure is to be effective, it must pay sufficient attention to the context in which the individual operates. Brown's account is only partially successful in this respect. It touches but briefly, for example, on the larger questions involving the United States as an emerging nation or the general factors underlying Adams' defeat for re-election. At times, however, Brown goes to the other extreme. He seldom criticizes Adams, but in the rare departures from this pattern, as in his abbreviated discussion of the Alien and Sedition acts, he spends most of his energies qualifying his criticism. Brown even devotes an entire chapter to defending Adams against charges concerning his possibly inflammatory rhetoric and his absences from the capital. In these and other instances, general readers may well feel buffeted about in a historiographical war neither of their making nor particularly of their concern, and scholars may suspect that the author has set up a straw man; the negative views of Adams which he seeks to counter are chiefly those perpetrated by historians of a much earlier period, not those of modern scholars. Ralph Adams Brown's book contributes to the continuing rejuvenation of John Adams, but it neither matches nor supplants previous studies of America's second president.

PAUL W. BREWER
Albuquerque
New Mexico

EDWARD M. COOK, JR. *The Fathers of the Towns: Leadership and Community Structure in Eighteenth-Century New England*. Pp. xvii, 265. Baltimore, Md.: The Johns Hopkins University Press, 1976. No price.

In this fine scholarly study, Edward Cook has successfully advanced historians' understanding of two very important aspects of colonial life: the nature of political leadership and the differences among towns in New England. Cook focuses on the local officials, describing the process by which they were chosen, their length of tenure, plus the significant role which wealth, family and religious participation played in their obtaining positions of leadership. The discussion on each topic naturally involves description, but the author consistently and skillfully integrates analysis into the text, raising and answering questions both broad and narrow as they arise out of his material. In fact, the book reads somewhat like a continuous, logical stream of thought punctuated by supporting evidence and explanations concerning the author's theoretical underpinnings and methodology—why he chose the variables he did, how he obtained his information, potential biases in his sources, and the like.

Cook's supporting evidence takes the form of laws, individual cases, and statistics. Frankly this book has too much detail and too many dry statistics to be either easy or enjoyable reading for any but the most enthusiastic student of the topic. And the insertion of an endless number of tables into the body of the text is made all the more annoying by the fact that the statistics provided are not always completely adequate. In order to fully answer the type of questions he has posed, the author really needed to go beyond the raw percentages he provides and deal more with the interaction of variables. Cook never really tests the degree to which his key factors of wealth, family and religious participation were dependent on each other. Essentially he treats them as independent and discusses their effects on leadership selection as if these were entirely discreet effects. Such a technique also means that he can't effectively weight them in terms of importance. But he has taken on a broad task here in trying to cover all of New England, and it would have been remarkable indeed if he had succeeded in presenting an analysis which was definitive in all respects.

Actually, the breadth of his study is one of its most valuable aspects, since up to now most of the significant books on New England community life have focused on individual towns, usually Massachusetts towns. Cook bases his generalizations on a much wider sample, including settlements in Connecticut, New Hampshire and Rhode Island. Moreover, he makes a concerted effort to actually categorize the different types of towns in New England, based on the constellation of leadership patterns which emerged in the different communities he studied. He comes up with a five-category breakdown which coincides roughly with the categories growing out of geographers' central place theory. In place of Jackson Turner Main's familiar divisions of frontier areas, subsistence farming areas, commercial farming areas and cities, Cook claims that in New England at least, the significant forms were frontier communities, farming villages, secondary urban centers, major county towns, and cities.

This aspect of his study, pre-figured in his important article on the typology of towns which appeared a few years back, should provide a structure for future studies of individual New England communities—a way of putting them in perspective. Hopefully other historians will fill out and support the picture Cook has drawn in his overview. In the meantime, *The Fathers of the Towns* is valuable reading for anyone interested in leadership patterns or community structure in early America.

LAURA BECKER
University of Pennsylvania
Philadelphia

LINO A. GRAGLIA. *Disaster by Decree: The Supreme Court Decisions on Race and the Schools*. Pp. 351. Ithaca, N.Y.: Cornell University Press, 1976. $11.50.

Professor Graglia's book is a penetrating assessment of the role of federal courts in the controversial and volatile area of schools and racial desegregation. Most of the evidence reviewed consists of a detailed analysis of court rulings, and their effects, over the last quarter century that have unearthed legally sanctioned racial discrimination and that have ordered busing in many school districts throughout the United States. The overall verdict of this book is that the federal courts, and especially the Supreme Court, have done less than a spectacular job, disrupting the political process through actions immune from direct public accountability, distorting and undermining the intents of other, more representative, branches of government, issuing orders barren of clear, logically (and Constitutionally) defensible principles, and creating havoc in the lives of many Americans, black and white, children and parents. In short, as the logo on the book jacket promises, Professor Graglia's work is "a sharply critical view of the court rulings that led to forced busing."

At the core of Professor Graglia's thesis is his interpretation of the principle enunciated by the Supreme Court when it first specifically declared legal racial discrimination in public schools unconstitutional (*Brown v. Board of Education of Topeka*, 1954). While expressing misgivings about the need and the desirability of court intervention in this policy arena, Professor Graglia contends that the most defensible principle emanating from the *Brown* case is that racial classification of *any* type in assigning young people to schools is Constitutionally prohibited. Professor Graglia argues that, subsequent to *Brown*, the Supreme Court has drifted from this principle, at times not fully employing it, at other times announcing that this is the rationale guiding court action when in *fact* the court has moved in an opposite direction. In the wake of this vacillation, the courts have ordered desegregation through requiring racial assignments to schools, even if busing were to be needed, and they have distorted legislative actions, especially the words and intent of the 1964 Civil Rights Act. And for what individual, social, or educational good? As Professor Graglia interprets the evidence, very little benefit has emerged. Indeed the losses in such things as educational achievement, efficiency in the financing of the public school system, defusing antipathy between the races, and instilling public confidence in governmental policy-makers, have far exceeded any gains.

The major strength of this book is the meticulous dissection of court decisions dealing with desegregation issued by judges at *all* levels of the federal judiciary. Sarcasm and outrage aside, Professor Graglia's industrious reconstruction of the court record provides an unusually complete probe into the writings of various members of the court system in their attempts to formulate public policy.

When evaluating the research about the effects of court opinions on human behavior, however, the presentation is less appealing. Here secondary sources provide the reservoir of impact information. Professor Graglia does not question either representativeness or possible spuriousness of these data, for instance. One becomes amused and dismayed in reading that an "independent researcher," assessing the consequences of court ordered busing in Denver, "reported [that] whites . . . will just quietly disappear in two to three years" (pp. 201–202) without any citation for this startling prediction to be found near the quote.

The most disturbing aspect of this book centers upon Professor Graglia's view of the principle that should guide Supreme Court actions in dealing with racial assignment and the public schools. To argue that a completely neutral position in racial classification is the favored rationale forecloses *any* governmental policy formulated to redress, through educational changes, inequities between the races deriving from previous political actions. Constitutional limitations don't just constrain the Supreme Court. Interpreting equal protection to mean a neutral racial orientation for political policy-makers is a gloomy prospect for those who feel that the existing Constitution provides a means to offset such inequities.

JAMES W. LAMARE

The University of Texas
El Paso

FRANCIS RUSSELL. *The President Makers.* Pp. 407. Boston, Mass.: Little, Brown and Company, 1976. $12.50.

Francis Russell writes well and does a service for those who want a synthesis of the secondary literature of eight 20th Century president-makers—Marcus Alonzo Hanna, Thomas Collier Platt, Theodore Roosevelt, George Harvey, Harry Micajah Daugherty, Louis McHenry Howe, Joseph Patrick Kennedy. There is no use of primary source material which might have taken the author into an exciting world of discovery of new motivations for presidential aspiration and of new hypotheses for presidential nomination and election. While such president-makers as Theodore Roosevelt and Louis Howe have been adequately researched, the others warrant fresh assessments. In his rush to publish—with the use of secondary sources—the author lost an opportunity. At that, he missed some of the valuable secondary sources, that is, Paola Coletta's and Louis W. Koenig's works on William J. Bryan, both of which discussed at some length the attributes of Marcus Hanna, the brilliant organizer of the Republican campaign which defeated the Democrats in 1896. And the author's use of some of the secondary sources is questionable. There is considerable doubt as to whether Claude Fuess wrote the definitive biography of Calvin Coolidge, given the fact that it was "authorized" and that Donald McCoy updated it considerably with his more recent biography, *The Quiet President*.

Aside from the above caveats, reading *The President Makers* is informative and fun—for example: the description of Harrison's last moments with McKinley; Platt hurriedly correcting himself about T.R.'s nomination for the Vice Presidency: "I am glad we had our way—the people, I mean, had their way"; T.R.'s affinity for the huge Taft (even though there is little on T.R.'s actual king-making role); Harvey's loyalty to Wilson until the President left for Versailles (although there is little on why that turned Harvey off); the 1920 Republican Convention where Brandegee quipped: "There ain't any first raters this year . . . Harding is the best of the second-raters"; Coolidge's nearly incredulous nomination for Vice President in 1920; vivid descriptions of Howe's gnome-like role in securing FDR's nomination and election; Joseph Kennedy's reaction of the assassination of his son, the President.

MARTIN L. FAUSOLD

State University of New York
College at Geneseo, New York

CYNTHIA EAGLE RUSSETT. *Darwin in America: The Intellectual Response, 1865–1912.* Pp. vii, 228. San Francisco, Calif.: W. H. Freeman & Co., 1976. $9.00.

Ms. Cynthia Russett has written an interesting book. A list of her sources, placed at the end of each chapter, evidence the scope and thoroughness of her research. Her style is simple and direct.

Although Charles Darwin was not the first scientist to think of evolution, he, in his *Origin of the Species*, treated the idea extensively. A careful reading of Darwin's book reveals the influence of others, especially Thomas Malthus' *Principle of Population*.

Darwin's theory was never received unanimously by Americans, but it initiated an intellectual revolution. The mental turmoil was expressed most bitterly between the scientists and the theologians. Of all religious groups, Protestants rejected Darwinianism most completely. Chancey Wright, however, found nothing in the theory that was religious at all. In contrast, Charles Peirce grasped the essential features of evolution—variation and natural selection—but he refused to accept Darwin's theory completely.

Before 1860, the author informs us, the emphasis was on Lockean individualism. Since that time, Americans were required to find a more solid foundation for the state. Industrialism and urbanism influenced our search, but the real problem was the city which drew the masses together, thereby intensifying many problems. Technology, argues the author, created independence but no community.

William Sumner believed that the state should only create favorable conditions for persons to pursue happiness: never create happiness. Lester Ward, however, opposed Sumner's laissez-faire attitude while John Dewey advocated exercising the human intellect to change the world around it.

Many intellectuals, declared Ms. Russett, at first favored Darwinianism with great gusto. By 1900, she contends, Darwin's theory was accepted in American intellectual life as a recapitulation of classical economics. Thorstein Veblen was the first economist to become a true disciple of Darwin. Today, certainly we Americans are far removed from the intellectual struggle over Darwinianism.

GEORGE OSBORN

Gainesville
Florida

P. D. G. THOMAS. *British Politics and the Stamp Act Crisis: The First Phase of the American Revolution, 1763–1767*. Pp. vi, 394. New York: Oxford University Press, 1975. $25.75.

This is an encyclopedic account of British politics regarding the American colonies from the Treaty of Paris to the enactment of Townshend's taxes. No one familiar with the "Namier school" will be surprised by the general view taken by Professor Thomas, an authority on Parliamentary history in the eighteenth century. Grenville, Townshend and George III are portrayed as responsible statesmen seeking to resolve imperial revenue difficulties while beset by political pressure of all sorts.

On this side of the Atlantic, those men are widely regarded as villains. But Thomas shows convincingly that their beliefs regarding Parliamentary authority over the colonies were not generally different from those held by our heroes Rockingham and Pitt. And in action the former were superior. According to Thomas' well-documented account, Grenville modified certain bills to account for possible or actual colonial objections, and delayed others to allow for colonial consideration. Townshend's well-known effort to enact the American distinction between internal and external taxation was actually supported by those Americans whom he could consult. Pitt, on the other hand, was something of a political opportunist, who once flirted with the idea of dictating all colonial economics, rather than merely trying to raise the badly needed revenue.

Anyone searching information about the day-by-day progress of the debates in Commons and Lords, private conversations among the principals in London, reports by provincial governors, or letters home by colonial agents, need look no further. Professor Thomas has included them all, to a fault. The reader is overwhelmed by dozens of passages about the papers, voting records, and changes of opinions of minor M.P.s like Conway and Dowdeswell, and conversations, letters, and anxieties of unknown businessmen like Trecothick and Whately; and by other passages about wholly irrelevant tidbits of information like what certain Committees of Parliament did on days they were not considering colonial matters, or how much the Rhode Island lieutenant governor sought in compensation for damage done by Stamp Act protestors. While enthusiastically applauding the research that produced such data—and no less the marvelously readable way the hundreds of footnotes are displayed—the reader wonders if the work did not need some significant pruning.

Finally, the book is grossly over-expensive. My guess is that this useful $12–$15 book has been taken right out of the market by Oxford University Press' price tag.

W. T. GENEROUS, JR.
Choate Rosemary Hall
Wallingford
Connecticut

BUCHANAN PARKER THOMSON. *Spain: Forgotten Ally of the American Revolution.* Pp. 250. North Quincy, Mass.: The Christopher Publishing Company, 1976. $9.75.

This book was written on the assumption that few Americans except historical specialists know that Spain gave the United States important assistance during the American Revolution. The author's purpose is to recount in a straightforward manner the story of Spain's significant aid.

On the basis of lengthy researches in Spanish and American archives she has woven together a very readable and, sometimes, dramatic account of Spain's aid—at first, surreptitious and, later, open.

The author is at her best in her sprightly treatment of those Spaniards whom she considers heroes—especially Bernardo de Gálvez and Don Diego de Gardoqui. At times the author's enthusiasm carries her away, but it makes for lively reading.

The first third of the book deals with Spanish aid during the period of official Spanish neutrality. The cooperation of France and Spain is discussed briefly and somewhat superficially. The remainder of the work concentrates on Spanish aid after Spain's declaration of war against Great Britain in 1779. It involved loans, supplies and direct naval and military assistance. Gálvez with his appointment as governor of Louisiana in 1777 early comes on center stage where he remains, and deservedly so. The account of his audacious and spectacular campaign resulting in the capture of heavily-fortified Pensacola from the British in May 1781 provides the climax of the book. A brief final section, a distinct anti-climax, attempts to present a reckoning in financial terms of Spain's assistance—a complex and dull subject. This might better have largely been relegated to an appendix with the heroics at Pensacola standing as the dramatic finale.

Overall the book presents much solid information in a pleasing narrative approach. It is nowhere highly analytical nor does it attempt to probe in depth the complex diplomacy of the major powers.

A serious drawback in this work is its deluge of gigantic quotations—in some cases running two to four pages (for example, pp. 65–69). Fewer, shorter quotations and resorting to brief summarization would improve readability. A check of several long quotations, incidentally, revealed some misspelled or omitted words and other transcription problems. The most serious drawback, however, is the lack of an index which sharply reduces its value for quick reference.

While the specialist will discover little that is new in fact or interpretation, the general reader will find this study of rarely-discussed aspects of the American Revolution enlightening and often absorbing.

ALBERT E. VAN DUSEN
University of Connecticut
Storrs

SOCIOLOGY

ALFRED W. CROSBY, JR. *Epidemic and Peace, 1918.* Pp. vi, 337. Westport, Conn.: Greenwood Press, 1976. $17.50.

The influenza pandemic of 1918–1919 killed at least 21 million human beings—twice as many as World War I. But except during its most virulent phase in September–November, 1918, when it sickened and destroyed life so rapidly that in many places neither medical nor mortuary facilities could keep pace with its devastation, the "Spanish" influenza attracted little attention. Even during its worst onslaught, the epidemic was overshadowed by the war and the armistice, and it had not received much attention from historians before the publication of this book. Based upon extensive research in medical and actuarial records, medical journals, periodical literature, and manuscript collections, Alfred W. Crosby, Jr. has reconstructed both the pandemic's attack upon the United States and modern medicine's search for its causes, and he has done so in a lucid and gripping narrative.

Professor Crosby traces the origins of the Spanish influenza to the United States where it began as a normally mild disease in the Spring of 1918. It was carried to Europe by American military personnel and overran much of Eurasia by mid-summer. Then in August, 1918, a much more deadly strain of the disease appeared almost simultaneously in Freetown, Sierra Leone, Brest, France, and Boston, Massachusetts. Striking with astonishing devastation, influenza afflicted between 25 and 40 percent of the American people by June, 1919, and killed some 675,000 Americans. Crosby surveys overall damage, but he concentrates on Philadelphia, San Francisco, troopships, the American Expeditionary Forces in France, American Somoa, and Alaska. Their diverse experiences ranged from a quarantined and disease-free Somoa to fantastic carnage and social paralysis in some native Alaskan settlements.

In 1918–1919 no one knew the cause of influenza, and Crosby makes clear the continuing uncertainty about the origins of the epidemic. Some researchers had suggested that influenza was produced by a filterable agent too small to observe, but a confused, frequently retrograde quest by medical researchers took ten years to establish the existence of viruses and still longer to show that the swine influenza that ravaged the hog population of the Middle West each fall after 1918 was the direct descendant of the Spanish influenza. Crosby points out also that even today's medical science cannot account for the absence in many of the epidemic's human victims of Peiffer's bacillus (which in combination with a virus produces swine influenza in hogs) or explain fully the startlingly heavy incidence of mortality among the Spanish influenza's young adult victims. One puts down this book with a sense of awe at the public apathy that met the pandemic and at the persistent mysteries of the disease's origins, pathology, and disappearance.

There was, in fact, little relation between the epidemic and the peacemaking of 1918–1919, and the book's suggestion of a connection is unfortunate. Crosby's view that the harshness and inequities of the peace settlement owed something to the effects of debilitating illness on the principal negotiators at Paris or on their staffs is simply unconvincing. Yet in spite of a misleading title, this book provides an excellent treatment of a major and neglected event. It serves a useful counterpoint to the concerns and pretensions of political and diplomatic historians, forcing us to recognize that a single, brief epidemic generated more fatalities, more suffering, and more demographic change in the United States than all the wars of the Twentieth Century.

THOMAS M. HILL

Miami University
Oxford
Ohio

SEYMOUR J. DEITCHMAN. *The Best-Laid Schemes: A Tale of Social Research and Bureaucracy*. Pp. 483. Cambridge, Mass.: MIT Press, 1976. $14.95.

The Best-Laid Schemes is the account of the now infamous Department of Defense's (DoD) ever-deepening involvement in the sponsorship and direction of social science research on the causes and mechanisms of revolutionary change, and how insurgency movements could be best combated using social science knowledge. The account is written in the first person by one of those directly involved in the establishment of Pentagon social science research projects into the problem of revolutionary warfare. Those who expect an exposé are cautioned to direct their attention elsewhere, for what *The Best-Laid Schemes* offers is a detailed historical description of the genesis of Project Camelot and similar ventures, and an analysis—and defense—of why DoD became involved in the sponsorship of applied behavioral research on social-political questions.

Deitchman, as Special Assistant for Counterinsurgency Programs in the Office of the Director of Defense Research and Engineering, was directly involved in Project Camelot—an aborted Army sponsored study of the sources of revolutionary movements and how social change could be influenced. Later, as Director of Project Agile—a post-Camelot attempt to continue doing military sponsored social research, but with a low profile—he was in an excellent position to describe the bureaucratic infighting and decision making from the heady days of the early 1960s, through the donnybrook of the ill-named and ill-starred Camelot, up until the Mansfield Amendment of 1969 (Section 203) finally banned the military from carrying out research not specifically related to military functions.

It would be difficult to find a practicing social scientist of note who does not hold a strong professional and moral position regarding DoD research. Thus, as a reviewer, I feel some obligation to state my own position. I consider DoD involvement in socio-political research to have been at best inappropriate, and at worst dangerous. Moreover, as a sociologist I would have to judge that most of the DoD projects were naive regarding both their goals and the state of the art. For example, Project Camelot, the most publicized of the projects, was not only ill conceived, it was also an example of poor research design and inadequate staffing. Researchers working for the Army through the Human Resources Research Office (HumRRO) at George Washington University of the Special Operations Research Office (SORO) at American University not only failed to ask the relevant questions, but also consistently overestimated what they could deliver.

Deitchman's own analysis of how and why the programs developed is far more sophisticated. Moreover, the volume is both detailed and well written. Deitchman carefully documents how DoD involvement in social science research grew out of the Kennedy era belief that social science knowledge could and should be applied to national defense problems. Viewed in perspective, the crucial decision was made during the mid-1960s, when segments of the social science community came to define internal war or counterinsurgency as an important problem for research, and accepted the premise that it was "researchable." Once this decision had been made all else followed logically. As put by Dietchman, "But however we might view it now in rueful retrospect over Vietnam, the point at the time was not whether the job *should* be done, or even whether it *could* be done, but rather how to do it better."

Logically, the Department of State should have been the agency most concerned with undertaking research on problems associated with Vietnam and the expanding "war of national liberation," but that agency was, at the time, intellectually and politically stagnant. Most government agencies were more than willing to let the McNamara Department of Defense take the lead. DoD, thus, became involved in sponsoring political studies, since the State Department had largely abdicated its role of providing information, and the military hierarchy recognized that they could not fight "wars of national liberation" in the conventional military manner. The Army, as a consequence, became directly involved in research on counterinsurgency and political instability. The DoD offered social scientists both the pot of gold of research support, plus a sense of mission. The question of whether social scientists could work on contract research, with the explicit goal of developing techniques for avoiding revolutionary change, without compromising their professional ethics and academic freedom was rarely asked until the Camelot debacle.

On the basis of his involvement in government sponsored social research, Deitchman now argues that there should be *less*, not more, governmental sponsorship of research into the workings of society. He suggests that the goals of government bureaucracies are inherently opposed to those of free and independent scholarly research. Key social issues can be approached with fewer conflicts of interest when done under private sponsorship—the constraints will be smaller, the researcher won't have to face public accountability for projects that the public doesn't approve, and there will be less (though still some) chance of being accused by subjects of being a representative of oppressors. As he concludes, "In the area of learning about societies, their values, and their behavior, I now believe that government can be most effective if it follows, rather than leads."

Although Deitchman is currently with the Institute for Defense Analysis, he has picked up a few of the more obvious Pentagon behavior patterns. One of these is a passion, even in a first person narrative, to avoid using names. In the preface Deitchman states that, "The reader will find that in many cases I have gone to some lengths of circumlocution to avoid naming scientists, civilian or military officials, or even countries, in connection with particular aspects of the events or particular research projects." Why, a decade later, is there a need for such secrecy? Deitchman obviously wants to protect those involved from further vilification, but by going to such lengths to cover up names he leaves the unintended impression that participation was something secretive and covert. Such secrecy makes about as much sense as the CIA's long-standing attempt to pretend that its massive complex across the Potomac from D.C. doesn't exist. During the 1960s it was common knowledge in the social science community who was doing what research for whom. Trying to maintain a cloak of secrecy a decade later merely lends a conspiratorial air to otherwise rather routine knowledge.

A second Pentagon characteristic Dietchman apparently fell prone to during his tours with DoD is Washington parochialism. In spite of his often excellent post-hoc analysis of what went wrong and why, Dietchman candidly admits that he and the others who had been involved in building DoD programs in problems of revolutionary warfare were amazed by the depth of the anti-Defense Department reaction to Project Camelot, and the virulent condemnation of the social scientists involved. While he recognizes that Camelot *per se* was merely the trigger for a bomb that had long been ticking, he still appears rather surprised that the bomb went off when it did. The question is, why were he and others in the DoD bureaucracy surprised? Given the campus ferment at the time, it seems remarkable that upper-level administrators in Washington could be so unaware of the changing mood of the nation. Yet they were. Those, such as this reviewer, who came to the upper reaches of Washington straight from the hinterland during the Vietnam years, were struck by the miasma that engulfed those who should have known better. By limiting himself largely to contact with scientists working for, or sympathetic to, DoD aims and involvement, Dietchman had effectively divorced himself from the changing temper of much of the academic community. Ironically, those attempting to implement programs to study changing attitudes and values in other nations were apparently among those least aware of the massive changes taking place within their own professions and country. To those researching social change, the furor over Camelot should not have come as a surprise, but rather as a foregone conclusion.

Finally, a particularistic nit-pick. The book is typed on an IBM selectric, and not set using standard type. Apparently the goal was to save money, but if that was the case, why not a softcover edition? For $14.95 one should, even in these days of inflation, expect a typeset volume.

The Best-Laid Schemes is must reading for those concerned with the interface between politics, policy and research. It is a thoughtful and intelligent review of a still painful period in the maturation of the American social science community.

J. JOHN PALEN

University of Wisconsin
Milwaukee

ANTHONY S. HALL. *Point of Entry: A Study of Client Reception in the Social Services.* Pp. 150. London: George Allen and Unwin Ltd., 1974. No price.

This is a report of a study of the influence of receptionists' attitudes and actions on the likelihood of applicants to a social service agency continuing beyond the point of intake. The study was conducted in four area offices of the public child welfare service of London, England. It grew out of the author's observations while conducting another study in one of the offices. In that study he found that a high proportion of applicants remained with it only a short time, many of them, indeed never coming back after they applied even though they had been accepted. (American studies have similar findings.) This led the author to undertake the present investigation, which centers on factors determining why the receptionists acted as they did.

The present study shows that requirements placed on the receptionists resulted in their becoming more involved with applicants than they were expected to, and that this fact was not known by the administrators of the program. The over-involvement resulted from such rules as that the receptionists should ensure the appropriateness of each applicant's request, that they should fill out a form about the problems and should also assess the urgency of the request. In addition they were often rebuked, gently or not so gently, for intruding on the busy social workers' time by referring inappropriate cases. As a result receptionists sometimes gave applicants their own opinion of what they should do about their problems or selected for referral the applicants they most liked. In general, these unexpected and undesired consequences depended largely on how difficult it was for the receptionists to make contact with the social workers.

The author offers several practical ideas about how to improve this situation. More important, however, he concludes, is the need for "a systematic approach to defining priorities that provides a rational basis for allocation of resources—accepting, rejecting, and closing cases. Without such a system . . . decisions on resource allocation and service provision tend to be made as a result of non-rational factors such as client pressures and chance."

Except for this rather cryptic conclusion, this is an excellent study. Many besides workers in social service agencies will find it interesting and its observations useful. It may even be of benefit to physicians and lawyers in private practice, who have much to lose if possible patients and clients are met by officious receptionists or those who give advice about how to deal with problems.

HELEN L. WITMER

Alexandria
Virginia

JACK NELSON. *Captive Voices: The Report of the Commission of Inquiry into High School Journalism.* Pp. xxi, 264. New York: Schocken Books, 1974. $10.95. Paperbound, $1.45.

Constitutional rights are rooted deep in American history but seem strangely threatened by school officials who can, and do, trim the life out of them. Where Congress shall make no law abridging freedom of the press, it appears that common school practices support and justify censorship to maintain social control, the status quo, or the school image.

These findings are reported by Jack Nelson of *The Los Angeles Times* in *Captive Voices*, an inquiry by educators and journalists into First Amendment rights and the function of journalism in high school.

Censorship is a matter of school policy, the report finds, and is directed toward image damaging materials, accepted as a routine part of the school process, is self-imposed, and is a fundamental cause of trivial and uniform high school newspapers.

"The great majority of high school journalism programs did not encourage free expression, independent inquiry, or investigation of important issues." Most publications are bland and serve as public relations tools for the schools.

Equally discouraging, but perhaps not as surprising, was the finding that members of racial, cultural, and ethnic minorities face subtle but real barriers in gaining access to student publications.

The report recommends that students have ultimate authority for their publications. And the only news that is not fit to print is "material that is legally obscene or libelous or likely to cause immediate and substantial disruption of the school."

A legal guide, suggestions for student publications, and a listing of resources are helpful additions to the report.

Captive Voices is well-intentioned but necessarily restricted in its critical analysis. It criticizes high school publications but many community papers suffer similar faults. Publishers, as well as principals, direct reports in the who-what-where-when-why-how of their stories. In fact, many observers have recognized the similarities between school and small community and a focus on their use of media would offer additional insight for comparative analysis.

This report is admittedly not designated as a scholarly investigation. Some of the many vignettes are superficial substitutes for more basic examinations of cause and consequence. And there is a disconcerting inconsistency in capitalizing, or not capitalizing "Black" and "Chicano."

The report is a needed commentary in support of Constitutional rights, although one might have hoped for a more emotionally convincing case.

As Eugene C. Patterson, editor of the *St. Petersburg Times*, suggests: "Freedom is a difficult art. To teach it, one must practice it." This is obviously true for the school and equally true for the community. One suspects there are unlimited opportunities for improvement.

TEDD LEVY

Norwalk
Connecticut

HARRY C. PAYNE. *The Philosophes and the People*. Pp. ix, 214. New Haven, Conn.: Yale University Press, 1976. $12.50.

This is an intellectual history of the philosophes' conception, attitude, and policies toward *le peuple*, especially as expressed in their *Encyclopedie* articles of the mid-eighteenth century.

Payne traces the movement in Enlightenment social thoughts from the harsh elitism of a Voltaire to the egalitarian social romanticism of Rousseau. He discusses such other Enlightenment thinkers as Montesquieu, Gibbon, Diderot, Turgot, Condorcet, Helvetius, Holbach and Smith.

It is movement *from* sheer contempt for *le peuple* as educable, moral agents and from naive or ideological insensitivity to their economic plight. The movement is *toward* "a maturing social awareness and growing sensitivity to the people's problems. . . ."

Payne takes particular note of the philosophes' debates about social legislation. It was during these confrontations with actual issues that their elitism was challenged. They generally disagreed about the social utility of religion and legislation regarding it. Regarding universal education, they came to favor at least the development of work related skills. Their economic policies never regarded "*pauvreté*" as eradicable, but concentrated on the alleviation of "misére," chiefly by cultivating charitable responsibility among the rich. Likewise, their occasional reference to civil equality among all persons was nearly always distinguished from political equality.

Payne's concluding chapter traces Rousseau's radically different conclusions from the Enlightenment presuppositions, and their impact on the other philosophes.

What he traces is actually less an historical trend—though there is something of a trend, as in *Encyclopedie* articles in the 1750s and 1760s—and more a fluctuation. For most of the philosophes there seems to be a dominant note of scorn, in sensitivity and separation regarding *le peuple*.

What Payne shows is how this note was tempered from time to time by themes inconsistent with it. The tempering themes he points out are those that resemble the social views of the nineteenth and twentieth centuries.

In Payne's words:

> The philosophes followed an elitist logic of economic and social realism, tempered by their sympathy for the lot of the people. They perceived society as a hierarchy justified not by sacred order but by its inevitability and its potential utility. Within this hierarchy, established by economics and talent, they saw both great possibilities for fairness and ability and great realities of oppression and misery.

GEORGE WILLIAMSON, JR.
Vassar College
Poughkeepsie, N.Y.

ROBERT F. RUSHMER. *Humanizing Health Care: Alternative Futures for Medicine*. Pp. x, 210. Cambridge, Mass.: MIT Press, 1975. No price.

BUDD N. SHENKIN. *Health Care for Migrant Workers: Policies and Politics*. Pp. v, 270. Cambridge, Mass.: Ballinger, 1975. No price.

These two books are concerned with the organization of medical care. The first was written by the Director of the Center for Bioengineering at the University of Washington; the second was written as the result of Dr. Shenkin's experiences as an administrator of the Migrant Health Program in Washington, D.C.

Dr. Rushmer, after discussing the limited applicability of some of the trends in medical research and the disproportion of health resources that are now devoted to a few "favored" illnesses such as cancer, heart disease, stroke, cystic fibrosis, multiple sclerosis, sickle-cell anemia and some others, argues that different facilities, personnel and organizational arrangements will be needed in the future. On the basis of cost/benefit and value added criteria, he shows the need for a greater amount of ambulatory and home based care with more use of paramedical personnel and a "new version" of the traditional physician. He feels that in the future individuals must be ever more responsible for their own health, particularly for the illnesses which do not require the services of physicians per se. We need to be aware of the cost/benefit of many expensive parts of our medical system, such as our hospitals, and try to find less expensive ways of bringing needed medical care to those who need it but cannot afford it. Dr. Rushmer is impressed with the Swedish hospital system and believes that the United States could adopt some phases of that system with benefit to its medical care delivery system.

The discussion of medical care in Dr. Shenkin's book is more restricted, as it is concerned with the medical and health needs of migrant workers. The analysis presented in this book served as a basis for Title IV of the Health Revenue Sharing and Health Services Act of 1974. Dr. Shenkin advises readers of his book to read first the summaries at the end of each chapter and then to read the summaries of each section within the chapters and finally to proceed to the basic text. This reviewer followed these instructions, but found it difficult to get an overall knowledge of a chapter from the summaries as written even though some of them were several pages in length.

The author first describes the migrant workers' characteristics and then the problem of their health and medical care which he feels is similar in general to the health problems of the rural poor. The second chapter describes the classical migrant health program which Shenkin claims is extremely weak. Next he discusses proposed alternatives to this classical program. In the discussion of administrative considerations of the Migrant Program the author points out two distinct phases: "The phase of innovation and the phase of support and management." Both these phases are necessary and in his estimation, each phase requires different personnel and organizational forms. Advisory groups made up of migrants and representatives of migrants with a significant degree of autonomy would also be required for each phase. The migrants have had too little input vis-à-vis the migrant health program in the past and there is great need for such input both in the planning and innovative phase and in the organizational phase. In conclusion, the author argues for some strong political input including pressure from the United Farm Workers. There is an Epilogue which describes in considerable detail the development and passage of Title IV.

Both of these books attempt to show how health could be improved by changing the medical care delivery system so that many now not getting medical care would have easier access to it. Better education and personal knowledge of health needs are recommended. Although those who can afford it can get excellent medical care in the United States, there is a great necessity to make it easier for rural residents, migrants and the poor to get such care. These two books advocate some changes in the medical care delivery system which their authors believe would work toward this end.

H. ASHLEY WEEKS
University of Michigan
Ann Arbor

JOYCE STEPHENS. *Loners, Losers, and Lovers: Elderly Tenants in a Slum Hotel*. Pp. ix, 118. Seattle: University of Washington Press, 1976. $8.95.

Imagine, if you can, a short book on the elderly which is simultaneously theoretically sound, revealing in its description, and both critical and humanistic in its approach. Fortunately, imagination is not necessary; Stephens has produced just such a book with *Loners, Losers, and Lovers*. Moreover, this monograph presents evidence and arguments which contradict certain widely held stereotypes of the elderly as necessarily passive, defeated, dependent and incompetent.

Employing the method of participant observation and the theoretical guidelines of the symbolic interactionist perspective of sociology, Stephens investigated the everyday lives and social milieu of elderly residents of a "SRO" (single-room occupancy) slum hotel. The usual criticisms of participant observation and case study methods are less valid in this instance due to the truly extraordinarily effective use of synthesizing concepts and generalizations. As an examplar of how sociological theory and language can be used to illuminate and explain, rather than obfuscate, social life, *Loners, Losers, and Lovers* is nothing less than superb. Particularly effective are the ways in which the contradictory demands of sufficient descriptive detail and integrative and generalizing commentary are balanced.

The text is organized as the reality was experienced by Stephens: a general description of the SRO hotel, then a view of the management and other "outsiders," and then a presentation of the behaviors and interpretations of the elderly residents. The contrast is vivid between the objective social situation in which these people live, in which money is always scarce, physical danger is prevalent, medical problems are calamitous, and effective public social agency support is nearly non-existent; and their personal interpretations and responses to these conditions, which reveal strength, courage, tenacity, and autonomy. After reading how these presumably incompetent people survive in what is unquestionably a very difficult and harsh environment, it is hard to maintain a conception of elderly persons as unable to care for themselves, or to manage their own lives. While they do not "win," they are in no sense of the word defeated.

The implications of this study are many and varied. Perhaps foremost among the questions raised is how the social conditions of the elderly who wish to remain autonomous can be made more humane and less punishing without necessarily infringing or limiting their right to self-determination. There are also obvious implications for changes in public assistance programs for the elderly, and for more general shifts in the political and social assumptions and beliefs upon which such programs are based. In addition, theories of aging and of social deviance must respond to the evidence presented in Stephens' study.

For all of the above reasons, and for others too specific and detailed to mention, *Loners, Losers, and Lovers* is recommended without qualification or hesitation to anyone interested in social gerontology, urban life, social deviance, or social theory; in sum, to anyone interested in gaining greater understanding of and insight into social life, and how social situations and social interaction can combine to produce a unique outcome: meaningful human encounters.

PAUL T. MCFARLANE

North Carolina State University
Raleigh

ANSELM L. STRAUSS. *Images of the American City*. Pp. 306. New Brunswick, N.J.: Transaction Books, 1976. $12.95.

This book can be reviewed in three different ways, each one appropriate. Therefore, to REVIEW #1:

Anselm Strauss has contributed a useful addition to the literature on American cities and what their images mean to their residents and interpreters. His work identifies major methods by which cities are symbolized, and how these configurations take form in mid-century America. His is an important contribution to urban studies, and no planner or urban sociologist should be without his volume for reference and historical reminder on the varying meanings of "city".

Strauss' book is flawed by the failure to cite recent literature on his subject, particularly the seminal work of Lynch and Clay. Indeed, this reviewer was not able to find references beyond 1960 in the volume.

Or, one might cast REVIEW #2:

Transaction Press has done the urbanist the favor of re-issuing Anselm Strauss' classic *Images of the City* some fifteen years after its original publication by the Free Press of Glencoe. Strauss' work is still useful as a reference, although it has been importantly updated in the interval by the contribution of Kevin Lynch, in particular. Strauss, though he focuses heavily on Chicago in the volume, and stints the West, did present a discussion no student of the growth of cities can afford to overlook in his comparative study of the growth of urban symbolism.

And, finally, REVIEW #3.

What is one to say about a publisher with the effrontery to reissue an important historical study in a field without acknowledging the original date of issue and source of publication? Indeed, Transaction Press presents Anselm Strauss' *Images of the City* in a format exactly that of an original issue, replete with a preface thanking Howard S. Becker and Blanche Geer of Community Studies, Incorporated, of Kansas City, Kai Erikson of the University of Pittsburgh, and Nathan Glazer of Bennington College. Issue in its present format is confusing to students, destructive of traditions of scholarly citation and accuracy, insulting to the author, and ignorant of basic principles of honesty and scholarship. The publisher should assume its moral obligation to rectify its egregious error by enclosing an errata page in all copies giving proper attribution to the work it has chosen to re-issue.

JON VAN TIL

Rutgers University
Camden, N.J.

DUANE F. STROMAN. *The Medical Establishment and Social Responsibility*. Pp. x, 193. Port Washington, N.Y.: Kennikat Press, 1976. $12.95.

Duane Stroman, Associate Professor of Sociology at Juniata College in Huntington, Pennsylvania, presents a well-documented critique of the health care system in the United States, focusing on the medical profession as the main cause of the "illness of our current health care system." Stroman outlined the signs of that illness as the extensive unmet medical need in the country, the uneven quality of American medicine, unnecessary medical services and the high costs of medical care.

The author accomplishes his purpose,

"to understand the complexity of our health care system and the forces for change within it," and the abundance of statistical detail and fact is somewhat overwhelming in sections of the book. However, the timeliness of the subject and the cogency of the author's arguments are well worth the effort.

The thrust of the critique of the health care system comes in chapters 5 and 6; there Stroman openly challenges the monopoly exerted by the medical establishment on health care. The author maintains that while the medical establishment sustains free enterprise medicine, it does so at the expense of the public. Instead of improving medical care for the majority, the medical professionals have worked to maintain their own closed system of providing services through the fee-for-service practice.

The author concludes his analysis with a "patient's bill of rights" and calls for a national health care system "to match the needs of our complex society."

Duane Stroman must be given credit for presenting an immense amount of information on such a problematic subject in a coherent perspective, and also for offering a necessary and convincing critique of the medical establishment in this country.

JOSEPH W. WEISS

Boston College
Chestnut Hill
Massachusetts

ECONOMICS

RUSTOW A. DANKWART and JOHN F. MUGNO. *OPEC: Success and Prospects*. Pp. ix, 179. New York: New York University Press, 1976. $12.50.

This short and eminently well written book should be read by every public and private official dealing with energy problems in general, and OPEC matters in particular.

This reviewer has seldom seen a multidisciplinary work that did not do grave injustice to one or all of the separate disciplines analyzing the subject matter. This is not the case with the work of Dankwart and Mugno on OPEC. Although the points of economic theory used in the analyses are not explained, the conclusions resulting from the theory are presented so the non-economist reader can perceive their significance as they relate to what OPEC is trying to accomplish. With the exception of several key tables, the empirical evidence used in support of the authors' arguments are neatly placed in an appendix, to be carefully scrutinized or ignored as the reader wishes. Similarly, the reader is not distracted by minute descriptions of the dozens of meetings, agreements, and government policy actions that made OPEC an international force. These descriptions also appear in neat chronological order in an appendix.

The book consists of three chapters and a short conclusion. Chapter one, of course, describes the creation and rise to power of OPEC. In 31 pages, the authors concisely and clearly discuss the roles played by the Persian Gulf Countries, Venezuela, the third world countries, the governments of industrialized countries, and the major oil companies in diplomatic and economic (price and tax) policies through the 1973–1974 petroleum crisis.

Although chapter 2 examines the way in which industrialized and third world countries view their positions vis-à-vis OPEC, and how OPEC funds are being recycled, the most interesting part of the chapter relates to the spending and investing objectives of OPEC. In that analysis Dankwart and Mugno look at such diverse objectives as: (1) the economic development of OPEC members, (2) the military security of some members, (3) direct investment in the private enterprises of industrialized countries, and (4) economic aid to third world countries. The chapter also examines how OPEC differs from other (potential) raw material cartels.

The main thrust of the third chapter and the conclusion is that OPEC stands strong in the immediate future because of (1) the futile nature of economic, military, and political retaliatory actions against OPEC; (2) the unlikelihood that OPEC members would gain much by price cuts, and (3) that economically viable alternative fuels are a long term solution.

MARY A. HOLMAN
The George Washington University
Washington, D.C.

ORVILLE F. GRIMES, JR. *Housing for Low-Income Urban Families: Economics and Policy in the Developing World.* Pp. xiv, 176. Baltimore, Md.: The Johns Hopkins University Press, 1976. $11.00. Paperbound, $3.65.

This World Bank Research Publication is a short but richly documented account of the urban housing problem in developing nations. It is descriptive—almost anecdotal—though the statistical appendix suggests that much empirical and some econometric effort underlies the terse text. An impressive Select Bibliography and consistently fine footnote source references enhance the credibility of author Grimes as commentator on this complex and surprisingly sensitive subject. The understated message of the book is that policy-makers in many developing nations are doing much less than they could to improve urban living conditions, mainly because they fail to appreciate the special kind of economics that is relevant.

Orville Grimes is billed on the jacket as an economist on the Development Policy Staff of the World Bank, a specialist on urban land and housing problems. The Preface seems to make it clear that the book was written for the Bank, representing collaboration by a number of Bank staff, and that abundant statistical material was developed through the Bank. The copyright page, however, has a disclaimer by the Bank for views and interpretations contained in the book. For those who may never have chanced upon the strange diplomacy of international assistance agencies, this apparent inconsistency means that the World Bank wants to avoid telling client governments how to conduct their internal affairs but at the same time hopes that a certain amount of enlightenment will make future financial discussions with those governments easier and more amicable. In short, it is reasonable to take this book as a primer on World Bank expectations with respect to urban housing efforts; client governments will be well advised to absorb its message.

The book is significantly more optimistic than Charles Abrams' elegant, explicit treatment of the same subject in *Man's Struggle for Shelter in an Urbanizing World* (MIT Press, 1964). Much of Abrams' book was a graphic description of the urban housing problem in numerous developing nations. Grimes' book is addressed primarily to people who already know what the problems are but fail to perceive how these problems can be solved. So it is a discussion of policy options and economic facts of life, documented as often as necessary with success stories such as Singapore and Hong Kong.

The physical problem is that a large fraction of these urban populations have grossly inadequate housing, in terms of space, sanitation, comfort and security. Incomes are low, but a large share of those who are underhoused could afford the economic cost of minimum standard housing if it were produced; the need for subsidy or income transfer is relatively minor in most places. The market economy does not supply housing because suitable financial institutions do not exist and because suitable land is not provided with utilities or transportation. Governmental housing agencies tend to produce the wrong kind of housing in the wrong places, at extravagant cost and frequently in token quantity. The real problem, as Grimes sees it, is public policy, because ". . . in most countries improvement in policy can contribute substantially to better housing without a major commitment of additional resources" (p. 91).

Specifically, there seems to be little need for loans or grants from international agencies: "In many developing countries poor people pay rents that yield returns on capital of from 30 to 100 percent a year" (p. 88, citing an AID publication). Housing can be financed internally if the nation will but "improve the workings of financial markets" (p. 58). Among the improvements suggested are removal of interest rate restrictions, encouragement for local building societies, diversion of social security funds to urban housing, and avoidance of rent control.

The other major policy option which Grimes supports is the "sites and services" approach. This often-repeated phrase refers to public provision of transportation and basic utilities to suitable, mostly peripheral, land. Houses themselves can best be built by private means, without government intervention or subsidy. For lack of such serviced land urban squatters in many metropolitan centers crowd illegally upon central sites better used for expanding businesses or not used at all. Getting government out of the business of building houses directly for the poor means that families get as much housing as they can afford and no more. In most cases this would be reasonably good, as long as cheap, serviced land is available. For the very poor there is often opportunity for "cross-subsidy"; if some of the resettled families pay a bit more for land, interest and the housing itself than those things actually cost the resulting surplus can be used to lower the rents of the poor—a kind of progressive rent scheme. The main thing is to discourage public agencies from putting scarce public resources into just a few projects which are developed at unrealistically high standards.

There are precedents and models for all the policy improvements which Grimes suggests, and he cites them. Brief as it is, this book ought to go far in persuading governments in developing nations that they could solve their urban housing problems if they really wanted to; they don't need help from the World Bank. This is the kind of frustrating advice often associated with bankers, a valid argument but somehow irrelevant. The book is a bit disingenuous in not anticipating how third world governments might respond to the lessons.

The large irrelevancies are two. First, there are few among the developing countries which actually have control over their internal financial system so that private capital for housing can be mobilized, and few also sufficiently benevolent to care. Showcase developments, externally financed and occupied mainly by favored officials can be photographed and displayed through a controlled press as proof that General X or Chairman Z has "solved" the nation's housing problem.

Second, the "sites and services" approach assumes a capacity for fiscal and development planning which scarcely exists in the most developed of nations, as well as a capital fund. Putting water, electricity and sewerage in a peripheral tract of land and extending good public transportation to that site requires public investment which may not be recouped through the existing fiscal system—that is, through user charges. Making that investment in advance of settlement is a gamble. How does one know that suitable development will occur? Information about the nature and extent of effective demand for housing and about real supplies of housing credit is just not available. Indeed, feasibility studies and infrastructure risk capital are just what developing nations most reasonably expect from agencies such as the World Bank. Grimes' book does not imply that such is forthcoming.

WALLACE F. SMITH

University of California
Berkeley

STEPHEN HERBERT HYMER. *The International Operations of National Firms: A Study of Direct Foreign Investments*. Pp. xxii, 253. Cambridge, Mass.: MIT Press, 1976. $12.50.

Back in 1960, the late Stephen Hymer completed a Ph.D. dissertation in the Department of Economics at MIT. It was probably the most read, unpublished dissertation in history. Everyone who was seriously interested in multinational corporations borrowed it. Hymer insisted foreign direct and portfolio investments were very different. He considered the theory of international capital movements applicable to portfolio investments. This theory argued that investors moved funds to get the best interest rates. He showed how it did not explain most foreign direct investments. He stressed control as crucial to foreign direct investment. "Cross-investments," direct foreign investments of U.S. companies abroad and foreign companies in the United States in the same industries, could not be accounted for by looking at interest rates. Economists, Hymer suggested, should not be using the theory of international capital movements but rather a theory of industrial or firm (enterprise) relationships in studying international operations of national firms. Considerations of oligopoly were more meaningful than those of interest rates.

The dissertation came as a breath of fresh air. It took observed phenomena and thoughtfully viewed the theoretical implications. It compared national and international operations of firms. I often wondered why Hymer never published the thesis. Charles Kindleberger in a sensitive introduction explains that the thesis was rejected for publication. What Hymer published later seemed to me less interesting and less original. As he grew older, he became interested in radical economics. Then in 1974, at age 39, he died in an automobile accident.

Now, MIT Press is publishing the thesis. As I reread it after more than a decade, I am struck by (1) the lucidity of the argument in the early chapters (Kindleberger tells us that one reader for MIT Press in 1960 found it too "simple and straightforward"); (2) how many of Hymer's ideas are now well accepted (I had forgotten that Hymer had stressed the necessity of a firm engaged in international business having advantage of some kind); (3) how Hymer neglected the vast antitrust literature on international business that was available in 1960 and would have helped him in his analysis; and (4) how much more sophisticated the literature on multinational corporations has become in the last sixteen years.

I welcome MIT Press's decision to publish this thesis. I wanted it for my library.

MIRA WILKINS
Florida International University
Miami

JOHN W. MELLOR. *The New Economics of Growth: A Strategy for India and the Developing World.* Pp. ix, 335. Ithaca, N.Y.: Cornell University Press, 1976. $11.50.

While conventional theories of economic development have consistently neglected the role of agriculture as the leading sector, proper credit should go to a remarkable group of agricultural economists who have heroically resisted the received wisdom. Now that time, technology and unconcealable mass poverty have reduced the appeal of convention in development studies, the recent works urging a revision of the established strategies of development should get a more patient reception than could be expected before. Fortunately, within about a year, two major works elaborating rural-oriented strategies of development have emerged. One is authored by Bruce Johnston and Peter Kilby, and the other by John Mellor is the subject of the present review.

Mellor's book presents a sustained critique of what he calls capital-intensive strategies of economic growth with a detailed analysis of the theory and practice of its Indian variant and at the same time offers a rural-led strategy as its alternative. Though the empirical materials are primarily derived from the recent economic experience of India, these are set in a comparative context of relevant Asian experience. The case study itself makes the book well worth reading but the comparative sensitivity and the new approach considerably increase its value for a wider circle of readership, including scholars and policy personnel.

Those who have followed the individual and the collaborative works of Mellor published earlier, will recognize that many of the ideas contained in his statement of the rural-led strategy are not unfamiliar. What is new, however, is the bold integration and elaboration of these ideas in the form of a consistent strategy explicitly designed to confront the issues of growth, employment and welfare together. The components of this strategy are deceptively simple. The new strategy will involve giving priority to increasing agricultural production through investment in new technology, reducing capital intensity in the industrial sector, simultaneously increasing exports and imports, and emphasizing the use of planning for productive inducement rather than unproductive regulation.

This strategy calls for a substantial shift from the established practice in India and some other countries which concentrated most of their attention on capital formation in the industrial sector. The basic emphasis in Mellor's strategy is on increased production of wage goods, particularly food, which if sustained by agro-technical innovation, is likely to generate cumulative production, employment, and welfare gains. That is why the first priority is accorded to agriculture where ensuring proper supply of inputs, adequate infra-structural provisions and assistance to small farmers can make a big difference. In short, a dynamic agricultural sector will imply not merely joining rural growth with economic participation but in addition, will ensure the needed intersectoral flow between agriculture, industry and trade without the cumbrous bureaucratic regulations that normally mark centralized planning.

Mellor is aware of the hard fact that it is not easy to switch strategic emphasis from industry to agriculture and from capital goods to wage goods. Not even the arguments of employment and welfare needs of the poorer masses are likely to shake the conventional ground very much since the established approach delivers a patronage effect that is congruent with the interests of the ruling coalition of social and political forces. His perceptive discussion of the internal and external political factors which can make a difference in the choice of a growth strategy is uncharacteristic of growth literature. While one may wish that he could elaborate this part further, he at least should be given due credit for recognizing the crucial political factors that are conventionally dismissed because of their untidy nature.

Whether one shares Mellor's high hopes regarding the promise of agro-technical innovations or his critique of conventional developmental planning and the value of the new strategy, he will have to recognize this book as a challenging contribution to the literature on economic growth and development. Reliance on technology, market mechanism, inducive planning and foreign compassion are, of course, unlikely to excite many scholars and politicians for a variety of reasons. No matter what these reasons are, they too will find the empirical part of this work highly rewarding. Those who would read this book for a novel approach to poverty-focused, rural-oriented development may question the author's austere detachment from the problems of the rural asset and authority structures. This neglect may be due to his interest in devising a strategy which may be feasible under the conditions of the existing regime. However, given the author's deep concern for the levels of living of the rural poor, it is not readily apparent to what extent a policy of switching investment unaccompanied by structural transformation in rural society will be able to accomplish substantial changes in the life situation of the poor such that they may have access to a life consistent with human dignity.

JYOTIRINDRA DAS GUPTA
University of California
Berkeley

LEO PANITCH. *Social Democracy and Industrial Militancy: The Labour Party, the Trade Unions and Incomes Policy, 1945–1974.* Pp. x, 318. New York: Cambridge University Press, 1976. $22.50.

The writer of this study of the role of the British trade union, as the direct object of the incomes policy, and ultimately the means of administering the policy to the rank and file, stresses the new social contact between the British Labour Government and unions. Assistant Professor Panitch of Carleton University, Canada, in his volume stresses the necessity of stabilizing the economy and restraining industrial militancy. His well-documented and indexed book formed a Ph.D. dissertation at the London School of Economics.

Professor Panitch reveals the trends of this development in the incomes policies of successive post-war governments, especially in the 1964–70 Labour Government. He also traces the way in which wage restraint was obtained from the unions, or imposed upon them, in the context of the attempted integration of the unions within the existing political and economic order.

The author emphasizes the role of the Labour Party in incomes policies generally—a stand which has emerged less from an interest in socialist economic planning than from the Party's integration ideology, particularly its rejection of the concept of class struggle in favour of affecting a compromise between the different classes in British society. Wage restraint, in the absence of effective price and profit controls, has given rise to repeated conflicts within the Labour Movement.

As Professor Panitch stresses, the basic aim of the 1964 Labour Government's incomes policy was to infuse the working people with national considerations at the level at which economic class considerations had persisted more stubbornly, namely, at the level of trade union wage bargaining. However, as the Labour Party extended its national integrative posture to attempt to employ trade unions as agencies of social control in restraining industrial conflict, the main political and class divisions in British society increasingly moved inside the Labour Movement itself. In a decade, the political and industrial issues became one, and the contradiction raised by an industrially militant working class affiliated with an ideologically integrative political party assumed new significance.

The volume follows an historical record of incomes policy, beginning with the 1945 Labour Government's attitude toward this policy and proceeding into the late 1960s—a complex period in which dividing lines did not fall into neat compartments. The author has provided an excellent description of the sharp divisions of left and right Ministers and backbenchers, Conference and Parliamentary Labour Party members, and within the union movement, between radical and moderate union leaders, militant shop stewards, the TUC and individual unions.

The conflict has not ended. However, the author concludes that *In Place of Strife* (issued in 1969) was a major step in integrating certain factions in the Labour Movement. His volume provides a general analysis of social democracy as it is defined in modern British society.

MARY E. MURPHY
California State University
Los Angeles

INGO WALTER. *International Economics of Pollution*. Pp. 208. New York: Halsted Press, 1976. $17.50.

Starting with the premise that environmental management places a 'shock' or pressure on the international economic system, Walter examines the impact of environmental quality standards on international trade, comparative advantage, multinational corporate operations, transfrontier pollution and economic development amongst other topics. The essential argument is that "international variations in collectively determined environmental priorities, systems of public administration and environmental assimilative capacity can be expected to produce significant differences in the economic impact of environmental management on national economies and, in turn, on economic relations between nations" (p. 33).

In order to assess the impact of environmental controls, Walter assumes the polluter pays principle. With this assumption the author concludes that, in the short term, enforcement of environmental controls, will not be critical to the balance of payments question. He notes, however, that the impact at the industry and firm level may be considerable. By implication the effect on particular regions in any one country, or on countries with a non-diversified economic base, may be significant. In the long term, the author argues that pollution control will have a relative impact on prices. The keys to both long and short term adjustments are the policies adopted by governments to control environmental pollution. Policies that deviate from a polluter pays principle tend to influence the competitiveness of firms primarily in the intermediate and long term periods. Subsidies to industry on the other hand tend to defeat the polluter pays principle in all time periods.

The focus of the book is on economic analysis, but there is a clear recognition of the political dimension, especially in the last four chapters. In these chapters Walter explores the impact of multinational corporations on economic interchange and particularly on the key role such organizations play in the transfer of environmental technology. He notes that developing countries in particular may very well benefit from the importation of technology for pollution control since this could lead to more sustained and orderly growth. These last four chapters lack the precise and vigorous argument apparent in the early chapters. This, in many respects can be attributed to the nature of the topics which are analyzed, but it could be disconcerting for an economist interested in a vigorous economic analysis of transfrontier pollution, multinational corporations and trade, environment and economic development. The book goes beyond the international economics of pollution implied in the title. The strongest point about the book is the theoretical discussion of the economic impact of pollution control and the recognition of a broad range of factors which are critical to sound environmental policy. The book would have been considerably enhanced had the author devoted more attention to specific cases and examples to illustrate his conclusions.

WILLIAM M. ROSS
University of Victoria
British Columbia
Canada

OTHER BOOKS

ALLMAND, C. T., ed. *War, Literature and Politics in the Late Middle Ages*. Pp. vi, 202. New York: Barnes & Noble, 1976. $26.50.

AMACHER, RYAN C. and RICHARD JAMES SWEENEY, eds. *The Law of the Sea: U.S. Interests and Alternatives*. Pp. 196. Washington, D.C.: American Enterprise Institute for Public Policy Research, 1976. $9.00. Paperbound, $4.00.

ANDERSON, ARTHUR J. O., FRANCES BERDAN and JAMES LOCKHART, eds. *Beyond the Codices: The Nahua View of Colonial Mexico*. Pp. 244. Berkeley: University of California Press, 1976. $12.00.

ANDERSON, PERRY. *Considerations on Western Marxism*. Pp. vii, 125. Atlantic Highlands, N.J.: Humanities Press, 1976. $9.00.

APTER, DAVID E. and LOUIS WOLF GOODMAN, eds. *The Multinational Corporation and Social Change*. Pp. vi, 234. New York: Praeger, 1976. $16.50. Paperbound, $5.95.

AUSTIN, DENNIS. *Ghana Observed*. Pp. vi, 199. New York: Holmes & Meier, 1976. $16.00.

AXELROD, ROBERT, ed. *Structure of Decision: The Cognitive Maps of Political Elites*. Pp. vii, 404. Princeton, N.J.: Princeton University Press, 1976. $25.00. Paperbound, $9.95.

BAAKLINI, ABDO I. *Legislative and Political Development: Lebanon, 1842–1972*. Pp. vii, 316. Durham, N.C.: Duke University Press, 1976. $11.50.

BARNDS, WILLIAM J., ed. *The Two Koreas in East Asian Affairs*. Pp. vi, 216. New York: New York University Press, 1976. $15.00.

BECKWITH, BURNHAM P. *The Case for Liberal Socialism*. Pp. iii, 182. Hicksville, N.Y.: Exposition Press, 1976. $7.50.

BENNETT, HAL. *Seventh Heaven*. Pp. 263. New York: Doubleday, 1975. $7.95.

BIBO, ISTVAN. *The Paralysis of International Institutions and the Remedies*. Pp. 152. New York: Halsted Press, 1976. $17.50.

BICKEL, ALEXANDER M. *The Morality of Consent*. Pp. vii, 156. New Haven, Conn.: Yale University Press, 1975. $10.00.

BLAKE, DAVID H. and ROBERT S. WALTERS. *The Politics of Global Economic Relations*. Pp. vii, 240. Englewood Cliffs, N.J.: Prentice-Hall, 1976. No price.

BOOTH, JOANNA STRANGWAYES. *A Cricket in the Thorn Tree: Helen Suzman and the Progressive Party*. Pp. 320. Bloomington: Indiana University Press, 1976. $12.50.

BREIT, WILLIAM and WILLIAM PATTON CULBERTSON, JR., eds. *Science and Ceremony: The Institutional Economics of C. E. Ayres*. Pp. viii, 210. Austin: University of Texas Press, 1976. $14.95.

BRUNN, KETTIL et al. *Alcohol Control Policies in Public Health Perspective*. Pp. 106. New Brunswick, N.J.: Rutgers Center of Alcohol Studies, 1975. $8.00.

CAMPBELL, ALAN K. and ROY W. BAHL, eds. *State and Local Government: The Political Economy of Reform*. Pp. v, 211. New York: The Free Press, 1976. $13.95.

CARALEY, DEMETRIOS, ed. *American Political Institutions in the 1970s*. Pp. vi, 407. New York: Columbia University Press, 1976. $17.50. Paperbound, $6.95.

CARTER, HUGH and PAUL C. GLICK. *Marriage and Divorce: A Social and Economic Study*. Revised Edition. Pp. v, 508. Cambridge, Mass.: Harvard University Press, 1976. $17.50.

CAUGHEY, JOHN and LAREE CAUGHEY. *Los Angeles: Biography of a City*. Pp. 523. Berkeley: University of California Press, 1976. $14.95.

CELL, JOHN W., ed. *By Kenya Possessed: The Correspondence of Norman Leys and J. H. Oldham, 1918–1926*. Pp. v, 382. Chicago, Ill.: University of Chicago Press, 1976. $20.00.

CHEETHAM, RUSSELL J. and EDWARD K. HAWKINS. *The Philippines: Priorities and Prospects for Development*. Pp. vii, 573. Washington, D.C.: The World Bank, 1976. $8.50. Paperbound.

CHRISTENSON, REO M. *Challenge and Decision: Political Issues of our Time*. 5th ed. Pp. ix, 244. New York: Harper & Row, 1976. $5.50. Paperbound.

COHAN, A. S. *Theories of Revolution: An Introduction*. Pp. 228. New York: Halsted Press, 1976. $9.95.

COHEN, PAUL A. and JOHN E. SCHRECKER, eds. *Reform in Nineteenth-Century China*. Pp. ix, 393. Cambridge, Mass.: Harvard University Press, 1976. $9.00. Paperbound.

COMBS, JAMES and MICHAEL W. MANSIELD, eds. *Drama in Life: The Uses of Communication in Society*. Pp. vi, 444. New York: Hastings House, 1976. $18.50. Paperbound, $10.50.

COOPER, CHESTER L., ed. *Growth in America*. Contributions in American Studies, no. 21. Pp. x, 262. Westport, Conn.: Greenwood Press, 1976. $15.00.

COUFOUDAKIS, VAN, ed. *Essays on the Cyprus Conflict*. Pp. v, 53. New York: Pella, 1976. $6.00. Paperbound, $3.00.

CULLEN, MICHAEL J. *The Statistical Movement in Early Victorian Britain: The Foundations of Empirical Social Research*. Pp. ix, 205. New York: Barnes & Noble, 1975. $22.50.

CZEMPIEL, ERNST-OTTO and RUSTOW A. DANKWART. *The Euro-American System*. Pp. 236. Boulder, Colo.: Westview Press, 1976. $25.00.

DAHL, ROBERT A. *Modern Political Analysis*. 3rd ed. Pp. vii, 156. Englewood Cliffs, N.J.: Prentice-Hall, 1976. $8.95.

DAYAL, RAJESHWAR. *Mission for Hammarskjold: The Congo Crisis*. P.. x, 335. Princeton, N.J.: Princeton University Press, 1976. $16.00.

DENNIS, PETER and ADRIAN PRESTON, eds. *Soldiers as Statesmen*. Pp. 184. New York: Barnes & Noble, 1976. $17.50.

Documents on Disarmament 1974. Pp. iii, 918. Washington, D.C.: U.S. Government Printing Office, 1976. $8.60. Paperbound.

DODD, LAWRENCE C. *Coalitions in Parliamentary Government*. Pp. viii, 283. Princeton, N.J.: Princeton University Press, 1976. $14.50.

DOUGLAS, JACK D. *Investigative Social Research: Individual and Team Field Research*. Pp. 229. Beverly Hills, Calif.: Sage, 1976. $11.00. Paperbound, $6.00.

DUNCAN, OTIS DUDLEY and ALBERT J. REISS. *Social Characteristics of Urban and Rural Communities, 1950*. Pp. vii, 421. New York: Russell & Russell, 1976. $25.00.

DYE, THOMAS R. *Who's Running America? Institutional Leadership in the United States*. Pp. v, 222. Englewood Cliffs, N.J.: Prentice-Hall, 1976. $8.95. Paperbound, $5.95.

EAGLETON, TERRY. *Marxism and Literary Criticism*. Pp. 96. Berkeley: University of California Press, 1976. $6.95. Paperbound, $2.65.

ESHERICK, JOSEPH W. *Reform and Revolution in China: The 1911 Revolution in Hunan and Hubei*. Pp. 335. Berkeley: University of California Press, 1976. $15.00.

FARER, TOM J. *War Clouds on the Horn of Africa: A Crisis for Détente*. Pp. vi, 157. Washington, D.C.: Carnegie Endowment for International Peace, 1976. $3.75. Paperbound.

FAY, BRIAN. *Social Theory and Political Practice*. Pp. 123. New York: Holmes & Meier, 1975. $10.00.

FIELD, MARK G., ed. *Social Consequences of Modernization in Communist Societies*. Pp. vii, 277. Baltimore, Md.: Johns Hopkins University Press, 1976. $14.50.

FILLER, LOUIS. *Crusaders for American Liberalism: The Story of the Muckrakers*. Pp. vii, 428. Yellow Springs, Ohio: The Antioch Press, 1964. $5.00.

FISCHER, HEINZ DIETRICH and JOHN C. MERRILL, eds. *International and Intercultural Communication*. Pp. xi, 524. New York: Hastings House, 1976. $22.50.

FOGELSON, RAYMOND D. et al. *Contributions to Anthropology: Selected Papers of A. Irving Hallowell*. Pp. vii, 534. Chicago, Ill.: University of Chicago Press, 1976. $24.00.

FONER, PHILLIP S., ed. *Frederick Douglass on Women's Rights*. Pp. x, 192. Westport, Conn.: Greenwood Press, 1976. $13.50.

FOWLER, ROBERT BOOTH and JEFFERY R. ORENSTEIN. *Contemporary Issues in Political Theory*. Pp. v, 168. New York: John Wiley & Sons, 1977. $10.95. Paperbound, $5.95.

FOWLES, JIB. *Mass Advertising as Social Forecast: A Method for Futures Research*. Pp. x, 156. Westport, Conn.: Greenwood Press, 1976. $10.95.

FRANKLIN, JOHN HOPE. *Racial Equality in America*. Pp. vii, 113. Chicago, Ill.: University of Chicago Press, 1976. $7.95.

FREEDMAN, ANNE E. and P. E. FREEDMAN. *The Psychology of Political Control*. Pp. vii, 269. New York: St. Martin's Press, 1976. $12.95.

FRIEDLANDER, WALTER A., ed. *Concepts and Methods of Social Work*. 2nd ed. Pp. v, 243. Englewood Cliffs, N.J.: Prentice-Hall, 1976. $9.95.

GAKENHEIMER, RALPH. *Transportation Planning as Response to Controversy: The Boston Case*. Pp. ix, 377. Cambridge, Mass.: MIT Press, 1976. $16.95.

GEANAKOPLOS, DENO JOHN. *Interaction of the "Sibling" Byzantine and Western Cultures in the Middle Ages and Italian Renaissance (330–1600)*. Pp. vii, 416. New Haven, Conn.: Yale University Press, 1976. $27.50.

GERSTI, JOEL and GLENN JACOBS, eds. *Professions for the People: The Politics of Skill*. Pp. 230. New York: Halsted Press, 1976. $9.50.

GILLESPIE, DAVID F., DENNIS S. MILETI and RONALD W. PERRY. *Organizational Response to Changing Community Systems*. Pp. 88. Kent, Ohio: Kent State University Press, 1976. $4.50. Paperbound.

GLACKEN, CLARENCE J. *Traces on the Rhodian Shore*. Pp. 791. Berkeley: University of California Press, 1976. $9.95. Paperbound.

GLOCK, CHARLES Y. and ROBERT N. BELLAH, eds. *The New Religious Consciousness*. Pp. 408. Berkeley: University of California Press, 1976. $14.95.

GOLDMAN, NANCY L. and DAVID R. SEGAL, eds. *The Social Psychology of Military Service*. Pp. 303. Beverly Hills, Calif.: Sage, 1976. $17.50. Paperbound, $7.50.

GOVE, SAMUEL K., RICHARD W. CARLSON and RICHARD J. CARLSON. *The Illinois Legislature: Structure and Process*. Pp. ix, 189. Urbana: University of Illinois Press, 1976. $5.95. Paperbound.

GREENBERG, MICHAEL R. and ROBERT M. HORDON. *Water Supply Planning: A Case Study and Systems Analysis*. Pp. 166. New Brunswick, N.J.: Rutgers University Press, 1976. $10.00. Paperbound.

GREENBERG, MICHAEL R. et al. *Solid Waste Planning in Metropolitan Regions*. Pp. 218. New Brunswick, N.J.: Rutgers University Press, 1976. $10.00. Paperbound.

GROTH, ALEXANDER J., ROBERT J. LIEBER and NANCY I. LIEBER. *Contemporary Politics: Europe*. Pp. v, 500. Cambridge, Mass.: Winthrop, 1976. $10.95.

HALLAHAN, DANIEL P. and JAMES M. KAUFFMAN. *Introduction to Learning Disabilities: A Psycho-Behavioral Approach*. Pp. v, 310. Englewood Cliffs, N.J.: Prentice-Hall, 1976. $10.95.

HALLOWELL, JOHN H., ed. *Prospects for Constitutional Democracy: Essays in Honor of R. Taylor Cole*. Pp. viii, 197. Durham, N.C.: Duke University Press, 1976. $9.75.

HAMBY, ALONZO L. *The Imperial Years: The U.S. Since 1939*. Pp. vii, 429. New York: Weybright and Talley, 1976. No price.

HELLMANN, DONALD C., ed. *China & Japan: A New Balance of Power*. Pp. v, 305. Lexington, Mass.: Lexington Books, 1976. No price.

HERGENHAHN, B. R. *An Introduction to Theories of Learning*. Pp. iii, 402. Englewood Cliffs, N.J.: Prentice-Hall, 1976. $12.95.

HERZ, JOHN H. *The Nation-State and the Crisis of World Politics*. Pp. 307. New York: David McKay, 1976. $4.95. Paperbound.

HILTON, GORDON. *Intermediate Politometrics*. Pp. viii, 282. New York: Columbia University Press, 1976. $15.00.

HIRST, PAUL O. *Social Evolution and Sociological Categories*. Pp. 135. New York: Holmes & Meier, 1976. $15.00.

HOLZER, MARC, ed. *Productivity in Public Organizations*. Pp. 328. Port Washington,

N.Y.: Kennikat Press, 1976. $18.50. Paperbound, $8.95.

HOOD, CHRISTOPHER C. *The Limits of Administration*. Pp. vi, 213. New York: John Wiley & Sons, 1976. $14.95.

HOY, JOHN C. and MELVIN H. BERNSTEIN, eds. *The Effective President*. Pp. ix, 183. Pacific Palisades, Calif.: Palisades, 1976. $8.95. Paperbound, $4.95.

JACOB, HERBERT and KENNETH N. VINES, eds. *Politics in the American States: A Comparative Analysis*. 3rd ed. Pp. ix, 509. Boston, Mass.: Little, Brown, 1976. $12.95.

JOHNSTON, OWEN DEAN, JR. *Miracle at Vaux: The Delightful Emergence of Black Literature in North Philadelphia*. Pp. 76. Philadelphia, Pa.: Dorrance, 1976. $3.95.

INGLE, HAROLD N. *Nesselrode and the Russian Rapprochement with Britain, 1836–1844*. Pp. 207. Berkeley: University of California Press, 1976. $11.75.

IPPOLITO, DENNIS S., THOMAS G. WALKER and KENNETH L. KOLSON. *Public Opinion and Responsible Democracy*. Pp. v, 330. Englewood Cliffs, N.J.: Prentice-Hall, 1976. $10.95.

KAHN, E. J., JR. *The China Hands: America's Foreign Service Officers and What Befell Them*. Pp. xi, 337. New York: Penguin Books, 1976. $3.95. Paperbound.

KALT, NEIL C. and SHELDON S. ZALKIND, eds. *Urban Problems: Psychological Inquiries*. Pp. v, 543. New York: Oxford University Press, 1976. $13.00. Paperbound, $8.00.

KALTER, ROBERT J. and WILLIAM A. VOGELY, eds. *Energy Supply and Government Policy*. Pp. 356. Ithaca, N.Y.: Cornell University Press, 1976. $18.50. Paperbound, $5.95.

KELLEY, DAVID HUMISTON. *Deciphering the Maya Script*. Pp. 334. Austin: University of Texas Press, 1976. $27.50.

KILSON, MARTIN L. and ROBERT I. ROTBERG, eds. *The African Diaspora: Interpretive Essays*. Pp. vii, 510. Cambridge, Mass.: Harvard University Press, 1976. $18.50.

KING, JEROME B. *Law versus Order: Legal Process and Free Speech in Contemporary France*. Pp. 206. Hamden, Conn.: Archon Books, 1975. $12.50.

KIRBY, R. G. and A. E. MUSSON. *The Voice of the People: John Doherty, 1798–1854. Trade Unionist, Radical and Factory Reformer*. Pp. 474. Totowa, N.J.: Rowman and Littlefield, 1976. $30.00.

KNORR, KLAUS, ed. *Historical Dimensions of National Security Problems*. Pp. v, 387. Lawrence: University Press of Kansas, 1976. $6.95. Paperbound.

KOURY, ENVER M. *The Crisis in the Lebanese System: Confessionalism and Chaos*. Pp. 92. Washington, D.C.: American Enterprise Institute for Public Policy Research, 1976. $3.00. Paperbound.

KRAINES, OSCAR. *The Impossible Dilemma: Who is a Jew in the State of Israel?* Pp. vi, 156. New York: Bloch, 1976. $6.95.

KUDRLE, ROBERT T. *Agricultural Tractors: A World Industry Study*. Pp. vii, 286. Cambridge, Mass.: Ballinger, 1976. No price.

KUHLMAN, JAMES A. and LOUIS J. MENSONIDES, eds. *Changes in European Relations*. Pp. vii, 214. The Netherlands: Sijthoff, 1976. $18.50.

LAMSON, PEGGY. *Roger Baldwin: Founder of the American Civil Liberties Union*. Pp. vi, 304. Boston, Mass.: Houghton Mifflin, 1976. $12.50.

LANGFORD, JOHN W. *Transport in Transition: The Reorganization of the Federal Transport Portfolio*. Pp. xiv, 267. Montreal, Ca.: McGill-Queen's University Press, 1976. $14.00. Paperbound, $7.00.

LANGFORD, PAUL. *The Eighteenth Century, 1688–1815*. Pp. v, 264. New York: St. Martin's Press, 1976. $15.95.

LARSEN, J. A. O. *Representative Government in Greek and Roman History*. Pp. 254. Berkeley: University of California Press, 1976. $11.50.

LEGAULT, ALBERT and GEORGE LINDSEY. *The Dynamics of the Nuclear Balance*. Revised Edition. Pp. 283. Ithaca, N.Y.: Cornell University Press, 1976. $14.50.

LEON, GEORGE B. *The Greek Socialist Movement and the First World War*. Pp. vi, 204. New York: Columbia University Press, 1976. $12.00.

LIKERT, RENSIS and JANE GIBSON LIKERT. *New Ways of Managing Conflict*. Pp. v, 375. New York: McGraw-Hill, 1976. $14.50.

LINDBERG, LEON N. *Politics and the Future of Industrial Society*. Pp. v, 286. New York: David McKay, 1976. $12.50. Paperbound, $6.95.

LISTOKIN, DAVID. *Fair Share Housing Allocation*. Pp. viii, 253. New Brunswick, N.J.: Rutgers University Press, 1976. $10.00. Paperbound.

LITTRELL, W. BOYD and GIDEON SJOBERG, eds. *Current Issues in Social Policy*. Pp. 248. Beverly Hills, Calif.: Sage, 1976. $15.00. Paperbound, $6.95.

LOEBEL, EUGEN. *Humanomics: How We Can Make The Economy Serve Us—Not Destroy Us*. Pp. 164. New York: Random House, 1976. $6.95.

MAANE, WILLIAM. *Lesotho: A Development Challenge*. Pp. iv, 98. Washington, D.C.: The World Bank, 1976. $4.75. Paperbound.

MACKIE, J. A. C., ed. *The Chinese in In-*

donesia. Pp. vi, 282. Honolulu: University Press of Hawaii, 1976. $12.00.

MADDOX, GEORGE L. and ROBIN B. KARASIK, eds. *Planning Services for Older People: Translating National Objectives into Effective Programs.* Pp. i, 186. Durham, N.C.: Duke University Press, 1975. $6.00. Paperbound.

MANSER, GORDON and ROSEMARY HIGGINS CASS. *Voluntarism at the Crossroads.* Pp. 262. New York: Family Service Association of America, 1976. $12.95.

MASOTTI, LOUIS H. and ROBERT L. LINEBERRY, eds. *The New Urban Politics.* Pp. v, 266. Cambridge, Mass.: Ballinger, 1976. $14.00.

MATHURIN, OWEN CHARLES. *Henry Sylvester Williams and the Origins of the Pan-African Movement, 1869–1911.* Pp. xvi, 183. Westport, Conn.: Greenwood Press, 1976. $16.50.

MAUDE, GEORGE. *The Finnish Dilemma: Neutrality in the Shadow of Power.* Pp. vi, 153. New York: Oxford University Press, 1976. $13.25.

MCCUBBIN, HAMILTON I., BARBARA B. DAHL and EDNA J. HUNTER, eds. *Families in the Military System.* Pp. 400. Beverly Hills, Calif.: Sage, 1976. $20.00.

MCLEOD, W. H. *The Evolution of the Sikh Community.* Pp. 119. New York: Oxford University Press, 1976. $8.75.

MEISNER, MAURICE and RHOADS MURPHY, eds. *The Mozartian Historian: Essays on the Works of Joseph R. Levenson.* Pp. 210. Berkeley: University of California Press, 1976. $10.00.

MELADY, THOMAS and MARGARET MELADY. *Uganda: The Asian Exiles.* Pp. vii, 86. Maryknoll, N.Y.: Orbis, 1976. $6.95.

MIROFF, BRUCE. *Pragmatic Illusions.* Pp. xi, 334. New York: David McKay, 1976. $9.95. Paperbound, $4.95.

MITCHELL, DANIEL J. B. *Labor Issues of American International Trade and Investment.* Pp. v, 112. Baltimore, Md.: Johns Hopkins University Press, 1976. $8.50. Paperbound, $2.95.

MOORE, BARRINGTON, JR. *Soviet Politics: The Dilemma of Power.* Pp. vi, 504. White Plains, N.Y.: IASP, 1976. $6.95. Paperbound.

MULCAHY, KEVIN V. and RICHARD S. KATZ. *America Votes: What You Should Know about Elections Today.* Pp. vii, 118. Englewood Cliffs, N.J.: Prentice-Hall, 1976. $8.95.

NEUMAN, STEPHANIE G., ed. *Small States and Segmented Societies: National Political Integration in a Global Environment.* Pp. vi, 238. New York: Praeger, 1976. $16.50.

NIEMI, RICHARD G. and HERBERT F. WEISBERG, eds. *Controversies in American Voting Behavior.* Pp. 543. San Francisco, Calif.: W. H. Freeman, 1976. $12.95. Paperbound, $6.95.

OGUL, MORRIS S. *Congress Oversees the Bureaucracy: Studies in Legislative Supervision.* Pp. ix, 237. Pittsburgh, Pa.: University of Pittsburgh Press, 1976. $9.95.

OWEN, BRUCE M. *Economics and Freedom of Expression: Media Structure and the First Amendment.* Pp. vii, 202. Cambridge, Mass.: Ballinger, 1975. No price.

PELTON, JOSEPH N. *Global Communications Satellite Policy: Intelsat, Politics and Functionalism.* Pp. v, 183. Mt. Airy, Md.: Lomond, 1976. $14.50.

PERROLLE, PIERRE M., ed. *Fundamentals of the Chinese Communist Party.* Pp. vii, 205. White Plains, N.Y.: IASP, 1976. $15.00.

PETIT, PAUL. *Pax Romana.* Pp. 368. Berkeley: University of California Press, 1976. $17.50.

PIERCE, JOHN C. and HARVEY R. DOERKSEN. *Water Politics and Public Involvement.* Pp. v, 294. Ann Arbor, Mich.: Ann Arbor Science, 1976. $15.00.

PLICE, STEVEN S. *Manpower and Merger: The Impact of Merger upon Personnel Policies in the Carpet and Furniture Industries.* Study no. 5. Philadelphia: University of Pennsylvania Press, 1976. $7.95. Paperbound.

Political Instability Abroad: A Contemporary Affairs Report. Pp. 203. Washington, D.C.: Congressional Quarterly, 1976. $5.25. Paperbound.

REDWOOD, JOHN. *Reason, Ridicule and Religion: The Age of Enlightenment in England, 1660–1750.* Pp. 287. Cambridge, Mass.: Harvard University Press, 1976. $12.00.

REGNERY, HENRY, ed. *¡Viva Vivas!* Pp. 379. Indianapolis, Ind.: Liberty Press, 1976. $7.95.

RICHARDS, PETER G. *The Local Government Act, 1972: Problems of Implementation.* Pp. 207. Beverly Hills, Calif.: Sage, 1975. $15.95.

RICHARDSON, DAN K. *The Cost of Environmental Protection: Regulating Housing Development in the Coastal Zone.* Pp. vii, 219. New Brunswick, N.J.: Rutgers University Press, 1976. $10.00. Paperbound.

RIESELBACH, LEROY N. *Congressional Reform in the Seventies.* Pp. 131. Morristown, N.J.: General Learning Press, 1977. No price.

ROBERTS, ROBERT W. and HELEN NORTHEN, eds. *Theories of Social Work with Groups.*

Pp. xii, 401. New York: Columbia University Press, 1976. $15.00.

RODEWALD, COSMO. *Money in the Age of Tiberius*. Pp. 154. Totowa, N.J.: Rowman and Littlefield, 1976. $16.00.

ROSE, RICHARD. *Managing Presidential Objectives*. Pp. ix, 180. New York: The Free Press, 1976. $12.95.

ROSECRANCE, RICHARD, ed. *America as an Ordinary Country: U.S. Foreign Policy and the Future*. Pp. 276. Ithaca, N.Y.: Cornell University Press, 1976. $9.75.

ROSETT, RICHARD N., ed. *The Role of Health Insurance in the Health Services Sector*. Universities National Bureau Conference Series, no. 27. Pp. ix, 548. New York: Neale Watson Publications, 1976. No price.

RUBIN, VERA and LAMBROS COMITAS. *Ganja in Jamaica: The Effects of Marijuana*. Pp. vi, 217. New York: Doubleday, 1976. $2.95. Paperbound.

RUBIN, VITALY A. *Individual and State in Ancient China: Essays on Four Chinese Philosophers*. Pp. x, 149. New York: Columbia University Press, 1976. $9.95.

ST. JOHN, JEFFREY. *Jimmy Carter's Betrayal of the South*. Pp. 161. Ottawa, Ill.: Green Hill, 1976. $1.75. Paperbound.

SALAS, RAFAEL M. *People: An International Choice*. Pp. vii, 154. New York: Pergamon Press, 1976. No price.

SALEM, MAHMOUD. *Organizational Survival in the Performing Arts: The Making of the Seattle Opera*. Pp. v, 210. New York: Praeger, 1976. $16.50.

SCHAUMBURG, FRANK D. *Judgment Reserved: A Landmark Environmental Case*. Pp. vii, 265. Reston, Va.: Reston, 1976. $11.95.

SCHLAFLY, PHILLIS and CHESTER WARD. *Ambush at Vladivostok*. Pp. 158. Alton, Ill.: Pere Marquette Press, 1976. $2.00. Paperbound.

SCHMITT, CARL. *The Concept of the Political*. Pp. 105. New Brunswick, N.J.: Rutgers University Press, 1976. $8.00. Paperbound, $3.50.

SELIGER, MARTIN. *Ideology and Politics*. Pp. 352. New York: The Free Press, 1976. $14.95.

SHAPIRO, YONATHAN. *The Formative Years of the Israeli Labour Party: The Organization of Power, 1919–1930*. Pp. 278. Beverly Hills, Calif.: Sage, 1976. $13.50.

SILVERMAN, MILTON and PHILIP R. LEE. *Pills, Profits, and Politics*. Pp. 421. Berkeley: University of California Press, 1976. $4.95. Paperbound.

SMITH, BRIAN. *Policy-Making in British Government: An Analysis of Power and Rationality*. Pp. 210. Totowa, N.J.: Rowman and Littlefield, 1976. $12.00.

SMOLE, WILLIAM J. *The Vanoama Indians: A Cultural Geography*. Pp. 272. Austin: University of Texas Press, 1976. $10.95.

SMOLINSKI, LEON. *L. V. Kantorovich: Essays in Optimal Planning*. Pp. ix, 251. New York: IASP, 1976. $15.00.

SPRAGENS, THOMAS A., JR. *Understanding Political Theory*. Pp. v, 155. New York: St. Martin's Press, 1976. $12.95. Paperbound, $4.50.

SPRAY, S. LEE, ed. *Organizational Effectiveness: Theory, Research, and Application*. Pp. 185. Kent, Ohio: Kent State University Press, 1976. $12.50.

STAHL, O. GLENN. *Public Personnel Administration*. 7th ed. Pp. v, 575. New York: Harper & Row, 1976. $16.95.

STEINER, STAN. *The Vanishing White Man*. Pp. vii, 309. New York: Harper & Row, 1976. $10.95.

STOESSINGER, JOHN G. *Henry Kissinger: The Anguish of Power*. Pp. 234. New York: W. W. Norton, 1976. $8.95.

STRETTON, HUGH. *Capitalism, Socialism and the Environment*. Pp. v, 332. New York: Cambridge University Press, 1976. $19.95. Paperbound, $6.95.

SUH, DAE-SOOK and CHAE-JIN LEE, eds. *Political Leadership in Korea*. Pp. vii, 272. Seattle: University of Washington Press, 1976. $9.50.

THOMPSON, DENNIS F. *John Stuart Mill and Representative Government*. Pp. vii, 241. Princeton, N.J.: Princeton University Press, 1976. $13.50.

TRIBE, LAURENCE H., CORINNE S. SCHELLING and JOHN VOSS, eds. *When Values Conflict: Essays on Environmental Analysis, Discourse, and Decision*. Pp. 208. Cambridge, Mass.: Ballinger, 1976. $15.00.

UNGER, ROBERTO MANGABEIRA. *Knowledge and Politics*. Pp. vii, 336. New York: The Free Press, 1976. $4.95. Paperbound.

VAN DEVENTER, DAVID E. *The Emergence of Provincial New Hampshire, 1623–1741*. Pp. v, 302. Baltimore, Md.: Johns Hopkins University Press, 1976. $14.50.

VARDY, STEVAN BELA. *Modern Hungarian Historiography*. Pp. viii, 333. New York: Columbia University Press, 1976. $20.60.

VON CLAUSEWITZ, CARL. *On War*. Edited by Michael Howard and Peter Paret. Pp. v, 717. Princeton, N.J.: Princeton University Press, 1976. $18.50.

WALKER, J. SAMUEL. *Henry A. Wallace and American Foreign Policy*. Pp. ix, 224. Westport, Conn.: Greenwood Press, 1976. $13.95.

WATSON, J. WREFORD and TIMOTHY O'RIORDAN, eds. *The American Environment: Perceptions and Policies*. Pp. vii, 340. New York: John Wiley & Sons, 1976. $19.50.

WEIGLEY, RUSSELL F., ed. *New Dimensions in Military History*. Pp. vii, 419. San Rafael, Calif.: Presidio Press, 1975. $14.95.

WELLS, ROBERT V. *The Population of the British Colonies in America before 1776: A Survey of Census Data*. Pp. vi, 342. Princeton, N.J.: Princeton University Press, 1975. $18.50.

WENDZEL, ROBERT L. *International Relations: A Policymaker Focus*. Pp. 286. New York: John Wiley & Sons, 1977. No price.

WHEELER, LESLIE. *Jimmy Who? An Examination of Presidential Candidate Jimmy Carter: The Man, His Career, His Stands on the Issues*. Pp. 352. Woodbury, N.Y.: Barron's, 1976. $2.95. Paperbound.

WIDICK, B. J., ed. *Auto Work and Its Discontents*. Pp. vii, 112. Baltimore, Md.: Johns Hopkins University Press, 1976. $8.00. Paperbound, $2.95.

WILLIAMS, WALTER and RICHARD F. ELMORE, eds. *Social Program Implementation*. Pp. v, 299. New York: Academic Press, 1976. $14.50.

WILSON, WILLIAM A. *Folklore and Nationalism in Modern Finland*. Pp. vii, 272. Bloomington: Indiana University Press, 1976. $10.00.

ZARUDNAYA, ELENA. *Trotsky's Diary in Exile, 1935*. Forward by Jean van Heijenoort. Pp. v, 218. Cambridge, Mass.: Harvard University Press, 1976. $8.00.

ZINNES, DINA A. and JOHN V. GILLESPIE, eds. *Mathematical Models in International Relations*. Pp. v, 397. New York: Praeger, 1976. $29.50.

INDEX

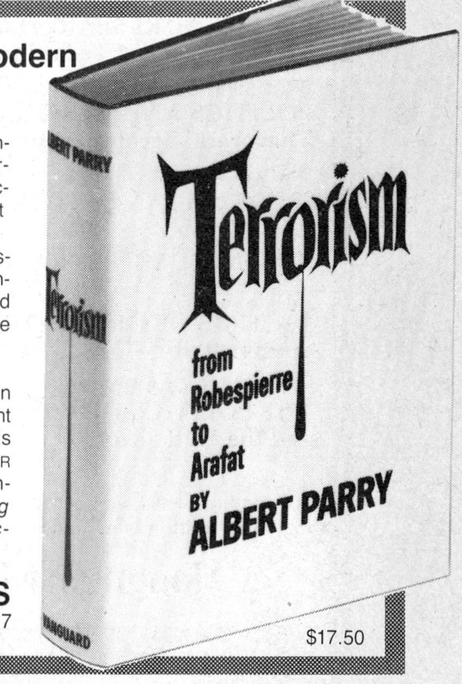
ALBERT PARRY
Terrorism
VANGUARD
Terrorism
from Robespierre to Arafat
BY
ALBERT PARRY
$17.50

The American Academy of Political and Social Science

3937 Chestnut Street **Philadelphia, Pennsylvania 19104**

Origin and Purpose. The Academy was organized December 14, 1889, to promote the progress of political and social science, especially through publications and meetings. The Academy does not take sides in controverted questions, but seeks to gather and present reliable information to assist the public in forming an intelligent and accurate judgment.

Meetings. The Academy holds an annual meeting in the spring extending over two days.

Publications. THE ANNALS is the bimonthly publication of The Academy. Each issue contains articles on some prominent social or political problem, written at the invitation of the editors. Also, monographs are published from time to time, numbers of which are distributed to pertinent professional organizations. These volumes constitute important reference works on the topics with which they deal, and they are extensively cited by authorities throughout the United States and abroad. The papers presented at the meetings of The Academy are included in THE ANNALS.

Membership. Each member of The Academy receives THE ANNALS and may attend the meetings of The Academy. Annual dues for individuals are $15.00 (for clothbound copies $20.00 per year). A life membership is $500. All payments are to be made in United States dollars.

Libraries and other institutions may receive THE ANNALS paperbound at a cost of $15.00 per year, or clothbound at $20.00 per year. Add $1.50 to above rates for membership outside U.S.A.

Single copies of THE ANNALS may be obtained by nonmembers of The Academy for $4.00 ($5.00 clothbound) and by members for $3.50 ($4.50 clothbound). A discount of 5 percent is allowed on orders for 10 to 24 copies of any one issue, and of 10 percent on orders for 25 or more copies. These discounts apply only when orders are placed directly with The Academy and not through agencies. The price to all bookstores and to all dealers is $4.00 per copy less 20 percent, with no quantity discount. Monographs may be purchased for $4.00, with proportionate discounts. Orders for 5 books or less must be prepaid (add $1.00 for postage and handling). Orders for 6 books or more must be invoiced.

All correspondence concerning The Academy or THE ANNALS should be addressed to the Academy offices, 3937 Chestnut Street, Philadelphia, Pa. 19104.